Exam Ref 70-533
Implementing Microsoft
Azure Infrastructure
Solutions

Michael Washam
Rick Rainey

PUBLISHED BY
Microsoft Press
A Division of Microsoft Corporation
One Microsoft Way
Redmond, Washington 98052-6399

Library of Congress Control Number: 2014951859
ISBN: 978-0-7356-9706-5

Printed and bound in the United States of America.

First Printing: February 2015

Microsoft Press books are available through booksellers and distributors worldwide. If you need support related to this book, email Microsoft Press Book Support at mspinput@microsoft.com. Please tell us what you think of this book at *http://aka.ms/tellpress*.

Acquisitions Editor: Karen Szall
Developmental Editor: Karen Szall
Editorial Production: Troy Mott, Ellie Volckhausen
Technical Reviewers: Jeremy Johnson; Technical Review services provided by Content Master, a member of CM Group, Ltd.
Copyeditor: Christina Rudloff
Indexer: Angela Howard
Cover: Twist Creative • Seattle

Contents at a glance

Contents

What do you think of this book? We want to hear from you!

Microsoft is interested in hearing your feedback so we can continually improve our books and learning resources for you. To participate in a brief online survey, please visit:

www.microsoft.com/learning/booksurvey/

Chapter 4: Implement storage 213

Chapter 5: Implement an Azure Active Directory   267

Chapter 6: Implement virtual networks   319

What do you think of this book? We want to hear from you!

Microsoft is interested in hearing your feedback so we can continually improve our books and learning resources for you. To participate in a brief online survey, please visit:

www.microsoft.com/learning/booksurvey/

Introduction

This book is written for IT professionals preparing for Exam 70-533 Implementing Microsoft Azure Infrastructure Solutions.

Microsoft Azure is the Microsoft cloud platform comprised of compute, data, application, and networking services. This book is written specifically for IT professionals who want to demonstrate their skills to implement and configure these services in Microsoft Azure.

At the time of this writing, two versions of the Web-based management portal for Azure are available. The current portal (the Azure management portal) is available at *https://manage.windowsazure.com*, and a preview portal (the Azure Preview Portal) is available at *https://portal.azure.com*. Throughout the book, as references to the portal are made, we use the Azure Preview Portal if the functionality is available in that portal. Otherwise, we use the Azure management portal. Chapters 3 and 5 reference only the Azure management portal because the topics discussed were not available in the Preview Portal at the time of this writing.

This book covers every exam objective, but it does not cover every exam question. Only the Microsoft exam team has access to the exam questions themselves and Microsoft regularly adds new questions to the exam, making it impossible to cover specific questions. You should consider this book a supplement to your relevant real-world experience and other study materials. If you encounter a topic in this book that you do not feel completely comfortable with, use the links you'll find in text to find more information and take the time to research and study the topic. Great information is available on MSDN, TechNet, and in blogs and forums.

Microsoft certifications

Microsoft certifications distinguish you by proving your command of a broad set of skills and experience with current Microsoft products and technologies. The exams and corresponding certifications are developed to validate your mastery of critical competencies as you design and develop, or implement and support, solutions with Microsoft products and technologies both on-premises and in the cloud. Certification brings a variety of benefits to the individual and to employers and organizations.

> **MORE INFO**   **ALL MICROSOFT CERTIFICATIONS**
>
> For information about Microsoft certifications, including a full list of available certifications, go to *http://www.microsoft.com/learning*.

Acknowledgments

Bringing a book to print involves the work and dedication of many individuals beyond the author's names you see on the front cover. Without their attention to detail and coordination during technical and editorial reviews, this book would simply not be possible. Therefore, we would like to extend the sincerest thank you to the following people:

- Alison Hirsch
- Christina Rudloff
- Karen Szall
- Jeremy Johnson
- Trevor Sullivan

Free ebooks from Microsoft Press

From technical overviews to in-depth information on special topics, the free ebooks from Microsoft Press cover a wide range of topics. These ebooks are available in PDF, EPUB, and Mobi for Kindle formats, ready for you to download at:

http://aka.ms/mspressfree

And, if you're new to Microsoft Azure, download the free ebook "Microsoft Azure Essentials: Fundamentals of Azure". It provides both conceptual and how-to content for key areas, including:

- Azure Websites and Azure Cloud Services
- Azure Virtual Machines
- Azure Storage
- Azure Virtual Networks
- Databases
- Azure Active Directory

Microsoft Virtual Academy

Build your knowledge of Microsoft technologies with free expert-led online training from Microsoft Virtual Academy (MVA). MVA offers a comprehensive library of videos, live events, and more to help you learn the latest technologies and prepare for certification exams. You'll find what you need here:

http://www.microsoftvirtualacademy.com

Errata, updates, & book support

We've made every effort to ensure the accuracy of this book and its companion content. You can access updates to this book—in the form of a list of submitted errata and their related corrections—at:

http://aka.ms/er533/errata

If you discover an error that is not already listed, please submit it to us at the same page.

If you need additional support, email Microsoft Press Book Support at *mspinput@microsoft.com*.

Please note that product support for Microsoft software and hardware is not offered through the previous addresses. For help with Microsoft software or hardware, go to *http://support.microsoft.com*.

We want to hear from you

At Microsoft Press, your satisfaction is our top priority, and your feedback our most valuable asset. Please tell us what you think of this book at:

http://aka.ms/tellpress

The survey is short, and we read every one of your comments and ideas. Thanks in advance for your input!

Stay in touch

Let's keep the conversation going! We're on Twitter: *http://twitter.com/MicrosoftPress*.

Preparing for the exam

Microsoft certification exams are a great way to build your resume and let the world know about your level of expertise. Certification exams validate your on-the-job experience and product knowledge. Although there is no substitute for on-the-job experience, preparation through study and hands-on practice can help you prepare for the exam. We recommend that you augment your exam preparation plan by using a combination of available study materials and courses. For example, you might use the Exam ref and another study guide for your "at home" preparation, and take a Microsoft Official Curriculum course for the classroom experience. Choose the combination that you think works best for you.

Note that this Exam Ref is based on publicly available information about the exam and the author's experience. To safeguard the integrity of the exam, authors do not have access to the live exam.

CHAPTER 1

Implement Websites

Microsoft Azure Websites is a fully managed platform-as-a-service (PaaS) that enables you to build, deploy, and scale enterprise-grade web applications in seconds. Whether your organization requires a global web presence for the organization's .com site, a solution to a Line-of-Business (LOB) intranet application that is secure and highly available, or a site for a digital marketing campaign, Azure Websites is the fastest way to create these web applications in Azure. Of all the Azure Compute options, Azure Websites is among the simplest to implement for scalability and manageability, and for capitalizing on the elasticity of cloud computing.

This chapter covers aspects of Azure Websites that are particularly important for the IT professional responsible for deploying, configuring, monitoring, and managing Azure Websites.

> **IMPORTANT**
> ## Have you read page xix?
> It contains valuable information regarding the skills you need to pass the exam.

Objectives in this chapter:

- Objective 1.1: Deploy Websites
- Objective 1.2: Configure Websites
- Objective 1.3: Configure diagnostics, monitoring, and analytics
- Objective 1.4: Configure scale and resilience
- Objective 1.5: Manage hosting plans

Objective 1.1: Deploy Websites

Microsoft Azure Websites is rich with features and services that meet the needs of some of the most demanding web application architectures in the cloud. As an IT professional, you need to be able to create the website environment and resources the site depends on in a way that meets the needs of the development teams and applications you are responsible for supporting.

> **This objective covers how to:**
> - Create an Azure Website
> - Define deployment slots
> - Publish an application
> - Swap deployment slots
> - Define and deploy WebJobs

Creating an Azure website

Before you can deploy an Azure website, you need to create the Azure website. When you create an Azure website, you are creating the unique DNS name, specifying the region the website will run in, and adding resources such as a Microsoft Azure SQL Database or Microsoft Azure Storage account. In other words, you are defining the infrastructure for the website that the web application will use. In an on-premises environment, a similar analogy would be creating a website in IIS Manager. When you do this, you simply create the site without any code. Later, application code is published to the site that users can reach through their browser.

A Microsoft Azure website can be created using a variety of tools, such as the following:

- Microsoft Azure management portal at *http://portal.azure.com*
- Azure PowerShell cmdlets
- Many other UI and command-line tools

Creating an Azure website using the Azure management portal

Using the Azure management portal to create an Azure website provides a rich and powerful UI experience. You can choose to create your website using a variety of templates. Some templates provide the option to include a database resource such as a SQL Database, MySQL Database, or Azure Storage account. Other templates can be used to create a fully functioning website for popular blogging and content management systems (CMSs), e-commerce, and more. All templates available are in the Web page in the Azure Gallery, as shown in Figure 1-1.

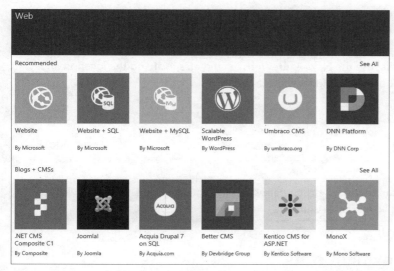

FIGURE 1-1 Web page in the Azure Gallery showing some of the templates available for creating an Azure website

Creating an Azure website using Azure PowerShell

Creating an Azure website using the Azure PowerShell cmdlets requires that you know the location (or region) you want to create the site in and a unique name for the site. To determine the website locations that are available to your Azure subscription, use the following Azure PowerShell cmdlet.

```
Get-AzureWebsiteLocation
```

> **MORE INFO** **AZURE POWERSHELL CMDLETS**
>
> An Azure PowerShell cmdlet reference is available at *https://msdn.microsoft.com/en-us/library/azure/jj554330.aspx*. You can also get detailed help on a cmdlet using the PowerShell Get-Help cmdlet.

The result will be a list of locations that are available to your subscription.

To determine if an Azure website name already exists, use the following Azure PowerShell command.

```
Test-AzureName -Website "contoso-web"
```

The result will be either true or false. If it is true, then the name specified already exists and therefore cannot be used. If it is false, then the Azure website name does not exist and therefore would be a valid unique name you can use.

To create the website, use the New-AzureWebsite cmdlet, specifying the location and name parameters as shown in the following example.

```
$wsLocation = "West US"
$wsName = "contoso-web"
New-AzureWebsite -Location $wsLocation -Name $wsName
```

EXAM TIP

All Azure Websites are created in the *Azurewebsites.net* domain. If you name your website Contoso-web, it will be reachable using the URL *contoso-web.azurewebsites.net*.

Defining deployment slots

Every Azure website, by default, includes one deployment slot, referred to as the production deployment slot, and is where the production version of your application will be deployed. You have the option of adding up to four additional deployment slots to your website. When you have two or more deployment slots, you can swap the contents of the deployment slots as new versions of your application are being developed. An example of how the deployment slots for a website might be configured is shown in Figure 1-2.

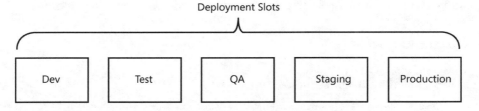

FIGURE 1-2 Example of how deployment slots can be used for different environments

EXAM TIP

Adding additional deployment slots to an Azure website requires that the website be configured for Standard mode.

Creating a deployment slot using the management portal

In the Deployment section of the blade for the Azure website is a *Deployment Slots* part that shows the number of deployment slots that have been created for the website. By clicking the Deployment Slots part, you can add additional deployment slots, as shown in Figure 1-3.

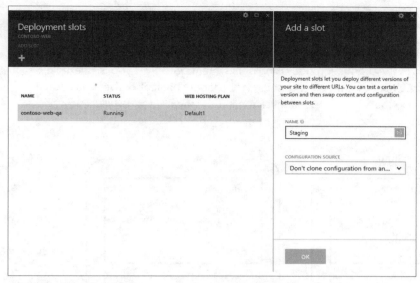

FIGURE 1-3 Adding a deployment slot named Staging using the management portal

> **NOTE CLONING AN EXISTING DEPLOYMENT SLOT**
>
> When creating a new deployment slot using the management portal, you have the option of cloning an existing deployment slot or creating a new deployment slot using default values.

Creating a deployment slot using Azure PowerShell

To create a deployment slot using the Azure PowerShell cmdlets, use the New-AzureWebsite cmdlet and provide the name of the existing website in the Name parameter, and the name of the new deployment slot in the Slot parameter. The following is an example.

```
$wsQASlot = "QA"
New-AzureWebsite -Location $wsLocation -Name $wsName -Slot $wsQASlot
```

EXAM TIP

A deployment slot is actually a completely separate Azure website linked to your production slot website. For example, if you create your website using the name Contoso-web and then later add a deployment slot named Staging, then the website name for the staging slot would be called Contoso-web-staging. Each website would be reachable from its unique URL. For example:

http://contoso-web.azurewebsites.net/

http://contoso-web-staging.azurewebsites.net/

Swapping deployment slots

When swapping deployment slots, you are swapping the contents of one slot with another. For example, you may have version 2.0 of an application in your staging slot and version 1.0 of the application in the production slot. Using deployment slots gives you the flexibility to test your version 2.0 application before pushing it to production. It also gives you a way to roll back (swap back) to the version 1.0 application if necessary. Figure 1-4 illustrates swapping between a staging and production environment.

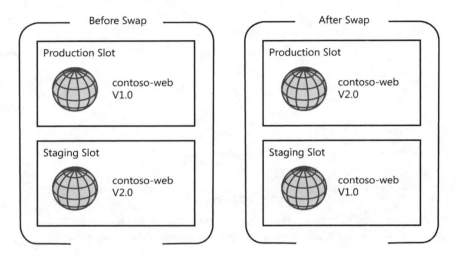

FIGURE 1-4 Swapping between production and staging deployment slots

You can swap deployment slots using the management portal and the Azure PowerShell cmdlets.

Swapping deployment slots using the management portal

In the Website blade for the Azure website, click the Swap button. If you have more than one deployment slot defined, then another blade will open where you can select the destination deployment slot to swap with.

Swapping deployment slots using Azure PowerShell

Use the Switch-AzureWebsiteSlot cmdlet to swap the slots specified in the Slot1 and Slot2 parameters. For example, the code shown here will swap the Staging and Production slots.

```
$wsStaging    = "Staging"
$wsProduction = "Production"
Switch-AzureWebsiteSlot -Name $wsName -Slot1 $wsStaging -Slot2 $wsProduction
```

Publishing an Azure website

Publishing an Azure website is the process by which the web application (or code) is copied to one of the deployment slots. A Microsoft Azure website can be published using a variety of tools, such as the following:

- Source control systems are often used in a continuous delivery (or deployment) model where the website is deployed as code changes are checked into the source control system
- FTP clients, such as FileZilla
- Windows PowerShell
- Web Deploy
- Visual Studio
- Git

Publishing a web deployment package using Azure PowerShell

Provided a web deployment package has already been created that contains the website, you can use the Publish-AzureWebsiteProject cmdlet to publish it to Azure. The example shown here publishes the application to the Staging slot for the website.

```
$pkgPath = "E:\Contoso-Web.zip"
Publish-AzureWebsiteProject -Name $wsName -Slot $wsStaging -Package $pkgPath
```

Deploying WebJobs

A WebJob is an application or script that can be run as a background task in an Azure website. The types of files that WebJobs supports as runnable tasks are:

- .cmd, .exe, .bat (using a Windows command prompt)
- .ps1 (using Windows PowerShell)
- .sh (Bash)
- .php
- .py (Python)
- .js (Node)

A WebJob can be configured as an On-Demand, Continuously Running, or Scheduled task.

Deploying an Azure WebJob using the management portal

To deploy a WebJob using the management portal, it is required that the application or script be zipped and deployed as a .zip file and that the size of the .zip file be a maximum size of 100 MBs.

If the WebJob is deployed as an *On-Demand or Continuously Running* task, then you need only to specify the name of the WebJob and the path to the .zip file.

If the WebJob is deployed as a *Scheduled* task, you have the choice to configure it as a *One-time job* or a *Recurring job*. For the Recurring job, you can set the granularity of the schedule to be as small as Minutes or as large as Months. Figure 1-5 shows how a job can be configured to run every 30 minutes.

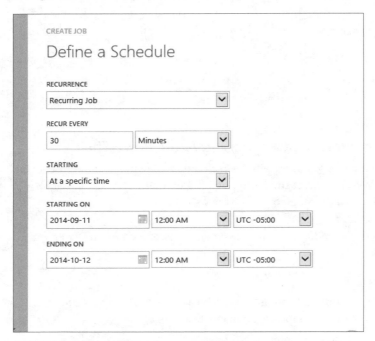

FIGURE 1-5 Define a WebJob to run every 30 minutes

Deploying an Azure WebJob using Azure PowerShell

To deploy a WebJob using Azure PowerShell, use the New-AzureWebsiteJob cmdlet as shown here.

```
$wjPath = "E:\Contoso-WebJob.exe"
$wjName = "Contoso-WebJob"
New-AzureWebsiteJob -Name $wsName -JobName $wjName -JobType Triggered -Slot $wsStaging
-JobFile $wjPath
```

> **NOTE DEPLOYING AN AZURE WEBJOB USING AZURE POWERSHELL**
>
> The New-AzureWebsiteJob cmdlet supports two types of jobs: Triggered and Continuous. Triggered jobs are the same as On-Demand. The JobType parameter does not support Scheduled WebJobs.

Thought experiment

Create an Azure website and SQL Database

In this thought experiment, apply what you've learned about this objective. You can find answers to these questions in the "Answers" section at the end of this chapter.

You are the IT Administrator for Contoso. One of Contoso's development teams you provide IT support for is tasked with building a new line-of-business web application. They are asking you to provide an Azure website environment to develop and test on.

As part of the requirements gathering, you learned that they intend to use SQL Database for relational data and Azure Blob Storage for document files used by the application. The development team needs a development environment and a testing environment that the QA team will use for testing. Your office is located in the Western US, but the development and QA team is located in West Europe.

1. You must provide an Azure website environment that supports these minimal requirements. How could you approach creating the environment?

2. Is the location of the development and test teams something you can take into consideration for your solution? If so, how?

Objective summary

- Azure Websites are created under the *.*azurewebsites.net* shared domain.
- Adding deployment slots to a website requires that the website be in Standard mode.
- A website has an implied production deployment slot. Up to four additional deployment slots can be added using any name, as long as the name is unique within the website.
- Azure WebJobs provides a way to run background tasks in an Azure website. WebJobs can be configured to run On-Demand, Continuously, or as a Scheduled task.

Objective review

Answer the following questions to test your knowledge of the information in this objective. You can find the answers to these questions and explanations of why each answer choice is correct or incorrect in the "Answers" section at the end of this chapter.

1. Which Azure PowerShell cmdlet is used to create a new Azure website?
    A. Publish-AzureWebsiteProject
    B. New-AzureWebsite
    C. New-AzureWebsiteJob

    D. Set-AzureWebsite

2. Which of the following are valid task types for a WebJob? (Choose all that apply.)

    A. Recurring

    B. On-Demand

    C. Scheduled

    D. Continuously

3. Which Azure Websites feature should you enable for continuously running WebJobs?

    A. Autoscale

    B. SSL

    C. Always-On

    D. Backup

4. 4. Which Azure PowerShell cmdlet is used to swap deployment slots in a website?

    A. Switch-AzureWebsiteSlot

    B. Get-AzureWebsite

    C. Restart-AzureWebsite

    D. Show-AzureWebsite

Objective 1.2: Configure websites

Every website has unique characteristics that need to be taken into consideration when configuring the environment that the site will run in. With Azure Websites, you have many choices when it comes to website configuration settings and the tools you use to configure the website.

This objective covers how to:

- Configure site settings
- Configure custom domains
- Configure SSL certificates
- Configure Microsoft Azure Traffic Manager
- Configure handler mappings
- Configure virtual applications and directories
- Use the Azure Cross-Platform Command-Line Interface tools for configuration tasks

Configuring site settings

Configuring the site settings for the site is among the first configuration tasks you will perform for an Azure website. The site settings section is where you can configure language versions, connection strings, application settings, and more. Table 1-1 shows some common settings and their possible values.

TABLE 1-1 General settings for Azure Websites

SETTING	VALUES
.NET Framework Version	V3.5, V4.5 (default)
PHP Version	OFF, 5.3, 5.4 (default), 5.5
Java Version	OFF (default), 1.7.0_51
Python Version	OFF (default), 2.7.3, 3.4.0
Platform	32-bit (default), 64-bit
Web Sockets	OFF (default), ON
Always On	OFF (default), ON
Remote Debugging	OFF (default), ON
Remote Visual Studio Version - Only applicable if Remote Debugging is ON.	2012, 2013

Connection strings and application settings

Just about any website will have a database for storing data. Azure Websites has a unique way of configuring *connection strings* to the database by enabling you to provide a connection string setting as part of the website environment. By storing a connection string as a site setting, the application can retrieve the connection string at runtime as an environment variable rather than storing it in a Web.config or Php.ini file. This approach is more secure because it avoids storing sensitive information, such as user id and password, in the configuration files for the site. Azure Websites support the following types of database connection strings:

- **SQL Database** A connection string for an Azure SQL Database.
- **SQL Server** A connection string for a SQL Server running on a physical machine or perhaps an Azure Virtual Machine.
- **MySQL** A connection string for a MySQL Database.
- **Custom** A connection string for other NoSQL storage options, such as an Azure Storage account.

Azure Websites uses this same technique for application settings that a website may depend on. Application settings can be anything, such as a URL to a web service the application may depend on, or a custom runtime setting that the application code understands.

Site settings for connection strings and application settings are defined as key/value pairs. The key can be any name you want and is how you will reference the application setting and/or connection string. For example, the following is a sample of how a key/value pair could be defined for a connection string to a SQL database.

```
Key = "ContosoDBConnStr"
Value = "Server=tcp:contosodbsrv01.database.windows.net,1433;Database=contoso-database;
User ID=AdminUser@contosodbsrv01;Password={your_password_here};Trusted_Connection=False;
Encrypt=True;Connection Timeout=30;"
```

The value for a connection string defined as a site setting can be retrieved at runtime by referencing the name of the environment variable for the setting. The name of the environment variable is a combination of a constant string based on the type of database connection string plus the name of the key. The constant strings are as follows:

- SQLAZURECONNSTR_
- SQLCONNSTR_
- MYSQLCONNSTR_
- CUSTOMCONNSTR_

Using the example from earlier, the environment variable name for the ContosoDBConnStr connection string is SQLAZURECONNSTR_ContosoDBConnStr.

Similarly, the value for an application setting defined as a site setting can also be retrieved at runtime by referencing the name of the environment variable for the setting. The constant string for application settings is APPSETTING_. As an example, if an application setting key is defined as ContosoHRWebServiceURL, then the environment variable name for the setting is APPSETTING_ ContosoHRWebServiceURL.

> **MORE INFO** **SETTING CONNECTION STRINGS AND APPLICATION SETTINGS**
>
> Although it's not a requirement to store connection strings and application settings as site settings for an Azure website, it's recommended to do so. Application developers still have the option of storing these settings in application configuration files such as Web.config or Php.ini files.

EXAM TIP

If an application setting, or connection string, is defined in both an application configuration file and as a site setting in the Azure website, the site setting value takes precedence over the setting in the application configuration file.

Configuring site settings using the management portal

There is a configuration section that contains a Site Settings icon in the Website blade for the Azure Website. Clicking this icon opens the Site Settings blade where you can make configuration changes. Figure 1-6 shows the General Settings section of the Site Settings blade.

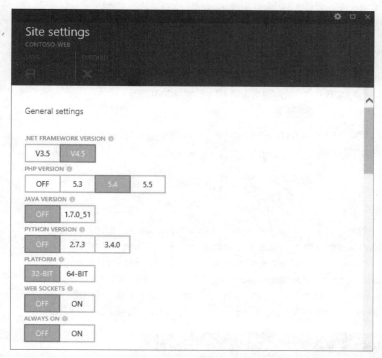

FIGURE 1-6 General Settings in the Site Settings blade

Configuring site settings using Azure PowerShell

To specify site settings using Azure PowerShell, use the Set-AzureWebsite cmdlet. For example, this code demonstrates enabling web sockets for a site.

```
$wsName = "contoso-web"
Set-AzureWebsite $wsName -WebSocketsEnabled $true
```

To define application settings using PowerShell, you will need to create a hashtable to define the setting. This is an example showing how to define a key/value pair for application settings.

```
$settings = New-Object Hashtable
$settings["Contoso_HR_WebService_URL"] = "https://contoso-webservices/hr"
Set-AzureWebsite $wsName -AppSettings $settings
```

This is an example of how to define a connection string using Azure PowerShell where a ConnectionStringInfo structure is used to define the connection string.

```
$connStrs = (@{Name="contosodb"; Type="SQLAzure"; ConnectionString="Server=tcp:.." })
Set-AzureWebsite -Name $wsName -ConnectionStrings $connStrs
```

Configuring a custom domain for a website

Azure Websites are assigned to the *azurewebsites.net* domain. So, if your site name is contoso-web, then it is reachable at the URL *contoso-web.azurewebsites.net*. During development and testing this may be acceptable. However, as you approach the release of your website, you will generally want to configure a custom domain for the site, such as *contoso.com*.

Configuring a custom domain name requires the following steps:

1. Obtain a custom domain from a domain registrar of your choice.
2. Add DNS records for your domain using your domain registrar.
3. Associate the custom domain with your Azure website.

Adding DNS records

The DNS records you add with your domain registrar can be either an A record or CNAME record. An A record resolves a domain to a specific IP address. For Azure Websites, that IP address is the IP address of the cluster of servers your website is running in. It is not the IP address of a specific virtual machine. You can obtain the IP address you should use for your A record from the management portal by clicking the Domains and SSL part in the Website blade for your site. This will open the SSL Settings blade for your site, as shown in Figure 1-7.

FIGURE 1-7 Locating the IP address to use for A records

If you use an A record, then Azure requires that you first add a CNAME record to verify that you own the domain. This CNAME must be formatted as awverify.*<yourdomain>*.com and map to awverify.*<your website name>*.azurewebsites.net. Table 1-2 illustrates how the A record and CNAME record are defined for the custom domain contoso.com.

TABLE 1-2 Example DNS records when using A records to configure a custom domain

RECORD TYPE	NAME	VALUE
A	*contoso.com*	23.100.46.198
CNAME	*awverify.contoso.com*	*awverify.contoso-web.azurewebsites.net*

EXAM TIP

The awverify CNAME record is only used when using an A record to configure a custom domain.

If you use CNAME records, then your DNS records only indicate the custom domain and the Azure website URL it maps to. It is also possible to map subdomains. Table 1-3 shows an example of how a CNAME record is defined for a custom domain contoso.com.

TABLE 1-3 Example DNS record when using CNAME records to configure a custom domain

RECORD TYPE	NAME	VALUE
CNAME	*contoso.com*	*contoso-web.azurewebsites.net*

Associating the custom domain with the website

After the CNAME records have been verified, the last step is to associate your custom domain with your Azure Website. This can be done using the management portal by clicking the Manage Domains button and adding the custom domain.

You can also add the custom domain using the Set-AzureWebsite cmdlet as shown here.

```
Set-AzureWebsite -Name "contoso-web" -HostNames @(www.contoso.com, "contoso.com")
```

NOTE MODE SETTING REQUIREMENTS FOR CUSTOM DOMAINS

Custom domains are not supported in the free tier of Azure Websites.

Configuring SSL certificates for an Azure website

Azure Websites provide SSL support for every site by default. If your website is named contoso-web, you can open a browser and access it using http or https, as shown here:

- *contoso-web.azurewebsites.net*
- *contoso-web.azurewebsites.net*

However, the azurewebsites.net domain is a shared domain and therefore the wildcard certificate providing SSL is also shared, making it less secure than if you had a custom domain and your own SSL certificate for the custom domain. You also probably wouldn't want to use the shared domain for a public-facing site. Still, it's good to know this support is there for cases where the shared domain is acceptable.

The majority of sites will have a custom domain and therefore will need to configure SSL with this in mind. The site must also be in Standard mode to support this configuration. Configuring SSL for an Azure website with a custom domain requires the following steps:

1. Obtain an SSL certificate.
2. Upload the SSL certificate to Azure.
3. Configure the SSL bindings.

EXAM TIP

To configure SSL for an Azure website with a custom domain, the website must be configured for Standard mode.

Obtaining an SSL certificate

A certificate authority must sign your SSL certificate, and the certificate must adhere to the following requirements:

- The certificate contains a private key.
- The certificate must be created for key exchange that can be exported to a Personal Information Exchange (.pfx) file.
- The certificate's subject name must match the custom domain. If you have multiple custom domains for your website, the certificate will need to be either a wildcard certificate or have a subject alternative name (SAN).
- The certificate should use 2048-bit (or higher) encryption.

Uploading the SSL certificate to Azure

After the SSL certificate is obtained, you can upload it to Azure using the management portal by clicking the Domains and SSL part in the Website blade for your site as shown in Figure 1-8. This opens the SSL Settings blade for your site where you can upload the certificate.

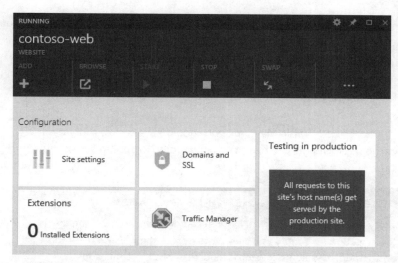

FIGURE 1-8 The Configuration section of the Website blade showing the Domains and SSL part

Configuring the SSL bindings

After the SSL certificate has been uploaded to your Azure Website, the last step in the process is to configure the SSL bindings. Azure Websites supports *Server Name Indication* (SNI) SSL and the traditional *IP-based SSL*. You can configure the SSL bindings in the management portal in the SSL Settings blade referenced earlier in Figure 1-7. For each binding you must specify the following:

- The custom domain name.
- The SSL certificate to use for the custom domain.
- Select either SNI SSL or IP-based SSL.

EXAM TIP

If you choose IP-based SSL for your SSL binding and your custom domain is configured using an A record, Azure will assign a new dedicated IP address to your website. This is a different IP address than what you previously used to configure the A record. Therefore, you must update the A record with your DNS registrar using the new virtual IP address. The virtual IP address can be found in the management portal by clicking the Properties part of the Website blade.

Configuring Azure Traffic Manager

Azure Traffic Manager is a network service that you can use to route users to website endpoints (deployments) in potentially different datacenters around the world. It provides services and settings that you can use to improve availability, performance for users, or load-balance traffic. It works by applying a policy engine to DNS queries for the domain names of your website.

To leverage the features of Azure Traffic Manager, you should have two or more deployments of your website. The deployments can be in the same region or spread across multiple regions around the world.

> **NOTE** **MULTIPLE DEPLOYMENTS FOR THE SAME WEBSITE APPLICATION**
>
> The implementation of an application will greatly influence how Azure Traffic Manager can be used for that application. As simple as it may be to deploy the website to multiple locations, careful consideration should be given to whether or not the application was designed for multiple deployments. How data is managed and accessed by the website, whether or not application state is a factor, and other important application design aspects need to be reviewed. Traffic Manager is a powerful service in the Azure platform that should be reviewed with application owners before configuring Traffic Manager for the application.

Configuring Azure Traffic Manager entails the following steps:

- Create an Azure Traffic Manager profile.
- Add endpoints to the profile.
- 3Update DNS records for your custom domain.

Creating an Azure Traffic Manager profile

To create an Azure Traffic Manager profile, you must select a unique DNS name for your profile. All Azure Traffic Manager profiles use the shared domain *.trafficmanager.net*. Therefore, your DNS name must be unique because it will form the Azure Traffic Manager domain name that you will use when updating your DNS records. As an example, a DNS name for Contoso might be *contoso-web-tm.trafficmanager.net*.

Related to the DNS name setting is the *DNS time-to-live (TTL)*, which tells DNS clients and resolvers on DNS servers how long to cache the name resolved by Azure Traffic Manager. The default value for this setting is five minutes.

You must select a load balancing method. The load balancing options are as follows:

- **Performance** Choose this option when your website is deployed in different regions and you want users to be routed to the closest data center you have deployed to.

- **Round Robin**   Choose this option when your website is deployed in the same or different regions and you want to distribute the load across multiple deployments.
- **Failover**   Choose this option when your website is deployed in the same or different regions and you want one deployment to be the primary for all traffic and the others to be available as backup if the primary becomes unavailable. If you have more than two deployments, then you can prioritize the order of the deployments that you want Traffic Manager to failover with.

For Azure Traffic Manager to determine the health of your website endpoints (deployments) you need to provide some basic *monitoring settings* so that Azure Traffic Manager can query your endpoints to determine if an endpoint should be taken out of the rotation. The monitoring settings consist of the following:

- **Protocol**   This can be HTTP or HTTPS.
- **Port**   Use standard HTTP and HTTPS ports, such as 80 or 443.
- **Relative Path And File Name**   This is the path and file name in the application that the monitoring service will perform an HTTP GET request against. This can be the root of the application, such as "/". Or, it could be a specific health check page the application may make available, such as /Healthcheck.aspx.

> *NOTE*   **USING HEALTH CHECK PAGES TO DETERMINE WEBSITE HEALTH**
>
> Some websites provide a health check page as part of the application and may name the page Healthcheck.aspx. The advantage of having a health check page is that the page can check the health of other services the application depends on, such as SQL Database connections, web service availability, or internal metrics the application developers have added as part of the health monitoring of the application. Just because a request for a page such as the root at "/" may return an HTTP 200 (OK), doesn't necessarily mean the application is healthy. By using a custom health check page, applications can more accurately determine the health of the application instance and return an error code, such as HTTP 503 (Service Unavailable). As a result, Azure Traffic Manager will remove the endpoint from the rotation until the application instance returns HTTP 200 (OK).

To create an Azure Traffic Manager profile using the management portal, specify the unique DNS name and the load balancing method. Next, configure the settings for the profile. Figure 1-9 shows the Configure page for an AzureTraffic Manager profile.

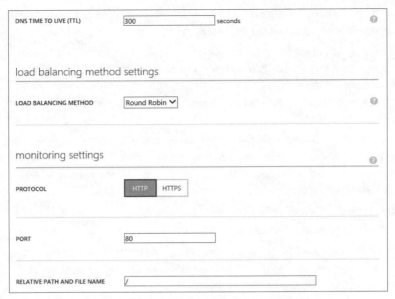

FIGURE 1-9 Configuring the Azure Traffic Manager profile

To create a Traffic Manager profile using Azure PowerShell, use the New-AzureTrafficManagerProfile cmdlet. For example, this code creates a profile named ContosoTM with a domain name of *contoso-web-tm.trafficmanager.net*, and a Failover load balancing method.

```
New-AzureTrafficManagerProfile -Name ContosoTM `
-DomainName contoso-web-tm.trafficmanager.net -LoadBalancingMethod Failover `
-MonitorPort 80 -MonitorProtocol Http -MonitorRelativePath "/" -Ttl 30
```

Adding endpoints to an Azure Traffic Manager profile

The endpoints are where Azure Traffic Manager will resolve DNS queries to for your domain. After creating the Azure Traffic Manager profile, you must add the endpoints to the profile that you want Azure Traffic Manager to resolve DNS queries to. In the management portal, you can add, delete, and disable endpoints on the *Endpoints* page of the Azure Traffic Manager profile, as shown in Figure 1-10.

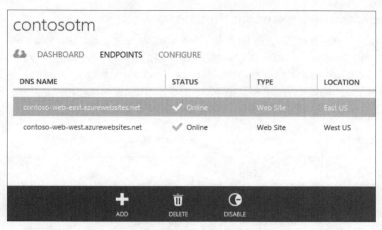

FIGURE 1-10 Adding, deleting, and disabling endpoints in an Azure Traffic Manager profile

You can use Azure PowerShell to add an endpoint by using the Get-AzureTrafficManagerProfile, Add-AzureTrafficManagerEndpoint, and Set-AzureTrafficManagerProfile cmdlets, as shown in the following code.

```
$tmProfile = Get-AzureTrafficManagerProfile -Name "ContosoTM"
Add-AzureTrafficManagerEndpoint -TrafficManagerProfile $tmProfile `

    -DomainName "contoso-web-west.azurewebsites.net" -Type AzureWebsite `
    -Status Enabled |
    Set-AzureTrafficManagerProfile
```

To remove an endpoint, use the Remove-AzureTrafficManagerEndpoint cmdlet as shown here.

```
$tmProfile = Get-AzureTrafficManagerProfile -Name "ContosoTM"

    Remove-AzureTrafficManagerEndpoint -TrafficManagerProfile $tmProfile `
    -DomainName "contoso-web-west.azurewebsites.net" |
    Set-AzureTrafficManagerProfile
```

To disable an endpoint, use the Set-AzureTrafficManagerEndpoint cmdlet as shown here.

```
$tmProfile = Get-AzureTrafficManagerProfile -Name "ContosoTM"
Set-AzureTrafficManagerEndpoint -TrafficManagerProfile $tmProfile `

    -DomainName "contoso-web-west.azurewebsites.net" -Status Disabled |
    Set-AzureTrafficManagerProfile
```

EXAM TIP

An Azure website must be in Standard mode to be added as an endpoint to an Azure Traffic Manager profile.

Updating DNS records for your custom domain

The last step to configuring Azure Traffic Manager is to update your custom domain to point to the Azure Traffic Manager DNS name using a CNAME record. As an example, assume your custom domain is *contoso.com* and your Azure Traffic Manager DNS name is *contoso-web-tm.trafficmanager.net*. Table 1-4 shows how the CNAME record should be configured in this scenario.

TABLE 1-4 Example DNS record for a custom domain and an Azure Traffic Manager DNS name

RECORD TYPE	NAME	VALUE
CNAME	*www.contoso.com*	*contoso-web-tm.trafficmanager.net*

EXAM TIP

As users navigate to an application configured with Azure Traffic Manager, there is not any actual traffic routed through Traffic Manager. When a user browses to a website configured with Azure Traffic Manager, such as *www.contoso.com*, the user's DNS server will send a new DNS query to the DNS name for the Traffic Manager profile, such as *contoso-web-tm.trafficmanager.net*. The Traffic Manager DNS name servers receive this query. Based on the load balancing method in the Azure Traffic Manager profile, Traffic Manager will select an endpoint from the profile, and return a CNAME record mapping *contoso-web-tm.trafficmanager.net* to the DNS name for the selected endpoint, such as *contoso-web-east.azurewebsites.net*. The user's DNS server will then resolve the endpoint DNS name to an IP address and return it to the user. The user's browser then calls the selected website using the IP address. The domain and IP address are cached on the client machine, so subsequent requests to the website are sent directly to the website until the local DNS cache expires.

Configuring handler mappings

Depending on the tools and language used to build a website, it may be necessary for you to configure additional handlers (or interpreters) to support the website code. To configure a handler mapping for an Azure website requires the following settings:

- **Extension**   The file extension that you want to be handled by the script processor. This can be a wildcard, a specific file extension, or even a specific file. For example, *, *.php, and Handler.fcgi. The script processor defined in the script processor path will process requests that match this pattern.

- **Script Processor Path**   The absolute path to the script processor that will process requests for files matching the pattern in the extension property.

- **Optional Arguments**   This can be a path to a script for the script processor to process or any other argument that you may need to define when invoking the script processor.

Configuring handler mappings using the management portal

In the management portal, you can add handler mappings by opening the Site Settings blade for your website. Scroll down towards the bottom of the blade until you find the Handler Mappings section, as shown in Figure 1-11.

FIGURE 1-11 Handler mappings in the Site Settings blade of the management portal

Configuring handler mappings using Azure PowerShell

Handler mappings can also be added using the Azure PowerShell cmdlets. The first task is to create a new HandlerMapping object and initialize it with your settings. Then, use the Set-AzureWebsite cmdlet and pass the handler mapping in using the HandlerMappings parameter. The script below demonstrates adding a handler mapping for *.php files.

```
$wsName = "contoso-web"

$handlerMapping = New-Object Microsoft.WindowsAzure.Commands.Utilities.Websites.
Services.WebEntities.HandlerMapping

$handlerMapping.Extension = "*.php"
$handlerMapping.ScriptProcessor = "d:\home\site\wwwroot\bin\php54\php-cgi.exe"

Set-AzureWebsite -Name $wsName -HandlerMappings $handlerMapping
```

Configuring virtual applications and directories

Some websites might require virtual applications or directories be added as part of the website configuration. Azure Websites supports these configuration requirements. Configuring a virtual application or directory for an Azure website requires the following settings:

- **Virtual Directory**   The path that users will use to access the directory or application.
- **Physical Path** (relative to site)   The path to the physical directory or application.
- **Application**   If selected, the virtual directory is configured as a web application. If the checkbox is clear, it will be a virtual directory.

Configuring virtual applications and directories using the management portal

In the management portal, you can add virtual applications and directories by opening the Site Settings blade for your website. Scroll down towards the bottom of the blade until you find the Virtual Applications and Directories section, as shown in Figure 1-12.

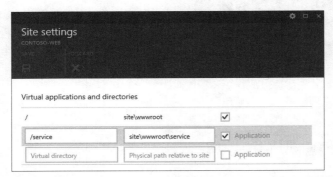

FIGURE 1-12 Virtual applications and directories in the Site Settings blade of the management portal

Using the Azure Cross-Platform Command-Line Interface tools for configuration tasks

For most of this book, the Azure PowerShell cmdlets are referenced for automating tasks using the script and that is a natural experience for users on the Windows platform. However, for users who are not running Windows or prefer an experience other than Azure PowerShell, Microsoft Azure offers the Azure Cross-Platform Command-Line Interface tools (xplat-cli).

The xplat-cli tools can be downloaded for free from the same download page the Azure PowerShell cmdlets are available at, which is *http://azure.microsoft.com/en-us/downloads/*. Scroll down to the Command-line tools section to locate the download links.

The xplat-cli tools are available for the following operating systems:

- Windows
- Mac
- Linux

To use the xplat-cli tools on Windows, open a command prompt and type Azure to list the version of the tools installed and the help for some of the commands, as shown in Figure 1-13.

FIGURE 1-13 The xplat-cli tools for Azure on Windows

Much of what you can do with the management portal and Azure PowerShell cmdlets you can also do with the xplat-cli tools. The Azure platform, features, and tools evolve at a very rapid pace, so it is important to make sure you update your tools regularly.

The xplat-cli tools are easy to use and offer help simply by typing the commands as shown in Figure 1-13. Since this chapter is about Azure Websites, type the following command to list all the commands specific to Azure Websites.

```
Azure site
```

One of the commands available is the command to list the sites in your subscription. To do this, type the following command.

```
Azure site list
```

As part of the list command, you can specify the *name* parameter to list only the site indicated. For example, to list the contoso-web website, type the following command.

```
Azure site list contoso-web
```

You can also create and edit websites. For example, Figure 1-14 shows how to create a new website in East US named contoso-web-01.

```
E:\>azure site create --location "East US" contoso-web-01
info:    Executing command site create
+ Getting sites
+ Getting locations
info:    Creating a new web site at contoso-web-01.azurewebsites.net
|info:    Created website at contoso-web-01.azurewebsites.net
+
info:    site create command OK
```

FIGURE 1-14 Creating a new website using the xplat-cli tools for Azure on Windows.

Thought experiment

Configure SSL with a custom domain

In this thought experiment, apply what you've learned about this objective. You can find answers to these questions in the "Answers" section at the end of this chapter.

You are the IT Administrator for Contoso. You have been asked to configure the Contoso website to use SSL for the root domain and all sub-domains (one level deep). The Contoso website already has a custom domain configured under the name *www.contoso.com* using CNAME records (no A records). During your requirements gathering you learned that your solution needs to work with recent browsers, such as Internet Explorer 7 (and newer), Safari 3.0 (and newer), and Google Chrome for Windows 6 (and newer).

1. What kind of SSL certificate will you need?

2. What are the steps required for you to deliver a solution?

Objective summary

- An Azure Website site setting is where you can configure language versions for .NET Framework, PHP, Java, and Python. This is also where you can set the site to run in 32-bit or 64-bit mode, enable web sockets and the Always-On feature, configure handler mappings, custom domains, and SSL.

- Application settings and connection strings can be defined in site settings and retrieved at application runtime using environment variables.

- An Azure website can have multiple custom domains associated with it. To configure a custom domain, you must first add an A and/or CNAME record using your DNS registrar. For A records, you must first add the awverify CNAME record.

- Azure Websites support Server Name Indication (SNI) SSL and IP-based SSL for websites with a custom domain.

- Azure Websites can be configured using the management portal, Azure PowerShell cmdlets, and the Cross-Platform Command-Line tools.

- The Cross-Platform Command-Line tools for Azure can be run on Windows, Mac, and Linux.

Objective review

Answer the following questions to test your knowledge of the information in this objective. You can find the answers to these questions and explanations of why each answer choice is correct or incorrect in the "Answers" section at the end of this chapter.

1. Which site settings can you define that can be read at application runtime using environment variables? (Choose all that apply.)

   A. Connection strings

   B. Handler mappings

   C. Application settings

   D. .NET Framework Version

2. Which Azure PowerShell cmdlet is used to add an endpoint to a Traffic Manager profile?

   A. Enable-AzureTrafficManagerProfile

   B. Set-AzureTrafficManagerEndpoint

   C. Set-AzureTrafficManagerProfile

   D. Add-AzureTrafficManagerEndpoint

3. Which Azure Traffic Manager load balancing method should be used to improve performance for users?

   A. Round Robin

   B. Failover

   C. Performance

   D. CDN

4. 4. Which operating system platforms are supported by the Azure Cross-Platform Command-Line tools? (Choose all that apply.)

   A. Windows

   B. Mac

   C. Azure

   D. Linux

Objective 1.3: Configure diagnostics, monitoring, and analytics

Monitoring websites to identify failures, potential performance issues, or metrics used to determine application health is a necessary function for IT. Azure Websites provides a rich set of monitoring and diagnostic features that you can use to easily monitor the website and quickly retrieve diagnostic data when you need to probe deeper into how the site is performing.

This objective covers how to:

- Enable application and site diagnostics
- Retrieve diagnostic logs
- View streaming logs
- Monitor website resources
- Configure endpoint monitoring and alerts
- Monitor Azure services
- Configure analytics
- Configure backup

Enabling application and site diagnostics

Diagnostic logging is not enabled by default. It is up to you to enable and configure logging in a way that provides the information you need to troubleshoot issues. There are two categories of Azure Website log files:

- Application diagnostic logs
- Site diagnostic logs

Application diagnostic logs contain information produced by the application code. This can be tracing that the developers instrumented when writing the code, or exceptions that were raised by the application. When you enable application logs, you must specify the logging level, which can be one of the following:

- Error
- Warning
- Information
- Verbose

Site diagnostic logs contain information produced by the web server that the web application is running on. Three types of site diagnostic logs can be enabled:

- **Web Server Logging**   Contains all HTTP events on a website and is formatted using the W3C extended log file format.

- **Detailed Error Messages**   Contains information on requests that resulted in a HTTP status code of 400 or higher.
- **Failed Request Tracing**   Contains detailed traces for any failed requests. This log also contains traces for all of the IIS components that were involved in processing the request. This can be useful when trying to isolate where in the system a failure is occurring.

EXAM TIP

Application diagnostic logs can be saved to the website's file system, Azure Table Storage, or Azure Blob Storage. The web server logging in site diagnostics can be saved to the website's file system or Azure Blob Storage.

Enabling diagnostics logs using the management portal

In the management portal, you can enable application and site diagnostic logs by opening the Website blade for your website and clicking the Diagnostics Logs part under the Operations section. This will open the Logs blade, where you can enable the logs and configure the logging level, as shown in Figure 1-15.

FIGURE 1-15 The Logs blade in the management portal where logging can be enabled and configured

Enabling diagnostics logs using Azure PowerShell cmdlets

You can enable and disable diagnostic logs using the Set-AzureWebsite cmdlet. As an example, the code shown here enables the *web server logging* and the *failed request tracing*.

```
$wsName = "contoso-web"
Set-AzureWebsite -Name $wsName -RequestTracingEnabled $true -HttpLoggingEnabled $true
```

Retrieving diagnostic logs

You have many choices when it comes to retrieving diagnostic logs or just viewing the contents of the logs. Regardless of how you choose to retrieve diagnostic logs, it's helpful to understand where the logs are stored on the website's file system. Table 1-5 lists the different logs and their location in the file system.

TABLE 1-5 Diagnostic log file locations on the file system for an Azure website

LOG FILE TYPE	LOCATION
Application Diagnostics	D:\Home\LogFiles\Application\
SITE DIAGNOSTICS (WEB SERVER)	D:\HOME\LOGFILES\HTTP\RAWLOGS\
Site Diagnostics (Detailed Errors)	D:\Home\LogFiles\DetailedErrors\
SITE DIAGNOSTICS (FAILED REQUEST TRACES)	D:\HOME\LOGFILES\W3SVC<RANDOM#>\

> **NOTE** **FAILED REQUEST LOGS STYLE SHEET FILE**
>
> When failed request logging is enabled, the folder where the logs are stored contains an .xml file and a file named Freb.xsl file. The .xml file contains the log data generated by the server. The Freb.xsl file is a style sheet document that enhances viewing the .xml file in your browser. When downloading failed request logs to your local computer, save the Freb.xsl in the same folder with .xml file. Then, open the .xml file using your browser for an enhanced viewing experience. This makes identifying errors and warnings in the log much easier.

Using FTP to retrieve log files

In the Logs blade of the management portal are settings identifying the FTP user and a URL that you can use to access the website's file system. Using this information you can connect using any FTP client you choose, navigate the file system, and download diagnostic logs.

Using Site Control Manager (Kudu) to retrieve log files

Site Control Manager, often referred to as "Kudu", is a website extension that you can use to retrieve log files, browse the file system, edit files, delete files, view environment variables, and even capture diagnostic dump files.

To access the Site Control Manager, open your browser and navigate to

https://<your site name>.scm.azurewebsites.net

EXAM TIP

Every Azure website gets the Site Control Manager site extension installed by default. There is nothing you have to do to enable it.

The URL is the same as the URL for your website, with the added scm. immediately after the website name. Figure 1-16 is an example of what the Site Control Manager screen looks like for a website.

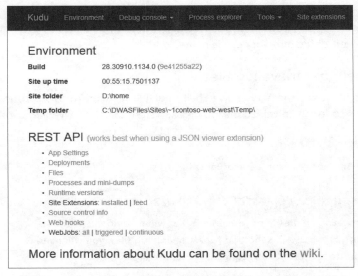

FIGURE 1-16 The home page of the Site Control Manager site extension

Using Site Control Manager, select the Debug Console and then select the CMD option. This opens a debug console that you can type directly into or use the navigation above. As you click the navigation links, the debug console will update to your current directory. Figure 1-17 shows the debug console screen and the contents of the LogFiles folder.

FIGURE 1-17 The debug console in Site Control Manager and viewing the LogFiles folder

Using Site Control Manager, you can download an entire folder or individual files by clicking the download link to the left of the directory or file name.

Using Azure PowerShell to retrieve log files

You can download all the log files using the Azure PowerShell cmdlet Save-AzureWebsiteLog, as shown in the code below. This code will download the log files and store them in E:\Weblogs.zip on the client computer.

```
$wsName = "contoso-web"
Save-AzureWebsiteLog -Name $wsName -Output e:\weblogs.zip
```

> **NOTE SAVING LOG FILES TO LOCAL COMPUTER USING POWERSHELL**
>
> Using the Save-AzureWebsiteLog cmdlet to download log files will download all logs except the Failed Request logs. If you use this method for retrieving log files, you will need to use one of the other options to retrieve failed request logs separately.

Viewing streaming logs

Sometimes it is preferable to view log data as it is being collected (almost real-time). Azure Websites provides a feature to enable streaming of log data via the log-streaming service. You can connect to the log-streaming service using the following methods:

- management portal
- Azure PowerShell Cmdlets
- Cross-Platform Command-Line Tools (xplat-cli)
- Site Control Manager (Kudu)
- Visual Studio

Viewing streaming logs using the management portal

The streaming log service is accessible from the Website blade of your website. Scroll down to the Operations section where you will see the Streaming Logs part, as shown in Figure 1-18.

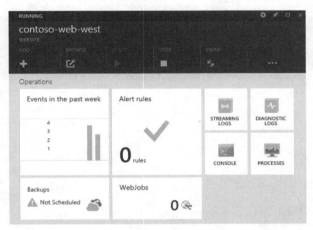

FIGURE 1-18 The Streaming Logs part on the Website blade of the management portal

In the Streaming Logs blade, you can toggle between application and web server logs, pause and start the log-streaming service, and clear the logs in the console. Figure 1-19 shows example output for the web server logs in the Streaming Logs blade.

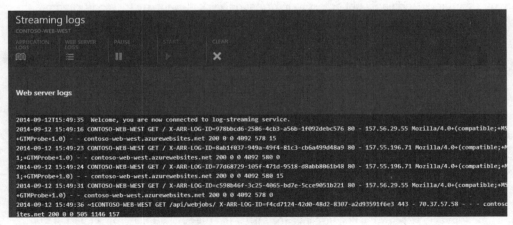

FIGURE 1-19 The Streaming Logs blade showing web server logs

Viewing streaming logs using Azure PowerShell

Using the Get-AzureWebsiteLog cmdlet, you can stream logs directly in the Azure PowerShell console window. The code shown here connects to the log-streaming service to start streaming the web server logs.

```
Get-AzureWebsiteLog -Name "contoso-web-west" -Tail -Path http
```

The Get-AzureWebsiteLog also supports a Message parameter that you can use to filter the output when streaming application logs. For example, the code shown here filters the log-streaming output to just application logs that are categorized as errors.

```
Get-AzureWebsiteLog -Name "contoso-web-west" -Tail -Message Error
```

Viewing streaming logs using Site Control Manager

The log-streaming service is available in the Site Control Manager as an option in the Tools menu, as shown in Figure 1-20.

FIGURE 1-20 The Tools menu in Site Control Manager showing the Log Stream option

Monitoring website resources

The management portal provides rich and visually appealing screens to monitor your Azure Website and resources included in the website's Resource group. The Website blade is where you can quickly and easily get access to information, click through metrics, parts and graphs, and in some cases just hover over part items to drill deeper into the data.

The Website blade is divided into sections such as Summary, Monitoring, Usage, Operations, Deployment, Networking, Configuration, and Access. Each section is pre-configured with live parts that provide various metrics for the website.

> *NOTE* **CUSTOMIZING BLADES IN THE MANAGEMENT PORTAL**
>
> Blades in the management portal can be customized to include or exclude information based on your preferences. You can also change the size of parts and reposition them. This is a very powerful feature of the management portal because not all websites are monitored equally. For example, you may have a line-of-business website where you want the summary to show the Backups and Alert parts. You may have a customer-facing site where you want the summary to show the Request and Errors part, and the Sessions Per Browser part. It's up to you how you customize the blade to give you the information important for your website.

You can quickly see the resources in the *resource group* of the website in the Summary section of the Website blade. Figure 1-21 is an example showing a resource group named ContosoWebSite that contains an Azure website, a virtual machine running SQL Server, and other resources. By clicking the ContosoWebSite resource group, you can then drill down further into all the resources in the group.

FIGURE 1-21 A resource group consisting of a website, virtual machine, and other resources

Azure Websites provide a number of useful performance counter metrics that you can monitor visually in a graph or in a line item detailed list using the management portal. Metrics that are available for websites are listed here:

- **CPUTime**   A measure of the website's CPU usage.
- **Requests**   A count of client requests to the website.
- **Data Out**   A measure of data sent by the website to clients.
- **Data In**   A measure of data received by the website from clients.
- **HTTP Client Errors**   Number of HTTP 4xx Client Error messages sent.
- **HTTP Server Errors**   Number of HTTP 5xx Server Error messages sent.
- **HTTP Successes**   Number of HTTP 2xx Success messages sent.
- **HTTP Redirects**   Number of HTTP 3xx Redirection messages sent.
- **HTTP 401 Errors**   Number of HTTP 401 Unauthorized messages sent.
- **HTTP 403 Errors**   Number of HTTP 403 Forbidden messages sent.
- **HTTP 404 Errors**   Number of HTTP 404 Not Found messages sent.
- **HTTP 406 Errors**   Number of HTTP 406 Not Acceptable messages sent.

Configuring endpoint monitoring and alerts

Endpoint monitoring is a feature that enables you to monitor your website from external geo-distributed locations. This feature is uniquely different from traditional performance counter monitoring where you are monitoring metrics on the server that the website is running on.

Azure Websites support up to two endpoints for endpoint monitoring. Each endpoint can be monitored (or tested) from up to three locations. For each endpoint you want to configure a web test for, the following information is required:

- **Test Name**   A name you will use to identify the test in the management portal.
- **URL**   The URL you want Azure to perform tests against. This can be your root website URL, such as *contoso.com*, or perhaps a custom health check page.
- **Test Locations**   The external locations you want Azure to perform the tests from. This can range from one to three locations.
- **Success Criteria**   The HTTP status code Azure should expect to indicate a successful test. Generally, this would be HTTP 200 (OK). Optionally, you can configure a content *match*, which is specific text in the response that Azure can look for to determine if the test was successful.
- **Alerts**   You can choose to enable an *alert* to notify by email service administrators and co-administrators on the subscription, or other administrators by specifying the email address.

EXAM TIP

Alerts can be configured with a sensitivity setting of low (1), medium (2), or high (3). A setting of low triggers an alert when all test locations detect a failure within 15 minutes. A setting of medium triggers an alert when at least half of the test locations detect a failure in 10 minutes. A setting of high triggers an alert any time a failure is detected.

With endpoint monitoring and alerts configured, you can let Azure perform the web tests as you have configured them, and wait for an email alert if a problem is detected. However, you can also get very useful information from the management portal relating to endpoint monitoring to see how the tests are performing, if any tests have failed and why, and metrics captured by the endpoint monitoring service.

The *Web Test* blade shows a graph of server response times, the number of successful tests, and the number of failed tests. The *Test Locations* section of the blade shows the locations the web test is being run from and the success rate in 20 minute, 1 hour, 24 hour, and 72 hour increments. The Failed Tests section will show tests that have failed per location, and you can click each one to see the test details and learn more about why the test failed.

The Web Test blade, as shown in Figure 1-22, provides a nice visual of how the web tests are performing, the number of successful tests, and the number of failed tests.

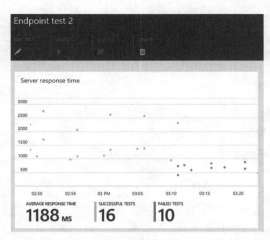

FIGURE 1-22 The server response time graph summarizing web tests performed

Configuring alerts based on metrics and events

Alerts can also be configured based on other metric conditions of the occurrence of certain events. The action taken when the alert is triggered is the same as discussed previously, which is to email service administrators and co-administrators on the subscription, and optionally other administrators with a specified email.

Configuring alerts based on performance counter metrics

To configure alerts based on performance counter metrics, open the Website blade for the website and scroll down to the Operations section to locate the Alert Rules web part. Click the Alert Rules part to open the Alert Rules blade, where you can add and edit alert rules. You can define an alert for any of the performance counter metrics mentioned in the earlier section.

The alert must define the performance counter metric, the condition, the threshold, and the action to take. Figure 1-23 shows an alert rule configured to email service administrators and co-administrators when the average response time takes longer than 15 seconds for a sustained period of five minutes or more.

FIGURE 1-23 Alert rule configuration for average response time

Configuring alerts based on events

The management portal also provides a way to define alerts based on events. For example, you can configure an alert on the following operation names:

- **All Operations**   Any operation being performed on the website.
- **Status**   The status of the operation, which can be succeeded or failed.
- **Aggregation**   The granularity to consider for the alert. Options are None (alert on every event) and Count (alert on a condition and threshold defined).
- **Period**   The duration of the period to consider for the alert to be triggered.

You can view all of the operations for a website by opening the Events blade.

Monitoring Azure services

To effectively monitor websites that you are responsible for means you also need to be able to monitor the Azure services your website depends on. The Microsoft Azure platform is very transparent when it comes to service availability and places a Service Health web part on the home page of the management portal, as shown in Figure 1-24.

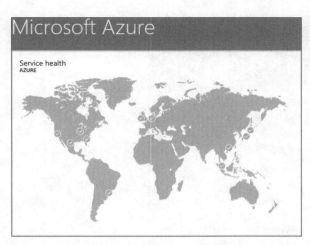

FIGURE 1-24 Service Health web part on the home page of the management portal

Green check marks on locations on the map in the Service Health web part, indicate that all services are running as expected. An orange exclamation mark indicates a warning. A red exclamation mark indicates an error. Finally, if you see a blue lower case "i", that is an indication of information you should be aware of, such as a service maintenance window in a particular region or for a particular service.

You can click the Service Health web part to get the status for services. From there, you can click each service to get the status per region.

> **MORE INFO**
>
> You can subscribe to an RSS feed to get updates from the Azure service dashboard at *http://azure.microsoft.com/en-us/status/feed/.* You can also see the history of service announcements at *http://azure.microsoft.com/en-us/status/#history.*

Configuring analytics

Azure Website analytics is a feature that can give you data about the different types of browsers your users are using, top pages viewed on your site, the slowest pages, the number of sessions per device, and more.

Analytics is collected client-side, not server-side. This means code needs to be inserted into the pages of the website you want to collect analytics for. The code is JavaScript code and can be generated directly from the management portal. From the Website blade, scroll to the Monitoring section, and click the Analytics web part. A blade displays the JavaScript code that should be inserted into the pages you want to collect analytics for, as shown in Figure 1-25.

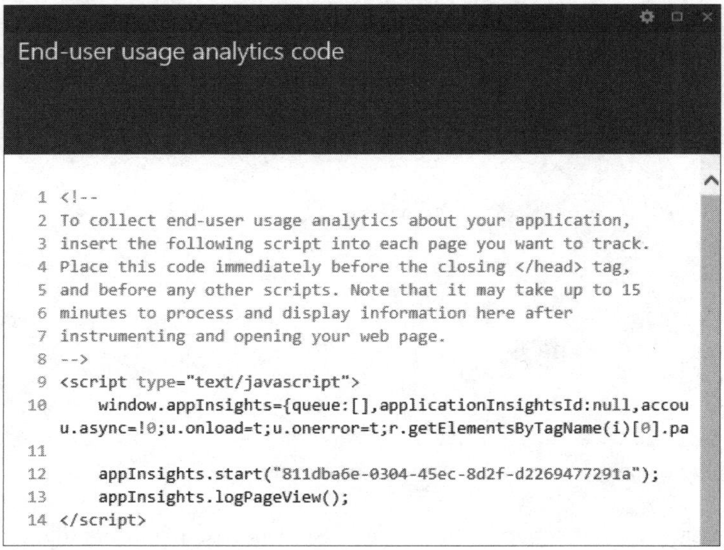

End-user usage analytics code

```
1  <!--
2  To collect end-user usage analytics about your application,
3  insert the following script into each page you want to track.
4  Place this code immediately before the closing </head> tag,
5  and before any other scripts. Note that it may take up to 15
6  minutes to process and display information here after
7  instrumenting and opening your web page.
8  -->
9  <script type="text/javascript">
10     window.appInsights={queue:[],applicationInsightsId:null,accou
   u.async=!0;u.onload=t;u.onerror=t;r.getElementsByTagName(i)[0].pa
11
12     appInsights.start("811dba6e-0304-45ec-8d2f-d2269477291a");
13     appInsights.logPageView();
14  </script>
```

FIGURE 1-25 JavaScript to insert in application pages to collect client-side analytics

After the JavaScript has been inserted into the pages, the user analytics will start showing up in the management portal.

> ***VIRTUAL ACADEMY*** **HYBRID CLOUD WORKLOADS - WEBSITES**
>
> Microsoft Virtual Academy provides an online training course that augments the content in this objective very well by covering how Azure Websites can be used in hybrid cloud scenarios. You can access the course at *http://www.microsoftvirtualacademy.com/training-courses/hybrid-cloud-workloads-websites*.

Configuring backup

While the Microsoft Azure platform is extremely resilient and has redundancy at many levels, a backup plan is still a best practice for any application running on-premises or in the cloud. Azure Websites offers an easy and effective backup service that can be used to back up your website configuration, file content, and even a SQL database or MySQL database that your application has a dependency on.

To configure backup for a website, you must have an Azure Storage account and a container where you want the backups stored.

Backups can be invoked on-demand or based on a schedule that you define. Regardless of how a backup is invoked, the contents of the backup will contain the following:

- **.zip file** A .zip file of the backed up data. If a SQL database is part of the backup, it will be in the root of the .zip file and stored as a BACPAC file.
- **.xml file** A manifest describing the contents of the .zip file.

The backup is a full backup of the website. It is not an incremental backup.

EXAM TIP

The storage account used to back up Azure Websites must belong to the same Azure subscription that the Azure website belongs to.

Restoring an Azure website backup

At some point it may be necessary to restore a website or a database from a backup. The management portal provides an intuitive interface to guide you through the process. As you start the restore process, you have the option to restore your website as follows:

- **Restore To Current Website** This option will overwrite your existing website with the backup website. As a result, your current website will be unavailable to users as the restore process completes.
- **Restore To A New Website Instance** This option will restore the backup to a new website instance.

The default option for database restore is to not *restore the database*. If you choose to restore the database, then you can choose to restore to the same database server or a new database server.

When restoring a SQL database to the same database server, you must choose a different database name to restore your database to. You cannot restore to the same name as the database that was backed up. When restoring a SQL database to a new database server, you can use the same database name.

When restoring a MySQL database, you can restore to the same database that was backed up, which will overwrite the existing database content.

Thought experiment

Configuring endpoint monitoring

In this thought experiment, apply what you've learned about this objective. You can find answers to these questions in the "Answers" section at the end of this chapter.

You are the IT Administrator for Contoso. The customer service group has been getting complaints from users lately indicating the public-facing website has been intermittently slow. Some users have also reported that they get an error message indicating a problem occurred processing their request.

The website has just one deployment in the North Central US region. All the services such as databases, web services, and storage accounts are in the same resource group as the website. Your user base has mostly been in the US. However, Contoso has lately been experiencing growth for users in Europe.

You need to configure monitoring to collect information that will help determine the root cause for the performance issues.

1. What kind of monitoring should you configure and how might you configure it?

Objective summary

- Azure Websites provides two categories of diagnostic logs: application diagnostics and site diagnostics. There are three site diagnostic log files available: Web Server, Detailed Errors, and Failed Request.
- When enabling application diagnostic logging, you must specify the logging level, which can be Error, Warning, Information, or Verbose.
- Site Control Manager (Kudu) is a website extension and is installed by default for every website. It is accessible at *https://<your site name>.scm.azurewebsites.net*. To authenticate, sign-in using the same credentials you use to sign-in to the management portal.
- When configuring endpoint monitoring, you can have up to two endpoints monitored per websites. For each endpoint, you can have up to three external locations perform web tests against the endpoint.
- Alerts can be configured for endpoints configured with endpoint monitoring, for performance counter metrics, and for events.
- Azure Website backups can be used to back up website configuration, file content, and databases. The databases supported for backup are SQL Database and MySQL.
- Azure Website backups can be performed on-demand or on a schedule.

Objective review

Answer the following questions to test your knowledge of the information in this objective. You can find the answers to these questions and explanations of why each answer choice is correct or incorrect in the "Answers" section at the end of this chapter.

1. Which are valid site diagnostic logs in Azure Websites? (Choose all that apply.)

   A. Application diagnostics

   B. Web server logging

   C. Detailed error messages

   D. Failed request tracing

2. Which Azure PowerShell cmdlet should you use to download the diagnostic logs from an Azure website to your local computer?

   A. Get-AzureWebsiteLog

   B. Enable-AzureWebsiteApplicationDiagnostic

   C. Save-AzureWebsiteLog

   D. Get-AzureWebsiteMetric

3. Which types of logs can be streamed using the log-streaming service? (Choose all that apply.)

   A. Application logs

   B. Failed request logs

   C. Detailed error messages

   D. Web server logs

4. When configuring endpoint monitoring, how many external website locations can you configure to perform web tests for an endpoint?

   A. Zero to three

   B. Two or more

   C. One to three

   D. One to two

5. Which is not part of the contents backed up when using the backup service for an Azure Website?

   A. Website configuration

   B. Website performance metrics

   C. Website file content

   D. Website databases

Objective 1.4: Configure scale and resilience

The Microsoft Azure platform is an extremely resilient platform. By leveraging the services and features available, users of the platform can implement solutions that can scale to meet the demand from users in a way that is cost effective for the business. The notion of elastic scale is a key driver for moving to the cloud, and Azure Websites delivers this with a rich set of scalability configurations you can apply to your websites that are configured for Standard mode.

Using the Autoscale feature, you can scale up and down the number of instances of your website based on schedules you set or metrics you define.

In cases where you just need more resources, such as CPU cores and RAM, you can manually scale up the size of website instances to meet the resource needs of the application.

This objective covers how to:

- Configure Autoscale using schedules
- Configure Autoscale using metrics
- Scale-up a website instance

Configuring Autoscale using schedules

Autoscale can be configured uniquely for different schedules. The schedule options you have available are as follows:

- **Recurring Schedules For Day And Night** This option is ideal when you need to scale up or down your website instances daily. You may need more instances running during the day than you need at night, and this schedule options gives you a way to define that.

- **Recurring Schedules For Weekdays And Weekends** This option is ideal when you need to scale up or down your website instances differently for weekdays and weekends.

- **Specific Dates** This option is ideal when you need to scale your website for specific dates and times that are not part of a recurring schedule. For example, if your website is an online retail website, then you may want to define a schedule for Cyber Monday or Black Friday.

EXAM TIP

Before you can access the Autoscale settings for an Azure website, the website's mode must first be set to Standard.

The management portal gives you a great deal of flexibility when it comes to defining a schedule that you can configure Autoscale for. Figure 1-26 shows the scheduling options covered above in more detail using the management portal.

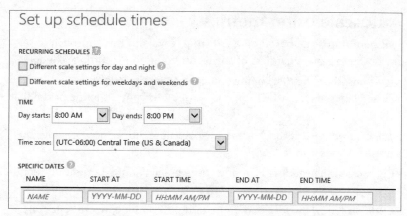

FIGURE 1-26 Options for defining recurring and non-recurring schedules

After schedules have been defined, you can configure Autoscale to scale the number of website instances by setting the instance count to a value between 1 and 10. For example, if you selected a schedule for weekday and weekend, you might configure weekday to run eight instances and configure weekend to run three instances. With these settings, the Autoscale feature in Azure Websites will scale your instances automatically. Figure 1-27 shows the Weekday Autoscale setting for such an example.

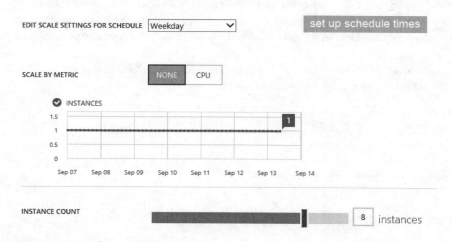

FIGURE 1-27 Weekday Autoscale setting in the management portal

EXAM TIP

You can scale website instances up and down, but it is not possible to start and stop the website on a schedule. For example, you cannot set the low end of your instance range to zero. It must be at least one.

Configuring Autoscale using metrics

You can choose to configure Autoscale based on a *CPU* metric. Taking this approach to Autoscale allows your website to scale regardless of any recurring or non-recurring schedules.

To configure Autoscale based on the CPU metric you need to first set the Scale By Metric setting to CPU. This will activate the Instance Count and Target CPU controls in the portal that you can customize.

The Instance Count and Target CPU settings are ranges of values, not a specific value. The way Azure interprets these settings is as follows:

- If the average CPU across all instances of your website are within the target CPU range, no action is taken.
- If the average CPU falls below the low-end of the target CPU range, Azure Autoscales your running instances down (once every two hours) until the number of running instances equals the low-end range defined in the Instance Count setting.
- If the average CPU exceeds the high-end of the target CPU range, Azure Autoscales your running instances up until the number of running instances equals the high-end range defined in the Instance Count setting.

> **NOTE** **AUTOSCALE USING OTHER METRICS BESIDES CPU**
>
> At the time of this writing, new metrics are being added to the Autoscale feature that include Memory Percentage, Disk Queue Length, HTTP Queue Length, Data In, and Data Out. These metrics are only available in the new management portal at *http://portal.azure.com*.

Figure 1-28 shows an example Autoscale configuration base on the CPU metric with an Instance Count between 3 and 8, and a Target CPU between 55 and 75 percent.

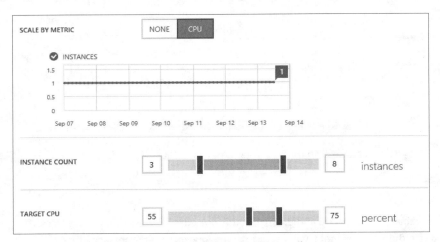

FIGURE 1-28 Autoscale configuration based on the CPU metric

Scaling up a website instance

Another aspect of managing scale for a website has to do with the resources per instance the website requires. For example, a website may initially only require the 1 core and 1.75 GB of memory to run as designed. However, over time and as more features are added, the website may require more resources, such as 2 cores and 3.5 GB of memory. Azure Websites provide a way for you to scale up the instance size of your running instances. There are three settings available for the instance size, as shown here:

- Small (1 core, 1.75 GB memory)
- Medium (2 cores, 3.5 GB memory)
- Large (4 cores, 7 GB memory)

The instance size setting is only available for websites running in a Basic and Standard-mode hosting plan. This setting is not applicable for websites running the Free or Shared plans.

EXAM TIP

It is not possible to autoscale the instance size for running instances of your website. If you define your instance size as Medium, all of your running instances will be Medium. In other words, you cannot have one instance of your website running a Small instance size and another instance of the same website running a Large instance.

Thought experiment
Autoscale an Azure website

In this thought experiment, apply what you've learned about this objective. You can find answers to these questions in the "Answers" section at the end of this chapter.

You are the IT Administrator for Contoso and responsible for managing the Contoso website. The public-facing website today is running in a Shared mode hosting plan. The development team is about to release a new version of the website that will require 1 dedicated core and 2.5 GB of memory to perform as designed.

As part of this new release, the marketing team is planning to run some television commercials and radio ads to notify new and existing customers of the new features and services offered by Contoso. The expectation is that these ads will generate large demand spikes as they are run during the campaign.

You need to provide a solution to meet the resource requirements for the new website version and to support the traffic spikes expected during the marketing campaign.

1. How will you scale the website to meet the new resource requirements?

2. How will you configure the website to support the traffic spikes during the marketing campaign?

Objective summary

- Autoscale can be configured to scale on a schedule or based on a metric.
- When configuring Autoscale schedules, you can define recurring schedules for day/night, recurring schedules for weekday/weekend, and specific schedules where you define the start time and end time for an Autoscale schedule.
- The instance size for a website can be set to Small (1 core, 1.75 GB memory), Medium (2 cores, 3.5 GB memory), or Large (4 cores, 7 GB memory). The instance size setting is only applicable to websites in the Basic and Standard mode hosting plans.
- The instance count for a website can be between 1 and 10.

Objective review

Answer the following questions to test your knowledge of the information in this objective. You can find the answers to these questions and explanations of why each answer choice is correct or incorrect in the "Answers" section at the end of this chapter.

1. Which Autoscale schedule setting is needed to configure Autoscale for a website such that the number of running instances can be increased during the day and decreased in the evening?

   A. Recurring schedule for weekday and weekend

   B. Recurring schedule for day and night

   C. Specific schedule with a start time in the morning and an end time in the evening

   D. Specific schedule with a start time in the evening and an end time in the morning

2. Which are valid instance size settings for an Azure website? (Choose all that apply.)

   A. A0 (Shared core, 768 MB memory)

   B. Small (1 core, 1.75 GB memory)

   C. Medium (2 cores, 3.5 GB memory)

   D. Large (4 cores, 7 GB memory)

Objective 1.5: Manage hosting plans

Azure Websites use web hosting plans to group features and capacity settings that can be shared across one or more websites. This enables you to control costs and resources for your websites. Web hosting plans are available as Free, Shared, Basic, or Standard plans. As you have seen from earlier objectives in this chapter, each plan (or mode) has a unique set of features and capabilities.

> **This objective covers how to:**
> - Create a new web hosting plan
> - Create a website within an existing web hosting plan
> - Migrate websites between hosting plans

Creating a new web hosting plan

You can create a new web hosting plan when you create a new website using the management portal. In the new Website blade, click the Web Hosting Plan setting to pick the web hosting plan that you want. The Pricing tier blade does a wonderful job showing all the web hosting plans available, the feature differences, and even the estimated monthly costs for each plan. After you have selected the plan you want, give the web hosting plan a name, and it will be saved as you continue through the process of creating the website. Figure 1-29 shows the Standard tier plans.

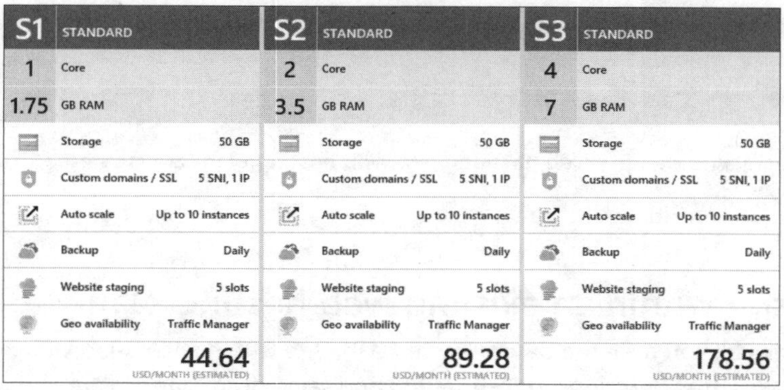
S1 STANDARD
1 Core
1.75 GB RAM
Storage 50 GB
Custom domains / SSL 5 SNI, 1 IP
Auto scale Up to 10 instances
Backup Daily
Website staging 5 slots
Geo availability Traffic Manager
44.64
USD/MONTH (ESTIMATED)
S2 STANDARD
2 Core
3.5 GB RAM
Storage 50 GB
Custom domains / SSL 5 SNI, 1 IP
Auto scale Up to 10 instances
Backup Daily
Website staging 5 slots
Geo availability Traffic Manager
89.28
USD/MONTH (ESTIMATED)
S3 STANDARD
4 Core
7 GB RAM
Storage 50 GB
Custom domains / SSL 5 SNI, 1 IP
Auto scale Up to 10 instances
Backup Daily
Website staging 5 slots
Geo availability Traffic Manager
178.56
USD/MONTH (ESTIMATED)

FIGURE 1-29 Standard tier web hosting plans

Figure 1-30 shows the Basic tier plans. Notice that features such as Autoscale, Backup, Staging slots, and Traffic Manager are not part of the Basic plans.

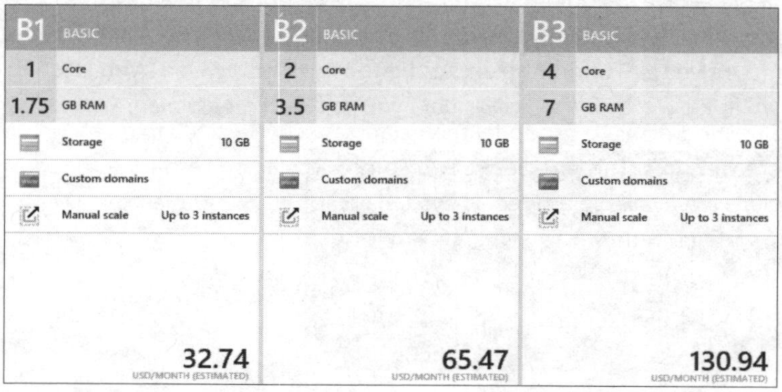
B1 BASIC
1 Core
1.75 GB RAM
Storage 10 GB
Custom domains
Manual scale Up to 3 instances
32.74
USD/MONTH (ESTIMATED)
B2 BASIC
2 Core
3.5 GB RAM
Storage 10 GB
Custom domains
Manual scale Up to 3 instances
65.47
USD/MONTH (ESTIMATED)
B3 BASIC
4 Core
7 GB RAM
Storage 10 GB
Custom domains
Manual scale Up to 3 instances
130.94
USD/MONTH (ESTIMATED)

FIGURE 1-30 Basic tier web hosting plans

Figure 1-31 shows the Free and Shared plans. As you can see, these are bare essential plans at little to no cost. This is a fantastic option for websites early in the development lifecycle phase. As the website needs grow, you can move it to another web hosting plan that offers the features and capacity needed.

FIGURE 1-31 Free and Shared tier web hosting plans

EXAM TIP

It is not possible to create a new empty web hosting plan. Web hosting plans are created during website creation.

Creating a website within an existing web hosting plan

When creating a new website, you have the option to create the site within an existing web hosting plan. To do this, click the Web Hosting Plan setting and select from one of your existing plans.

Migrating websites between hosting plans

As your website requirements evolve, it could make sense to move your site to a new web hosting plan that offers the capacity and features needed. To do this, open the Website blade for the website you want to move to a different plan. At the top of the blade is a Web Hosting Plan toolbar button, shown in Figure 1-32 that will enable you to select a new plan.

FIGURE 1-32 Website blade toolbar with the Web Hosting Plan button

When moving a website to a new web hosting plan, the new plan must be in the same region and resource group as the plan it is currently in.

Thought experiment

Managing web hosting plans for a website

In this thought experiment, apply what you've learned about this objective. You can find answers to these questions in the "Answers" section at the end of this chapter.

You are the IT Administrator for Contoso. The development team has asked you to create a website environment for a new website they have been working on. They have been using the Free tier to build a minimum viable product for the site and are ready to engage a few select customers to get their early feedback. The only additional feature they need at the moment is a custom domain without SSL support. They aren't concerned about availability of the site at this time.

Shortly after the site is deployed, the development team will be iterating quickly (several times a day) to implement features, fix bugs, and other things captured during customer feedback. Therefore, they will also need a way to quickly and easily test changes internally before making them available for the customer to review.

You need to provide a solution at a minimum cost.

1. Which web hosting plan would you choose for the development team?

2. How will you support the rapid pace for deployments that the development team will need?

Objective summary

- Web hosting plans are a way to group together capacity and features that can be shared by multiple websites.

- Web hosting plans are available as Free, Shared, Basic, and Standard plans. Each plan offers unique capacity and feature settings.

- The Basic and Standard plans can be scaled up such that all website instances have the same instance size, which can be Small, Medium, and Large. This translates into three Basic plans and three Standard plans that you can choose from which are B1, B2, B3, and S1, S2, and S3.

- As a website's features and capacity requirements evolve, the website can be migrated to a different web hosting plan that meets the website's requirements.

Objective review

Answer the following questions to test your knowledge of the information in this objective. You can find the answers to these questions and explanations of why each answer choice is correct or incorrect in the "Answers" section at the end of this chapter.

1. Which web hosting plan would be appropriate for a website requiring SSL for a custom domain, 3 GB of memory, and a minimum of two instances?

   A. Standard (S2)

   B. Basic (B3)

   C. Shared

   D. Basic (B2)

2. Which web hosting plans can you configure a specific instance size for all websites in the web hosting plan? (Choose all that apply.)

   A. Standard

   B. Shared

   C. Basic

   D. Free

Answers

This section contains the solutions to the thought experiments and answers to the objective review questions in this chapter.

Objective 1.1: Thought experiment

1. Using the management portal, create a new Azure website using the Website + SQL template. This will provide you with options to create a SQL database. As a result, the SQL database and the Azure website will also be in the same resource group.

    A. When creating the SQL database, select the option to allow Azure Services to connect to it so that the Website will be able to access the database.

    B. Create an Azure Storage account in the same resource group as the Website and SQL database to support the requirement for storing document files.

    C. Configure the Website for Standard Mode to enable adding additional deployment slots.

    D. Add a deployment slot for "dev" and another deployment slot for "qa."

2. Yes, the location is something you should take into consideration when creating the resources in your resource group. Use the West Europe location when creating the Website, Storage account, and SQL database.

Objective 1.1: Review

1. **Correct answer:** B

    A. **Incorrect:** Publish-AzureWebsite is the cmdlet used to publish the web application (or code) into a deployment slot of the website.

    B. **Correct:** New-AzureWebsite is the cmdlet used to create a new Azure website. At a minimum, you need to specify the location for the website and a unique DNS name.

    C. **Incorrect:** New-AzureWebsiteJob is the cmdlet used to create a WebJob.

    D. **Incorrect:** Set-AzureWebsite is the cmdlet used to set website properties, such as application settings, connection strings, framework versions, and more.

2. **Correct answers:** B, C, and D

    A. **Incorrect:** Recurring is not a valid task type.

    B. **Correct:** On-Demand is a valid task type.

    C. **Correct:** Scheduled is a valid task type.

    D. **Correct:** Continuous is a valid task type.

3. **Correct answer:** C

   A. **Incorrect:** Autoscale is used to scale the number of standard instances of a website up and down.

   B. **Incorrect:** SSL is used to encrypt traffic on the wire.

   C. **Correct:** Always-On is recommended for continuously running WebJobs.

   D. **Incorrect:** Backup is a feature to back up the website contents and databases to Azure Blob Storage.

4. **Correct answer:** A

   A. **Correct:** Switch-AzureWebsiteSlot is the cmdlet used to swap deployment slots. If a website has only 1 additional deployment slot (additional to the production deployment slot), it is not necessary to specify the Slot2 parameter. If there are more than 2 deployment slots, it is necessary to specify Slot1 and Slot2 parameters.

   B. **Incorrect:** Get-AzureWebsite is the cmdlet used to get a list of the websites in the current subscription or configuration settings for a specified website.

   C. **Incorrect:** Restart-AzureWebsite is the cmdlet used to stop and then restart a specified website.

   D. **Incorrect:** Show-AzureWebsite is the cmdlet you can use to launch a browser and navigate to the URL of a specified website.

Objective 1.2: Thought experiment

1. Because your requirements indicate that your solution must work for sub-domains, you will need to obtain either a wildcard certificate or a certificate with subject alternate name (SAN) identifying all of the domains.

2. The steps required to deliver the solution are as follows:

   A. Configure the website for Standard mode if it is not already configured.

   B. Obtain an SSL certificate that is signed from a certificate authority (CA).

   C. Upload the Public Information Exchange (.pfx) file to Azure using the management portal. The SSL settings blade provides the user interface to upload the certificate for the website.

   D. Configure the SSL binding. Because you only have to be concerned with newer browsers, you should choose the SNI SSL option. If you had to support browsers older than what was specified in the requirements, you could use IP-based SSL.

Objective 1.2: Review

1. **Correct answers:** A, C

   A. **Correct:** Connection strings can be retrieved at runtime as environment variables. The environment variable name will have a prefix of SQLAZURECONNSTR_, SQLCONNSTR_, MYSQLCONNSTR_, or CUSTOMCONNSTR_.

   B. **Incorrect:** Handler mappings is not a setting that can be retrieved at runtime as an environment variable. The handler mapping is used to define a custom processing script for a particular file extension.

   C. **Correct:** Application settings can be retrieved at runtime as environment variables. The environment variable name will have a name starting with APPSETTING_.

   D. **Incorrect:** The .NET Framework version is a configuration setting in the site settings and is not something you define. You can only change its value.

2. **Correct answer:** D

   A. **Incorrect:** Enable-AzureTrafficManagerProfile is used to enable an existing Traffic Manager profile that was previously disabled.

   B. **Incorrect:** Set-AzureTrafficManagerEndpoint is used to update the properties of an existing Traffic Manager endpoint.

   C. **Incorrect:** Set-AzureTrafficManagerProfile is used to update the properties of an existing Traffic Manager profile. However, after updating the profile to include the new endpoint, this cmdlet would have to be called to update the profile in Azure.

   D. **Correct:** Add-AzureTrafficManagerEndpoint adds a new endpoint to a Traffic Manager profile. The result of this cmdlet is piped into (or passed as a parameter) to the Set-AzureTrafficMaanagerProfile cmdlet to apply the change in Azure.

3. **Correct answer:** C

   A. **Incorrect:** Round Robin will result in traffic being evenly distributed across all available endpoints, regardless of performance for the user.

   B. **Incorrect:** Failover will result in all traffic being routed to a primary endpoint, with backup endpoints on standby in case the primary goes down.

   C. **Correct:** The Performance method will determine the closest endpoint to the user with the lowest latency.

   D. **Incorrect:** CDN is a Content Delivery Network and is generally used for serving up static files to users in regions around the world. Although this is a very useful service to improve performance for users, it is not a valid Traffic Manager load balancing method.

4. **Correct answers:** A, B, D

    A. **Correct:** Windows is supported by the xplat-cli tools.

    B. **Correct:** Mac operating system is supported by the xplat-cli tools.

    C. **Incorrect:** Azure is not a client operating system.

    D. **Correct:** Linux is supported by the xplat-cli tools.

Objective 1.3: Thought experiment

1. Because the complaints are intermittent and largely around the speed of website responses, you should configure endpoint monitoring with web test from locations in the US, Europe, and locations where Contoso has high customer density. You might also choose to set up performance counter monitoring for HTTP Client Errors, and HTTP Server Errors. This may help validate the complaints from users that requests sometimes result in an error. As an added measure, you may configure an alert based on response time to notify you or other administrators when slow responses are being detected by the monitoring service.

Objective 1.3: Review

1. **Correct answers:** B, C, D

    A. **Incorrect:** Application diagnostics is the other category of diagnostic logs. It is used to capture logging from the application.

    B. **Correct:** Web server logging is part of site diagnostics. It contains all requests to the website in W3C extended log file format.

    C. **Correct:** Detailed error messages is part of site diagnostics. It contains error information for requests that result in an HTTP 400 code or higher.

    D. **Correct:** Failed request tracing is part of site diagnostics. It contains information about failed requests to the website and also traces from the IIS components that were involved in processing the request. The Freb.xsl file is present in the same folder to enhance the viewing experience of the failed request log.

2. **Correct answer:** C

    A. **Incorrect:** Get-AzureWebsiteLog is used to enable log streaming.

    B. **Incorrect:** Enable-AzureWebsiteApplicationDiagnostic is used to enable application diagnostics and configure logging level.

    C. **Correct:** Save-AzureWebsiteLog is the cmdlet to download the log files from Azure to your local computer.

    D. **Incorrect:** Get-AzureWebsiteMetric is used to get detailed metrics for the website.

3. **Correct answers:** A, D

   A. **Correct:** Application logs are available using the log-streaming service.

   B. **Incorrect:** Failed request logs cannot be streamed. You must download these logs to view them.

   C. **Incorrect:** Detailed error messages cannot be streamed. You must download these logs to view them.

   D. **Correct:** Web server logs are available using the log-streaming service.

4. **Correct answer:** C

   A. **Incorrect:** Zero to three is not correct. You must have at least one external website location.

   B. **Incorrect:** Two or more is not correct. You could have one external website location but no more than three.

   C. **Correct:** One to three external website locations is correct.

   D. **Incorrect:** One to two external website locations is not correct. You can have up to three.

5. **Correct answer:** B

   A. **Incorrect:** Website configuration is part of the backup.

   B. **Correct:** Website performance metrics is not part of an Azure website backup.

   C. **Incorrect:** Website file content is part of the backup.

   D. **Incorrect:** Website databases (SQL database or MySQL) is part of the backup.

Objective 1.4: Thought experiment

1. The new version of the website requires 1 core and 2.5 GB of memory. Configuring the website to run in Small mode meets the core requirement, but not the memory requirement. Setting the mode to Medium would be the most cost-effective solution that meets both requirements.

2. The marketing campaign for the new website release is a short-lived event and not an on-going recurring event. Also, you are not able to predict exactly when the ads will be run on television and radio. To handle these traffic spikes during the campaign, you should use a specific data and time schedule that aligns with the campaign period. After the schedule is defined you should configure the number of running instances required during the campaign.

3. Another solution could be to autoscale the website based on CPU. However, autoscale does not happen instantly and so your website instances are not likely to scale fast enough to support the traffic spikes.

Objective 1.4: Review

1. **Correct answer**: B

   A. **Incorrect:** Recurring schedule for weekday and weekend enables you to scale Monday through Friday and Saturday through Sunday.

   B. **Correct:** Recurring schedule for day and night enables you to indicate the start and end time for your day, and scale on that schedule.

   C. **Incorrect:** Specific schedule with a start time in the morning and an end time in the evening enables you to scale up or down during that time period only. It doesn't give you an option to scale up and down.

   D. **Incorrect:** Specific schedule with a start time in the evening and an end time in the morning enables you to scale up or down during that time period only. It doesn't give you an option to scale up and down.

2. **Correct answers:** B, C, D

   A. **Incorrect:** A0 (Shared core, 768 MB memory) is not a valid website instance size. However, this is a valid size for a virtual machine.

   B. **Correct:** Small (1 core, 1.75 GB memory) is a valid instance size setting.

   C. **Correct:** Medium (2 cores, 3.5 GB memory) is a valid instance size setting.

   D. **Correct:** Large (4 cores, 7 GB memory) is a valid instance size setting.

Objective 1.5: Thought experiment

1. The Shared web hosting plan would be the most cost-effective solution that offers the support for custom domains.

2. The development team will need the Staging deployments feature to support their rapid pace for deployments as they implement changes based on the customer feedback loop. This feature is available in the Standard tier only, so creating a new web hosting plan using the S1 pricing tier would be the most cost-effective approach. When the development team needs this feature, you can migrate the website from the Shared plan to the S1 plan.

Objective 1.5: Review

1. **Correct answer:** D

   A. **Incorrect:** Standard (S2) meets all the requirements for the website but is not the most cost-effective choice.

   B. **Incorrect:** Basic (B3) meets all the requirements for the website but is not the most cost-effective choice.

   C. **Incorrect:** Shared doesn't meet any of the requirements.

   D. **Correct:** Basic (B2) meets all the requirements and is the most cost-effective choice.

2. **Correct answers:** A, C

   A. **Correct:** Standard mode lets you define the instance size, and is offered as S1, S2, and S3 for instance sizes Small, Medium, and Large.

   B. **Incorrect:** Shared does not let you define an instance size.

   C. **Correct:** Basic mode lets you define the instance size, and is offered as B1, B2, and B3 for instance sizes Small, Medium, and Large.

   D. **Incorrect:** Free does not let you define an instance size.

CHAPTER 2

Implement virtual machines

Virtual machines are one of the key compute options for deploying workloads in Microsoft Azure. Virtual machines can provide the on-ramp for migrating workloads from on-premises (or other cloud providers) to Azure because they are usually the most compatible with existing solutions. The flexibility of virtual machines makes them a key scenario for many workloads. For example, you have a choice of server operating systems, with various versions of Windows and Linux distributions supported. Azure virtual machines also provide you full control over the operating system, along with advanced configuration options for networking and storage.

Objectives in this chapter:

- Objective 2.1: Deploy workloads on Azure virtual machines (VMs)
- Objective 2.2: Implement images and disks
- Objective 2.3: Perform configuration management
- Objective 2.4: Configure VM networking
- Objective 2.5: Configure VM for resiliency
- Objective 2.6: Design and implement VM storage
- Objective 2.7: Monitor VMs

Objective 2.1: Deploy workloads on Azure virtual machines (VMs)

Microsoft Azure Virtual Machines is a flexible and powerful option for deploying workloads into the cloud. The support of both Windows and Linux-based operating systems allows for deploying a wide variety of workloads.

> **This objective covers how to:**
> - Identify supported Microsoft workloads
> - Create virtual machines
> - Managing the lifecycle of a virtual machine
> - Connect to virtual machines

Identifying supported workloads

Azure virtual machines are based on Windows Server Hyper-V but not all features within Hyper-V are directly supported. With that in mind, it should not come as a total surprise that all workloads from Microsoft (including roles and features of Windows Server itself) are not supported when running within Azure Virtual Machines. The best way to keep track of what is, and is not supported, is through the Microsoft support article: *http://support.microsoft.com/kb/2721672*. This article details which Microsoft workloads are supported within Azure. Also, the article is kept up-to-date as new workloads are brought online, or the support policy changes when new capabilities within Azure enhance what is supported.

Creating virtual machines

You can create virtual machines using the Azure management portal, the Azure PowerShell cmdlets, the Azure cross-platform command-line tools, or the management REST API. Each method brings with it their own capabilities and tradeoffs, and it is important to understand which tool should be used in the right scenario.

Using the Azure management portal

The Azure management portal allows you to use a wide variety of virtual machine images, and pre-defined templates for entire solutions such as SQL Server AlwaysOn, or even a complete SharePoint farm. For individual virtual machines you can specify some, but not all, configuration options at creation time. Some options, such as configuring the load balancer, and specifying data disk configuration, are not available at creation time through the management portal but can be set after the virtual machine is created. Using the management portal, you must create virtual machines in the same cloud service, one virtual machine at a time. This can be cumbersome for large deployments with many virtual machines and automation may make more sense those scenarios. The management portal is cross-platform and is supported in most modern browsers.

Using the cross-platform command-line tools

The Azure cross-platform command-line tools allow you to provision and manage virtual machines and many other Azure resources. The commands in these tools can be scripted to provide automated deployments. The cross-platform command-line tools are built using Node.js, and as the name implies will work across multiple platforms. The tools are supported on Windows, Mac, and Linux.

Using the Azure PowerShell cmdlets

Using the Azure PowerShell cmdlets, you can define the entire configuration of a virtual machine, including advanced configuration options such as: network endpoints, data disks, and Active Directory domain join information. You have full control over the names and locations of the underlying VHD (virtual hard disk) files for the virtual machine during creation. Like the

on the virtual machine. Input endpoints allow network traffic into the virtual machine on a specific port. This cmdlet can also be used to add load-balanced endpoints, and can attach access control lists.

To create the virtual machine using this technique you must pass the configuration object to the New-AzureVM cmdlet. The New-AzureVM cmdlet does the bulk of the work of creating the virtual machine with the passed in configuration. Table 2-1 shows the differences between the two approaches for creating virtual machines.

TABLE 2-1 Capabilities for virtual machine creation with the Azure PowerShell cmdlets

New-AzureQuickVM	New-AzureVMConfig and New-AzureVM
Windows and Linux supported	Windows and Linux supported
Create only from image	Create from image or operating system disk
Specify availability set name	Specify availability set name
Specify subnet and virtual network	Specify subnet and virtual network
Deploy to location or affinity group	Deploy to location or affinity group
Deploy X509 certificates	Deploy X509 certificates
Deploy SSH certificates on Linux virtual machines	Deploy SSH certificates on Linux virtual machines
	Specify Active Directory domain join information
	Require admin password reset on first login
	Create new or attach existing data disks
	Configure endpoints (including internal and external load balancing)
	Disable Windows Update
	Specify the time zone
	Specify static IP addresses
	Specify reserved IP address of the cloud service/domain name

Creating from a virtual machine image

Creating a virtual machine requires you to specify either an existing operating system disk, or a virtual machine image. Virtual machine images have different provisioning settings depending on whether the source image is Windows or Linux-based. That being said, a significant portion of the configuration options will be the same regardless of the operating system type. Within the management portal, you select the image name from the Gallery view, as Figure 2-1 shows.

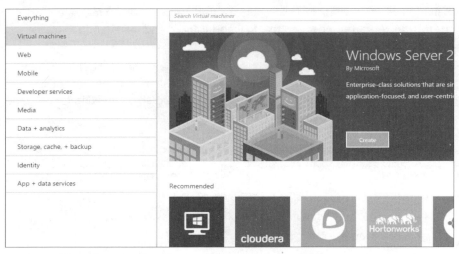

FIGURE 2-1 The Gallery view for virtual machines

Using the Azure PowerShell cmdlets you can enumerate the available images using the Get-AzureVMImage cmdlet. This cmdlet will return all of the image information that is available (including some images that do not appear in the management portal). It can be quite overwhelming without applying some basic filters.

To only return images available for the Windows Server 2012 R2 Datacenter family, you can filter on the $_.ImageFamily property, as shown in the following example and Figure 2-2.

```
$imageFamily = "Windows Server 2012 R2 Datacenter"
Get-AzureVMImage | where { $_.ImageFamily -eq $imageFamily }
```

```
PS C:\> $imageFamily = "Windows Server 2012 R2 Datacenter"
Get-AzureVMImage | where { $_.ImageFamily -eq $imageFamily }


ImageName            : a699494373c04fc0bc8f2bb1389d6106__Windows-Server-2012-R2-201409.01-en.us-127GB.vhd
OS                   : Windows
MediaLink            :
LogicalSizeInGB      : 128
AffinityGroup        :
Category             : Public
Location             : East Asia;Southeast Asia;Australia East;Australia Southeast;Brazil South;North
                       Europe;West Europe;Japan East;Japan West;Central US;East US;East US 2;North Central
                       US;South Central US;West US
Label                : Windows Server 2012 R2 Datacenter, September 2014
Description          : At the heart of the Microsoft Cloud OS vision, Windows Server 2012 R2 brings
                       Microsoft's experience delivering global-scale cloud services into your
                       infrastructure. It offers enterprise-class performance, flexibility for your
                       applications and excellent economics for your datacenter and hybrid cloud environment.
                       This image includes Windows Server 2012 R2 Update.
```

FIGURE 2-2 Enumerating available images by image family

The Azure PowerShell cmdlets use the ImageName property to specify the image to use during creation. You can take the previous example one step further by sorting the PublishedDate in descending order, and then select the ImageName to only return the latest ImageName for the requested image family as shown in the following example and Figure 2-3.

```
$imageFamily = "Windows Server 2012 R2 Datacenter"
$imageName = Get-AzureVMImage |
            where { $_.ImageFamily -eq $imageFamily } |
            sort PublishedDate -Descending |
            select -ExpandProperty ImageName -First 1
```

```
PS C:\> $imageFamily = "Windows Server 2012 R2 Datacenter"
$imageName = Get-AzureVMImage |
            where { $_.ImageFamily -eq $imageFamily } |
            sort PublishedDate -Descending |
            select -ExpandProperty ImageName -First 1

PS C:\> $imageName
a699494373c04fc0bc8f2bb1389d6106__Windows-Server-2012-R2-201411.01-en.us-127GB.vhd
```

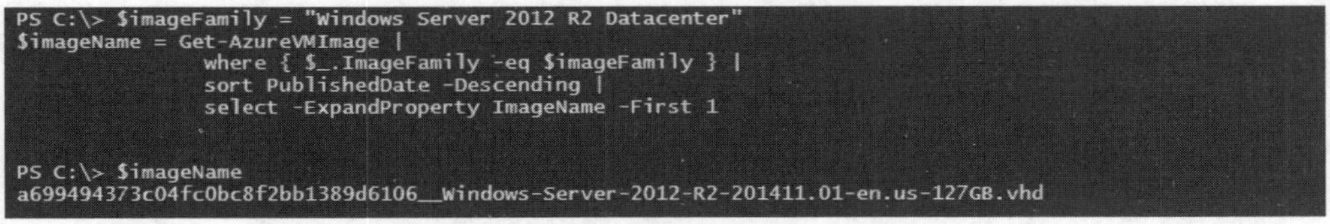

FIGURE 2-3 Identifying the newest image by image family

When the image name has been determined, it is passed to the New-AzureQuickVM, or the New-AzureVMConfig cmdlet with the ImageName parameter.

Creating a virtual machine from an operating system disk

In addition to creating a virtual machine from an image, you can create a virtual machine directly from a virtual hard disk (VHD) as long as the disk is associated as an operating system disk as shown in Figure 2-4. This scenario is useful for disks that have been uploaded from on-premises, or recreating a previously deleted virtual machine where the operating system disk was retained.

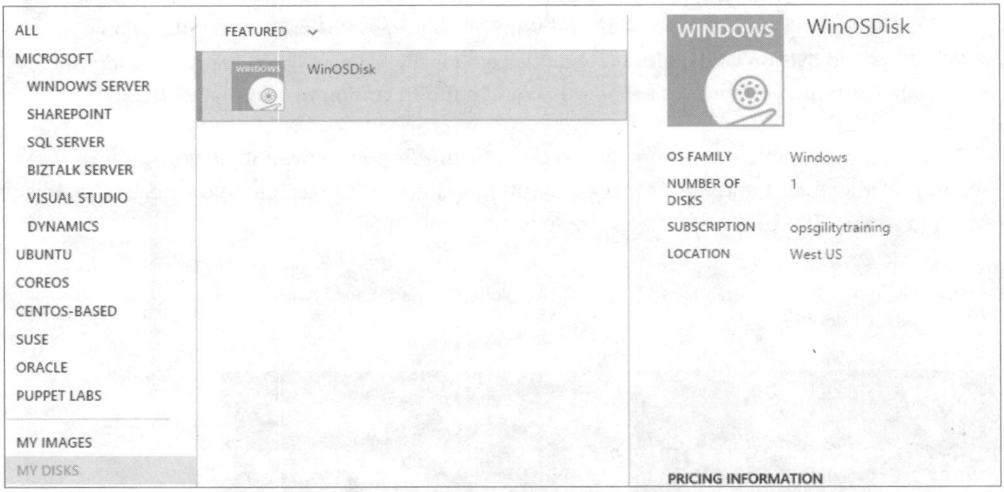

FIGURE 2-4 Provisioning a virtual machine from an operating system (OS) disk

Using the Azure PowerShell cmdlets, the New-AzureVMConfig cmdlet supports passing a DiskName parameter instead of using ImageName. The following example creates a small virtual machine named vm3 in the contoso-vms3 cloud service. It assumes an operating system disk named WinOSDisk is already created in the subscription. This example also adds an endpoint for remote desktop at creation time using the Add-AzureEndpoint cmdlet.

```
$adminUser    = "[admin user name]"
$password     = "[admin password]"
$serviceName  = "contoso-vms3"
$location     = "West US"
$size         = "Small"
$vmName       = "vm3"
$diskName     = "WinOSDisk"
New-AzureVMConfig -Name $vmName `
                  -InstanceSize $size `
                  -DiskName $diskName |

Add-AzureEndpoint -Name "RDP" `
                  -Protocol tcp `
                  -LocalPort 3389 `
                  -PublicPort 3389 |

New-AzureVM -ServiceName $serviceName -Location $location
```

EXAM TIP

Creating a virtual machine from a disk using the Azure PowerShell cmdlets has several key differences that you should be aware of. First, New-AzureQuickVM doesn't support creating from a disk (only images are supported). Second, the Add-AzureProvisioningConfig cmdlet isn't used because it only sets options available for provisioning from an image. Third, the default endpoints for RDP and WinRM (Windows PowerShell remoting) on Windows and SSH on Linux aren't created automatically for you. If you want the endpoints available at boot, you must use the Add-AzureEndpoint cmdlet to add them.

To view the available operating system disks from Windows PowerShell, you can use the Get-AzureDisk cmdlet and filter for the operating system and AttachedTo properties, as this example shows. The output of the example is displayed in Figure 2-5.

```
Get-AzureDisk |
    where { $_.OS -eq "Windows" -and $_.AttachedTo -eq $null} |
    select DiskName
```

```
PS C:\> Get-AzureDisk |
    where { $_.OS -eq "Windows" -and $_.AttachedTo -eq $null} |
    select DiskName


DiskName
--------
WinOSDisk
```

FIGURE 2-5 Querying for all Windows-based disks that are unattached

Specifying the virtual machine size and tier

You can set the size and tier of the virtual machine in the management portal by configuring the Pricing Tier option, as shown in Figure 2-6.

FIGURE 2-6 Selecting the Pricing Tier for a virtual machine

The size and tier of the virtual machine is set using Windows PowerShell by specifying the InstanceSize parameter of the New-AzureVMConfig, or New-AzureQuickVM cmdlets.

Each size and tier brings with it different capabilities: load balancing, and Autoscale, as well as compute resources, such as number of cores, data disks, IOPS on data disks, and the amount of memory allocated to the virtual machine. Table 2-2 provides more details on each of the available configurations for the Basic tier, and Table 2-3 contains information for the Standard tier.

TABLE 2-2 Basic tier instance sizes

Size	CPU Cores	Memory	Resource Disk	Data Disks	IOPS
A0	Shared (.025)	768 MB	20 GB	1	1x300
A1	1	1.75 GB	40 GB	2	2x300
A2	2	3.5 GB	60 GB	4	4x300
A3	4	7 GB	120 GB	8	8x300
A4	8	14 GB	240 GB	16	16x300

TABLE 2-3 Standard tier instance sizes

Size	CPU Cores	Memory	Resource Disk	Data Disks	IOPS
A0	Shared (.025)	768 MB	20 GB	1	1x500
A1	1	1.75 GB	40 GB	2	2x500
A2	2	3.5 GB	60 GB	4	4x500
A3	4	7 GB	120 GB	8	8x500
A4	8	14 GB	240 GB	16	16x500
A5	2	15 GB	135 GB	4	4x500
A6	4	28 GB	285 GB	8	8x500
A7	8	56 GB	605 GB	16	16x500
A8	8	56 GB	382 GB	16	16x500
A9	16	112 GB	382 GB	16	16x500
STANDARD_D1	1	3.5 GB	50 GB (SSD)	1	1x500
STANDARD_D2	2	7 GB	100 GB (SSD)	2	2x500
STANDARD_D3	4	14 GB	200 GB (SSD)	4	4x500
STANDARD_D4	8	28 GB	400 GB (SSD)	8	8x500
STANDARD_D11	2	14 GB	100 GB (SSD)	2	2x500
STANDARD_D12	4	28 GB	200 GB (SSD)	4	4x500
STANDARD_D13	8	56 GB	400 GB (SSD)	8	8x500
STANDARD_D14	16	112 GB	800 GB (SSD)	16	16x500

There are several differences between the Basic and Standard tiers. The first difference to note is that the Basic tier only supports up to the A4 size. The second difference is the number of IOPS per disk: 300 IOPS with Basic, where Standard supports 500 IOPS per disk. Additionally, virtual machines using the Basic tier do not support load balancing, or the Autoscale feature. The Standard tier also offers high performance SSD drives for the temporary resource disk.

You can identify the currently available virtual machine configurations through MSDN at *http://msdn.microsoft.com/en-us/library/azure/dn197896.aspx*, or by using the Windows PowerShell cmdlet Get-AzureRoleSize.

The Get-AzureRoleSize cmdlet returns all of the available sizes for virtual machines and cloud services (web and worker roles) if the InstanceSize parameter is not specified. If you specify a size, the cmdlet only returns information for that size. This cmdlet also exposes two properties: SupportedByWebWorkerRoles and SupportedByVirtualMachines. These properties identify whether the size is supported on web and worker roles, virtual machines, or both.

Figure 2-7 shows an example of the A5 size, as returned from the Get-AzureRoleSize cmdlet. The output contains all of the form factor information such as cores, memory, local storage on the resource disks and data disks, and the supported compute type properties.

```
PS C:\> Get-AzureRoleSize -InstanceSize A5

InstanceSize                         : A5
RoleSizeLabel                        : A5 (2 cores, 14336 MB)
Cores                                : 2
MemoryInMb                           : 14336
SupportedByWebWorkerRoles            : True
SupportedByVirtualMachines           : True
MaxDataDiskCount                     : 4
WebWorkerResourceDiskSizeInMb        : 501760
VirtualMachineResourceDiskSizeInMb   : 138240
OperationDescription                 : Get-AzureRoleSize
OperationId                          : 4cb4c528-ab9a-3248-92f6-8705bf2df822
OperationStatus                      : Succeeded
```

FIGURE 2-7 Using the Get-AzureRoleSize cmdlet

The original size names ExtraSmall, Small, Medium, Large, and ExtraLarge are still required when used from the command-line tools or the REST API. Table 2-4 shows how to specify the A0-A4 sizes, and also what values to use when specifying sizes using the Basic tier.

TABLE 2-4 Size values used with the command-line and REST API

Official name	Basic tier	Standard tier
A0	Basic_A0	ExtraSmall
A1	Basic_A1	Small
A2	Basic_A2	Medium
A3	Basic_A3	Large
A4	Basic_A4	ExtraLarge
A5		A5
A6		A6
A7		A7
A8		A8
A9		A9
STANDARD_D1		STANDARD_D1
STANDARD_D2		STANDARD_D2
STANDARD_D3		STANDARD_D3
STANDARD_D4		STANDARD_D4
STANDARD_D11		STANDARD_D11
STANDARD_D12		STANDARD_D12
STANDARD_D13		STANDARD_D13
STANDARD_D14		STANDARD_D14

Specifying the subscription

If the account you are logged in to the management portal with has access to multiple subscriptions, selecting the correct subscription should be one of the first configuration settings to make. All resources for your virtual machine (domain names, storage accounts, virtual networks, and so on) are filtered in the management portal based on the subscription you specify. If you are using the Azure PowerShell cmdlets it is just as important to specify the correct subscription. To select the correct subscription use the Select-AzureSubscription cmdlet.

Specifying the virtual machine location

The location is the Azure region the virtual machine will be created in. The location of the virtual machine also determines the location requirement of the underlying storage, and if specified the virtual network. The virtual network and storage account must reside in the same location as the virtual machine. As shown in Figure 2-8, the management portal enforces this behavior by only allowing you to select a storage account or virtual network that matches the location of the virtual machine. The service management API enforces this requirement as well. Attempting to create a virtual machine with the storage account or the virtual network in a remote region will result in an error.

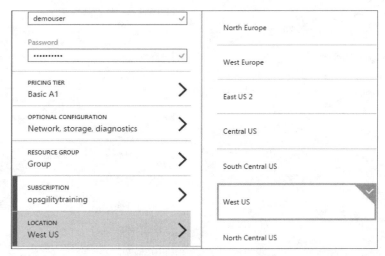

FIGURE 2-8 Specifying the location of a virtual machine at create time

Figure 2-9 shows how the Get-AzureLocation Azure PowerShell cmdlet is used to identify the available locations and their capabilities. When new sizes are introduced, they might not be available immediately in all regions.

```
PS C:\> Get-AzureLocation

DisplayName           : North Europe
Name                  : North Europe
AvailableServices     : {Compute, Storage, PersistentVMRole, HighMemory}
WebWorkerRoleSizes    : {A5, A6, A7, A8, A9, ExtraLarge, ExtraSmall, Large, Medium, Small, Standard_D1,
                        Standard_D11, Standard_D12, Standard_D13, Standard_D14, Standard_D2, Standard_D3,
                        Standard_D4}
VirtualMachineRoleSizes : {A5, A6, A7, A8, A9, Basic_A0, Basic_A1, Basic_A2, Basic_A3, Basic_A4, ExtraLarge,
                        ExtraSmall, Large, Medium, Small, Standard_D1, Standard_D11, Standard_D12,
                        Standard_D13, Standard_D14, Standard_D2, Standard_D3, Standard_D4}
OperationDescription  : Get-AzureLocation
OperationId           : f4fce516-7a75-32e3-b0bb-8c973ba04121
OperationStatus       : Succeeded
```

FIGURE 2-9 Using the Get-AzureLocation cmdlet

The virtual machine's location can only be set at creation time and cannot be changed later. When creating a virtual machine using the Azure PowerShell cmdlets, use the -Location parameter of the New-AzureQuickVM or New-AzureVM cmdlets, as the following partial examples demonstrate.

```
New-AzureQuickVM -Location $location (other parameters)
New-AzureVM -Location $location (other parameters)
```

Configuring the network

Through the management portal you can specify the virtual network, subnet, DNS name (the host name of the DNS name is also known as the cloud service name), and whether the IP address will be dynamic or static. Setting a static IP address is not available in the current management portal (*https://manage.windowsazure.com*), but you can specify one in the Azure Preview Portal (*http://portal.azure.com*), or through Windows PowerShell.

Domain names and cloud services

One of the most important concepts for deploying virtual machines is using the domain name container correctly. The host portion of the domain (contoso-vms in Figure 2-10) is also known as the cloud service name, and is referenced that way in the management portal (*https://manage.windowsazure.com*) and the Azure PowerShell cmdlets. Figure 2-10 shows creating a new domain name to host a virtual machine in. When creating a new domain name, the host portion of the name must be globally unique in the *cloudapp.net* domain.

FIGURE 2-10 Creating a new domain name (cloud service)

Adding a virtual machine to an existing domain name

Figure 2-11 shows that during virtual machine creation you can choose an existing domain name if it already exists in your subscription. This is required to configure virtual machines for load balancing, availability sets, and direct network connectivity (without using a virtual network). All virtual machines within the same domain name must reside in the same Azure region.

FIGURE 2-11 Selecting an existing domain name (cloud service) using the management portal

> **NOTE** **LIMIT TO THE NUMBER OF VIRTUAL VMS**
>
> You can add at most 50 virtual machines into the same domain name/cloud service. This puts an upper limit on how many virtual machines can be load-balanced, Autoscaled, or configured for availability using availability sets.

Cloud Services and Windows PowerShell

The Azure PowerShell cmdlets require you to specify the cloud service name to interact with an Azure virtual machine. To create a new cloud service (or domain name) the name must be unique within the *cloudapp.net* domain. The management portal validates this for you automatically. To validate the availability of the name using the Azure PowerShell cmdlets, use the Test-AzureName cmdlet as shown in the following example.

```
$serviceName = "contoso-vms"
Test-AzureName -Service -Name $serviceName
```

If Test-AzureName returns true, the service name already exists and is not available for you to create. That does not necessarily mean you cannot use it. If the cloud service exists in your subscription and is in the same region as the virtual machine you want to create, you can specify it when creating a virtual machine. You can identify whether the service is in your subscription from Windows PowerShell by calling the Get-AzureService cmdlet and passing the cloud service name to the ServiceName parameter. If Get-AzureService returns an error, it is not available in your subscription.

The cloud service name is specified by passing it to the ServiceName parameter of the New-AzureQuickVM or New-AzureVM cmdlets. Specify the Location parameter to create a new cloud service as in the following partial example.

```
New-AzureQuickVM -ServiceName $serviceName -Location $location (other parameters)
```

To add a new virtual machine in an existing cloud service with New-AzureQuickVM, do not pass the Location parameter and just specify the existing cloud service name, as this partial example shows.

```
New-AzureQuickVM -ServiceName $serviceName (other parameters)
```

To create a new cloud service container using the New-AzureVM cmdlet, you must specify the ServiceName parameter and the Location parameter, as this partial example shows.

```
New-AzureVM -ServiceName $serviceName -Location $location (other parameters)
```

To add a new virtual machine in an existing cloud service with New-AzureVM, you can omit or specify the Location parameter (either option works).

> **NOTE CLOUD SERVICE LOCATION**
> New-AzureQuickVM will fail if you specify the location and also if the cloud service name specified in ServiceName already exists. New-AzureVM will produce a warning that the cloud service already exists but will continue.

Specifying the storage account

The storage account is used to store the virtual machine's operating system disk and data disks. By default, the operating system virtual hard disks (.vhd files) for the virtual machine will be created in a container called vhds. The management portal will filter to only storage accounts in the same location, as specified for the virtual machine, as shown in Figure 2-12.

FIGURE 2-12 Specifying the Storage Account for a virtual machine

Set a default storage account at the subscription level with Windows PowerShell by using the Set-AzureSubscription cmdlet, as the example shows. The Azure PowerShell cmdlets will use this storage account as the default location for new virtual hard disk files unless otherwise specified.

```
Set-AzureSubscription -SubscriptionName $subscriptionName `
                -CurrentStorageAccountName $storageAccount
```

Overriding virtual hard disk locations

Using Windows PowerShell you can override the default location and name of the virtual hard disks for your virtual machines. This is helpful to establish a naming and location convention that may be more understandable for your organization.

The New-AzureVMConfig cmdlet supports passing the uniform resource identifier (URI) to the location in storage that the operating system disk will be created in using the MediaLocation parameter. To override the creation location of data disks, you can specify the URI to the location in storage with the MediaLocation property of the Add-AzureDataDisk cmdlet.

In the following example, the operating system disk and both data disks have specific paths in an Azure storage account specified using the MediaLocation parameter of New-AzureVMConfig and Add-AzureDataDisk. When the virtual machine is created, the virtual hard disk files will be created in the specified locations. The bold code shows the changes necessary to specify the virtual hard disk locations.

```
$adminUser   = "[admin user name]"
$password    = "[admin password]"
$serviceName = "contoso-vms-storage"
$location    = "West US"
$size        = "Small"
$vmName      = "customdisks"
$imageFamily = "Windows Server 2012 R2 Datacenter"
$imageName = Get-AzureVMImage |
                 where { $_.ImageFamily -eq $imageFamily } |
                      sort PublishedDate -Descending |
                 select -ExpandProperty ImageName -First 1

$storage = "examref1"
$osDisk = "https://$storage.blob.core.windows.net/disks/os.vhd"
$data1 = "https://$storage.blob.core.windows.net/disks/data1.vhd"
$data2 = "https://$storage.blob.core.windows.net/disks/data2.vhd"

New-AzureVMConfig -ImageName $imageName
                          -MediaLocation $osDisk `
                          -InstanceSize  $size `
                          -Name $vmName |

Add-AzureDataDisk -CreateNew  `
                  -MediaLocation $data1 `
                  -LUN 0 `
                  -Label "data 1"  |

Add-AzureDataDisk -CreateNew `
                  -MediaLocation $data2 `
                  -LUN 0 `
                  -Label "data 2" |

New-AzureVM -ServiceName $serviceName `
            -Location $location
```

Specifying the resource group

Resource groups are logical containers that are used to group resources such as virtual machines, storage accounts, databases, websites, and others that share a common life cycle. Resource groups are currently only available with virtual machines when using the Azure Preview Portal (*http://portal.azure.com*), as shown in Figure 2-13.

FIGURE 2-13 Specifying the resource group using the Azure Preview Portal

Operating system specific settings

In addition to the common deployment settings we just reviewed, Windows and Linux-based images also have operating system specific settings. Some can be set through the management portal, and some can only be set through Windows PowerShell or the API.

Specifying the user name and password

Virtual machines created from Windows-based images require the local administrator user name and password at creation. With Linux-based images, setting the password is optional because it is possible through the management portal, Windows PowerShell, and the cross-platform CLI tools to deploy an SSH certificate to use instead of a password. Azure restricts the user name and password to non-obvious values. For example, you cannot specify administrator and password, as those values are easy to guess.

Currently, using Linux-based images you cannot specify the password using the Azure Preview Portal (*https://portal.azure.com*). The management portal (*https://manage.windowsazure.com*) does support this ability. Using the management portal, you must specify the user name and an SSH authentication key for Linux-based images. The Azure Preview Portal allows you to specify the user name, password, or an SSH certificate.

There are several techniques for creating a certificate to use for SSH. One option is to use the Openssl.exe utility to generate the certificate. The following is an example of what this command looks like.

```
openssl.exe req -x509 -nodes -days 365 -newkey rsa:2048 -keyout myPrivateKey.key -out myCert.pem
```

On Windows, you can use the PuttyGen.exe utility, as shown in Figure 2-14, to load the created private key (myPrivateKey.key) and copy the value into the SSH Authentication Key field of the Create VM blade.

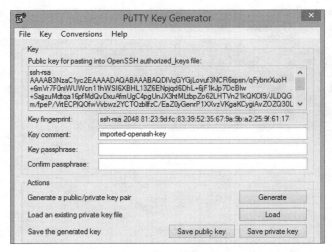

FIGURE 2-14 Specifying the user name and SSH key for a Linux virtual machine

To accomplish the same task using Windows PowerShell, upload the .pem file to an existing cloud service. If you are deploying a virtual machine for the first time, and no cloud service exists, you can create an empty cloud service using the following New-AzureService cmdlet.

```
New-AzureService -ServiceName $serviceName -Location $location
```

After the cloud service is created, call the Add-AzureCertificate cmdlet specifying the path to the previously created certificate (.pem), and the cloud service name to install the certificate to.

```
$certPath = "C:\MyCerts\myCert.pem"
$cert = Get-PfxCertificate -FilePath $certPath
Add-AzureCertificate -CertToDeploy $certPath `
                     -ServiceName $serviceName
```

After the certificate is uploaded, pass the configuration information to Azure so that the certificate will be deployed correctly on the Linux virtual machine.

```
$sshKey = New-AzureSSHKey -PublicKey -Fingerprint $cert.Thumbprint `
                     -Path "/home/$linuxUser/.ssh/authorized_keys"
```

The $sshKey variable is passed to the creation process by passing it as a parameter to the SSHPublicKeys parameter of the Add-AzureProvisioningConfig cmdlet, as this partial example shows.

```
Add-AzureProvisioningConfig -SSHPublicKeys $sshkey (other parameters)
```

The following is a complete example of how to provision a Linux virtual machine using an SSH certificate from Windows PowerShell. The MyCert.pem file was created using Openssl.exe. The user can log in using the specified user name and password, or the user name and SSH certificate.

```
$location     = "West US"
$serviceName  = "contosolinux1"
$vmName       = "linuxvm1"
$size         = "Small"
$adminUser    = "[admin user name]"
$password     = "[admin password]"

$imageFamily = "Ubuntu Server 14.10 DAILY"
$imageName = Get-AzureVMImage |
                where { $_.ImageFamily -eq $imageFamily } |
                    sort PublishedDate -Descending |
                select -ExpandProperty ImageName -First 1

$certPath     = "$PSScriptRoot\MyCert.pem"

New-AzureService -ServiceName $serviceName `
                -Location $location

$cert = Get-PfxCertificate -FilePath $certPath

Add-AzureCertificate -CertToDeploy $certPath `
                    -ServiceName $serviceName

$sshKey = New-AzureSSHKey -PublicKey -Fingerprint $cert.Thumbprint `
                    -Path "/home/$linuxUser/.ssh/authorized_keys"

New-AzureVMConfig -Name $vmName `
                -InstanceSize $size `
                -ImageName $imageName |

Add-AzureProvisioningConfig -Linux `
                    -AdminUsername $adminUser `
                    -Password $password `
                    -SSHPublicKeys $sshKey |

New-AzureVM -ServiceName $serviceName
```

Windows Update

Windows-based Azure images have the default Windows Update behavior set to Install Updates Automatically. As part of the creation process you can disable automatic updates using the new Azure Preview Portal (*https://portal.azure.com*). This capability is not available in the previous version of the management portal (*https://manage.windowsazure.com*).

This setting can be specified during creation from Windows PowerShell as well by adding the DisableAutomaticUpdates parameter to Add-AzureProvisioningConfig, as shown in this partial example.

```
Add-AzureProvisioningConfig -DisableAutomaticUpdates (other parameters)
```

Setting the time zone

Setting the time zone at creation time is another feature specific to Windows-based virtual machines. You can set the time zone that the virtual machine will use when it boots for the first time using the new management portal, or Windows PowerShell as shown here.

```
Add-AzureProvisioningConfig -TimeZone "Tokyo Standard Time" (other parameters)
```

Deploying certificates

With Windows PowerShell, you can automatically deploy certificates to virtual machines that you create. This can be useful for configuring SSL on a web server or other authentication scenarios that require a certificate. The following example loads an X509 certificate .pfx file into the $cert variable. From there, the certificate is passed to the X509Certificates parameter of Add-AzureProvisioningConfig. This parameter accepts an array of values so that multiple certificates could be specified and deployed at one time. The cmdlets will automatically upload the certificates to the cloud service container, and then deploy them onto the virtual machine.

```
$pfxName = Join-Path $PSScriptRoot "ssl-certificate.pfx"

$cert = New-Object System.Security.Cryptography.X509Certificates.X509Certificate2
$cert.Import($pfxName,$certPassword,'Exportable')

Add-AzureProvisioningConfig -X509Certificates $cert
```

Resetting password at first log on

A common security technique on Windows-based images is to provision a virtual machine and require that the local administrator account's password be changed the very first time the user logs in. To enable this feature on Windows-based virtual machines, pass the ResetPasswordOnFirstLogon parameter to the Add-AzureProvisioningConfig cmdlet, as shown here.

```
Add-AzureProvisioningConfig -ResetPasswordOnFirstLogon (other parameters)
```

Managing the lifecycle of a virtual machine

Although not specifically called out in this objective, understanding how to stop, start, restart, and delete virtual machines are critical tasks that are required for the management of virtual machines in Azure.

Stopping a virtual machine

Stopping a virtual machine from the management portal, or using Windows PowerShell with the Stop-AzureVM cmdlet will by default put the virtual machine in the StoppedDeallocated state. It is important to understand the difference between StoppedDeallocated and just Stopped. In the Stopped state a virtual machine is still allocated in Azure, and the operating system is simply shut down. You will still be billed for the compute time for a virtual machine in this state. A virtual machine in the StoppedDeallocated state is no longer occupying physical hardware in the Azure region, and you will not be billed for the compute time (you are still billed for the underlying storage).

Why would you ever not put a virtual machine in the StoppedDeallocated state if you do not have to pay for it? The drawback to this state is that if all virtual machines in the same cloud service are in the StoppedDeallocated state, you can lose the virtual IP (VIP) assigned to your cloud service. This can be mitigated with a reserved IP, which is described later in this chapter. The following example shows how to stop a virtual machine using the Stop-AzureVM cmdlet.

```
Stop-AzureVM -ServiceName $serviceName -Name $vmName
```

The Stop-AzureVM cmdlet has two parameters that you will need to be aware of. The first is StayProvisioned. When this parameter is passed, it tells Azure to keep the virtual machine allocated on the physical server. This is the same result as shutting the virtual machine down from within the guest operating system, and will result in the virtual machine state set to Stopped instead of StoppedDeallocated. You will still be billed for the compute usage. The second parameter is Force. If you are attempting to shut down all of the virtual machines in a cloud service (putting them in the StoppedDeallocated state) the Stop-AzureVM cmdlet will prompt you when it hits the last virtual machine, to make you aware that you will lose the public IP address of your cloud service. Using Force ignores this prompt. This allows you to chain commands together using the Windows PowerShell pipeline without an interactive prompt, as the following example demonstrates.

```
Get-AzureVM -ServiceName $serviceName  | Stop-AzureVM -Force
```

Starting virtual machines

Starting virtual machines is much simpler. There are no complexities around losing IP addresses with this capability. Simply click Start in the management portal for the specific virtual machine, or use the Start-AzureVM or Restart-AzureVM cmdlet. The syntax for both cmdlets is the same.

```
Start-AzureVM -ServiceName $serviceName -Name $vmName
```

Deleting virtual machines

There are several options you should be aware of when deleting a virtual machine. Both the management portal and Windows PowerShell offer the ability to delete a virtual machine along with its underlying disks. You can optionally delete the virtual machine and retain the disks as well, which allows you to create another virtual machine from them, or just attach the disks to another virtual machine. Creating a virtual machine from a disk and attaching disks is covered in more detail in Objective 2.2.

In the following example, the virtual machine will be deleted, but the underlying disks will be retained. To remove the disks, you should also specify the DeleteVHD parameter.

```
Remove-AzureVM -ServiceName $serviceName -Name $vmName
```

You can also delete a virtual machine by deleting the cloud service it is contained in, using both the management portal and with the Remove-AzureService Azure PowerShell cmdlet. Removing the cloud service removes all of the virtual machines in the service. This cmdlet supports the Force parameter to override its default behavior of prompting for confirmation. It also supports the DeleteAll parameter, which deletes all of the underlying disks for all of the virtual machines, as shown below.

```
Remove-AzureService -ServieName $serviceName -Name $vmName -Force -DeleteAll
```

Connecting to virtual machines

Without hybrid connectivity options, such as site-to-site, point-to-site, or Microsoft Azure ExpressRoute which are discussed in depth in Chapter 6, you will connect and manage virtual machines through the public (VIP) of the cloud service. Windows-based virtual machines by default will have an endpoint for Remote Desktop Protocol (RDP) and Windows PowerShell remoting (WinRM) enabled. Linux-based virtual machines will have SSH enabled by default.

Connecting using remote desktop

From a client operating system that has a remote desktop client installed, you can use the management portal or the Azure PowerShell cmdlets to generate an .rdp file for each virtual machine that has an endpoint with a private port of 3389. The public port does not matter in this situation because its value will be added to the .rdp file automatically at creation.

To generate the .rdp file from the management portal, simply open the virtual machine's settings in the management portal, and click the Connect button. Depending on your browser settings, you will either be prompted to open the .rdp file, which will prompt you to initiate the connection, or to optionally save the file to the local file system.

> **NOTE** **CONNECTION BUTTON DISABLED**
>
> If the connect button is disabled in a virtual machine property page, it can mean that the virtual machine is currently stopped, or that there is no endpoint with a private port of 3389 on that virtual machine.

You can launch a remote desktop session from Windows PowerShell by using the Get-AzureRemoteDeskopFile cmdlet. The Get-AzureRemoteDeskopFile cmdlet performs the same validation as the management portal. The API it calls enumerates the endpoints on the virtual machine specified with the ServiceName and Name parameters looking for an endpoint with the private port set to 3389. If the endpoint exists, it will generate an .rdp file consumable with a Remote Desktop client. The .rdp file will have the IP address of the VIP and public port of the virtual machine specified embedded. There are two parameters that alter the behavior of what happens with the generated file.

Use the Launch parameter to retrieve the .rdp file and immediately open it with a Remote Desktop client. The following example will launch the Mstsc.exe (Remote Desktop client), and the client will prompt you to initiate the connection.

```
Get-AzureRemoteDesktopFile -ServiceName $serviceName -Name $vmName -Launch
```

The second behavior is specifying the LocalPath parameter, as the following example shows. Use this parameter to save the .rdp file locally for later use.

```
Get-AzureRemoteDesktopFile -ServiceName $serviceName -Name $vmName -LocalPath $path
```

Connecting remotely with Windows PowerShell

By default, a Windows-based virtual machine will have Windows PowerShell remoting enabled for connectivity through the cloud service public IP (VIP) like the Remote Desktop Protocol (RDP). This endpoint is setup to use SSL on private port 5986. If you do not specify a certificate, Azure will automatically generate a self-signed certificate that can be used for SSL to encrypt the connection. This certificate is installed in the cloud service container for the virtual machine at creation time, as well as installed on the virtual machine itself. Azure will configure a listener on the Windows Remote Management service in the virtual machine using port 5986, and configured with the generated certificate.

Use the generated certificate to secure your connection by downloading and installing the certificate on the client machine that will initiate the connection. For an example of how to do this, visit *http://gallery.technet.microsoft.com/scriptcenter/Configures-Secure-Remote-b137f2fe*. Optionally, you can specify your own certificate by passing an X509Certificate object to the WinRMCertificate parameter of the Add-AzureProvisioningConfig or New-AzureQuickVM cmdlets.

The Azure PowerShell cmdlets provide a helper cmdlet called Get-AzureWinRMUri that is used to generate the connection string to the virtual machine. In the following example, Get-AzureWinRMUri is called with the cloud service name and the virtual machine name. This cmdlet will enumerate the endpoints looking for an endpoint with a private port of 5986 and return a URI object for your use.

```
$uri = Get-AzureWinRMUri -ServiceName $serviceName -Name $vmName
```

The returned URI object can then be passed to native Windows PowerShell remoting cmdlets, such as Enter-PSSesson, to start a remote Windows PowerShell session.

```
$credentials = Get-Credentials
Enter-PSSession -ConnectionUri $uri -Credential $credentials
```

> **NOTE** **WINDOWS POWERSHELL REMOTING AUTHENTICATION**
>
> Connecting to a virtual machine with Windows PowerShell remoting only allows access to resources on the virtual machine itself. To access remote resources, such as install files on a file share, requires you to enable CredSSP authentication. This is also known as multi-hop support. More information on CredSSP can be found at *http://msdn.microsoft.com/en-us/library/ee309365(v=vs.85).aspx*.

Connecting to Linux-based virtual machines

Secure Shell (SSH) is the most common protocol for remotely managing a Linux-based virtual machine. Just like RDP and WinRM endpoints, the public port for an SSH endpoint might not be the common port 22. It might be picked from a list of available public ports in the cloud service. Unlike the Azure PowerShell cmdlet Get-AzureWinRMUri, it is up to you to identify the public port for the SSH client to connect to.

To connect to the Linux-based virtual machine, you need the domain name and the public port of the SSH endpoint. For example, the server linuxvm1 is in the *contoso-vms.cloudapp.net* domain name. The public port for the example SSH endpoint shown in Figure 2-15 is 5009.

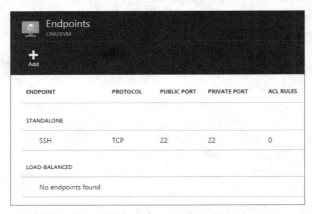

FIGURE 2-15 Endpoint view of a virtual machine

To connect to this virtual machine using an SSH client such as Putty.exe, simply specify the domain name (or public IP) and the public port of the SSH endpoint.

FIGURE 2-16 Using Putty.exe to connect using a SSH

The same information could be used to login to the server using a command line SSH client as shown.

```
ssh contoso-vms.cloudapp.net -p 5009 -l demouser
```

If the virtual machine was created with a user name and an SSH certificate instead of a password, the syntax is slightly different.

```
ssh -i myPrivateKey.key contoso-vms.cloudapp.net -p 5009 -l demouser
```

Modifying the default connection settings

You can specify that these endpoints should not be created when using the Azure PowerShell cmdlets by specifying the following parameters of Add-AzureProvisioningConfig.

- **-NoWinRMEndpoint** will not create an endpoint for WinRM.
- **-NoSSHEndpoint** will not create an endpoint for SSH.
- **-NoRDPEndpoint** will not create an endpoint for RDP.

It is also possible to disable SSH and Windows PowerShell remoting altogether by specifying parameters on New-AzureQuickVM and Add-AzureProvisioningConfig:

- New-AzureQuickVM
    - -DisableWinRMHttps does not enable Windows PowerShell remoting
- Add-AzureProvisioningConfig
    - -DisableSSH does not enable SSH
    - -DisableWinRMHttps does not enable Windows PowerShell remoting

Thought experiment
Deploying a Linux-based solution

In this thought experiment, apply what you have learned about this objective. You can find answers to these questions in the "Answers" section at the end of this chapter.

You are the IT administrator for Contoso. A new team has come online that needs to deploy a solution based on Apache. The solution has features that are not supported directly on Windows.

This solution must support deploying two servers that will be used as web servers, and two servers that will be used as database servers. All of the servers must be reachable on the same network.

1. What features should be configured on the web servers to provide external connectivity and high availability?

2. Should all of the servers be deployed into the same domain name (or cloud service), or should they be deployed in their own?

Objective summary

- There are several methods of creating Azure virtual machines. The management portal is cross-platform and is supported by most modern browsers. To create virtual machines from the command line, the Azure cross-platform command-line tools are available on Windows, Mac, and Linux. The Azure PowerShell cmdlets are available for Windows PowerShell users.

- One or more virtual machines (up to 50) can be created in a cloud service. Creating virtual machines in the same cloud service is required to configure the virtual machines to be in the same load balanced set or availability set. Virtual machines in the same cloud service can connect to other virtual machines in the same cloud service by using their internal IP.

- Using the Azure PowerShell cmdlets, you must select the subscription prior to use with the Select-AzureSubscription cmdlet. To specify the default storage account to use for virtual machine disks, set the CurrentStorageAccountName parameter of the Set-AzureSubscription cmdlet.

- There are several operating system specific settings when creating a virtual machine from a Windows or Linux-based image. Not all of these settings are accessible from the management portal. Many can only be set with Windows PowerShell using the New-AzureQuickVM, New-AzureVM, or Add-AzureProvisioningConfig cmdlets.

- The Azure PowerShell cmdlets can manage the lifecycle of your virtual machines with cmdlets such as Start-AzureVM, Restart-AzureVM, Stop-AzureVM, and Remove-AzureVM. You can delete all of the virtual machines in a cloud service with one operation by using the Remove-AzureService cmdlet.

- By default, virtual machines will have connectivity enabled for Remote Desktop and PowerShell remoting on virtual machines created from a Windows-based image. For virtual machines created from a Linux-based image, SSH will be enabled by default.

Objective review

Answer the following questions to test your knowledge of the information in this objective. You can find the answers to these questions and explanations of why each answer choice is correct or incorrect in the "Answers" section at the end of this chapter.

1. To avoid losing the public virtual IP of a cloud service, what is the correct way to shut down the last virtual machine in the cloud service?

    A. Stop-AzureVM -ServiceName $serviceName -Name $vmName.

    B. Use the management portal to shut down the virtual machine.

    C. Stop-AzureVM -ServiceName $serviceName -Name $vmName -StayProvisioned or shutting down the virtual machine from within the guest operating system.

    D. Use a reserved IP address.

2. How many virtual machines can be deployed into a cloud service?

   A. Unlimited

   B. 25

   C. 50

   D. 1

3. How many virtual machines can be in the same availability set?

   A. Unlimited

   B. 25

   C. 50

   D. 1

4. Which cmdlet must be run first to deploy a Linux-based virtual machine into a new cloud service and deploy an SSH certificate using the Azure PowerShell cmdlets?

   A. New-AzureService

   B. New-AzureVM

   C. New-AzureVMConfig

   D. Set-AzureService

Objective 2.2: Implement images and disks

Azure virtual machines support multiple image types (generic and specialized) that can be used for provisioning virtual machines in several scenarios for quick deployments, and even a simple backup. Other common tasks that are related to images and disks include the ability to upload and download virtual hard disk files and copy them between storage accounts and subscriptions. The virtual hard disk files must be registered as operating system disks or data disks to be directly usable by an Azure virtual machine as a mountable disk.

This objective covers how to:

- Upload and download virtual hard disk files (.vhd)
- Copy virtual hard disks between storage accounts and subscriptions
- Implement specialized and generic virtual machine images
- Manage virtual hard disk (VHD) files and disks

Uploading and downloading virtual hard disks

A common task when dealing with Azure virtual machines is uploading disks and images from on-premises to the cloud. The management portal does not support this capability directly, but it is possible using either third-party tools or the Azure PowerShell cmdlets. There are two cmdlets that can help with this: Add-AzureVHD and Save-AzureVHD.

The Add-AzureVHD cmdlet is designed to efficiently upload a virtual hard disk (.vhd) to an Azure Storage account. This cmdlet uses the VHD data structures to determine what bytes are actually written in the file, and only uploads those bytes instead of the empty bytes of the entire disk as an optimization. The following example shows how to upload a virtual hard disk file to an Azure Storage account.

```
$storage = "[storage account name]"
$storagePath = "https://$storage.blob.core.windows.net/uploads/myosdisk.vhd"
$sourcePath = "C:\mydisks\myosdisk.vhd"
Add-AzureVhd -Destination $storagePath `
            -LocalFilePath $sourcePath
```

It is important to understand the following disk requirements and limitations in Azure for using an uploaded virtual hard disk file.

- Maximum file size for an Azure operating system disk: 127 GB
- Maximum file size for an Azure data disk: 1023 GB (~1 TB)
- Azure does not currently support the VHDX file format
- Azure currently only supports fixed virtual hard disks

The last limitation is made somewhat easier with Add-AzureVHD because it will automatically convert a dynamic virtual hard disk (.vhd) to fixed format during upload. The Add-AzureVHD cmdlet supports three additional parameters that can modify its behavior. The NumberOfUploaderThreads parameter allows you to override the default number (8) of threads to use for upload operations. The BaseImageUriToPatch parameter supports specifying the URI of an existing image in Azure Storage that will be patched if you are uploading a differencing disk. The Overwrite parameter tells the cmdlet to overwrite an existing virtual hard disk file in the same location if it already exists. If the virtual hard disk file is already associated as a disk in Azure,gf fgh ht it will have a storage lease which blocks outside code from modifying it, and Overwrite will still fail.

The Save-AzureVHD cmdlet works in a similar fashion to Add-AzureVHD, except the source is now a URI to an existing virtual hard disk (.vhd) file in an Azure Storage account, and the path specified to LocalFilePath will be the destination of where the .vhd file will be downloaded to on the local file system. This cmdlet also supports the Overwrite parameter to overwrite an existing file in the same location and the same name.

```
Save-AzureVhd -Source $storagePath `
            -LocalFilePath $localPath
```

Copying virtual hard disks between storage accounts and subscriptions

A common operation when implementing virtual machines is copying virtual hard disk files between storage accounts in the same or separate subscriptions. This could be to move or copy a virtual machine between regions or subscriptions, or to use a virtual machine image in a separate region. The Azure Storage service provides the asynchronous blob copy API. This API makes it easy to specify a source blob file URI and a destination URI, and the service will perform the copy on your behalf. To use this API from Windows PowerShell, the Start-AzureStorageBlobCopy cmdlet can be used. This cmdlet will be covered in depth in Chapter 4.

Virtual machine images

Azure virtual machines can be provisioned from the platform images provided by Azure as you saw in Objective 2.1. Azure also supports the creation of your own custom images. These images are used for the deployment of custom software and configuration, or as a simple but effective backup.

Azure supports three distinct image types. The first type is the legacy operating system image, which only supports creating a generic image with the operating system disk. The virtual machine image type was introduced later, and it supports creating both generic and specialized images. This image type also supports the capture of data disks in addition to the operating system disk.

Generic images

Generic images are referred to as generic because as part of their creation, a tool that generalizes the operating system is run. On Windows-based images this tool is Sysprep.exe, and on Linux-based images this is the Azure Agent (waagent). These tools put the operating system in a pre-deployment state (no computer/host name, domain join information, removal security identifiers (SIDs), or local credentials), but your customizations remain intact.

The use case for a generic image is if you need to deploy custom software or configuration changes that will then be applied to multiple virtual machines for nearly identical instances. A web farm deployment is a good example. For a given server in a web farm, you may install a webserver, deploy custom frameworks, runtimes, and potentially management services. Applying those customizations one time to a virtual machine and then capturing that as an image makes more sense than applying that configuration manually across each server in a web farm.

To create a generic image, boot up a starting image based on Windows or Linux. From there, customize the virtual machine by installing software or making changes to the operating system configuration. Finally, you run the generalization tool.

In Windows, this is accomplished using the Sysprep.exe utility. Using Sysprep.exe, select the Generalize check box and change the Shutdown Options to Shutdown, as shown in Figure 2-17. After you click OK, Sysprep.exe will generalize the operating system and automatically shut down the virtual machine when it is complete.

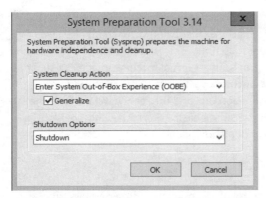

FIGURE 2-17 Using the Sysprep.exe utility to generalize the virtual machine for imaging

In Linux, this is accomplished by using the Azure Agent waagent. Using sudo, run the waagent command line with the Deprovision parameter, as shown in Figure 2-18. After the command has completed, you must manually shut down the virtual machine using the Linux command line, either with the management portals or the Azure command-line tools.

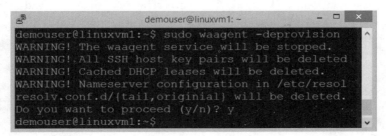

FIGURE 2-18 Using the Azure Agent to prepare a Linux virtual machine for imaging

After the virtual machine is generalized and is in the Stopped state, using the management portal, click the Capture button and ensure you select the box labeled I Have Run Sysprep On The Virtual Machine (Windows) or I Have Run The Windows Azure Linux Agent On The Virtual Machine (Linux) before capturing, as shown in Figure 2-19.

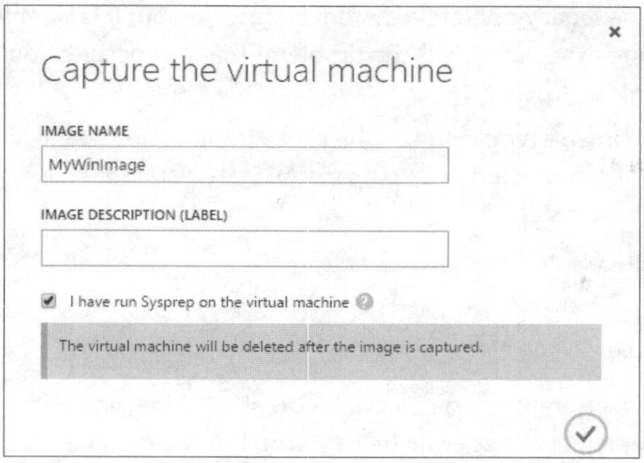

FIGURE 2-19 Capturing a Windows-based generalized image using the management portal

You can also capture a generic image using the Azure PowerShell cmdlet Save-AzureVMImage, and specifying the value Generalized to the OSState parameter, as shown here.

```
Save-AzureVMImage  -ServiceName $serviceName `
              -Name $vmName `
              -ImageName $imageName `
              -ImageLabel $imageLabel `
              -OSState Generalized
```

Specialized images

As the name suggests, specialized images are virtual machine images that are not generalized. This means you do not run Sysprep.exe on Windows or waagent on Linux prior to capturing the image. When the image is captured, the virtual machine's operating system disk has all of initial provisioning configuration at the time it was created. Customizations such as machine name, user name, and password are exactly as they were at the time of capture.

To capture a specialized image using the management portal, do not select the check box labeled I Have Run Sysprep On The Virtual Machine before capturing. The virtual machine does not need to be in the Stopped state as capturing a generic image does. One word of warning, if the virtual machine is not shut down, the disks might be in a dirty state because they were captured while they were running.

To capture a specialized image using Windows PowerShell, specify the value Specialized to the OSState parameter in the call to Save-AzureVMImage, as shown here.

```
Save-AzureVMImage  -ServiceName $serviceName `
              -Name $vmName `
              -ImageName $imageName `
              -ImageLabel $imageLabel `
              -OSState Specialized
```

There is not a lot of reason to create the legacy operating system image type but it is worth calling out due to its potential to be on the exam, as well as the problems that can occur if you accidently create one when you did not mean to.

To create the legacy operating system image type, you use the same cmdlet and parameters as specialized and generic VM images, but you do not pass the OSState parameter, as the following example shows.

```
Save-AzureVMImage -ServiceName $serviceName `
                  -Name $vmName `
                  -ImageName $imageName `
                  -ImageLabel $imageLabel
```

The risk with this approach is if you are attempting to capture a virtual machine with data disks and you accidently omit this parameter, the image will be captured but the data disks will be deleted in the process and will not be part of your image. This behavior is only available through Windows PowerShell and the service management API.

Changing the configuration of a captured image

An image captured from a virtual machine using The management portal or the OSState parameter of Save-AzureVMImage retains the disk configuration when it is captured. Each virtual machine image has two properties that contain the disk configuration for the image: OSDiskConfiguration and DataDiskConfiguration. You can modify these properties using the New-AzureDiskConfigSet, Get-AzureVMImage, Set-AzureVMImageOSDiskConfig, Set-AzureVMImageDataDiskConfig, and Update-AzureVMImage cmdlets. The following example changes the HostCache setting and the label of an existing data disk in a previously captured virtual machine image.

```
$diskName   = "[data disk name]"
$imageName  = "[image name]"
$imageLabel = "[new image label]"

$imageCtx = Get-AzureVMImage $imageName
$config = Get-AzureVMImageDiskConfigSet -ImageContext $imageCtx
Set-AzureVMImageDataDiskConfig -DataDiskName $diskName `
                               -HostCaching ReadWrite `
                               -DiskConfig $config
Update-AzureVMImage -ImageName $diskName `
                    -Label $imageLabel `
                    -DiskConfig $config
```

Creating images and disks from a virtual hard disk

A virtual hard disk file must have a disk or image associated in Azure in order for it to be mounted to an Azure virtual machine. When you create a virtual machine, an image, or create a data disk on an existing virtual machine, this association is created for you automatically. You can view the existing disks and custom images in your subscription using Windows PowerShell or the current management portal (*http://manage.windowsazure.com*).

FIGURE 2-20 Viewing the available custom images in the management portal

You have already seen how to use the Get-AzureVMImage and Get-AzureDisk cmdlets to view existing images and disks associated in your subscription in Objective 2.1. To associate an existing virtual hard disk (.vhd) file as an operating system disk using the management portal, click the Create button at the bottom of the page on the Disks tab. The dialog box that opens allows you to browse to the virtual hard disk file and select the next to The VHD Contains An Operating System check box, as shown in Figure 2-21. To associate a data disk, the same dialog box is used, but you do not select the check box.

Create a disk from a VHD

NAME

MyOSDisk

VHD URL

https://examref1.blob.core.windows.net/disks/Wi

☑ The VHD contains an operating system.

OPERATING SYSTEM FAMILY

Windows ▼

FIGURE 2-21 Associating a virtual hard disk with an operating system disk using the management portal

To associate a virtual hard disk (.vhd) file as a disk (not an image) in Azure using Windows PowerShell, use the Add-AzureDisk cmdlet. The Add-AzureDisk cmdlet requires the DiskName, MediaLocation, and Label parameters, and optionally the OS parameter. If you are registering a disk with an operating system, specify Windows or Linux as the value for the OS parameter. In the following example, the Add-AzureDisk cmdlet registers the disk named MyOSDisk with the underlying virtual hard disk file in the container named Uploads, within the storage account specified in the $storage variable.

```
$storage = "[storage account name]"
$storagePath = "https://$storage.blob.core.windows.net/uploads/myosdisk.vhd"
```

```
$diskName = "MyOSDisk"
$label = "MyOSDisk"
Add-AzureDisk -DiskName $diskName -Label $label -MediaLocation $storagePath -OS Windows
```

When the call to Add-AzureDisk completes, a virtual machine can be created by passing the $diskName variable to the DiskName parameter of New-AzureVMConfig instead of ImageName.

If the virtual hard disk file only has data on it, you would create it using the same technique except omitting the OS parameter as the following example demonstrates.

```
$storage = "[storage account name]"
$storagePath = "https://$storage.blob.core.windows.net/uploads/mydatadisk.vhd"
$diskName = "MyDataDisk"
$label = "MyDataDisk"
Add-AzureDisk -DiskName $diskName -Label $label -MediaLocation $storagePath
```

Registering a virtual hard disk file as an image is a similar process. Using the management portal, browse to the virtual hard disk in the Azure Storage account, specify the name, description, and operating system type. If you are creating a Windows image and you ran Sysprep on the virtual machine, select the I Have Run Sysprep On The Virtual Machine check box. This will create a generalized image. To create a specialized image, do not select the check box.

FIGURE 2-22 Associating a virtual hard disk with an operating system image using the management portal

A significant difference between creating images based on Windows or Linux, is that Linux images are required to have the Azure Agent installed prior to associating the virtual hard disk file with an image. The Agent can be installed using the yum or rpm package managers, or manually from *https://github.com/Azure/WALinuxAgent*. Associating a Linux-based image with a virtual hard disk is the same process as Windows except in the management portal the check box will say I Have Ran Waagent -Deprovision On The Virtual Machine, instead of mentioning Sysprep.

To accomplish the same task using Windows PowerShell, as shown in Figure 2-22, use the Add-AzureVMImage cmdlet. The minimum parameters that are required are the ImageName, MediaLocation, and the OS parameter, as shown in the following example.

```
$storage = "[storage account name]"
$storagePath = https://$storage.blob.core.windows.net/uploads/myosimage.vhd
$imageName = "MyGeneralizedImage"
$label      = "MyGeneralizedImage"
Add-AzureVMImage -ImageName $imageName `
                 -MediaLocation $storagePath `
                 -OS Windows
```

The Add-AzureVMImage cmdlet supports several optional parameters to help describe the image. Many of these properties are used by the platform images but are available for your own custom images if you want to use them.

TABLE 2-5 Capabilities for virtual machine creation using the Azure PowerShell cmdlets

EULA	Optional end user license agreement text
ImageFamily	Optional value that can be used for grouping images into an image family.
Label	Optional label for the image.
PrivacyUri	Optional URI to a page that describes privacy policy.
PublishedDate	The date the image was published.
RecommendedVMSize	The recommended size of the virtual machine for this specific image. When this is set the management portal will automatically set this value as the default size when creating a virtual machine from the image.

Here is an example of creating an image using all of the optional parameters when creating a new image from an existing virtual hard disk.

```
$storage = "[storage account name]"
$storage = "examref1"
$storagePath = https://$storage.blob.core.windows.net/uploads/myosimage.vhd
$imageName = "MyGeneralizedImage"
$label = "MyGeneralizedImage"
Add-AzureVMImage -ImageName $imageName `
                 -MediaLocation $storagePath `
                 -OS Windows `
                 -Eula "some eula language" `
                 -Label "image label" `
                 -Description "image descripion" `
                 -RecommendedVMSize "A5" `
                 -ImageFamily "My Custom Image Family" `
                 -PublishedDate "10/5/2014" `
                 -PrivacyUri "http://contoso.com/privacy"
```

Managing data disks

You can attach an existing data disk, or create a new empty data disk and attach it to an existing virtual machine using the Management portal (*http://manage.windowsazure.com*) and Windows PowerShell. If an unattached data disk is in your subscription and in the same region as your virtual machine, the Attach button in the management portal will allow you to attach it to the virtual machine, as shown in Figure 2-23.

FIGURE 2-23 Associating a virtual hard disk as a data disk using the Management portal

You can also click Attach and click the New Empty Disk drop-down instead. This will launch the dialog box in Figure 2-24. You can specify the disk name, location, and a size of up to 1023 GB.

FIGURE 2-24 Associating a virtual hard disk as a data disk using the Management portal

You can attach an existing data disk or create a new data disk by using the Add-AzureDataDisk cmdlet. This cmdlet supports three separate parameter sets:

- -CreateNew for creating a new disk
- -Import for referencing an existing disk by name
- -ImportFrom for referencing a virtual hard disk file directly in storage

This cmdlet works during virtual machine creation, as you saw in Objective 2.1, or on a virtual machine that already exists. Now look at a slightly simpler version of that example for reference. This example creates a virtual machine with a 10 GB data disk already attached when the virtual machine is provisioned.

```
$adminUser    = "[admin user name]"
$password     = "[admin password]"
$serviceName  = "contoso-vms"
$location     = "West US"
$size         = "Small"
$vmName       = "vm1"

$imageFamily = "Windows Server 2012 R2 Datacenter"
$imageName = Get-AzureVMImage |
                where { $_.ImageFamily -eq $imageFamily } |
                        sort PublishedDate -Descending |
                select -ExpandProperty ImageName -First 1

New-AzureVMConfig -Name $vmName `
                  -InstanceSize $size `
                  -ImageName $imageName |

Add-AzureProvisioningConfig -Windows `
                            -AdminUsername $adminUser `
                            -Password $password |

Add-AzureDataDisk -CreateNew `
                  -DiskSizeInGB 10 `
                  -LUN 0 `
                  -DiskLabel "data" |
New-AzureVM -ServiceName $serviceName `
            -Location $location
```

The example shows how to attach a second data disk on the virtual machine as part of an update. Since the first data disk is already attached on LUN 0, the LUN parameter is set to 1.

```
$serviceName = "contoso-vms"
$vmName      = "vm1"
Get-AzureVM -ServiceName $serviceName -Name $vmName |
Add-AzureDataDisk -CreateNew `
                  -DiskSizeInGB 500 `
                  -LUN 1 `
                  -DiskLabel "data 2" |
Update-AzureVM
```

You can view the data disk configuration of your virtual machine through the management portal (on the Dashboard tab) or using Windows PowerShell by piping the configuration object to the Get-AzureDataDisk cmdlet, as shown in Figure 2-25.

```
PS C:\> Get-AzureVM -ServiceName $serviceName -Name $vmName | Get-AzureDataDisk

HostCaching         : None
DiskLabel           : data
DiskName            : contoso-vms-vm1-0-201412022301300406
Lun                 : 0
LogicalDiskSizeInGB : 10
MediaLink           : https://examref1.blob.core.windows.net/vhds/contoso-vms-vm1-data-2014-12-2-52.vhd
SourceMediaLink     :
ExtensionData       :

HostCaching         : None
DiskLabel           : data 2
DiskName            : contoso-vms-vm1-1-201412022301340020
Lun                 : 1
LogicalDiskSizeInGB : 500
MediaLink           : https://examref1.blob.core.windows.net/vhds/contoso-vms-vm1-data 2-2014-12-2-54.vhd
SourceMediaLink     :
ExtensionData       :
```

FIGURE 2-25 Associating a virtual hard disk as a data disk using the Management portal

To import an existing data disk instead of using the CreateNew parameter, use the Import or ImportFrom parameters. Using the Import parameter assumes the disk is already associated and you just need to specify the existing disk name and the LUN on the virtual machine. The following example demonstrates how to use the Import parameter to reference an existing data disk by name, and attach it to a virtual machine configuration object.

```
Add-AzureDataDisk -Import -DiskName "mydatadisk" -LUN 1
```

If the virtual hard disk file was not associated with the Add-AzureDisk cmdlet, you can reference it in storage directly using the ImportFrom parameter, as shown in the following example. This has the effect of registering the disk and attaching it to the virtual machine at the same time.

```
$storagePath = https://$storage.blob.core.windows.net/uploads/mydatadisk.vhd
Add-AzureDataDisk -ImportFrom `
                  -DiskLabel "Data 2" `
                  -MediaLocation $storagePath `
                  -LUN 1
```

Deleting images and disks

The current management portal (*https://manage.windowsazure.com*) allows you to delete disks and images directly as long as the disk is not attached to a virtual machine. When you delete the disk using the management portal, you will be prompted to Delete The Associated VHD or to Retain The Associated VHD. This controls whether the virtual hard disk file is removed from Azure Storage.

Using the Azure PowerShell cmdlets, you can delete images and disks using the Remove-AzureVMImage and Remove-AzureDisk cmdlets. Both cmdlets support the DeleteVHD parameter, which will delete the associated virtual hard disk files (.vhd) if specified. They will remain in your Azure Storage account if the parameter is not specified. Here is an example of deleting a virtual machine image and the associated .vhd file.

```
Remove-AzureVMImage -ImageName "MyGeneralizedImage" -DeleteVHD
```

Here is another example, this time showing how to delete a disk and the associated .vhd file.

```
Remove-AzureDisk -DiskName "mydatadisk" -DeleteVHD
```

Thought experiment
Deploying a web farm

In this thought experiment, apply what you have learned about this objective. You can find answers to these questions in the "Answers" section at the end of this chapter.

You are the network administrator of Contoso. You are responsible for deploying an IIS-based web application using 10 virtual machines. The virtual machines will be identical in configuration except for their machine names.

1. Which image type would be best for this type of deployment?

2. What tool must be run on the source virtual machine before capturing the image?

Objective summary

- Virtual hard disk files (.vhd) can be uploaded to an Azure Storage account using the Add-AzureVHD cmdlet. The Save-AzureVHD cmdlet can be used to download a .vhd file to the local file system.

- To copy a virtual hard disk (.vhd) file from one storage account to another, use the Start-AzureStorageBlobCopy cmdlet.

- Generic images are captured after generalizing the operating system using the Sysprep.exe tool in Windows or the Azure Agent (waagent) on Linux. The operating system must be shut down before the image can be captured. Specialized images are captured without running a generalization tool. Specialized images don't need to go through the provisioning process again.

- When provisioning a virtual machine using a generic image, you must specify provisioning configuration, such as user name and password. Using Windows PowerShell, this is specified using the Add-AzureProvisioningConfig cmdlet. When provisioning a specialized image, don't specify a user name and password (because the local credentials are already set) and, to create from Windows PowerShell, don't call the Add-AzureProvisioningConfig cmdlet.

- To associate a disk with a virtual hard disk (.vhd) file, you can use the management portal or the Azure PowerShell Add-AzureDisk cmdlet. To associate an image with a virtual hard disk (.vhd) file you can use the management portal or the Azure PowerShell Add-AzureVMImage cmdlet.

- To delete a custom image or disk using the management portal, select the image or disk and click Delete. For Azure PowerShell, use the Remove-AzureVMImage and Remove-AzureDisk cmdlets.

Objective review

Answer the following questions to test your knowledge of the information in this objective. You can find the answers to these questions and explanations of why each answer choice is correct or incorrect in the "Answers" section at the end of this chapter.

1. What is the maximum disk size supported for an operating system (OS) disk in Azure?

   A. 1023 GB

   B. 64 TB

   C. 2 TB

   D. 127 GB

2. Which Azure PowerShell cmdlet should you use to upload a virtual hard disk file?

   A. Add-AzureDisk

   B. Add-AzureDataDisk

   C. Set-AzureOSDisk

   D. Add-AzureVHD

3. Your Hyper-V based virtual machines disks are dynamic. What, if anything, do you need to do to the disks prior to upload?

   A. Nothing; the Azure PowerShell cmdlets will convert to fixed format automatically.

   B. Nothing; Azure natively supports dynamic disks.

   C. First convert the disk to fixed using Hyper-V Manager.

   D. First convert the disk to fixed by using Windows PowerShell.

Objective 2.3: Perform configuration management

Azure virtual machines have a variety of built-in extensions that can enable configuration management. There are two extensions for Windows PowerShell. The custom script extension allows you to run a script on a virtual machine at provisioning time or after it is running. The Windows PowerShell DSC Extension allows you to define the state of a virtual machine using the PowerShell Desired State Configuration language and apply it. There are also extensions that allow you to configure your virtual machines to use open source configuration management utilities such as Chef or Puppet.

This objective covers how to:

- Use the custom script extension
- Implement Windows PowerShell Desired State Configuration (DSC)
- Use the Virtual Machine Access Extension
- Enable the Chef virtual machine extension
- Enable the Puppet virtual machine extension

Using the custom script extension

Objective 2.2 describes how to connect externally using Windows PowerShell remoting. That is not your only option for executing scripts against virtual machines. The Azure PowerShell cmdlets and the Azure virtual machine Agent also support two additional methods, the custom script extension and the Windows PowerShell DSC extension. You can use both options to run scripts and update the configuration of an Azure virtual machine.

To use the Azure custom script extension, you create a Windows PowerShell script that can optionally accept parameters, and upload it to an Azure Storage account. The custom script extension takes as parameters the script name, the container, and the parameters you want to pass to the script, and you can run the script at any time as long as the virtual machine is running. Figure 2-26 shows how to enable this extension using the Management portal.

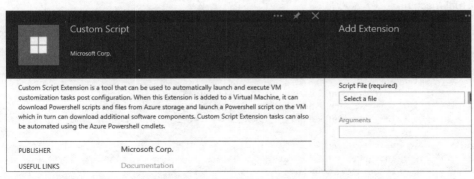

FIGURE 2-26 Specifying a custom script using the Management portal

The Azure PowerShell cmdlets can also be used to run scripts using the custom script extension. For example, the following script deploys the Active Directory Domain Services role. It accepts two parameters: one is for the domain name and the other is for the administrator password.

```
param(
  $domain,
  $password
)
$smPassword = (ConvertTo-SecureString $password -AsPlainText -Force)
```

```
Install-WindowsFeature -Name "AD-Domain-Services" `
                        -IncludeManagementTools `
                        -IncludeAllSubFeature

Install-ADDSForest -DomainName $domain `
                    -DomainMode Win2012 `
                    -ForestMode Win2012 `
                    -Force `
                    -SafeModeAdministratorPassword $smPassword
```

Use the Set-AzureVMCustomScriptExtension cmdlet to run this script on an Azure virtual machine. This scenario can be used for installing roles or any other type of iterative script you want to run on the virtual machine.

The script must reside in an Azure Storage account. Upload the file to storage using the Set-AzureStorageBlobContent cmdlet, a separate tool like Visual Studio, or one of the several third-party storage tools available. The script doesn't have to be in a public container because you can also pass the Azure Storage account name and key to the Set-AzureVMCustomScriptExtension cmdlet using the StorageAccountKey and StorageAccountName parameters.

To run the script at provisioning time, modify the virtual machine configuration with the Set-AzureVMCustomScriptExtension cmdlet to specify the scripts to run. In the following example, the bolded code shows the code necessary to run a script during the provisioning of a virtual machine.

```
$scriptName = "install-active-directory.ps1"
$scriptUri = http://$storageAccount.blob.core.windows.net/scripts/$scriptName
$scriptArgument = "fabrikam.com $password"
$imageFamily = "Windows Server 2012 R2 Datacenter"
$imageName = Get-AzureVMImage |
                where { $_.ImageFamily -eq $imageFamily } |
                    sort PublishedDate -Descending |
                select -ExpandProperty ImageName -First 1

New-AzureVMConfig -Name $vmName `
                    -InstanceSize $size `
                    -ImageName $imageName |

Add-AzureProvisioningConfig -Windows `
                            -AdminUsername $adminUser `
                            -Password $password |
Set-AzureSubnet -SubnetNames $subnet |
Set-AzureStaticVNetIP -IPAddress $ipAddress |
Set-AzureVMCustomScriptExtension -FileUri $scriptUri `
                                    -Run $scriptname `
                                    -Argument "$domain $password" |
New-AzureVM -ServiceName $serviceName `
                -Location $location `
                -VNetName $vnetName
```

The FileUri parameter of the Set-AzureVMCustomScriptExtension cmdlet, accepts the URI to the script in the Azure Storage account, and the Run parameter tells the cmdlet the script to run on the virtual machine. The script can also be specified using the StorageAccountName, StorageAcountKey, ContainerName, and FileName parameters.

To run a script after the virtual machine is configured, use the Azure PowerShell cmdlets update pattern of Get-AzureVM, modify, Update-AzureVM. The following example returns the existing virtual machine configuration using the Get-AzureVM cmdlet. Then, it modifies the configuration with Set-AzureVMCustomScriptExtension. Finally, the script updates the virtual machine by calling the Update-AzureVM cmdlet and piping in the updated configuration.

```
Get-AzureVM -ServiceName $serviceName -Name $vmName |
Set-AzureVMCustomScriptExtension -FileUri $scriptUri `
                                 -Run $scriptname `
                                 -Argument "$domain $password" |
Update-AzureVM
```

To run multiple scripts, make multiple calls to the Set-AzureVMCustomScriptExtension cmdlet on the same configuration object, or you can pass multiple scripts to the FileUri parameter.

Implementing Windows PowerShell Desired State Configuration

Windows PowerShell Desired State Configuration (DSC) allows you to declaratively configure the state of the virtual machine. Using built-in resource providers or custom providers with a DSC script enables you to declaratively configure settings such as roles and features, registry settings, files and directories, firewall rules, and most settings available to Windows. One of the compelling features of DSC is that, instead of writing logic to detect and correct the state of the machine, the providers do that work for you and make the system state as defined in the script.

For example, the following DSC script declares that the Web-Server role should be installed, along with the Web-Asp-Net45 feature. The WindowsFeature code block represents a DSC resource. The resource has a property named Ensure that can be set to Present or Absent. In this example, the WindowsFeature resource will verify whether the Web-Server role is present on the target machine and if it is not, the resource will install it. It will repeat the process for the Web-Asp-Net45 feature.

```
Configuration ContosoSimple
{

    Node "localhost"
    {
        #Install the IIS Role
        WindowsFeature IIS
        {
          Ensure = "Present"
          Name = "Web-Server"
        }
        #Install ASP.NET 4.5
        WindowsFeature AspNet45
```

```
            {
                Ensure = "Present"
                Name = "Web-Asp-Net45"
            }


        }
    }
```

In addition to the DSC resources that come with Windows Server 2012 R2, there are several "waves" of DSC resources that have been released by the Windows PowerShell engineering team, and of course you can write your own. To install a custom resource, download it and unzip it into the C:\Program Files\WindowsPowerShell\Modules folder. To download the latest DSC resources from Microsoft and the community, navigate to the TechNet Script Center at *https://gallery.technet.microsoft.com/scriptcenter* and search for "DSC Resource".

The following example (ContosoAdvanced.ps1) uses a downloadable resource xWebAdministration to create a new IIS website, stop the default website, and deploy an application from a file share to the destination website folder.

```
# ContosoAdvanced.psd1

configuration ContosoAdvanced
{
    # Import the module that defines custom resources
    Import-DscResource -Module xWebAdministration
    Node "localhost"
    {
        # Install the IIS role
        WindowsFeature IIS
        {
            Ensure          = "Present"
            Name            = "Web-Server"
        }
        # Install the ASP .NET 4.5 role
        WindowsFeature AspNet45
        {
            Ensure          = "Present"
            Name            = "Web-Asp-Net45"
        }
        # Stop an existing website
        xWebsite DefaultSite
        {
            Ensure          = "Present"
            Name            = "Default Web Site"
            State           = "Stopped"
            PhysicalPath    = "C:\Inetpub\wwwroot"
            DependsOn       = "[WindowsFeature]IIS"

        }
        # Copy the website content
        File WebContent
        {
            Ensure          = "Present"
            SourcePath      = "\\vmconfig\share\app"
            DestinationPath = "C:\inetpub\contoso"
```

```
            Recurse           = $true
            Type              = "Directory"
            DependsOn         = "[WindowsFeature]AspNet45"
        }
        # Create a new website
        xWebsite Fabrikam
        {
            Ensure            = "Present"
            Name              = "Contoso Advanced"
            State             = "Started"
            PhysicalPath      = "C:\inetpub\contoso"
            DependsOn         = "[File]WebContent"
        }

    }
}
```

Using the Azure PowerShell cmdlets and the DSC Script Extension, you can publish this configuration complete with the custom resources and have them deployed to an Azure virtual machine. The first step is to publish the DSC configuration (including the resources) to an Azure Storage account. The following example does just that.

```
Publish-AzureVMDscConfiguration .\ContosoAdvanced.ps1
```

The Publish-AzureVMDscConfiguration cmdlet takes the Windows PowerShell DSC Script, imports all of the resources such as xWebAdministration in the example, and produces a .zip file that it then uploads to the storage account specified with CurrentStorageAccount name in your subscription. The .zip file's name is in the format of scriptname.ps1.zip and by default will be uploaded to the windows-powershell-dsc container in the storage account.

To see the .zip file created by the Publish-AzureVMDscConfiguration cmdlet, specify the ConfigurationArchivePath parameter with the path, and a complete file name, and the cmdlet will produce the .zip file locally as shown here.

```
$dscFileName = "ContosoAdvanced.ps1.zip"
Publish-AzureVMDscConfiguration .\ContosoAdvanced.ps1 `
                        -ConfigurationArchivePath $dscFileName
```

You can upload the generated .zip file directly using the same cmdlet. If the .zip file already exists in the storage account, specify the Force parameter to overwrite it as shown below.

```
Publish-AzureVMDscConfiguration $dscFileName -Force
```

To specify an alternative storage account instead of the account specified with Set-AzureSubscription $subscription CurrentStorageAccount, you can pass a storage context object to the Publish-AzureVMDscConfiguration cmdlet, as shown in this example.

```
$storageAccount = "[storage account name]"
$storageKey = (Get-AzureStorageKey -StorageAccountName $storageAccount).Primary
$ctx = New-AzureStorageContext -StorageAccountName $storageAccount `
                        -StorageAccountKey $storageKey
Publish-AzureVMDscConfiguration -ConfigurationPath ".\ContosoAdvanced.ps1" `
                        -StorageContext $ctx
```

After the configuration is published, it can be applied to any virtual machine at provisioning time or after the fact using the Set-AzureVMDscExtension cmdlet. To show how this works, this example uses the same code previously used with the custom script extension. The first example shows creating a new virtual machine and specifying a DSC configuration. The changes specific to the DSC configuration are in bold.

```
$configArchive = "ContosoAdvanced.ps1.zip"
$configName    = "ContosoAdvanced"
$imageFamily = "Windows Server 2012 R2 Datacenter"
$imageName = Get-AzureVMImage |
                where { $_.ImageFamily -eq $imageFamily } |
                        sort PublishedDate -Descending |
                select -ExpandProperty ImageName -First 1
New-AzureVMConfig -Name $vmName `
                        -InstanceSize $size `
                        -ImageName $imageName |
Add-AzureProvisioningConfig -Windows `
                        -AdminUsername $adminUser `
                        -Password $password |
Set-AzureSubnet -SubnetNames $subnet |
Set-AzureVMDscExtension -ConfigurationArchive $configArchive `
                        -ConfigurationName $configName |
New-AzureVM -ServiceName $serviceName `
            -Location $location `
            -VNetName $vnetName
```

The example to apply the DSC configuration to an existing virtual machine uses the same pattern to update the virtual machine as using the custom script extension. The change is calling Set-AzureVMDscExtension with the name of the produced .zip file, and the name of the configuration in the script instead of Set-AzureVMCustomScriptExtension.

```
$configArchive = "Contoso.ps1.zip"
$configName    = "ContosoAdvanced"
Get-AzureVM -ServiceName $serviceName -Name $vmName |
Set-AzureVMDscExtension -ConfigurationArchive $configArchive `
                        -ConfigurationName $configName |
Update-AzureVM
```

The Set-AzureVMDscExtension downloads the .zip package specified with ConfigurationArchive and unzips it to a temporary directory. It installs any resources that were previously imported into the .zip file, and then looks for a script with the same name (minus the .zip extension), and runs it on the virtual machine.

The previous example is a good start, but because the script is pointing to a specific file share and most of the configuration values are defined inline in the script, its reusability is limited. Windows PowerShell DSC scripts support specifying a secondary file that contains variables to be applied at runtime.

For example, to make the previous example flexible enough to deploy any web application with the same dependencies, you could move some of the parameters to a Windows PowerShell data file (file with a .psd1 extension) and create a hashtable with the configuration values specific to the web application for deployment, as in the following example of ContosoConfig.psd1.

```
#ContosoConfig.psd1

@{
    AllNodes = @(
        @{
            NodeName            = "localhost"
            WebsiteName         = "ContosoWebApp"
            SourcePath          = "\\vmconfig\share\app"
            DestinationPath     = "C:\inetpub\contoso"
        }
    );
}
```

The Windows PowerShell DSC script itself could reference the variable names inline using the $Node.Variable name syntax. In the following example, $Node.SourcePath, $Node.DestinationPath, and $Node.WebsiteName are all used in place of the hard coded values in the earlier example. The Node syntax is also introduced to the script. This line allows you to selectively apply the configuration based on the node name, which in this case is localhost, because you are applying it to a single virtual machine at a time. The changes to reference the parameters file are in bold.

```
#DeployWebApp.ps1
configuration WebsiteConfig
{
    # Import the module that defines custom resources
    Import-DscResource -Module xWebAdministration

    Node "localhost"
    {
        # Install the IIS role
        WindowsFeature IIS
        {
            Ensure          = "Present"
            Name            = "Web-Server"
        }
        # Install the ASP .NET 4.5 role
        WindowsFeature AspNet45
        {
            Ensure          = "Present"
            Name            = "Web-Asp-Net45"
        }
        # Stop an existing website
        xWebsite DefaultSite
        {
            Ensure          = "Present"
            Name            = "Default Web Site"
            State           = "Stopped"
            PhysicalPath    = "C:\Inetpub\wwwroot"
            DependsOn       = "[WindowsFeature]IIS"

        }
```

```
        # Copy the website content
        File WebContent
        {
            Ensure        = "Present"
            SourcePath      = $Node.SourcePath
            DestinationPath = $Node.DestinationPath
            Recurse        = $true
            Type          = "Directory"
            DependsOn      = "[WindowsFeature]AspNet45"
        }
        # Create a new website
        xWebsite WebSite
        {
            Ensure        = "Present"
            Name          = $Node.WebsiteName
            State         = "Started"
            PhysicalPath   = $Node.DestinationPath
            DependsOn      = "[File]WebContent"
        }
    }
}
```

Because the script and configuration has changed, the Publish-AzureVMDscConfiguration cmdlet is used to publish this configuration, as shown below. Note in the following example that the Windows PowerShell script has changed from ContosoApp.ps1 to DeployWebApp. ps1 to reflect that the script is now generic and not specific to the Contoso application.

```
Publish-AzureVMDscConfiguration .\DeployWebApp.ps1
```

> **NOTE** **OVERWRITING AN EXISTING DSC CONFIGURATION**
>
> If the DSC configuration already exists in the Azure Storage account, you can use the Force parameter to overwrite it.

Use the Set-AzureVMDscExtension to apply the configuration as before. The following example also uses the ConfigurationDataPath parameter to specify the ContosoConfig.psd1 file, which contains the application-specific deployment information. Changes to the script are in bold.

```
$configArchive = "DeployWebApp.ps1.zip"
$configName    = "WebsiteConfig"

Get-AzureVM -ServiceName $serviceName -Name $vmName |
Set-AzureVMDscExtension -ConfigurationArchive $configArchive `
                        -ConfigurationName $configName `
                        -ConfigurationDataPath .\ContosoConfig.psd1 |
Update-AzureVM
```

In addition to publishing and setting the DSC configuration, the Azure PowerShell cmdlets allow you to view the current DSC extension configuration using the Get-AzureVMDscExtension cmdlet, as shown in Figure 2-27. This cmdlet shows whether the extension is applied and the URL in Azure Storage to the .zip file if it is. The following example shows how to call the cmdlet.

```
Get-AzureVM -ServiceName $serviceName -Name $vmName | Get-AzureVMDscExtension
```

```
PS C:\> Get-AzureVM -ServiceName $serviceName -Name $vmName | Get-AzureVMDscExtension

ModulesUrl             : https://examref1.blob.core.windows.net/windows-powershell-dsc/DeployWebApp.ps1.zip
ConfigurationFunction  : DeployWebApp.ps1\WebsiteConfig
Properties             : {}
ExtensionName          : DSC
Publisher              : Microsoft.Powershell
Version                : 1.*
PrivateConfiguration   :
PublicConfiguration    : {"SasToken":"?sv=2014-02-14&sr=b&sig=FU6NFDsdD1kL4MJbN%2F79yKBDCFu64qnf8AonpRLtUEw%3D&
                         se=2014-12-03T00%3A10%3A26Z&sp=r","ModulesUrl":"https://examref1.blob.core.windows.net
                         /windows-powershell-dsc/DeployWebApp.ps1.zip","ConfigurationFunction":"DeployWebApp.ps
                         1\WebsiteConfig","Properties":[],"ProtocolVersion":{"Major":2,"Minor":0,"Build":0,"Re
                         vision":0,"MajorRevision":0,"MinorRevision":0}}
ReferenceName          : DSC
```

FIGURE 2-27 Viewing the current DSC extension configuration of a virtual machine

One more cmdlet to be aware of is the Remove-AzureVMDscExtension. This cmdlet, as the name implies, will remove the DSC extension from the virtual machine. Its usage follows the familiar update pattern of returning the virtual machine configuration with the Get-AzureVM cmdlet, modifying the configuration, and using the Update-AzureVM cmdlet to complete the update as the example shows.

```
Get-AzureVM -ServiceName $serviceName -Name $vmName |
Remove-AzureVMDscExtension |
Update-AzureVM

$config = Get-AzureVM -ServiceName $serviceName -Name $vmName
$config | Remove-AzureVMDscExtension
$config | Update-AzureVM
```

The configuration could be passed on using the VM parameter like this:

```
Remove-AzureVMDscExtension -VM $config.
```

EXAM TIP

Just a reminder that Windows PowerShell examples like the previous example can be written in multiple ways. For instance the configuration could be piped as a separate variable.

Using the Virtual Machine Access Extension

Another extension that can come in handy is the VM Access Extension. Currently, the extension can only be enabled using the Set-AzureVMAccessExtension cmdlet. This cmdlet can reset the local administrator name, password, and also enable Remote Desktop access if it is accidently disabled. Because this is an extension, it does have a dependency on the Azure Virtual Machine Guest Agent. This cmdlet accepts a UserName and Password parameter, as the example shows. If an existing user name is specified, the extension will set the password to the value specified.

```
Get-AzureVM -ServiceName $serviceName -Name $vmName |
Set-AzureVMAccessExtension -UserName $userName -Password $password |
Update-AzureVM
```

Enabling the Puppet virtual machine extension

Beyond using Windows PowerShell for configuration management, this objective also has the requirements of enabling the virtual machine extensions for Puppet and Chef.

The Puppet virtual machine extension can be enabled through the Management portal, as shown in Figure 2-28. Simply specify the Puppet master server name and install the extension.

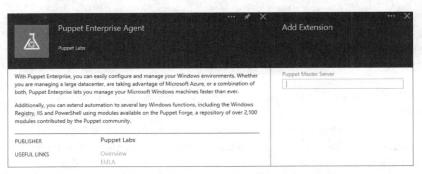

FIGURE 2-28 Enabling the puppet client by specifying a Puppet master server

You can also enable the Puppet extension using the Set-AzureVMPuppetExtension Azure PowerShell cmdlet. The cmdlet accepts a parameter PuppetMasterServer to reference the Puppet master server just like the management portal. The Set-AzureVMPuppetExtension cmdlet can be used at provisioning time my modifying the virtual machine configuration object, as the example shows.

```
$puppetServer = "puppetmaster.cloudapp.net"
$imageFamily = "Windows Server 2012 R2 Datacenter"
$imageName = Get-AzureVMImage |
             where { $_.ImageFamily -eq $imageFamily } |
                    sort PublishedDate -Descending |
             select -ExpandProperty ImageName -First 1

New-AzureVMConfig -Name $vmName `
                         -InstanceSize $size `
                         -ImageName $imageName |

Add-AzureProvisioningConfig -Windows `
                         -AdminUsername $adminUser `
                         -Password $password |

Set-AzureVMPuppetExtension -PuppetMasterServer $puppetServer |

New-AzureVM -ServiceName $serviceName `
            -Location $location
```

The Set-AzureVMPuppetExtension cmdlet can also be enabled on a provisioned virtual machine by returning the virtual machine configuration with Get-AzureVM, modifying it with Set-AzureVMPuppetExtension, and then updating the configuration using the Update-AzureVM cmdlet, as shown here.

```
$puppetServer = "puppetmaster.cloudapp.net"
Get-AzureVM -ServiceName $serviceName -Name $vmName |
Set-AzureVMPuppetExtension -PuppetMasterServer $puppetServer |
Update-AzureVM
```

Enabling the Chef virtual machine extension

The Chef client does not currently have a specific Azure PowerShell extension cmdlet. It can still be enabled easily through the Management portal in the same way as the Puppet virtual machine extension, as shown in Figure 2-29.

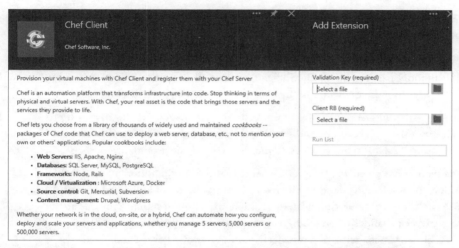

FIGURE 2-29 Enabling the Chef client by specifying the Client.rb file and a validation key

Extensions without cmdlets

As the example with Chef shows, not all virtual machine extensions have their own specific Azure PowerShell cmdlet. To view the extensions that are available, use the Get-AzureVMAvailableExtension cmdlet. Piping the results to the Out-GridView cmdlet makes it easy to read.

```
Get-AzureVMAvailableExtension | Out-GridView
```

Virtual machine extensions can be enabled directly using the Set-AzureVMExtension cmdlet. This cmdlet accepts the extension name, the publisher name, the version of the extension, and the public and private configuration to be set. Extensions like the Chef extension, and the Linux custom script extension are both examples of extensions that currently can only be enabled through this technique. An example of how to implement the custom script extension for Linux can be found in the Azure blog at
http://azure.microsoft.com/blog/2014/08/20/automate-linux-vm-customization-tasks-using-customscript-extension/.

EXAM TIP

To use virtual machine extensions like DSC, Puppet, and Chef on Windows, the Azure virtual machine agent must be installed on the virtual machine. By default, the agent is installed on virtual machines created after February 2014 (when the feature was added). But, it's also possible to not install the agent by using the management portal, or by using the DisableGuestAgent parameter of the Add-AzureProvisioningConfig and New-AzureQuickVM cmdlets. If the agent is not installed at provisioning time, or if you have migrated a virtual hard disk from on-premises, you can manually install the agent on these virtual machines by downloading and installing the agent from Microsoft at *http://go.microsoft.com/fwlink/?LinkID=394789&clcid=0x409*.

Thought experiment
Implementing configuration management

In this thought experiment, apply what you've learned about this objective. You can find answers to these questions in the "Answers" section at the end of this chapter.

You are the network administrator of Contoso. You are responsible for deploying applications through several environments, including the production environment. You're using Azure virtual machines as your deployment environment.

Management has given you the requirements that the configuration management solution you implement should avoid manual configuration of individual servers, which can cause configuration drift. In addition, the solution should provide the ability to track changes when modifying the configuration. The majority of your team is either familiar with, or has expertise with Windows PowerShell.

1. You have to come up with a configuration management solution to support your management's requirements. What is the best solution?

2. What additional component should be involved with your solution to help track changes?

Objective summary

- The Management portal or the Get-AzureVMAvailableExtension cmdlet can enumerate the available extensions for Azure virtual machines.
- Azure Windows-based virtual machines support executing standard or DSC-based Windows PowerShell scripts using the Management portal or the Azure PowerShell cmdlets.
- To apply a DSC script to a virtual machine using Windows PowerShell, publish it to an Azure Storage account using the Publish-AzureVMDscConfiguration cmdlet. The Azure Storage account can be specified using the CurrentStorageAccount setting of the subscription, or the cmdlet accepts a storage context object.

- To apply the published configuration to an individual virtual machine, use the Set-AzureVMDscExtension cmdlet, or the Management portal. This configuration can be applied at provisioning time or later.

- The Set-AzureVMAccessExtension cmdlet is used to execute the VM Access Extension. This extension can enable Remote Desktop access on a virtual machine, change the local administrator password, and rename the local administrator account user name. This extension does not work against Active Directory domain accounts or on domain controllers.

- Windows-based Azure virtual machines natively support the Puppet extension by enabling it through the Management portal, or using the Set-AzureVMPuppetExtension cmdlet. You can enable the Chef extension on both platforms using the Management portal.

Objective review

Answer the following questions to test your knowledge of the information in this objective. You can find the answers to these questions and explanations of why each answer choice is correct or incorrect in the "Answers" section at the end of this chapter.

1. Which Azure PowerShell cmdlet can be used to enable Remote Desktop on an Azure virtual machine?

   A. Set-AzureServiceRemoteDesktopExtension

   B. Set-AzureVMAccessExtension

   C. Set-AzureServiceADDomainExtension

   D. Add-AzureEndpoint

2. When publishing a PowerShell DSC configuration using Windows PowerShell, how do you specify a Windows PowerShell data file (.psd1) that contains parameters for the configuration?

   A. Specify the ConfigurationName parameter of the Set-AzureVMDscExtension cmdlet.

   B. Specify the ConfigurationArchivePath of the parameter of the Publish-AzureVMDscConfiguration cmdlet.

   C. Specify the ConfigurationDataPath parameter of the Set-AzureVMDscExtension cmdlet.

   D. This is only possible through the Management portal.

3. How do you identify all of the available virtual machine extensions using Windows PowerShell?

   A. Get-AzureVMExtension

   B. Get-AzureServiceExtension

   C. Get-AzureVMAvailableExtension

   D. Get-AzureVM

Objective 2.4: Configure VM networking

Configuring the network for Azure virtual machines is a broad topic. This objective covers network-related topics that do not require a virtual network, such as configuring the load balancer on the external VIP, access control lists, and reserved and instance level (public) IP address. It touches on configuring the guest operating system network settings for Azure.

> **This objective covers how to:**
> - Understand cloud services
> - Configure endpoints
> - Configure access control lists
> - Configure reserved IP addresses
> - Configure public IP addresses
> - Configure the guest operating system network

Understanding cloud services

Any discussion of Azure virtual machine networking needs to start with cloud services. Virtual machines are always created in a cloud service (or domain name as referenced in the new management portal). Virtual machines that are inside of the same cloud service are on the same private network, and can communicate with each other directly using their internal IP addresses. Each cloud service has a unique name that is part of the *cloudapp.net* domain.

To access virtual machines inside of the cloud service externally, you create an endpoint (also referred to as an input endpoint). An endpoint can refer to a single virtual machine, or it can be configured as part of a load balanced set. To access an individual virtual machine, you create an endpoint with an unused public port that forwards traffic to the private port on the virtual machine itself. Figure 2-30 depicts two virtual machines deployed inside of a cloud service. Both virtual machines are exposing port 3389 (Remote Desktop) to the outside world through separate endpoints. To access the virtual machines individually through the single IP address of the cloud service (the VIP), an unused public port must be used for each virtual machine endpoint (6510 and 6511 in this case) that is configured to forward to the internal port 3389 on each virtual machine.

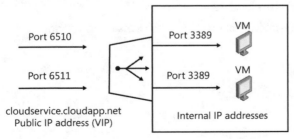

FIGURE 2-30 The architecture of a cloud service with two endpoints configured to forward traffic to two virtual machines

Name resolution within a cloud service

Virtual machines deployed into the same cloud service will have name resolution by default. This is possible because Azure provides a multi-tenant DNS server for your virtual machines. The Azure DNS server does not support the advanced records needed for workloads like Active Directory. In those workloads, deploying your own DNS server is a requirement.

EXAM TIP

Chapter 6 covers deploying multiple cloud services on the same virtual network, which allows virtual machines even in separate cloud services to have direct connectivity. For the exam, you should know that the built-in DNS server supports name resolution automatically for virtual machines within the same cloud service. However, it does not support name resolution across cloud services even if the virtual machines are deployed in a virtual network.

Configuring endpoints

Allowing external traffic from the cloud service VIP to the virtual machines within your cloud service is accomplished through the configuration of endpoints. Endpoints can allow simple port forwarding from one external port to an internal port on a single virtual machine, or they can be configured to allow load balanced traffic to multiple virtual machines.

Figure 2-31 shows the default endpoints for a Windows-based virtual machine and the dialog box to add a new endpoint. Each endpoint has a name, the protocol (TCP or UDP), and the public port and private port (in Windows PowerShell this is specified as LocalPort). The public port and the private port do not have to match (as in the example of the remote desktop endpoints in Figure 2-31). There is also an option to enable floating IP. This feature is also known as *direct server return*, and allows a client to have a direct connection to the virtual machine without the load balancer. This feature is currently only supported for SQL Server Always On Availability Group listeners.

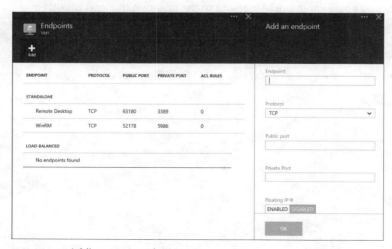

FIGURE 2-31 Adding a new endpoint

To create a port forwarded endpoint using Windows PowerShell, the Add-AzureEndpoint cmdlet is used, as shown in the following example.

```
Get-AzureVM -ServiceName $serviceName -Name $vmName |
        Add-AzureEndpoint -Name "SQL" `
                        -Protocol tcp `
                        -LocalPort 1433 `
                        -PublicPort 1433 |

        Update-AzureVM
```

A port forwarded endpoint can be modified after it is created using the Set-AzureEndpoint cmdlet or through the management portal. This example shows how to change the previously created endpoint named SQL, to listen on public port 2000.

```
Get-AzureVM -ServiceName $serviceName -Name $vmName |
        Set-AzureEndpoint -Name "SQL" `
                        -Protocol tcp `
                        -LocalPort 1433 `
                        -PublicPort 2000 |
Update-AzureVM
```

To remove an endpoint, use the management portal or the Remove-AzureEndpoint cmdlet, as shown.

```
Get-AzureVM -ServiceName $serviceName -Name $vmName |
        Remove-AzureEndpoint -Name "SQL" |
        Update-AzureVM
```

Load balanced endpoints

Load balancing endpoints allows you to distribute TCP or UDP traffic over one or more virtual machines (up to 50 in the same cloud service). This is useful in cases where you want to scale out processing power horizontally by adding more virtual machines.

To create a load balanced endpoint in the Management portal, open the load balanced set tile, select Public or Internal (internal load balancing will be discussed in-depth in Chapter 6), choose the Load Balanced Set menu item, then click Create A Load Balanced Set. This will display the blade for creating a load balanced set, as shown in Figure 2-32. Further down on this same blade, you can specify the probe configuration for the load balanced endpoint.

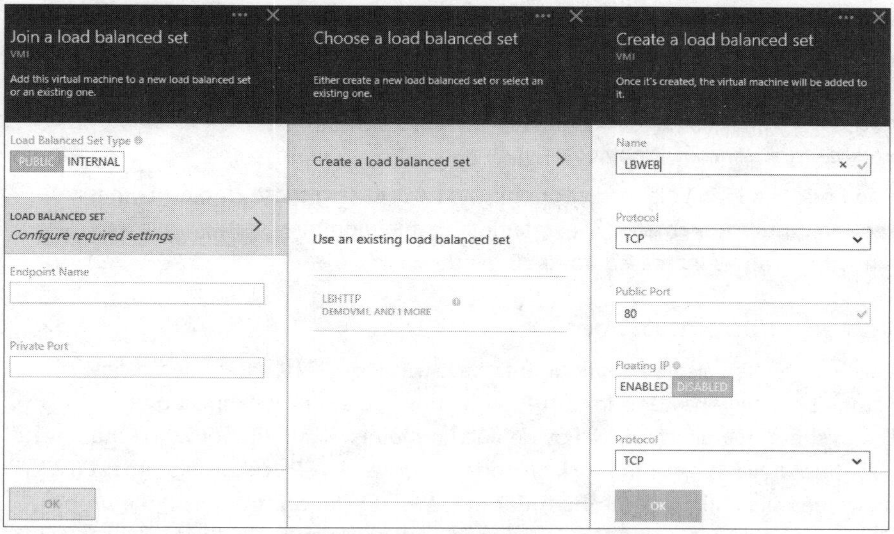

FIGURE 2-32 Creating a load balanced endpoint

The Azure load balancer uses the Name property of the endpoint to know which virtual machines to forward the load balanced traffic to. To add additional virtual machines to the load balanced set, you must create an endpoint on each virtual machine with the same load balanced set name. As Figure 2-33 shows, this is easy using the Management portal because it provides a list of the existing load balanced sets within the same cloud service that you can choose from.

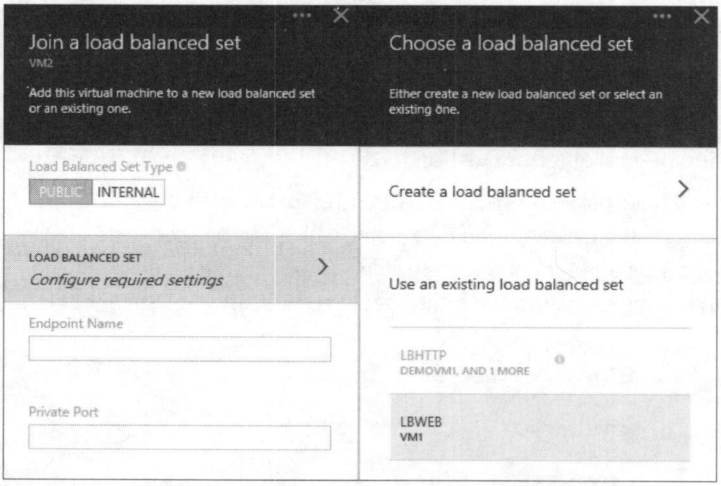

FIGURE 2-33 Adding an endpoint to an existing load balanced set

To create a load balanced endpoint using Windows PowerShell, use the Add-AzureEndpoint cmdlet, and specify the load balanced set name with the LBSetName parameter. You will also be required to specify the probe configuration using the DefaultProbe, NoProbe, or specific probe configuration. A load balanced endpoint cannot be modified using the Set-AzureEndpoint cmdlet. Use the Set-AzureLoadBalancedEndpoint cmdlet instead.

The idle timeout of a load balanced endpoint can be set using these cmdlets by passing the IdleTimeoutInMinutes parameter. The default (and minimum) timeout value is four minutes, but this setting can be increased up to 30 minutes.

Load balanced endpoint probes

Each load balanced set can also be configured to have a TCP or HTTP based load balancer probe. The default probe behavior is for a TCP probe to make a socket connect on the port specified as the probe port. This will by default (in the management portal) be the private port, but it does not have to be. If the socket connect receives a TCP acknowledgement (ACK), the virtual machine will continue receiving traffic in the load balancer rotation. If the probe does not receive a response (two failures, 15 seconds each by default), the load balancer will take the virtual machine in question out of the load balancer rotation. The load balancer does continue to probe, and if the service starts to respond, the virtual machine will be put back into rotation.

An HTTP probe works in a similar manner, except instead of looking for a TCP ACK, the HTTP probe is looking for a successful response from HTTP (HTTP 200 OK). This option allows you to specify the probe path, which is a relative path to an HTTP endpoint that will respond with the code. For example, you could write custom code that responds on the relative path of /Healthcheck.aspx that checks whether the application on the virtual machine is functional (database connectivity and queue access). This allows a much deeper inspection of your application, and programmatic control over whether the virtual machine should be in rotation or not. The probe can be set through the management portal or through Windows PowerShell using the Add-AzureEndpoint cmdlet (creation), or the Set-AzureLoadBalancedEndpoint cmdlet (after creation).

This example shows adding a load-balanced endpoint with a TCP probe with the ProbePort set to 80. This cmdlet also supports the DefaultProbe parameter, which can be used instead of the ProbeProtocol and ProbePort parameters, and will result in the exact same configuration (a TCP probe configured with the ProbePort set to the same port as the LocalPort of the endpoint).

```
$config | Add-AzureEndpoint -Name "WEB" `
                            -Protocol tcp `
                            -LocalPort 80 `
                            -PublicPort 80 `
                            -LBSetName "LBWEB" `
                            -ProbeProtocol tcp `
                            -ProbePort 80
```

The probe can be set on an existing load balanced endpoint using the Set-AzureLoadBalancedEndpoint cmdlet. This cmdlet uses the ProbeProtocolHTTP or

ProbeProtocolTCP parameters instead of ProbeProtocol parameter that Add-AzureEndpoint uses.

In the following example, the cloud service name is passed to the Set-AzureLoadBalancedEndpoint cmdlet with the ServiceName parameter, and the name of the load balanced set, along with specifying the new probe configuration.

```
Set-AzureLoadBalancedEndpoint -ServiceName $serviceName `
                              -LBSetName "LBWEB" `
                              -ProbeProtocolHTTP `
                              -ProbePort 80 `
                              -ProbePath "/healthcheck.aspx"
```

Both TCP and HTTP probes also support specifying the timeout and interval for the probe. Both values are in seconds. These can be specified using the management portal, or with the ProbeIntervalInSeconds and ProbeTimeoutInSeconds parameters of Add-AzureEndpoint or Set-AzureLoadBalancedEndpoint.

Configuring access control lists

Access control lists are lists of rules to either permit or deny a remote network range to access an endpoint. You can specify up to 50 access control lists per endpoint.

Figure 2-34 shows the dialog box to add an access control list to an existing endpoint. Each access control list rule requires a name, the order the rule is processed in, the action to execute (Permit or Deny), and the remote subnet in CIDR format.

FIGURE 2-34 Adding an access control list (ACL) to the Windows PowerShell endpoint

Access control lists work by applying the rules in the order you specify. A permit rule implicitly blocks traffic to all remote networks that do not match the rule unless the incoming IP address matches another permit rule later in the access control list. Likewise, a deny rule allows traffic for source remote networks that do not match the deny rule.

You can specify an access control list from Windows PowerShell as well. This allows you to specify the access control list at the time you open the endpoint so the endpoint is always secured.

The example shows how to use the New-AzureAclConfig cmdlet to create an empty ACL object. The Set-AzureAclConfig cmdlet accepts the ACL object as a parameter, whether it is a Permit or Deny rule, the order to process the rule, a user-defined subscription, and of course the remote subnets the rule applies to in CIDR format. The ACL is applied to the endpoint by calling the Set-AzureEndpoint cmdlet and specifying it as a parameter.

```
$permitSubnet1    = "[remote admin IP 1]/32"
$permitSubnet2    = "[remote admin IP 1]/32"
$acl = New-AzureAclConfig
Set-AzureAclConfig -ACL $acl `
                   -AddRule Permit `
                   -RemoteSubnet $permitSubnet1 `
                   -Order 1 `
                   -Description "remote admin 1"
Set-AzureAclConfig -ACL $acl `
                   -AddRule Permit `
                   -RemoteSubnet $permitSubnet2 `
                   -Order 2 `
                   -Description "remote admin 2"
Get-AzureVM -ServiceName $serviceName -Name $vmName |
Set-AzureEndpoint -Name "PowerShell" -ACL $acl |
Update-AzureVM
```

The cmdlets Add-AzureEndpoint, and Set-AzureLoadBalancedEndpoint both support the ACL parameter. This means that an ACL can be applied to a simple input endpoint or a load balanced endpoint, and can be set at creation time or later.

Configuring reserved IP addresses

Recall that each cloud service has an associated public IP address (or VIP) associated with it. This IP address is only allocated to the cloud service if there are one or more virtual machines not in the StoppedDeallocated state. A virtual machine can get into this state by running Stop-AzureVM or stopping the virtual machine in the management portal. If all of the virtual machines in a cloud service are in the StoppedDeallocated state (or deleted), the public IP address of the cloud service is lost. You can mitigate this by using a reserved IP address. As the name implies, a reserved IP address does not change unless it is deleted. The example shows how to create a new reserved IP using the New-AzureReservedIP cmdlet.

```
$reservedIPName = "WebFarm"
$label = "IP for WebFarm"
$location = "West US"
New-AzureReservedIP -ReservedIPName $reservedIPName `
                    -Label $label `
                    -Location $location
```

After the reserved IP has been created, you can only associate it with the cloud service hosting your virtual machines at creation time. Both the New-AzureVM and New-AzureQuickVM cmdlet support specifying the name to the ReservedIPName parameter, as shown here.

```
New-AzureQuickVM -ReservedIPName $reservedIPName (other parameters)
New-AzureVM -ReservedIPName $reservedIPName (other parameters)
```

There are two other cmdlets involving reserved IPs. The Get-AzureReservedIP cmdlet will enumerate all of the available reserved IP addresses in your subscription. It also accepts a ReservedIPName parameter so that you can view the details of a specific IP. The second cmdlet is Remove-AzureReservedIP. This cmdlet accepts the name of the IP address and will delete it from your subscription. The reserved IP address can only be deleted if it is not associated with an existing cloud service. You can delete an existing cloud service from the management portal, or by using the Remove-AzureService cmdlet.

Configuring public IP addresses

An instance level (or public IP) address is an IP address that is assigned directly to the virtual machine instead of the cloud service. This IP address does not replace the cloud service VIP, but is instead an additional IP that you can use to connect to your virtual machine directly. There are several use cases for a public IP address. Connecting to a virtual machine through its public IP address bypasses the cloud service so there is no need to open endpoints separately. One of the more common is using it for passive FTP, which requires dynamic ports. Also, in some cases a solution might require the outbound request to be the IP address of the virtual machine instead of the cloud service VIP. Figure 2-35 shows the route a user accesses to reach a virtual machine using an instance level IP.

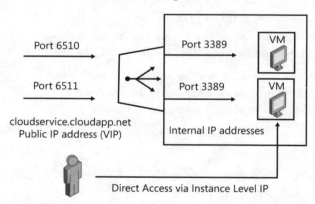

FIGURE 2-35 User accessing a virtual machine using an instance level IP

To create a public IP, use the Set-AzurePublicIP cmdlet. This cmdlet works by modifying the virtual machine configuration object so it can be used at virtual machine provisioning time or later. The Set-AzurePublicIP cmdlet also supports setting the idle timeout (default is four minutes) with the IdleTimeoutInMinutes parameter. This example shows how to add a new public IP address named PassiveFTP to an existing virtual machine.

```
Get-AzureVM -ServiceName $serviceName -Name $vmName |
    Set-AzurePublicIP -PublicIPName "PassiveFTP" |
    Update-AzureVM
```

After the virtual machine has been updated, you can return the updated virtual machine configuration with Get-AzureVM, and extract the new public IP address from it using the Get-AzurePublicIP address cmdlet as the example shows.

```
Get-AzureVM -ServiceName $serviceName -Name $vmName | Get-AzurePublicIP
You can remove the public IP address using the same pattern to update a virtual machine
and the Remove-AzurePublicIP cmdlet. Removing the virtual machine with Remove-AzureVM
works too.
```

```
Get-AzureVM -ServiceName $serviceName -Name $vmName |
    Remove-AzurePublicIP -PublicIPName "PassiveFTP" |
    Update-AzureVM
```

EXAM TIP

Although this objective is focused mostly on the Azure-specific networking, you might see questions related to configuring the network in the guest operating system. In general, you should avoid applying settings such as IP addresses or DNS servers within the guest operating system because those settings should be set through Azure Virtual Networks (covered in Chapter 6). However, you will still be responsible for settings like firewall rules, and algorithm- and protocol-specifc settings, such as the keep alive settings.

Thought experiment
Implementing Configuration Management

In this thought experiment, apply what you've learned about this objective. You can find answers to these questions in the "Answers" section at the end of this chapter.

You are responsible for deploying a web application using IIS and hosted on several virtual machines. The domain name *contoso.com* will have a new A record added (www) to allow users to resolve the application using their browsers.

1. How will you deploy the virtual machines to ensure that the A record is always accurate?

2. What additional changes do you need to make on each virtual machine to support this solution?

Objective summary

- Azure virtual machines that are grouped into cloud services have automatic name resolution supplied by the Azure name resolution service.
- Create an input endpoint to allow traffic to a virtual machine from the Internet. Each endpoint requires a public port, private port, name, and protocol (TCP or UDP). Use

the Management portal or the Add-AzureEndpoint, Set-AzureEndpoint, and Remove-AzureEndpoint cmdlets to manage.

- To load balance an endpoint, create a load balanced set. Virtual machines must reside in the same cloud service to be part of the same load balanced set.

- The Set-AzureEndpoint cmdlet cannot be used to manage a load balanced endpoint. Use the Set-AzureLoadBalancedEndpoint cmdlet instead.

- To enable custom code to control the load balancer probe, use an HTTP health probe.

- A cloud service VIP will change if all of the virtual machines in the cloud service are deleted or put in the StoppedDeallocated state. Use a reserved IP address to retain the IP. A reserved IP address is created using the New-AzureReservedIP cmdlet and can only be set when creating the first virtual machine in a cloud service.

- A public IP can be used to enable direct network access to a virtual machine. This is useful when solutions that require dynamic ports are needed. Use the Set-AzurePublicIP cmdlet to configure.

Objective review

Answer the following questions to test your knowledge of the information in this objective. You can find the answers to these questions and explanations of why each answer choice is correct or incorrect in the "Answers" section at the end of this chapter.

1. You create a virtual machine named vm1 in cloudservice1, and vm2 in cloudservice2. You have added a load balanced endpoint on vm1 but the management portal does not show the load-balanced set on vm2. What is the problem?

   A. You must use Windows PowerShell to configure load balanced endpoints.

   B. The virtual machines must be in the same cloud service.

   C. You must refresh the management portal after the first endpoint is created.

   D. The virtual machines are not in the same availability set.

2. Which cmdlet should be used first to retain the IP address of the cloud service VIP even if all of the virtual machines are stopped?

   A. Set-AzurePublicIP

   B. Set-AzureEndpoint

   C. New-AzureReservedIP

   D. Set-AzureLoadBalancedEndpoint

3. Which CIDR notation would you use to permit access to an endpoint ACL for the following IP address: 134.170.188.221?

   A. 134.170.188.221/24

   B. 134.170.188.221/8

   C. 134.170.188.221/32

   D. 134.170.188.221/16

Objective 2.5: Configure VM for resiliency

Resiliency is a critical part of any application architecture, whether the servers are physical or virtual Azure provides several features and capabilities to make virtual machine deployments resilient. The platform helps you to avoid single point of failure at the physical hardware level, and also provides techniques to avoid downtime during host updates. Using features like Autoscale, and the ability to change the size of a given virtual machine (up or down), Azure can also be used to provide resiliency for deployments at large scale.

> **This objective covers how to:**
> - Configure availability sets
> - Scaling a virtual machine up and down
> - Implementing Autoscale

Configuring availability sets

Availability sets are used to control availability for multiple virtual machines in the same application tier. To provide redundancy for your virtual machines, it is recommended to have at least two virtual machines in an availability set. This configuration ensures that at least one virtual machine will be available in the event of a host update or a problem with the physical hardware the virtual machines are hosted on. Having at least two virtual machines in an availability set is a requirement for the service level agreement (SLA) for virtual machines of 99.95 percent.

> **NOTE AVAILABILITY SETS IMPACT YOUR SERVICE LEVEL AGREEMENT (SLA)**
>
> For more information on managing availability and service level agreements see the following article: *http://azure.microsoft.com/en-us/documentation/articles/virtual-machines-manage-availability/*.

Virtual machines should be deployed into availability sets according to their workload or application tier. For instance, if you are deploying a three-tier solution that consists of web servers, a middle tier, and a database tier, each tier would have its own availability set, as Figure 2-36 demonstrates.

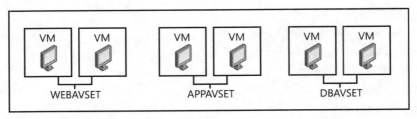

FIGURE 2-36 Application tiers grouped by availability set

Each virtual machine in your availability set will be assigned a fault domain and an update domain. Each availability set will have five non-configurable update domains available, which indicates the groups of virtual machines and the underlying physical hardware that can be rebooted at the same time for host updates. Each availability set will also be comprised of two fault domains. Fault domains represent which virtual machines will be on separate physical hardware for redundancy. This limits the impact of physical hardware failures such as server, network, or power interruptions.

It is important to understand that virtual machines must be created in the same cloud service to be joined in the same availability set.

To create an availability set, specify a name for the availability set that is not in use by any other availability sets within the same cloud service. A virtual machine can be added to an availability set at creation time or after. To join a virtual machine to an existing availability, simply select the existing availability set name.

> **NOTE MOVING A VM TO AN AVAILABILITY SET MAY CAUSE A REBOOT**
>
> Adding an existing virtual machine to an availability set may cause the virtual machine to restart if it has to move to another physical server.

To specify the availability set using Windows PowerShell at provisioning time, use the New-AzureQuickVM or New-AzureVMConfig Azure PowerShell cmdlets with the AvailabilitySetName parameter. If the availability set does not exist it will be created, or if the availability does exist on another virtual machine in the same cloud service, the new virtual machine will join the existing availability set.

The Set-AzureAvailabilitySet cmdlet can be used to add an existing virtual machine to an availability set using the virtual machine update pattern, as shown in this example.

```
Get-AzureVM -ServiceName $serviceName -Name $vmName |
Set-AzureAvailabilitySet WebACVSet |
Update-AzureVM
```

Scaling a virtual machine up and down

Objective 2.1 covered the various instance sizes an Azure virtual machine could be hosted in. To change the size of a virtual machine between instance sizes, you must ensure that the instance size you are changing the virtual machine to supports the same number of data disks the virtual machine currently has attached. For instance, if you are changing from an ExtraLarge (A4) that has 16 data disks attached to a Medium (A2), you will receive an error. To change the size of a virtual machine, use the Management portal or the Set-AzureVMSize cmdlet, as shown in the following example.

```
$newSize = "A9"
Get-AzureVm -ServiceName $serviceName -Name $vmName |
Set-AzureVMSize -InstanceSize $newSize |
Update-AzureVM
```

Implementing Autoscale

Autoscale for Azure virtual machines provides the ability to have Azure automatically start or stop virtual machines in a workload based on a performance metric like CPU, memory usage, the number of messages in a queue, or even based on a schedule. Not all workloads are ideally suited for Autoscale workloads. The workload must be linearly scalable. This means simply adding more servers performing the same operation will increase the overall throughput.

To implement Autoscale in Azure virtual machines, you first create the virtual machines that will be automatically scaled in an availability set. For instance, if you want four web servers to be automatically scaled as a group, create four web servers in the same availability set, as shown in Figure 2-37.

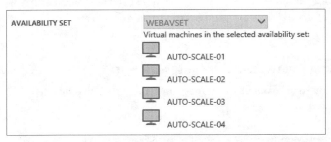

FIGURE 2-37 Virtual machines in an availability set

After the virtual machines are in the availability set, it is a simple matter of choosing to Autoscale using a schedule, CPU, or a Queue, as shown in Figure 2-38.

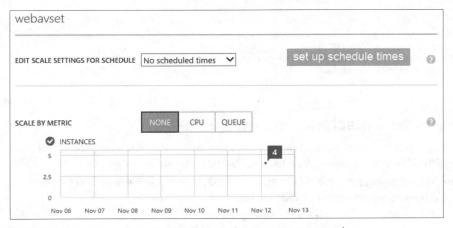

FIGURE 2-38 The Autoscale metrics available in the Management portal

Scaling by CPU

Figure 2-39 shows the available options when scaling by the CPU metric. The available options allow you to specify the instance range (minimum and maximum number of instances to scale), the target CPU range, and the number of instances to scale up or down by, along with a configurable delay between scaling actions. The target CPU metric is important to understand. If the average CPU utilization of your workload falls below the target CPU, Azure will remove the number of instances specified in the scale down option. If the average CPU utilization of your workload is above the target CPU, Azure will add the number of instances specified in the scale up option. The average CPU utilization includes all instances averaged over the period of an hour.

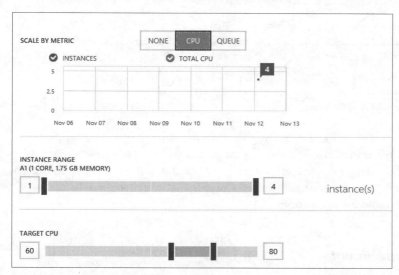

FIGURE 2-39 Autoscale by CPU metric options

Scaling by queue

If your workload processes messages out of a storage queue you can enable Autoscale based on the number of messages in the queue. To configure, select the queue metric, a storage account, and the storage queue your workload is using. Set the scale metric by specifying the number of messages using the target per machine setting. Instances will scale up or down based on the total number of messages in the queue divided by the instances.

Using a schedule

The Autoscale feature allows you to configure different Autoscale settings based on a schedule. Figure 2-40 shows the options available, including settings based on day and night, weekdays and weekends, or even specific date and time ranges. After the schedules are selected, you can specify custom Autoscale settings for each option.

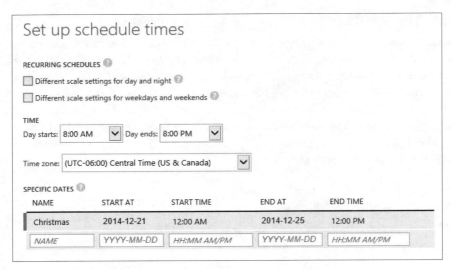

FIGURE 2-40 Autoscale by schedule options

To monitor how Autoscale is behaving, you can open management services in the management portal, and under operation logs, change the type to Autoscale. Each change in the Autoscale state will generate a new entry (including the initial configuration change). This entry will show the configuration, the metric that triggered the Autoscale event, and the new and old instance count.

Thought experiment
Solving over capacity

In this thought experiment, apply what you've learned about this objective. You can find answers to these questions in the "Answers" section at the end of this chapter.

You are the system administrator for Contoso. You have successfully moved a large intranet workload with 10 load balanced virtual machines from on-premises to Azure virtual machines. Your manager has asked you to optimize the costs of this deployment. The workload has heavy usage between the hours of 7:00 to 18:00 with little usage on the weekends.

1. How must you configure the virtual machines to enable the Autoscale feature?

2. How would you configure the Autoscale feature?

Objective summary

- Configure two or more virtual machines in each application tier into separate availability sets for availability and to qualify for the virtual machine service level agreement (SLA).
- Availability sets provide physical redundancy in the Azure data center by hosting some of the virtual machines in the same availability set on separate physical hardware.
- Availability sets provide Azure information on which servers can be rebooted for a host update without taking down the entire application.
- Virtual machine sizes can be changed in the management portal or using the Set-AzureVMSize cmdlet. They cannot be changed to a size that does not support the number of data disks currently attached.
- Virtual machines must be created inside of an availability, set to be scaled using the Autoscale feature.
- Autoscale supports scaling by CPU or Queue.
- You can setup separate scale settings by a schedule including, days and nights, weekdays and weekends, or even custom date and time ranges.

Objective review

Answer the following questions to test your knowledge of the information in this objective. You can find the answers to these questions and explanations of why each answer choice is correct or incorrect in the "Answers" section at the end of this chapter.

1. How many upgrade domains are assigned to an availability set?

   A. 20

   B. 5

   C. 2

   D. One per virtual machine

2. Which Azure PowerShell cmdlet should you use to change the size of a virtual machine?

   A. Set-AzureVMSize

   B. Set-AzureService

   C. New-AzureVMConfig

   D. The virtual machine size can only be changed through the management portal.

3. What is the maximum number of virtual machines that can be scaled as a set?

   A. 10

   B. 2

   C. 50

   D. Unlimited

Objective 2.6: Design and implement VM storage

Virtual machine storage includes managing the virtual machine operating system and data disks. This includes configuring for performance using the available caching options, managing redundancy to avoid data loss, and just as important, implementing strategies such as disk striping or using Storage Pools for increased IO performance by utilizing multiple disks. This objective also provides an introduction to Azure Files, which is currently in preview.

> **This objective covers how to:**
> - Configure virtual machine disk caching
> - Plan for storage capacity
> - Implement disk redundancy for durability
> - Implement disk redundancy for performance
> - Implement Azure Files
> - Encrypt disks

Configuring virtual machine disk caching

Azure disks (operating system and data) have configurable cache settings that you should be aware of. You can cache reads or writes (depending on the configuration) for up to four data disks plus the operating system disk. The reads and writes are buffered on the local physical disk that on the host server the virtual machine is running on. This is the same disk that the temporary drive D is backed by.

The cache setting for data disks can be set when the disk is attached using the management portal or Windows PowerShell. The operating system disk setting can only be set through Windows PowerShell, but it can be set at creation time or as part of an update.

To specify the operating system cache setting at creation time, specify one of the supported values (ReadOnly or ReadWrite) to the HostCaching parameter of the New-AzureQuickVM or New-AzureVMConfig cmdlets. The default cache setting is ReadWrite. This value can be changed later using the Set-AzureOSDisk cmdlet (this does require a reboot). For instance, the following example changes the operating system disk HostCaching property from ReadWrite to ReadOnly of an existing virtual machine.

```
Get-AzureVM -ServiceName $serviceName -Name $vmName |
Set-AzureOSDisk -HostCaching ReadOnly |
Update-AzureVM
```

The HostCaching property of a data disk can be set using Windows PowerShell at any time. To specify when attaching a new or existing data disk use the HostCaching parameter of the Add-AzureDataDisk cmdlet with a supported value (None, ReadOnly, or ReadWrite). The Set-AzureDataDisk cmdlet is used to update an existing data disk. Use the LUN parameter to specify which disk to update.

```
Get-AzureVM -ServiceName $serviceName -Name $vmName |
Set-AzureDataDisk -LUN 0 -HostCaching ReadWrite |
Update-AzureVM
```

Planning for storage capacity

Planning for storage capacity is a key exercise when you are deploying a new workload or migrating an existing workload. In Azure Storage, there are really two primary limits to be aware of. The first is the size of the disks themselves. For an Azure virtual machine, the maximum capacity of the operating system disk on drive C is 127 GB. The maximum capacity of additional data disks is 1023 GB (~1 TB). Currently, the most disks you can attach to a single virtual machine are 16 for a total storage capacity of 16 TB.

In addition to the size limitations, it is important to understand that each Azure Storage account that your virtual machine hosts its disks in has scalability targets of its own. It is very important to understand from a capacity planning perspective what these limits are.

For instance, an Azure Storage account supports a maximum of 20,000 IOPS. An Azure Virtual Machine in standard tier supports 500 IOPS per disk and basic tier supports 300 IOPS per disk. If the disks are used at maximum capacity, a single Azure Storage account could handle 40 disks hosted on standard virtual machines, or 66 disks on basic virtual machines. Storage accounts also have a maximum storage capacity of 500 TB per Azure Storage account. When performing capacity planning, the number of Azure Storage accounts per the number of virtual machines can be derived from these numbers.

Implementing disk redundancy for durability

The operating system disk and data disks used in Azure virtual machines are implemented as page blobs hosted in Azure Storage. From a disaster recovery perspective there is little need to create disk configurations with software mirroring within the operating system such as RAID 1, or striped with parity, such as RAID 5. Azure Storage provides this redundancy by replicating each disk a minimum of three times within the same region if the storage account is configured for the Local Redundant tier. There is also the Geo-Redundant and Read-Access Geo-Redundant tiers. Both of these options will replicate data from the Azure Storage account to a remote region. For instance, an Azure Storage account created in East US will have a replica created in West US. The second of these tiers Read-Access Geo-Redundant allows read only access to the replicated data where the first option Geo-Redundant does not. The replication options available on your Azure Storage account include the following options available in Figure 2-41. These options can also be set using the Set-AzureStorageAccount cmdlet.

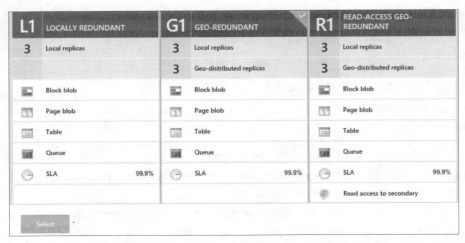

FIGURE 2-41 Redundancy options for an Azure Storage account hosting virtual machine disks

Implementing disk redundancy for performance

If your workload throughput requirements exceed the IOPS capabilities of a single disk (500 IOPS per second), or your storage requirements are greater than 1 TB, you do have options. The first option is to add multiple data disks (depending on the virtual machine size) and implement RAID 0 disk striping, and create one or more volumes with multiple data disks. This gives you increased capacity (up to 16 TB per disk) and increased throughput.

If your virtual machine is hosted on Server 2012 or above, you can use storage pools. You can use storage pools to virtualize storage by grouping industry-standard disks into pools, and then create virtual disks called Storage Spaces from the available capacity in the storage pools. You can then configure these virtual disks to provide striping capabilities across all disks in the pool, combining good performance characteristics. Storage pools make it easy to grow or shrink volumes depending on your needs (and the capacity of the Azure data disks you have attached).

This example creates a new storage pool named VMStoragePool with all of the available data disks configured as part of the pool. The code identifies the available data disks using the Get-PhysicalDisk cmdlet and creates the virtual disk using the New-VirtualDisk cmdlet.

```
New-StoragePool –FriendlyName "VMStoragePool" `
                –StorageSubsystemFriendlyName "Storage Spaces*" `
                –PhysicalDisks (Get-PhysicalDisk –CanPool $True)
$disks = Get-StoragePool –FriendlyName "VMStoragePool" `
                    –IsPrimordial $false |
                    Get-PhysicalDisk
New-VirtualDisk –FriendlyName "VirtualDisk1" `
                –ResiliencySettingName Simple `
                –NumberOfColumns $disks.Count `
                –UseMaximumSize –Interleave 256KB `
                –StoragePoolFriendlyName "VMStoragePool"
```

The NumberOfColumns parameter of New-VirtualDisk should be set to the number of data disks utilized to create the underlying storage pool. This allows IO requests to be evenly distributed against all data disks in the pool. The Interleave parameter enables you to specify the number of bytes written in each underlying data disk in a virtual disk. Microsoft recommends that you use 256 KB for all workloads.

After the virtual disk is created, the disk must be initialized, formatted, and mounted to a drive letter or mount point just like any other disk.

EXAM TIP

Mounting data disks may come up on the exam. It is important to remember that on Windows, the drive D is mapped to the local resource disk, which is only for temporary data since it is actually backed by the local physical disk on the host server. The resource disk will be mounted on the /Dev/Sdb1 device on Linux with the actual mount point varying by Linux distribution.

Implementing Azure Files

Azure Files is currently in preview so the following information may be outdated when the service is officially released. Azure Files offers an SMB 2.1 endpoint directly from an Azure Storage account. This service allows you to create file shares directly on an Azure Storage account and access the shares from multiple virtual machines or cloud services (web and worker role instances).

To implement Azure Files you must currently download and install a separate Windows PowerShell module from *http://go.microsoft.com/fwlink/?LinkID=398183*. To create a share, first create an Azure Storage context object using the New-AzureStorageContext cmdlet. Pass the context object to the New-AzureStorageShare cmdlet along with the name of the share to create as the next example shows.

```
$storage    = "[storage account name]"
$accountKey = "[storage account key]"
$shareName  = "sharedStorage"
Import-Module .\AzureStorageFile.psd1
$ctx=New-AzureStorageContext $storage $accountKey
$s = New-AzureStorageShare $shareName -Context $ctx
```

The returned value $s can be used as a parameter to other Azure Storage cmdlets for performing IO against the share. The other option for using the newly created share (not counting the REST API) is through the operating system by mapping a drive. To map a drive, the native net use command can be used with the following syntax.

```
net use z: \\[storage account name].file.core.windows.net\<share name> /u: \\[storage
account name] [storage account key]
```

Encrypting disks

Disk encryption is a topic that due to its importance and the specifics of using it in the cloud, is bound to be on the exam. Within Windows, a common disk encryption solution is to use BitLocker for disk encryption of boot and data volumes.

Within Azure virtual machines, BitLocker is not supported for boot volumes. This is partially because guest virtual machines don't have the Trusted Platform Modules (TPMs), which normally store encryption keys. Also, it isn't possible to input a decryption key during the virtual machine's boot process. However, BitLocker is supported on a virtual machine's data disks and there are also third-party solutions available that enable encryption of the boot volume, as well as the data volumes to protect all data at rest.

Thought experiment
Planning for storage capacity

In this thought experiment, apply what you've learned about this objective. You can find answers to these questions in the "Answers" section at the end of this chapter.

You are the system administrator for Contoso. You are planning to deploy a solution that will initially require 10 virtual machines with a total of 80 individual data disks. The data disks should be durable and accessible from a remote region if the primary Azure region has a failure.

1. How many Azure Storage accounts would you recommend for this solution?

2. What is the best option for enabling the disks to be durable and available from a remote Azure region?

Objective summary

- The operating system disk and data disks both support disk caching using the local resource disk. The operating system disk has the HostCaching property set to ReadWrite by default, and data disks have the HostCaching property set to None by default.

- For capacity planning, an Azure Storage account can support a maximum of 20,000 IOPs per second, and an Azure disk can support a maximum of 500 IOPs per second in Standard Tier (40 disks). A Basic Tier can support a maximum of 300 IOPs per second (66 disks). Each Azure Storage account has a maximum capacity of 500 TB.

- Azure Storage accounts offer three levels of redundancy for virtual machine disks: local redundancy (three replicas of each blob in the same region), geo-redundancy (three replicas of each blob locally, and three replicas to a remote region), and read-access geo-redundancy (the same as geo-redundancy, but you also have read only access to the replicated data).

- Group multiple data disks using a striped set or with Server 2012 or above a storage pool for increased IO throughput.

- Azure Files is a service in preview that allows you to create a file share directly on an Azure Storage account that can be shared by multiple virtual machines or cloud services.

- Encrypting the operating system disk using BitLocker is not supported. However, encrypting the data disk is. Using third-party services allows for encryption of the operating system, and data disks.

Objective review

Answer the following questions to test your knowledge of the information in this objective. You can find the answers to these questions and explanations of why each answer choice is correct or incorrect in the "Answers" section at the end of this chapter.

1. What is the maximum size of an Azure operating system disk?
   A. 2 TB
   B. 127 GB
   C. 1 TB
   D. 30 GB

2. What is the best RAID configuration for multiple data disks to increase IO throughput?
   A. RAID 1 (Mirroring)
   B. RAID 5 (Striped with parity)
   C. RAID 0 (Striped without parity)
   D. Software RAID is not supported in Azure

3. What is the minimum number of Azure Storage accounts to use for a solution that requires 30,000 IOPs?
   A. 1
   B. 2
   C. 3
   D. 4

Objective 2.7: Monitor VMs

There are several options for monitoring virtual machines. The management portal offers built-in capabilities, such as monitoring HTTP endpoints for response time and uptime and configuring alerts on performance metrics, such as CPU and network. Azure virtual machines also have the ability to enable virtual machine diagnostics using the Azure virtual machine agent.

The option of using an existing monitoring solution such as Operations Manager to monitor your virtual machines through a hybrid connection, will be discussed in-depth in Chapter 6.

> **This objective covers how to:**
> - Configure metrics and alerts
> - Configure endpoint monitoring
> - Configure diagnostics

Configuring metrics and alerts

You can collect metrics and display them in tiles on the management portal. To configure the metrics displayed, right-click the monitoring tile within your Azure virtual machine and click Edit Chart, as shown in Figure 2-42. Check the metrics you want to monitor and click Save. The chart supports displaying the monitored metrics over pre-configured time range or a custom range.

FIGURE 2-42 Configuring metrics to display for a virtual machine

You can configure an alert to email you when one of the monitored metrics passes a configurable threshold. Open the metric configuration by clicking the monitoring tile. Figure 2-43 shows that you can click the Add Alert button at the top of the new blade.

FIGURE 2-43 The metric configuration menu

An alert needs a name, description, metric (such as CPU), threshold value, and the time period. Figure 2-44 shows an example alert configuration that will trigger when the CPU utilization is at 80 percent for over five minutes. You can configure an alert to email you, or the Azure subscription administrator and co-administrators.

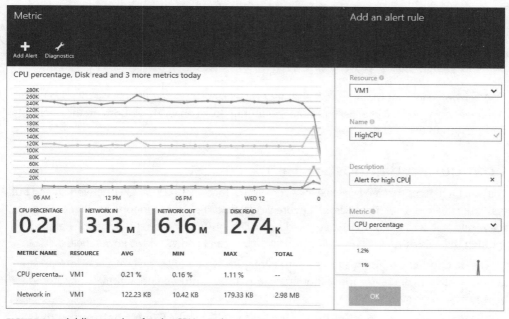

FIGURE 2-44 Adding an alert for the CPU metric

Configuring endpoint monitoring

Azure endpoint monitoring is currently in preview and at the time of this writing is only available in the current Management portal (*https://manage.windowsazure.com*). This service allows you to configure Azure to monitor two of your web endpoints from up to three global locations per endpoint.

Figure 2-45 shows how you could potentially configure two endpoints. The first endpoint named US could have all locations in the United States monitoring where the second endpoint named EUASIA could reference endpoints in Europe and Asia (up to three).

FIGURE 2-45 Configuring web endpoint monitoring

After web endpoint monitoring is enabled, you will have two additional metrics available, Uptime and Response Time. Each remote monitoring location will have both metrics available for monitoring and alerts.

Configuring diagnostics

The default metrics that are available for Azure virtual machines include CPU, network in and out, and disk read and write. The Microsoft Azure virtual machine agent supports another extension for Windows-based virtual machines called Azure Diagnostics. This extension can be enabled through the Azure Preview Portal (*https://portal.azure.com*) and Windows PowerShell.

The diagnostics extension allows you to configure event logs, a rich set of performance counters, IIS logs, and even application trace logs to be captured and automatically stored in an Azure Storage account.

The diagnostics data for all of the log files (except IIS) can be filtered for based on the severity. For instance, to only view logs that have errors, you could set the criteria to be Error. Other logging levels include Verbose, Warning, and Informational.

Figure 2-46 shows how to enable this capability through the management portal. After diagnostics is enabled, a much longer list of performance metrics becomes available for monitoring your virtual machines.

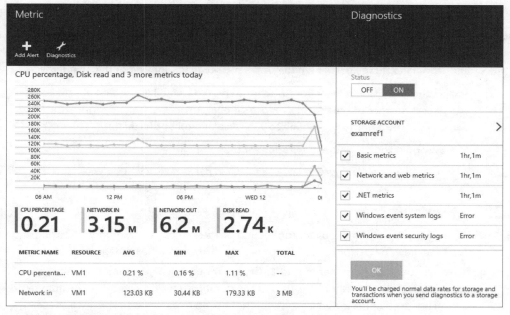

FIGURE 2-46 Metrics available through the Azure diagnostics extension

This capability can also be enabled through Windows PowerShell with the Set-AzureVMDiagnosticsExtension cmdlet. This cmdlet accepts a storage context object to specify the storage account and key to use for configuring the diagnostics agent. The cmdlet also requires the path to an XML configuration file that defines the diagnostics agent configuration. The schema for the diagnostics configuration is beyond the scope of this book, but I would highly recommend reviewing the capabilities for the exam. The schema documentation is located on MSDN at *http://msdn.microsoft.com/en-us/library/azure/hh411551.aspx*. Like other extension cmdlets, the Set-AzureVMDiagnosticsExtension modifies a virtual machine configuration object so that it can be enabled at provision time, or after the fact, as the example shows.

```
$configPath="c:\Diagnostics\diagnosticsConfig.xml"
$storageContext = New-AzureStorageContext -StorageAccountName $storage
-StorageAccountKey $accountKey
Get-AzureVM -ServiceName $serviceName -Name $vmName |
Set-AzureVMDiagnosticsExtension -DiagnosticsConfigurationPath $configPath `
                                -Version "1.*" `
                                -StorageContext $storageContext |
Update-AzureVM -ServiceName $serviceName -Name $vmName
```

> ### *Thought experiment*
> ### Monitoring global response time
>
> In this thought experiment, apply what you've learned about this objective. You can find answers to these questions in the "Answers" section at the end of this chapter.
>
> You are the web site administrator for *contoso.com*. You would like to find out the overall performance of the site for Contoso's global customers. If the performance is poor, you would like to be notified so you can troubleshoot further.
>
> 1. How would you configure monitoring for the solution?
> 2. What would you configure to be notified when performance was slow?

Objective summary

- Using Azure monitoring you can configure metrics such as CPU, Memory, Network, and Disk, and view the performance of your virtual machines in the management portal.
- Alerts can be configured per metric. Each alert requires a name, metric, threshold, and duration. After the threshold has passed the duration, an alert can email the administrators or co-administrators of the subscription, and you can also specify a specific email address to receive the alert.
- Use Azure endpoint monitoring to remotely monitor the uptime and response time for up to two endpoints on your virtual machine, from up to three global locations for each endpoint.
- Enable Azure diagnostics to have a much richer selection of performance counters. Azure diagnostics can also automatically transfer event logs, web logs, and application trace logs to an Azure Storage account. There are several third-party tools that allow you to monitor the diagnostics of a virtual machine.

Objective review

Answer the following questions to test your knowledge of the information in this objective. You can find the answers to these questions and explanations of why each answer choice is correct or incorrect in the "Answers" section at the end of this chapter.

1. You need to monitor the number of ASP.NET errors on your virtual machine. Which monitoring solution do you use?

   A. Add the default metrics and configure an alert in the management portal.

   B. Enable the Azure diagnostics extension and configure monitoring for the ASP.NET Errors metric.

   C. There is no method to capture this data through the management portal or Windows PowerShell. Login to the server and run Perfmon.exe instead.

   D. Instrument the application to log a count of the exceptions.

2. You need to configure Azure to email a specific address when the CPU of an application is on average over 75 percent over 15 minutes.

    A. Add an alert to the CPU metric, and configure the alert threshold to send email to administrators and co-administrators of the subscription.

    B. Add an alert to the CPU metric, and configure the alert threshold to send email to a specific email address.

    C. Enable Azure Diagnostics, then add an alert to the CPU metric, and configure the alert threshold to send email to a specific email address.

    D. There is no way to configure an alert to use a specific email. You must build a custom solution.

3. What configuration changes do you need to make to transfer web logs from your virtual machines to Azure Storage?

    A. Enable Azure Diagnostics

    B. Configure Diagnostics Infrastructure Logs to be transferred

    C. Configure IIS Logs to be transferred

    D. Specify a Storage account for Azure Diagnostics

MICROSOFT VIRTUAL ACADEMY **MICROSOFT AZURE IAAS DEEP DIVE JUMP START**

Microsoft Virtual Academy offers free online courses delivered by industry experts, including a course relevant to this exam. We recommend the Microsoft Azure IaaS Deep Dive Jump Start. You can access the course at *http://www.microsoftvirtualacademy.com/training-courses/windows-azure-iaas-deep-dive-jump-start*.

Answers

This section contains the solutions to the thought experiments, and answers to the lesson review questions, in this chapter.

Objective 2.1: Thought experiment

1. The web servers and database servers should be deployed into two availability sets (one for each tier). The web servers should have load balanced endpoints enabled to allow web traffic in.

2. All of the servers should be deployed into the same cloud service to allow direct network connectivity.

Objective 2.1: Review

1. **Correct answers:** C and D

   A. **Incorrect:** By default, the Stop-AzureVM cmdlet will put the virtual machine in the StoppedDeallocated state. If all of the virtual machines in the cloud service are in this state, the cloud service VIP is lost unless you have specified a reserved IP.

   B. **Incorrect:** Stopping a virtual machine using the Management portal will put the virtual machine in the StoppedDeallocated state. If all of the virtual machines in the cloud service are in this state the cloud service VIP is lost unless you have specified a reserved IP.

   C. **Correct:** Using the StayProvisioned parameter of Stop-AzureVM, or shutting the operating system down within the guest operating system, will put the virtual machine in the Stopped state, which does not release the cloud service VIP.

   D. **Correct:** Using a reserved IP address for the cloud service would also retain the IP address if all virtual machines in the cloud service were shutdown.

2. **Correct answer:** C

   A. **Incorrect:** Each cloud service can contain up to 50 virtual machines and not an unlimited number.

   B. **Incorrect:** Each cloud service can contain up to 50 virtual machines and is not limited to 25.

   C. **Correct:** Each cloud service can contain up to 50 virtual machines.

   D. **Incorrect:** Each cloud service can contain up to 50 virtual machines and is not limited to 1.

3. **Correct answer:** C

   A. **Incorrect:** The Get-AzureVMExtension cmdlet returns information about an extension installed on an existing virtual machine.

   B. **Incorrect:** The Get-AzureServiceExtension cmdlet returns information about an extension installed on an existing cloud service (web and worker role) deployment.

   C. **Correct:** The Get-AzureVMAvailableExtension cmdlet is used to the available extensions.

   D. **Incorrect:** The Get-AzureVM cmdlet is used to return information about a virtual machine.

Objective 2.4: Thought experiment

1. Prior to deploying the web servers, use the New-AzureReservedIP cmdlet to create a reserved IP address. Reference the reserved IP name when deploying the web servers.

2. You will need to add load balanced endpoints to all of the web servers deployed.

Objective 2.4: Review

1. **Correct answer:** B

   A. **Incorrect:** Adding load balanced endpoints can be accomplished using Azure PowerShell, but it is not required and can be configured through the management portal.

   B. **Correct:** Virtual machines must be created in the same cloud service in order to be part of the same load balanced set.

   C. **Incorrect:** While the management portal may occasionally need to be refreshed since the virtual machines are in separate cloud services, they still cannot be load balanced together.

   D. **Incorrect:** Virtual machines do not have to be in the same availability set to be load balanced (it is usually recommended though).

2. **Correct answer:** C

   A. **Incorrect:** The Set-AzurePublicIP cmdlet is used to add a public IP to a specific virtual machine but not the VIP of the cloud service.

   B. **Incorrect:** The Set-AzureEndpoint cmdlet is used to modify the configuration of an input endpoint.

   C. **Correct:** The New-AzureReservedIP is used to create a reserved IP address that can then be referenced during creation of the first virtual machine.

   D. **Incorrect:** The Set-AzureLoadBalancedEndpoint cmdlet is used to modify a load balanced endpoint, but will not help with VIP reservation.

3. **Correct answer:** C

   A. **Incorrect:** Using /24 in CIDR notation represents using just the first 24 bits of the network or an equivalent network mask of: 255.255.255.0.

   B. **Incorrect:** Using /8 in CIDR notation represents using just the first 8 bits of the network or an equivalent network mask of: 255.0.0.0.

   C. **Correct:** Using /32 in CIDR notation represents using the entire network, which leaves just the IP address specified.

   D. **Incorrect:** Using /16 in CIDR notation represents using just the first 16 bits of the network or an equivalent network mask of: 255.255.0.0.

Objective 2.5: Thought experiment

1. The virtual machines must be created in the same cloud service and availability set to be configured for Autoscale.

2. Autoscale should be configured with a minimum of 1 virtual machine and a maximum of 10. The CPU metric is the correct configuration to use. Using the default of a minimum of 60 percent and a maximum of 80 percent should accomplish the task.

Objective 2.5: Review

1. **Correct answer:** B

   A. **Incorrect:** For a given Availability Set, up to five non-user-configurable update domains are assigned and not 20.

   B. **Correct:** For a given Availability Set, five non-user-configurable update domains are assigned.

   C. **Incorrect:** For a given Availability Set, five non-user-configurable update domains are assigned and not 2.

   D. **Incorrect:** For a given Availability Set, five non-user-configurable update domains are assigned. An upgrade domain is not assigned per virtual machine.

2. **Correct answer:** A

   A. **Correct:** The Set-AzureVMSize cmdlet can be used to change the size of a virtual machine.

   B. **Incorrect:** The Set-AzureService cmdlet is used to change the configuration of a cloud service.

   C. **Incorrect:** The New-AzureVMConfig cmdlet sets the size of the virtual machine at creation.

   D. **Incorrect:** The size of a virtual machine can be set from or the command line.

3. **Correct answer:** C

   A. Incorrect: 10 is incorrect. The maximum number of virtual machines to be scaled is the same number as the maximum number of virtual machines in a cloud service, which is 50.

   B. Incorrect: 2 virtual machines is incorrect. The maximum number of virtual machines to be scaled is the same number as the maximum number of virtual machines in a cloud service, which is 50.

   C. Correct: The maximum number of virtual machines to be scaled is the same number as the maximum number of virtual machines in a cloud service, which is 50.

   D. Incorrect: The maximum number of virtual machines to be scaled is the same number as the maximum number of virtual machines in a cloud service, which is 50 and is not unlimited.

Objective 2.6: Thought experiment

1. An Azure Storage account has a maximum throughput of 20,000 IOPs. Each disk can have up to 500 IOPS per disk. At maximum capacity, this is 40 disks per Azure Storage account. For this solution you should use at least two Azure Storage accounts.

2. Azure Storage automatically keeps three local replicas of each file in storage for durability. Enabling geo-replication on the Azure Storage account will allow the disks to be replicated to a remote region for additional durability.

Objective 2.6: Review

1. **Correct answer:** B

   A. Incorrect: An operating system disk in Azure has a maximum capacity of 127 GB and currently does not support a disk size of 2TB.

   B. Correct: An operating system disk in Azure has a maximum capacity of 127 GB.

   C. Incorrect: An operating system disk in Azure has a maximum capacity of 127 GB and currently does not support a disk size of 1TB.

   D. Incorrect: An operating system disk in Azure has a maximum capacity of 127 GB and is not limited to 30GB.

2. **Correct answer:** C

   A. **Incorrect:** RAID 1 mirroring is designed for redundancy but is not necessary because disks in Azure are already replicated three times in storage. Mirroring also does not increase IO throughput.

   B. **Incorrect:** RAID 5 disk striping with parity is meant for redundancy and performance but is not necessary because disks in Azure are already replicated three times in storage.

   C. **Correct:** RAID 0 disk striping without parity allows the operating system to spread IO across multiple disks, which can increase overall IO throughput.

   D. **Incorrect:** Software RAID configurations are supported in Azure virtual machines.

3. **Correct answer:** B

   A. **Incorrect:** An Azure Storage account has a scalability target of a maximum of 20,000 IOPS. This is not enough capacity for a solution that requires 30,000 IOPS.

   B. **Correct:** An Azure Storage account has a scalability target of a maximum of 20,000 IOPS. Two Azure Storage accounts would provide a maximum of 40,000 IOPS.

   C. **Incorrect:** An Azure Storage account has a scalability target of a maximum of 20,000 IOPS. Three Azure Storage accounts would provide a maximum of 60,000 IOPS, which is more than the minimum necessary.

   D. **Incorrect:** An Azure Storage account has a scalability target of a maximum of 20,000 IOPS. Four Azure Storage accounts would provide a maximum of 80,000 IOPS, which is more than the minimum necessary.

Objective 2.7: Thought experiment

1. Configure web endpoint monitoring for up to two endpoints. Configure each endpoint using regions from up to three locations in the United States, Europe, and Asia.

2. Add an alert to the response time metrics for each of the endpoints, and set the threshold to a duration that is outside of your response time goal. Have the alert configured to send an email when the threshold is hit.

Objective 2.7: Review

1. **Correct answer:** B

   A. **Incorrect:** The default metrics do not include ASP.NET error data.

   B. **Correct:** Enabling the Azure Diagnostics virtual machine extension allows you to specify detailed metrics, such as ASP.NET Errors to capture for later analysis.

   C. **Incorrect:** This goal can be accomplished by using the Azure Diagnostics virtual machine extension.

   D. **Incorrect:** You are not required to instrument your application to capture this data. Diagnostics can capture it and make it available for later analysis.

2. **Correct answer:** B

A. **Incorrect:** The question asked for a specific email address. This option will send an email to the email address of the co-administrators or administrator of the subscription.

B. **Correct:** This option allows you to specify a specific email address if an alert is triggered.

C. **Incorrect:** Azure Diagnostics is not required for this scenario.

D. **Incorrect:** You do not need to build a custom solution for this scenario because alerts can be configured to send an email to a specific address.

3. **Correct answers:** A, C, and D

A. **Correct:** Enabling the Azure Diagnostics extension is required to automatically transfer web logs to storage.

B. **Incorrect:** This option is not required to transfer IIS Logs.

C. **Correct:** This option is required to use the Azure Diagnostics extension to transfer IIS Logs to storage.

D. **Correct:** This option is required to specify the Azure Storage account for Azure Diagnostics to use.

CHAPTER 3

Implement Cloud Services

When Microsoft first launched the Azure platform in February of 2010, the cloud service compute model was the sole model for running applications in the cloud. Microsoft Azure Cloud Services provides a platform as a service (PaaS) environment that is ideal for running multi-tier web applications, where each tier can be scaled up and out independently of the other. In this model, the underlying infrastructure for the cloud service is maintained by Azure, freeing you from tasks such as performing operating system updates, and recovering from hardware failure. Yet, with all this happening for you, the IT pro, tasks such as configuring, deploying, managing, and monitoring Azure Cloud Services still requires the skills and knowledge to ensure Cloud Services run optimally. This chapter identifies and teaches those skills needed to perform such tasks successfully.

Objectives in this chapter:

- Objective 3.1: Configure Cloud Services and roles
- Objective 3.2: Deploy and manage Cloud Services
- Objective 3.3: Monitor Cloud Services

Objective 3.1: Configure Cloud Services and roles

Many of the configuration settings for Cloud Services, and the roles that make up a cloud service, are set during application development and packaging. It is not the goal of this objective to teach those *developer* experiences to the IT professional. Instead, the objective is to equip the IT professional with the skills needed to identify these configuration settings, know how to configure them when needed, and how to configure aspects of an Azure cloud service to meet requirements that the development and packaging process does not enable.

Configuring role instance count

The roles comprising an Azure cloud service can be scaled independently of one another. The ability to scale roles independently like this is one reason Azure Cloud Services is so well suited for multi-tier application architectures. For example, a cloud service may require three instances of a web front end, running in a web role to meet customer demand. The cloud service may also have five instances of a back end worker role to process orders created in the web front end.

The number of instances for a role is defined in the cloud service configuration (.cscfg) file of a cloud service. This is an XML file that is generated as part of the packaging process for a cloud service. The setting is located in the <Instances> element within each <Role> element that comprises the cloud service. Listing 3-1 shows a web role configured for three instances, and a worker role configured for five instances.

LISTING 3-1 Configuration of role instance count in a cloud service configuration (.csfg) file

```
<ServiceConfiguration serviceName="Demo.CloudService"
  xmlns=http://schemas.microsoft.com/ServiceHosting/2008/10/ServiceConfiguration
  osFamily="4" osVersion="*" schemaVersion="2014-06.2.4">
  <Role name="Demo.WebRole">
    <Instances count="3" />
    <ConfigurationSettings>
      ...
    </ConfigurationSettings>
  </Role>
  <Role name="Demo.WorkerRole">
    <Instances count="5" />
    <ConfigurationSettings>
      ...
    </ConfigurationSettings>
  </Role>
</ServiceConfiguration>
```

It is important that you verify your subscription has the core capacity to support the instance count settings for a role. Using the sample in Listing 3-1, if each of the roles were configured to use a medium (2 cores) instance size, this would result in 16 cores being used by the cloud service. An Azure subscription has a maximum core count setting and this value can be different for each subscription. To find out how many cores are being used and what the core capacity is for a subscription, you can use the Get-AzureSubscription cmdlet as shown here.

```
Get-AzureSubscription -Current -ExtendedDetails `
    | Select CurrentCoreCount, MaxCoreCount `
    | Format-List
```

EXAM TIP

It is possible to publish a cloud service where one of the roles has an instance count of one. However, the cloud service must have at least two instances for every role in order to qualify for the Azure service level agreement (SLA) that guarantees connectivity of 99.95 percent.

Configuring role instance count for a cloud service using Azure PowerShell

To set the instance count for a role in an existing cloud service, you can use the Azure PowerShell cmdlet Set-AzureRole. The code in Listing 3-2 demonstrates setting the instance count for a web role to four in a cloud service.

LISTING 3-2 Setting the role instance count for an existing cloud service role using Azure PowerShell

```
$csName = "Contosocloudservice"
$csRole = "Demo.WebRole"
$roleCount = 4
Set-AzureRole -ServiceName $csName -RoleName $csRole -Slot Staging -Count $roleCount
```

Configuring role instance count for a cloud service using the Microsoft Azure management portal

The instance count for a role can also be configured in the Azure management portal. This is accomplished by going to the *Scale* page for the cloud service. This page will show a summary at the top of the page for all of the roles in the cloud service. Under the summary section, there are scale settings for each role in the cloud service, where you can configure the number of instances and also configure Autoscale settings for the role. As an example, see Figure 3-1 where the instance count for the web role Demo.webrole is updated to 8 instances.

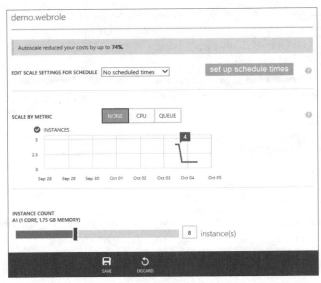

FIGURE 3-1 Instance count setting in the scale page of the Azure management portal

> **MORE INFO**   **UPGRADE DOMAINS AND FAULT DOMAINS**
>
> Setting the role instance count to a value of two or more is an important part of a cloud service's availability strategy and is required to get the financially-backed service level agreement (SLA) for a cloud service deployment. In the Azure platform, the roles for a cloud service are strategically allocated into logical units called upgrade domains, and a physical unit called *fault domains*. By setting the instance count for cloud service roles to two or more, you are enabling the Azure platform to spread your service instances across upgrade domains and fault domains in a manner so that the platform can guarantee 99.95 percent connectivity to your cloud service.
>
> An upgrade domain is a logical unit used to group role instances in a cloud service for updating purposes. By default, a cloud service has up to five upgrade domains. As you increase your role instance count, instances will be allocated to the next subsequent upgrade domain. As an example, if you have 7 instances for a web role, then upgrade domains 0 through 1 will have two instances, and upgrade domains 2 through 4 will have one instance. When updates to the cloud service are applied, Azure will roll through the upgrade domains applying the update to one upgrade domain at a time. This insures that only a minimum number of instances are offline during an upgrade.
>
> A fault domain is a physical unit used to avoid a single point of failure for the cloud service. When a cloud service role has more than one instance, Azure will provision the instances in multiple fault domains. In a datacenter, you can think of a fault domain as a rack of physical servers. By spreading the deployment for cloud service roles across multiple fault domains, Azure is better able to resolve hardware failures without your service being completely unavailable.

Determining upgrade domain and fault domain for role instances

You can determine the upgrade domain and fault domain for role instances by opening the Instances page of a cloud service in the management portal, as shown here in Figure 3-2.

NAME	STATUS	ROLE	SIZE	UPDATE DOMAIN	FAULT DOMAIN
Demo.CacheWorkerRole_IN_0	Running	Demo.CacheWorkerRole	Standard_A1	0	0
Demo.CacheWorkerRole_IN_1	Running	Demo.CacheWorkerRole	Standard_A1	1	1
Demo.CacheWorkerRole_IN_2	Waiting...	Demo.CacheWorkerRole	Standard_A1	2	0
Demo.CacheWorkerRole_IN_3	Waiting...	Demo.CacheWorkerRole	Standard_A1	3	1
Demo.CacheWorkerRole_IN_4	Waiting...	Demo.CacheWorkerRole	Standard_A1	4	0
Demo.CacheWorkerRole_IN_5	Waiting...	Demo.CacheWorkerRole	Standard_A1	0	1
Demo.CacheWorkerRole_IN_6	Waiting...	Demo.CacheWorkerRole	Standard_A1	1	0

DASHBOARD · MONITOR · CONFIGURE · SCALE · INSTANCES · LINKED RESOURCES · CERTIFICATES

PRODUCTION · STAGING

TRANSITIONING — The deployment is transitioning. 10 Instances: 5 Running, 5 Waiting for the status

FIGURE 3-2 Observing the upgrade domain and fault domain for role instances in the management portal

Configuring role operating system settings

The operating system settings for a cloud service apply to all roles that make up the cloud service. It is not a configuration that can be applied separately for each role. There are two settings applicable when configuring operating system settings for a cloud service. These are:

- Operating system family
- Operating system version

The operating system family defines which Windows Server operating system each role instance will use. This is referred to as the guest operating system and is identified numerically in the cloud service configuration (.cscfg) file. In Listing 3-1, the *osFamily* property of the <ServiceConfiguration> element configures the Windows Server operating system for all roles in the cloud service. The available options are shown here with the numerical value in parentheses:

- Windows Server 2008 SP2 (1)
- Windows Server 2008 R2 (2)
- Windows Server 2012 (3)
- Windows Server 2012 R2 (4)

The operating system version defines a version of the guest operating system to use for the role instances. Azure makes available different versions of each operating system family that include the latest updates for the operating system at the time the version was created. If a cloud service is developed and tested using a specific version of an operating system, configuring the service to use only that version when provisioning virtual machine instances for the roles insures the application is always running in the environment it was tested in.

Some Cloud Services may not have requirements for a specific version of an operating system and instead always use the latest version available. This configuration choice is available as the Automatic setting.

In Listing 3-1, the *osVersion* property of the <ServiceConfiguration> element configures the version of the Windows Server operating system for all roles in the cloud service. The value "*" instructs Azure to use the *Automatic* setting, which is the latest version available for the *osFamily* specified.

The available options for *osVersion* can be identified using the Get-AzureOSVersion cmdlet as shown below. Notice that the output has been abbreviated to only show the last two versions for each operating system family to save space and therefore is not a full listing of all the operating system versions available.

```
PS E:\> Get-AzureOSVersion | Format-Table Family, FamilyLabel, Version

Family    FamilyLabel              Version
------    -----------              -------
...
1         Windows Server 2008 SP2  WA-GUEST-OS-1.8_201010-01
1         Windows Server 2008 SP2  WA-GUEST-OS-1.9_201011-01
...
2         Windows Server 2008 R2   WA-GUEST-OS-2.9_201112-02
2         Windows Server 2008 R2   WA-GUEST-OS-2.9_201112-03
...
3         Windows Server 2012      WA-GUEST-OS-3.8_201310-01
3         Windows Server 2012      WA-GUEST-OS-3.9_201311-01
...
4         Windows Server 2012 R2   WA-GUEST-OS-4.8_201405-01
4         Windows Server 2012 R2   WA-GUEST-OS-4.9_201406-01
```

To configure a cloud service for a specific version of an operating system, use the *osVersion* property of the <ServiceConfiguration> element and set the version string for the operating system as shown here.

```
<ServiceConfiguration serviceName="Demo.CloudService" xmlns=http://schemas.microsoft.
com/ServiceHosting/2008/10/ServiceConfiguration osFamily="4" osVersion=" WA-GUEST-
OS-4.9_201406-01" schemaVersion="2014-06.2.4">
...
</ServiceConfiguration>
```

Configuring role operating system settings using the management portal

You can change the operating system setting for an existing cloud service in the management portal in the *Configure* page for the cloud service. Figure 3-3 shows where the Operating System Family and Operating System Version settings can be set.

FIGURE 3-3 Operating system settings for a cloud service in the management portal

Configuring In-Role Cache for Microsoft Azure Cache

In-Role Cache is a caching solution unique to Cloud Services. It is referred to as in-role be-cause it is hosted within the Azure roles that the cloud service consists of. The roles that are hosting the cache form a cache cluster in the cloud service. The cluster can be formed from two possible topologies as follows:

- Co-located
- Dedicated

In a co-located cache, the cache is hosted on the web and/or worker roles comprising the cloud service. In this topology, the resources (primarily memory) of the virtual machines host-ing the web and/or worker roles are also used to host the distributed cache. Figure 3-4 shows a co-located cache on a web role with three instances.

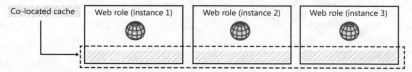

FIGURE 3-4 Co-located cache hosted on a web role with three instances

In a dedicated cache, the cache is hosted on worker role instances specifically for the pur-pose of caching. In this topology, the full resources of the virtual machine are used to host the distributed cache. Figure 3-5 shows a dedicated cache using cache worker roles.

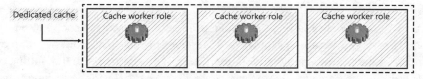

FIGURE 3-5 Dedicated cache hosted on a cache worker role with three instances

A cache cluster requires a Microsoft Azure Storage account to store the cache settings that the role instances will use to read the settings from. A cache consists of the following configuration settings:

- **Caching.ConfigStoreConnectionString** The connection string to the Azure storage account used to store the cache settings.

- **Caching.CacheSizePercentage** The percentage of role instance memory to use for the cache. This setting is only applicable for a *co-located* cache. For a *dedicated* cache, the value should be left empty.

- **Caching.DiagnosticLevel** The diagnostic level for the cache can be a value between 0 and 4 and identifies the logging level as shown here:

  - **Level 0** Logs only critical events, such as crash dumps. Crash dump format is mini crash dumps.

  - **Level 1** Logs diagnostic data at a level that helps identity usage patterns for the cache, overall health, and potential errors. Crash dump format is mini crash dumps. This level is the default level.

  - **Level 2** Logs diagnostic data at fine grain granularity of all requests and includes important system information. Crash dump format is full crash dumps.

  - **Level 3** Logs diagnostic data that is more verbose and includes system information. Crash dump format is full crash dumps.

  - **Level 4** Logs all requests and system information hosting the cache cluster. Crash dump format is full crash dumps.

A cache cluster can have one or more Named Caches, each with different cache settings. A default named cache exists and is named "default." Additional Named Caches can exist using any name you choose. The following settings can be set independently for each Named Cache:

- **Name** The name used to reference and identify the cache.

- **High Availability** A flag indicating whether a cached object is allocated on a second role instance hosting the cache.

- **Notifications** A flag indicating whether notifications are raised for cache operations, such as an object being added or removed from the cache.

- **Eviction Policy** A policy setting to use for deleting items in the cache when the cache approaches its capacity. The setting can be *None* or *Least Recently Used (LRU)*. LRU is the default setting for a Named Cache.

- **Time To Live (TTL)** The number of minutes an object is kept in the cache before it expires.

- **Expiration Type** A policy setting that applies expiration behaviors in cooperation with the TTL setting. The setting can be *None*, *Absolute*, or *Sliding Window*. A setting of *None* indicates items expire and therefore the TTL must be also be set to 0. A setting of *Absolute* indicates an item in the cache will expire after it has been in the cache for the number of minutes specified by the TTL setting. A setting of *Sliding Window* indicates an item's expiration timer is reset each time an item is retrieved from the cache.

EXAM TIP

The dedicated In-Role Cache is only supported for cloud service worker roles. It is not possible to use a web role for dedicated in-role caching.

Cache capacity planning

There are several factors that should be considered when choosing a cache topology, role instance count and sizes, percentage of resources (for co-located caches), and settings for named caches. An improperly configured cache can have a detrimental impact on the applications using it. As an example, a co-located cache topology is not recommended for the following scenarios:

- The cache size exceeds 1.5 GB
- The cache cluster exceeds 400 caching transactions per second per role instance
- The cache cluster exceeds 1.2 MB of bandwidth used for caching operations per second per role instance

Azure provides a capacity planning guide spreadsheet that you can use to determine the correct configuration for your applications. The spreadsheet and instructions on how to use it are available at *http://msdn.microsoft.com/en-us/library/azure/hh914129.aspx*.

EXAM TIP

A cache with high availability enabled will reduce the capacity of the cache because each item added to the cache will be added twice. It also requires a role instance count of two or more.

Configuring In-Role Cache using the management portal

You can configure an In-Role Cache cluster using the management portal. The *Configure* page of the cloud service shows the cache settings for the role that is configured to host the cache. Figure 3-6 shows the cache settings for a *dedicated* cache hosted in a role name Demo.CacheWorkerRole.

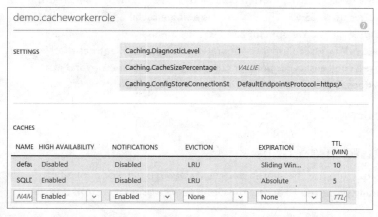

FIGURE 3-6 Cache settings for a dedicated cache in the management portal

Caching options in the Azure platform have changed several times since caching was first made available in the platform. This has led to a lot of confusion about what the caching options are today and which caching option you should choose for your applications.

There are three caching options in the Azure platform; In-Role Cache, Managed cache, and the Redis cache. The In-Role Cache has been the focus of this section and is unique to cloud services. As you know, this cache uses all or part of resources for web or worker roles in the cloud service to host the cache. As a result, there is specific guidance about how the cache should be configured and capacity planning considerations at *http://msdn.microsoft.com/en-us/library/azure/hh914129.aspx*. The In-Role Cache continues to be a viable option in the platform supporting traditional key-value pair entries in the cache. However, since it is self-hosted on the role instances of the cloud service, there is no cache-specific SLA beyond the SLA you get for cloud services.

The Managed cache is a fully managed cache service managed by Microsoft that does come with a financially backed SLA. Like the In-Role Cache, it is a key-value pair cache available in three different tiers, which are Basic, Standard, and Premium. The size of the cache and features depends on the tier. For example, the Standard and Premium tiers offer notifications, high availability, up to 10 named caches, and a maximum size of 10 GB to 150 GB respectively. However, Microsoft is very clear in its messaging that this cache offering exists primarily to support existing applications that are using the service. It is not recommended for new applications and the management portal doesn't support creating a Managed Cache. The only way to create a Managed Cache today is to use Azure PowerShell and the New-AzureManagedCache command.

The Redis Cache is the latest and most feature-rich cache service in the platform and is what Microsoft recommends you use going forward. It is a fully Managed Cache service built on the open source Redis Cache and comes with a 99.99 percent financially backed SLA in the Standard tier. The Redis Cache is offered in two tiers; Basic and Standard, both accommodating cache sizes up to 55 GB. The Basic tier is a single cache node that is ideal for non-critical workloads such as development and test. The Standard tier is a replicated cache in with a two-node primary/secondary configuration. Some of the features that make this a superior cache choice is its support for complex data structures beyond just key-value pairs, transactions, incrementing values in a hash, pushing values to a list, and many more.

Configuring a custom domain

Cloud Services deployed in Azure use the shared domain **.cloudapp.net*. For public-facing Cloud Services, it is generally preferred to access the cloud service using a custom domain such as contoso.com.

Configuring a custom domain for a cloud service involves adding CNAME and A records to your domain registrar. The CNAME record will use the site URL for the cloud service while the A record will use the public virtual IP (VIP) address of the cloud service. These values can be found under the quick glance section on the *Dashboard* page for the cloud service in the management portal, as shown here in Figure 3-7.

quick glance

⊞ View Applicable Add-ons

⊕ Set up publishing with Visual Studio
   Online

STATUS
Running

MANAGEMENT SERVICES
Operation Logs

SITE URL
http://contosocloudservice.cloudapp.net/

DEPLOYMENT NAME
d0f5b236635aa4a0eb96f1622680642cf

DEPLOYMENT LABEL
Deployment 1

PUBLIC VIRTUAL IP (VIP) ADDRESS
191.234.50.39

INPUT ENDPOINTS
Demo.WebRole : 191.234.50.39:80
Demo.WebRole : 191.234.50.39:443

FIGURE 3-7 Quick glance of Dashboard page in the management portal

You can also find the site URL and public VIP using Azure PowerShell as shown here:

```
$csName = "ContosoCloudService"
Get-AzureDeployment –ServiceName $csName –Slot Production | Select Url

URL
---
http://contosocloudservice.cloudapp.net/

Get-AzureVM –ServiceName $csName | Get-AzureEndpoint | Select Vip

VIP
---
191.234.50.39
191.234.50.39
```

After obtaining the necessary values, you can register the necessary CNAME and A records with your domain registrar. A detailed guide on how to add the records is available at *http://support2.microsoft.com/kb/2990804*.

EXAM TIP

As long as a cloud service deployment exists, the public virtual IP (VIP) will remain unchanged. However, if you delete a cloud service deployment and later re-deploy the cloud service, the public VIP will be different in the new deployment. As a result, A records registered with your domain registrar will have to be updated to reference the new IP address.

Configuring SSL

Cloud service endpoints should be protected using SSL for any application transferring sensitive or confidential information. Before configuring SSL for a cloud service, you must first obtain a certificate that meets the following requirements:

- The certificate contains a private key.

- The certificate supports key exchange and can be exported to a personal information exchange (.pfx) file.

- The subject name must match the custom domain used to access the cloud service.

- The certificate uses a minimum 2048-bit encryption.

Configuration for the HTTPS endpoint of a cloud service is applied during development and incorporated into the package and configuration files of the cloud service during the packaging process. After obtaining a certificate to be used for SSL, you will need to provide the thumbprint of the certificate to the developer so it can be incorporated into the cloud service definition (.csdef) file. This is typically applied using the cloud service SDK tools for Visual Studio but could be added manually as XML to the .csdef file for the service. Regardless of how settings are applied, it will surface in the cloud service configuration (.cscfg) file that will be used when deploying the service. Listing 3-3 shows the <Certificates> element that will be added during packaging.

LISTING 3-3 Setting the role instance count for an existing cloud service role using PowerShell

```
<ServiceConfiguration serviceName="Demo.CloudService" xmlns=http://schemas.
microsoft.com/ServiceHosting/2008/10/ServiceConfiguration osFamily="4" osVersion="*"
schemaVersion="2014-06.2.4">
  <Role name="Demo.WebRole">
    <Instances count="2" />
      <ConfigurationSettings>
        ...
      </ConfigurationSettings>
    <Certificates>
      <Certificate name="ContosoSSLCert" thumbprint="a74cbf58406b848000cf77a2fc09b1220b6
f1f43" thumbprintAlgorithm="sha1" />
    </Certificates>
  </Role>
</ServiceConfiguration>
```

A cloud service configured for SSL must include the certificate file in the cloud service environment and can be uploaded during the initial deployment of the cloud service by selecting the Add Certificates option, as shown below in Figure 3-8.

FIGURE 3-8 Adding a SSL certificate to a cloud service during publishing using the management portal

After you select the Add Certificates option, you will an option to select the certificate file (.pfx) and enter the password. Figure 3-9 shows the dialog used to attach a certificate to the cloud service deployment.

FIGURE 3-9 Attaching a certificate to a cloud service deployment using the management portal

You can also add a certificate to a cloud service environment using the Add-AzureCertificate PowerShell cmdlet, as shown here.

```
$cert = Get-Item E:\contoso-cs-ssl.pfx
$certPwd = "[YOUR PASSWORD]
$csName = "ContosoCloudService"
Add-AzureCertificate -ServiceName $csName -CertToDeploy $cert -Password $certPwd
```

Microsoft provides a detailed guide for securing a cloud service with an SSL certificate, which can be found at *http://support2.microsoft.com/kb/2990804*.

Configuring a reserved IP address

The ability to reserve an IPv4 address in your Azure subscription and associate it with a cloud service is a feature that solves problems relating to addressing a cloud service using its IP address. For example, in the earlier section about custom domains you learned that if a cloud service deployment is deleted, its public virtual IP (VIP) address will be reassigned when the service is re-deployed, resulting in you having to update the A record with your domain registrar. Reserved IP addresses are a fantastic solution when you need an IP address to remain the same for a cloud service.

An Azure subscription allows up to five reserved IP addresses by default. You can add more if needed by contacting Microsoft support. IP addresses are a limited resource and therefore you can expect to pay for reserved IP addresses. Details on the pricing structure for reserved IP addresses can be found at *http://azure.microsoft.com/en-us/pricing/details/ip-addresses/*.

Reserving an IP address

Before you can configure a reserved IP address for a cloud service, you must first reserve (or obtain) one from Azure. The only way to reserve an IP address is using the Azure PowerShell cmdlets; the management portal does not support this.

To reserve an IP address using Azure PowerShell, the New-AzureReservedIP cmdlet can be used as shown here.

```
PS E:\New-AzureReservedIP -ReservedIPName "contosocloudserviceip" -Location "East US"

OperationDescription    OperationId                           OperationStatus
--------------------    -----------                           ---------------
New-AzureReservedIP     8aa9c279-d81d-1392-bd25-bf713a955728  Succeeded
```

To retrieve the IP addresses reserved in a subscription, use the Get-AzureReservedIP cmdlet as shown here.

```
PS E:\> Get-AzureReservedIP | Select ReservedIPName, Address
ReservedIPName          Address
--------------          -------
contosocloudserviceip   104.45.147.167
```

Configuring a cloud service to use a reserved IP address

After an IP address has been reserved, you can configure a cloud service to use the IP address by adding necessary configuration to the cloud service configuration (.cscfg) file. Alternatively, you can pass the ReserverdIPName you used to reserve the IP address to the developer and have him/her include it in the cloud service configuration during packaging. Listing 3-4 shows the resulting cloud service configuration (.cscfg) file for a cloud service configured to use the reserved IP address named Contosocloudserviceip.

LISTING 3-4 Cloud service configuration file for a service configured to use a reserved IP address

```
<ServiceConfiguration serviceName="Demo.CloudService" xmlns=http://schemas.
microsoft.com/ServiceHosting/2008/10/ServiceConfiguration osFamily="4" osVersion="*"
schemaVersion="2014-06.2.4">
  <Role name="Demo.WebRole">
    <Instances count="2" />
      <ConfigurationSettings>
        ...
      </ConfigurationSettings>
    <Certificates>
      <Certificate name="ContosoSSLCert" thumbprint=
      "a74cbf58406b848000cf77a2fc09b1220b6f1f43" thumbprintAlgorithm="sha1" />
    </Certificates>
  </Role>
  <NetworkConfiguration>
    <AddressAssignments>
      <ReservedIPs>
        <ReservedIP name="contosocloudserviceip" />
      </ReservedIPs>
    </AddressAssignments>
  </NetworkConfiguration>
</ServiceConfiguration>
```

After deploying the cloud service with this configuration, the web role for the cloud service that contains public facing endpoints, will use the reserved IP address as shown here in Figure 3-10.

SITE URL
http://contosocloudservice.cloudapp.net/

DEPLOYMENT NAME
d0b6a109e7ad845b292c98157bd126132

DEPLOYMENT LABEL
Deployment 1

PUBLIC VIRTUAL IP (VIP) ADDRESS
104.45.147.167

INPUT ENDPOINTS
Demo.WebRole : 104.45.147.167:80
Demo.WebRole : 104.45.147.167:443

FIGURE 3-10 Quick glance section of dashboard page for a cloud service using a reserved IP address

If a reserved IP address is no longer needed by a cloud service or virtual machine in the Azure subscription, you can remove it from the Azure subscription using the Remove-AzureReservedIP command as shown here.

```
Remove-AzureReservedIP -ReservedIPName "contosocloudserviceip" -Force
```

> **NOTE   REMOVING A RESERVED IP ADDRESS FROM AN AZURE SUBSCRIPTION**
>
> If an Azure cloud service is currently using a reserved IP address, then you won't be able to remove the Azure reserved IP address. You must first either delete the cloud service deployment or redeploy it with network configuration using a different reserved IP address or no reserved IP address.

Configuring network traffic rules

Cloud Services define external (input) endpoints and optionally internal endpoints that are used for communication with roles. An external endpoint is used for communication with external clients. For example, a web role running a web application would be accessible to users through an external endpoint. An internal endpoint is used for communication between role instances and is accessible only to the roles within the cloud service. For example, a web role may consume a web service in a worker role using an internal endpoint.

In cloud service architectures comprising multiple roles with internal endpoints, roles are free to communicate between each other on the internal endpoints. For some cloud service architectures, this may not be the desired behavior. Instead, it may be preferred to restrict the flow of communication between roles. Network traffic rules are a feature of Cloud Services that can be used to define how roles communicate.

EXAM TIP

A role can have a maximum of five internal endpoints. A cloud service can have a maximum of 25 internal endpoints across all roles.

Network traffic rules are defined in the cloud service definition (.csdef) file within the <NetworkTrafficRules> element. There can be only one instance of this in the cloud service definition file. The schema for network traffic rules provides for the following elements that may be configured within the <NetworkTrafficRules> element:

- **<OnlyAllowTrafficTo>**   Defines a collection of destination endpoints and names of roles that can communicate on the endpoints.
- **<Destinations>**   Contains a collection of <RoleEndpoint> elements.
- **<RoleEndpoint>**   Defines the name of the endpoint to allow traffic to, and the name of, the role to allow communication to.
- **<AllowAllTraffic>**   A rule allowing all roles to communicate on the role endpoints defined in <Destinations>.

- **<FromRole>**   Defines which roles can communicate with role endpoints defined in <Destinations>.

Figure 3-11 illustrates an example of a cloud service architecture with one web role that is accessible to external clients on a defined input endpoint, and two worker roles that are accessible to other roles in the cloud service only on internal endpoints. In this architecture, the WebRole is able to communicate directly with WorkerRole1 and WorkerRole2 while WorkerRole1 is only able communicate directly with WorkerRole2.

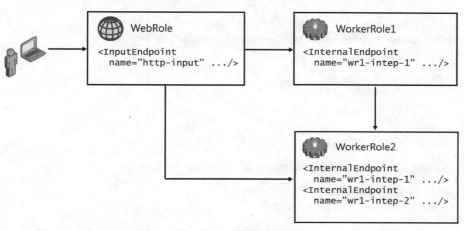

FIGURE 3-11 Communication flow between one web role and two worker roles

Listing 3-5 shows network traffic rules configured for the cloud service architecture shown in Figure 3-11.

LISTING 3-5 Cloud service definition with network traffic rules used to define communication between roles

```
<ServiceDefinition name="ContosoCloudService" xmlns=http://schemas.microsoft.com/
ServiceHosting/2008/10/ServiceDefinition schemaVersion="2014-06.2.4">
  <WebRole name="WebRole" vmsize="Medium">
    <Sites>
      <Site name="Web">
        <Bindings>
          <Binding name="HttpIn" endpointName="http-input" />
        </Bindings>
      </Site>
    </Sites>
    <Endpoints>
      <InputEndpoint name="http-input" protocol="http" port="80" />
    </Endpoints>
  </WebRole>

  <WorkerRole name="WorkerRole1">
    <Endpoints>
      <InternalEndpoint name="wr1-intep-1" protocol="tcp" />
    </Endpoints>
```

```
      </WorkerRole>

      <WorkerRole name="WorkerRole2">
        <Endpoints>
          <InternalEndpoint name="wr2-intep-1" protocol="tcp" />
          <InternalEndpoint name="wr2-intep-2" protocol="tcp" />
        </Endpoints>
      </WorkerRole>

      <NetworkTrafficRules>
        <OnlyAllowTrafficTo>
          <Destinations>
            <RoleEndpoint endpointName="wr1-intep-1" roleName="WorkerRole1"/>
          </Destinations>
          <AllowAllTraffic/>
          <WhenSource matches="AnyRule">
            <FromRole roleName="WebRole"/>
          </WhenSource>
        </OnlyAllowTrafficTo>

        <OnlyAllowTrafficTo>
          <Destinations>
            <RoleEndpoint endpointName="wr2-intep-1" roleName="WorkerRole2"/>
          </Destinations>
          <WhenSource matches="AnyRule">
            <FromRole roleName="WorkerRole1"/>
          </WhenSource>
        </OnlyAllowTrafficTo>

        <OnlyAllowTrafficTo>
          <Destinations>
            <RoleEndpoint endpointName="wr2-intep-2" roleName="WorkerRole2"/>
          </Destinations>
          <WhenSource matches="AnyRule">
            <FromRole roleName="WebRole"/>
          </WhenSource>
        </OnlyAllowTrafficTo>
      </NetworkTrafficRules>
    </ServiceDefinition>
```

Restricting web role access

By default, a web role in a cloud service is bound to the IIS site bindings using its external input endpoint. This is part of the underlying infrastructure that makes the web role accessible to external clients, typically over HTTP/HTTPS using a browser. However, there are situations where a public facing web role needs to have access limited to clients from specifically identified IP addresses to reduce the attack surface. The concept is the same as configuring access control lists (ACLs) on an endpoint for a virtual machine. However, in Cloud Services, the approach is different and is accomplished by configuring the IIS instance in the virtual machine the web role is hosted on.

Azure provisions the virtual machine instances hosting a web role or worker role automatically, using the configuration files associated with the cloud service. Therefore, the configuration of the IIS instance has to be done at the time the virtual machine is provisioned and the application is deployed, which can be accomplished using a startup task and some configuration in the Web.config file for the web application.

> **MORE INFO**   **STARTUP TASKS IN CLOUD SERVICES**
>
> A startup task is a unique feature of Cloud Services that enable you to perform configuration changes to the virtual machine for a role instance before the role is started. A scenario where this is particularly useful is when a third-party component or application that the role depends on needs to be installed and configured before the role can be started. Or, perhaps an environment variable the role will be looking for needs to be added.
>
> A startup task is defined in the cloud service definition (.csdef) file using the <Task> element within a <WebRole> or <WorkerRole> element. A <Task> element contains three properties that you can use to influence permissions and behaviors for the task, which are:
>
> - **commandLine**   Identifies the program or script you want to execute.
> - **executionContext**   Sets the permission level needed by the script, and can be either limited or elevated. Configuration changes such as changing IIS settings will require that the task be run in an elevated mode.
> - **taskType**   Can be either simple, foreground, or background. A simple task is executed synchronously before a role starts. Foreground and background tasks are executed asynchronously in parallel with the role. A foreground task can keep a role running and prevent it from shutting down or recycle. A background task will be stopped if a role needs to shut down or be recycled.
>
> More information about startup tasks and best practices for using them can be found at *http://msdn.microsoft.com/en-us/library/azure/hh180155.aspx*.

To configure the IIS instance for the role, the startup task needs only to unlock the ipSecurity section of the Applicationhost.config file on the virtual machine. By unlocking the ipSecurity section, the Web.config file can define the rules regarding which ipAddresses to allow access to the web role. To unlock this section, the startup task can call Appcmd.exe to perform this step as shown here.

```
%windir%\system32\inetsrv\AppCmd.exe unlock config -section:system.webServer/security/
ipSecurity
```

Next, update the cloud service definition file to include the startup task. Listing 3-6 shows the cloud service definition file for a web role configured to execute the startup task. Notice that the execution context is set to elevated, which is required to apply changes to the Applicationhost.config file.

LISTING 3-6 Cloud service definition with a startup task to unlock the ipSecurity section of Applicationhost.config

```
<?xml version="1.0" encoding="utf-8"?>
<ServiceDefinition name="Contoso.CloudService" xmlns="http://schemas.microsoft.com/
```

```
    ServiceHosting/2008/10/ServiceDefinition" schemaVersion="2014-06.2.4">
      <WebRole name="ContosoWebRole" vmsize="Small">
        <Sites>
          <Site name="Web">
            <Bindings>
              <Binding name="Endpoint1" endpointName="http-in" />
            </Bindings>
          </Site>
        </Sites>

        <Endpoints>
          <InputEndpoint name="http-in" protocol="http" port="80" />
        </Endpoints>
        <Imports>
          <Import moduleName="Diagnostics" />
        </Imports>
        <Startup>
          <Task commandLine="startup\startup.cmd" executionContext="elevated"
taskType="simple" />
        </Startup>
      </WebRole>
    </ServiceDefinition>
```

The final step is to add the <ipSecurity> settings in the Web.config to configure which IP addresses will be able to access the service. Listing 3-7 shows configuration restricting access to a single IP address.

LISTING 3-7 Configuration of <ipSecurity> element in Web.config to restrict access to a single IP address

```
<system.webServer>
  <security>
    <ipSecurity allowUnlisted="false">
      <add allowed="true" ipAddress="72.110.72.113" subnetMask="255.255.255.255"/>
    </ipSecurity>
  </security>
</system.webServer>
```

> **NOTE** **CONFIGURING <IPSECURITY>IN WEB.CONFIG**
>
> Generally, you would provide this information to the developer to include it in the Web.config for the web role. The Web.config file for a web role or worker role is packaged into the cloud service package (.cspkg) and therefore is not something that should be edited after the package is created.

Configuring local storage

Local storage resources provide a way to reserve a named directory on the local file system of the virtual machine a role is running on. The role instance can read and write to the directory as needed. This can be particularly useful in a scenario where a web role needs to cache images that are stored in an Azure Storage container. Reading the images from Azure Storage uses bandwidth. Instead, the role can pull all of the files needed locally, store them in local storage when the role starts, and then read from the local directory for the duration of the of the role instance.

To configure local storage for a role, you set the following three properties:

1. The name of the local storage resource. This name will be the name the role will use to reference the local storage.

2. The size (in MBs).

3. A flag indicating whether or not the contents of the local storage should be cleaned (that is, deleted) if/when the role is restarted.

Local storage is configured in the cloud service definition file using the <LocalStorage> element. Listing 3-8 shows two local storage resources configured for a web role.

LISTING 3-8 Configuration of <ipSecurity> element in web.config to restrict access to a single IP address

```xml
<?xml version="1.0" encoding="utf-8"?>
<ServiceDefinition name="Contoso.CloudService" xmlns="http://schemas.microsoft.com/
ServiceHosting/2008/10/ServiceDefinition" schemaVersion="2014-06.2.4">
  <WebRole name="ContosoWebRole" vmsize="Small">
    <Sites>
      <Site name="Web">
        <Bindings>
          <Binding name="Endpoint1" endpointName="http-in" />
        </Bindings>
      </Site>
    </Sites>

    <Endpoints>
      <InputEndpoint name="http-in" protocol="http" port="80" />
    </Endpoints>
    <LocalResources>
      <LocalStorage name="webGraphics" sizeInMB="40" cleanOnRoleRecycle="true" />
      <LocalStorage name="MiscStore" sizeInMB="20" cleanOnRoleRecycle="false"/>
    </LocalResources>
  </WebRole>
</ServiceDefinition>
```

Local resources are allocated on the drive C of the virtual machine running the role instance. The directory is located under the path C:\Resources\Directory\<random id>\ <role name>.<local resource name>, as shown in Figure 3-12.

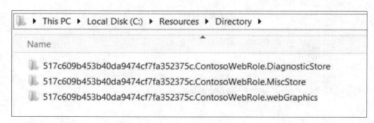

FIGURE 3-12 Local resources directory on a role instance virtual machine

The capacity for local resources will vary depending on the size of the virtual machine that has been configured for the role. Although the configuration may appear acceptable, the application will fail when it attempts to write to the local resource if the SizeInMB setting exceeds the capacity of the local drive.

Configuring role instance size

Throughout this objective you have seen references to the role instance size (virtual machine size) in consideration for things such as capacity planning for an In-Role Cache or configuring local storage resources. This section identifies where the role instance size is defined and what the available options are.

Determining role instance sizes that are available

It is a reasonable assumption that because cloud service role instances are virtual machines, any size available to virtual machines would also be available for Cloud Services. However, that is not the case. When choosing the role instance size for roles in a cloud service, you need to make sure you're selecting from the sizes that are available to Cloud Services.

The Azure PowerShell cmdlets offer a cmdlet called Get-AzureRoleSize that makes this very easy to determine. Shown below, Get-AzureRoleSize returns the number of cores, memory, and available resource disk size of all instance sizes that are supported by web roles and worker roles.

```
Get-AzureRoleSize `
  | where { $_.SupportedByWebWorkerRoles -eq $true } `
  | Select InstanceSize, Cores, MemoryInMb, WebWorkerResourceDiskSizeInMb
```

InstanceSize	Cores	MemoryInMb	WebWorkerResourceDiskSizeInMb
A5	2	14336	501760
A6	4	28672	1024000
A7	8	57344	2088960
A8	8	57344	1861268
A9	16	114688	1861268
ExtraLarge	8	14336	2088960
ExtraSmall	1	768	20480
Large	4	7168	1024000
Medium	2	3584	501760
Small	1	1792	230400
Standard_D1	1	3584	51200
Standard_D11	2	14336	102400
Standard_D12	4	28672	256000
Standard_D13	8	57344	512000
Standard_D14	16	114688	1024000
Standard_D2	2	7168	102400
Standard_D3	4	14336	256000
Standard_D4	8	28672	512000

The instance size for a role is defined in the <WebRole> or <WorkerRole> element in the cloud service definition file. The *vmsize* property specifies the instance size and must be set to one of the values in the InstanceSize column from above as shown here.

```
<ServiceDefinition name="Contoso.CloudService" xmlns="http://schemas.microsoft.com/
ServiceHosting/2008/10/ServiceDefinition" schemaVersion="2014-06.2.4">
  <WebRole name="ContosoWebRole" vmsize="Standard_D2">
    ...
  </WebRole>
</ServiceDefinition>
```

If you know your requirements for cores, memory, and local resource storage capacity, you can get a list of instance sizes matching those requirements by applying some filters to the output of Get-AzureRoleSize as shown here, where the request is for instance size that match the following requirements:

- At least 3 cores
- At least 48 GB of memory
- At least 500 GB of local resource storage

```
Get-AzureRoleSize `
 | where { $_.SupportedByWebWorkerRoles -eq $true } `
 | where { ($_.Cores -ge 4) -and ($_.MemoryInMb -ge 48000) -and ($_.
VirtualMachineResourceDiskSizeInMb -ge 500000) } `
 | Select InstanceSize, Cores, MemoryInMb, WebWorkerResourceDiskSizeInMb
```

InstanceSize	Cores	MemoryInMb	WebWorkerResourceDiskSizeInMb
A7	8	57344	2088960
Standard_D13	8	57344	512000
Standard_D14	16	114688	1024000

Configuring multiple websites on a web role

Configuring multiple websites on a single web role presents a potentially significant cost savings when you have multiple websites to run. The default behavior for cloud service web roles is to host one website per role. If you have additional sites to host, that normally means adding another web role for each site, which equates to one or more role instances (virtual machines) for each website added. In cases where multiple websites don't need the full capacity of resources a virtual machine provides, it can be advantageous to host those websites on the same web role to minimize the additional role instances that would otherwise be required.

Listing 3-8 above is an example web role hosting a single website. The <Sites> element within the <WebRole> is where the default website referred to as Web is defined. The <Site> element configures a binding in IIS using the web role's <InputEndpoint> settings for the binding. The configuration in Listing 3-8 results in a single site hosted in IIS, as shown in Figure 3-13.

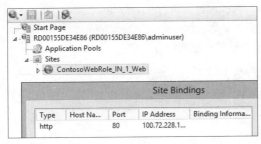

FIGURE 3-13 Website and site bindings in IIS Manager for a web role deployed to Azure

Adding another website to the web role essentially means adding another <Site> configuration within the <Sites> element. Listing 3-9 shows a second <Site> configuration added for the web role.

LISTING 3-9 Cloud service definition with two sites configured for a single web role

```
<?xml version="1.0" encoding="utf-8"?>
<ServiceDefinition name="Contoso.CloudService" xmlns="http://schemas.microsoft.com/
ServiceHosting/2008/10/ServiceDefinition" schemaVersion="2014-06.2.4">
  <WebRole name="ContosoWebRole" vmsize="Small">
    <Sites>
      <Site name="Web">
        <Bindings>
          <Binding name="Endpoint1" endpointName="http-in" />
        </Bindings>
      </Site>
      <Site name="ContosoWeb2" physicalDirectory="..\..\..\..\ContosoWeb2">
        <Bindings>
          <Binding name="Endpoint1" endpointName="http-in" hostHeader="contoso2.com"/>
        </Bindings>
      </Site>
    </Sites>

    <Endpoints>
      <InputEndpoint name="http-in" protocol="http" port="80" />
    </Endpoints>
    <LocalResources>
      <LocalStorage name="webGraphics" sizeInMB="40" cleanOnRoleRecycle="true" />
      <LocalStorage name="MiscStore" sizeInMB="20" cleanOnRoleRecycle="false"/>
    </LocalResources>
  </WebRole>
</ServiceDefinition>
```

The configuration in Listing 3-9 results in a role instance configuration with two sites for the web role, as shown in Figure 3-14.

FIGURE 3-14 Two websites and the site bindings for the second site in IIS Manager for a single web role deployed to Azure

Although the focus in this section has been about running multiple websites in a single web role, there are scenarios where you may not need to host a separate site, but instead an additional web application within a website. You can do this by adding a <VirtualApplication> element within the <Site> element you want the web application to be available from, as shown in Listing 3-10.

LISTING 3-10 Cloud service definition with two sites and a virtual application configured in one web role

```xml
<?xml version="1.0" encoding="utf-8"?>
<ServiceDefinition name="Contoso.CloudService" xmlns="http://schemas.microsoft.com/
ServiceHosting/2008/10/ServiceDefinition" schemaVersion="2014-06.2.4">
  <WebRole name="ContosoWebRole" vmsize="Small">
    <Sites>
      <Site name="Web">
        <VirtualApplication name="ContosoApp2" physicalDirectory="..\..\..\
ContosoApp2"/>
        <Bindings>
          <Binding name="Endpoint1" endpointName="http-in" />
        </Bindings>
      </Site>
      <Site name="ContosoWeb2" physicalDirectory="..\..\..\..\ContosoWeb2">
        <Bindings>
          <Binding name="Endpoint1" endpointName="http-in" hostHeader="contoso2.com"/>
        </Bindings>
      </Site>
    </Sites>

    <Endpoints>
      <InputEndpoint name="http-in" protocol="http" port="80" />
    </Endpoints>
    <LocalResources>
      <LocalStorage name="webGraphics" sizeInMB="40" cleanOnRoleRecycle="true" />
      <LocalStorage name="MiscStore" sizeInMB="20" cleanOnRoleRecycle="false"/>
    </LocalResources>
  </WebRole>
</ServiceDefinition>
```

Configuring remote desktop

The ability to connect to a virtual machine for a role instance can be handy in situations where you need to troubleshoot a role instance. This is also often used during development and testing to experiment with different configurations for the role.

Azure Cloud Services support connecting to the virtual machine hosting a role instance using Remote Desktop (RDP). Configuring a cloud service for RDP access involves registering a management certificate with the cloud service and setting up credentials to sign in to the virtual machine.

Configuring RDP access using the management portal

In the management portal, you configure RDP access for a cloud service by going to the *Configure* page. At the bottom of the *Configure* page is a Remote button. Click the Remote button to open a window where you can configure RDP access for all the roles in a cloud service, or a specific role in the cloud service. Figure 3-15 shows setting up RDP access for a web role.

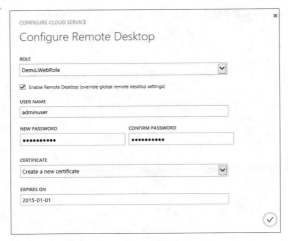

FIGURE 3-15 Configuring RDP access for a web role using the management portal

The certificate field shown in Figure 3-15 can be an existing management certificate that was previously uploaded to Azure, or as shown, you can have Azure create a management certificate for you that will expire on a future date you specify.

Configuring RDP access using Azure PowerShell

You can use the Azure PowerShell cmdlets to configure RDP access for a cloud service. The Set-AzureServiceRemoteDesktopExtension cmdlet enables RDP for a cloud service or a specific role, as shown here.

```
$creds = Get-Credential
$csName = "ContosoCloudService"
```

```
$csRole = "DemoWorkerRole"
$certThumbprint = "[YOUR MGMT CERTIFICATE THUMBPRINT]"
$cert = Get-Item Cert:\CurrentUser\My\$certThumbprint

Set-AzureServiceRemoteDesktopExtension -ServiceName $csName -Role `
  $csRole -Credential $creds -X509Certificate $cert
```

To disable the RDP access, use the Remove-AzureServiceRemoteDesktopExtension cmdlet as shown here.

```
Remove-AzureServiceRemoteDesktopExtension -ServiceName $csName -Role $csRole
```

Thought experiment
Configure an In-Role Cache

In this thought experiment, apply what you've learned about this objective. You can find answers to these questions in the "Answers" section at the end of this chapter.

You are the IT Administrator for Contoso and responsible for managing Cloud Services. One of the Cloud Services you manage is a dedicated cache that other Cloud Services use. The development team is updating one of the Cloud Services that uses the cache, and the update requires a new named cache be added to support the change.

Items stored in the cache must exist for 20 minutes before they expire. If a request is made for an item in the cache, then it should not expire until 20 minutes after the last time it was accessed. Notifications for the cache should be disabled.

1. What additional information do you need to be able to configure the cache?

2. What settings will you use to configure the cache?

3. How will this impact the capacity of the cache?

Objective summary

- Operating system settings enable you to configure the operating system family and the operation system version for a cloud service. Operating system settings apply to all roles in a cloud service and cannot be configured uniquely for each role.

- The operating system family can be set in the cloud service configuration (.cscfg) file using the osFamily property of the <ServiceConfiguration> element.

- The operating system version can be set in the cloud service configuration (.cscfg) file using the osVersion property of the <ServiceConfiguration> element.

- Remote desktop can be enabled for all roles in a cloud service or for individual roles. To configure remote desktop access, you need to provide a certificate and credentials that will be used to connect to the virtual machine. You can retrieve the remote desktop (.RDP) file for a virtual machine role instance using the Get-AzureRemoteDesktopFile

PowerShell cmdlet. You can also retrieve it from the management portal by clicking the Connect button for a role that has remote desktop access enabled.

- In-Role Cache can be configured as either a co-located or dedicated topology. A co-located cache is hosted using the same resources of the virtual machine that is hosting the web role or worker role in the cloud service. A dedicated cache is hosted using the dedicated worker role instances. The full resources of the virtual machine instances are used for the cache.

- Network traffic rules can be added to the cloud service definition file to control how roles communicate with one another using their internal endpoint configurations.

- Blocking access to a web role requires updating the <ipSecurity> section of the Applicationhost.config file on the virtual machine instance the web role runs on. This can be accomplished using a startup task and updating the Web.config of the web role to apply the configuration at the time the virtual machine is provisioned.

Objective review

Answer the following questions to test your knowledge of the information in this objective. You can find the answers to these questions and explanations of why each answer choice is correct or incorrect in the "Answers" section at the end of this chapter.

1. Which are valid in-role caching topologies for a cloud service? (Choose all that apply).

    A. Managed Cache

    B. Co-located cache

    C. Redis Cache

    D. Dedicated cache

2. You need to configure a cloud service to use a specific version of the Windows Server 2012 R2 operating system. Which setting in the cloud service configuration (.cscfg) file will you use?

    A. osFamily

    B. <ConfigurationSettings>

    C. osVersion

    D. <Instances>

3. You have been asked to configure Remote Desktop (RDP) access for a cloud service. Which Azure PowerShell cmdlet will you use to configure RDP access?

    A. New-AzureServiceRemoteDesktopExtensionConfig

    B. Set-AzureServiceRemoteDesktopExtension

    C. Get-AzureRemoteDesktopFile

    D. Enable-AzureServiceProjectRemoteDesktop

4. You need to upload a certificate for SSL to an existing cloud service deployment. Which Azure PowerShell cmdlet should you use?

   A. Add-AzureCertificate

   B. New-AzureCertificateSetting

   C. Set-AzureDeployment

   D. Get-AzureCertificate

5. You need to reserve an IP address for a cloud service. Which three tasks are necessary in this to accomplish this task?

   A. Use the New-AzureReservedIP PowerShell cmdlet to reserve an IP address in a specified region and assign a name to reference the reserved IP address.

   B. Add the <NetworkConfiguration> to the cloud service configuration file identifying the reserved IP address by name.

   C. Delete any existing cloud service deployments.

   D. Re-deploy the cloud service with the updated service configuration file to the same region the reserved IP address was reserved in.

6. To configure network traffic rules between role instances of a cloud service, which XML element must you use to define the rules in the cloud service definition file?

   A. <ServiceDefinition>

   B. <NetworkTrafficRules>

   C. <InternalEndpoint>

   D. <InputEndpoint>

7. You need to provide configuration to store image files in a local storage resource for a web role. Which XML element will you use to define the local resource properties?

   A. <LocalStorage>

   B. <LocalResources>

   C. <WebRole>

   D. <Destinations>

8. You need to recommend an instance size for a worker role that requires at least 3 cores, 48 GB of memory, and local resource storage capacity of 500 GB. Which instance size would meet these requirements and be the most cost effective?

   A. Large

   B. ExtraLarge

   C. Standard_D13

   D. A7

Objective 3.2: Deploy and manage Cloud Services

Deploying a cloud service to Microsoft Azure involves uploading the cloud service package (.cspkg) and the cloud service configuration (.cscfg) files to the staging or production slot of a cloud service. Although much of the configuration for a cloud service is done during the packaging of the service, there are still several deployment options and environment settings that you should consider.

> **This objective covers how to:**
> - Package a cloud service
> - Deploy a cloud service
> - Perform a VIP swap
> - Update a cloud service deployment
> - Scale a cloud service
> - Create a service bus namespace

Packaging a cloud service

Before a cloud service can be deployed to Microsoft Azure, it must be packaged in a format that Azure expects. The development team using Visual Studio and the SDK tools in their environment usually handles the process of packaging a cloud service. Alternatively, a cloud service can be packaged using the *CSPack* command-line tool. This tool is ideal in situations when you are not using Visual Studio or don't have Visual Studio installed.

> *TIP* **GET THE CSPACK TOOL**
>
> The CSPack command-line tool is part of the Azure SDK. The Azure SDK can be installed without having Visual Studio installed using the Web Platform Installer. The default location for the tool is at C:\Program Files\Microsoft SDKs\Windows Azure\.NET SDK\<sdk-version>\bin.
>
> Use the Microsoft Azure SDK command prompt to open a command prompt. This command prompt includes the paths and environment variables you will need when using the CSPack tool.

The CSPack tool uses the cloud service definition file and the binaries for each of the roles in the cloud service to construct a cloud service package (.cspkg) file. As an example, consider a cloud service named Contoso.CloudService with a single web role named ContosoWebRole. The command to generate a package file for this application is shown here.

```
E:\Contoso.CloudService.Solution>cspack .\Contoso.CloudService\ServiceDefinition.csdef
/role:ContosoWebRole;.\ContosoWebRole\bin /sites:ContosoWebRole;Web;.\ContosoWebRole
/out:.\ContosoDeployment\ContosoCloudService.cspkg /useCtpPackageFormat
```

The first parameter in the command above is the path to the cloud service definition (.csdef) file.

The second parameter is /Role, which consist of two parts separated by a semicolon. The first part is the name of the web role while the second part is the path to the binaries for that role. If a cloud service has multiple roles, you would repeat the /Role parameter for each role in the cloud service.

The third parameter is /Sites which consists of three parts separated by a semicolon. The first part is the name of the web role that includes the site binding configuration as part of the role. Recall from earlier that this is identified in the cloud service definition file as the <Sites> element. The second part is the name of the site, which is identified as a property in the <Site> element. The third part is the path to the files for the web role.

The fourth parameter is /Out which identifies the location where you want the package file stored. This can be any path you prefer.

The last parameter is the /UseCtpPackageFormat switch that tells CSPack to generate the package using the latest packaging format that was introduced in version 1.7 of the Azure SDK.

> **NOTE   CLOUD SERVICE PACKAGE FORMAT**
>
> The cloud service package format introduced in version 1.7 of the Azure SDK uses the standard ZIP format. The default extension for a package file is .cspkg. However, if you re-name the package file to a .zip extension, you can unzip it and explore or edit the package contents.
>
> The new package format is particularly useful as it provides a way to edit and repackage (zip back up) the package contents without requiring any SDK tools. It is also a format that can be used on non-Windows operating systems.

Cloud service configuration files

You may recall from earlier sections of this objective references to the cloud service configuration (.cscfg) file. The CSPack command-line tool does not generate this file. Instead, the file is typically generated and edited during the development phase of the cloud service using Visual Studio and the SDK tools. The Azure PowerShell cmdlets provide the New-AzureServiceProject command that can also be used to initially create the cloud service project.

Regardless of which tools are used to create the cloud service project, two versions of the cloud service configuration file likely exist. They are usually named as follows:

- ServiceConfiguration.Cloud.cscfg
- ServiceConfiguration.Local.cscfg

The ServiceConfiguration.Cloud.cscfg file contains the configuration to deploy and run the cloud service in Microsoft Azure. The ServiceConfiguration.Local.cscfg file contains the configuration to deploy and run the cloud service in a local development environment such as the Azure Compute Emulator. A common difference found in the service configuration files is the connection strings to a storage account. In the cloud version, the connection string is for an Azure storage account hosted in Azure. In the local version, the connection string is often a value indicating that the Azure Storage Emulator should be used, which simulates an Azure Storage account using local developer resources.

Deploying a cloud service

After you package a cloud service, you can deploy it using the management portal or the Azure PowerShell command Publish-AzureServiceProject. If you have a development environment with Visual Studio and the Azure SDK tools installed, you can publish using Visual Studio.

Publish using the management portal

To publish a cloud service package using the management portal, select the option to custom create the cloud service, as shown in Figure 3-16. The Custom Create option gives you an opportunity to select a cloud service package to upload after the cloud service is created.

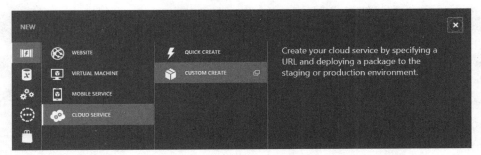

FIGURE 3-16 Custom Create option for creating a cloud service in the management portal

When using the Custom Create option to create a cloud service, you will have the option to deploy a cloud service package, as shown in Figure 3-17. If you don't check this option, you can create an empty cloud service without any deployments.

FIGURE 3-17 Dialog in management portal with option to Deploy A Cloud Service Package

After you select the option to deploy a cloud service package, the next dialog box prompts you for additional information needed to deploy your package, as shown in Figure 3-18.

FIGURE 3-18 Dialog in management portal to publish a cloud service package

The first field is the Deployment Label and this can be any text value you want to use to identify the deployment.

The Package field is where you specify the cloud service package (.cspkg) that you want to deploy. There are two options for locating this file. The first is to locate it From Local, which would be a location on your local file system. The second is to locate it From Storage, which would be an Azure Storage container where the file has been previously uploaded.

The Configuration field is identical to the Package field except that the file selected is the cloud service configuration (.cscfg) file.

The Environment field is where you can indicate which environment you want to deploy to. This can be either the production or staging environment. Generally it is a good idea to deploy to your staging environment first, and then later swap the staging and production environments after you have verified the application is working as expected.

The check box labeled Deploy Even If One Or More Roles Contain A Single Instance is necessary if your instance count for any role is set to one. By selecting this box, you are acknowledging that you are intentionally deploying a cloud service that won't be subject to the financially backed SLA of 99.95 percent. Recall from earlier, to get the SLA, all roles in the cloud service must have a minimum of two instances.

The check box labeled Start Deployment will result in Azure starting the role instances after the deployment completes.

If the check box labeled Add Certificates is selected, a third dialog will be added to the wizard where you can select the certificate (.pfx) file to use for SSL.

> **NOTE** **PUBLISH A CLOUD SERVICE PACKAGE TO AN EXISTING CLOUD SERVICE**
>
> There may be situations where the cloud service already exists in Azure and you are deploying the package to either the staging or production environment for the cloud service. The experience for deploying the package is almost the same. To deploy the package, you need to open the Dashboard page for the cloud service and then click either the Staging or Production environment tab at the top of the screen. At the bottom of the screen, you can use the Upload button to upload the package. The dialog will be exactly the same with one exception being that you won't have the option to attach an SSL certificate to the deployment. It is assumed that, if the cloud service was previously created, any SSL certificates have also already been uploaded in the Certificates page of the management portal.

Publish using Azure PowerShell

To publish a cloud service package using Azure PowerShell, use the Publish-AzureServiceProject cmdlet as shown here.

```
$csLocation = "West US"
$deployName = "V1-BETA"
$pathCSPKG = Get-Item E:\Contoso.CloudService.Solution\ContosoDeployment\
ContosoCloudService.cspkg
$pathCSCFG = Get-Item E:\Contoso.CloudService.Solution\Contoso.CloudService\
ServiceConfiguration.Cloud.cscfg

Publish-AzureServiceProject -Location $csLocation -Slot "Staging" `
  -Package $pathCSPKG -Configuration $pathCSCFG -DeploymentName $deployName
```

Deploy a cloud service into a virtual network

A cloud service can be deployed into a Microsoft Azure Virtual Network with some configuration added to the cloud service configuration file. A few reasons why you may want to deploy a cloud service to a virtual network are as follows:

- You use a virtual network in Azure to connect to an on-premises network.
- You have resources, such as SQL Server, running in virtual machines that your cloud service depends on.
- You have web roles or worker roles in another cloud service that the web roles or worker roles in your cloud service need to communicate with.
- You want to increase security of your cloud services and virtual machines by isolating them in a virtual network.
- You want to reduce network latency between the cloud service and virtual machines it needs to communicate with.

> **MORE INFO** **MICROSOFT AZURE VIRTUAL NETWORK**
>
> The networking service in Microsoft Azure that lets customers create and manage virtual private networks in Microsoft Azure and securely link them to other virtual networks or their own on-premises networking infrastructure. Microsoft Azure Virtual Networks is discussed in Chapter 6 of this text.

As an example, consider an existing virtual network called ContosoVNET that has a subnet called Apps, as shown in Figure 3-19.

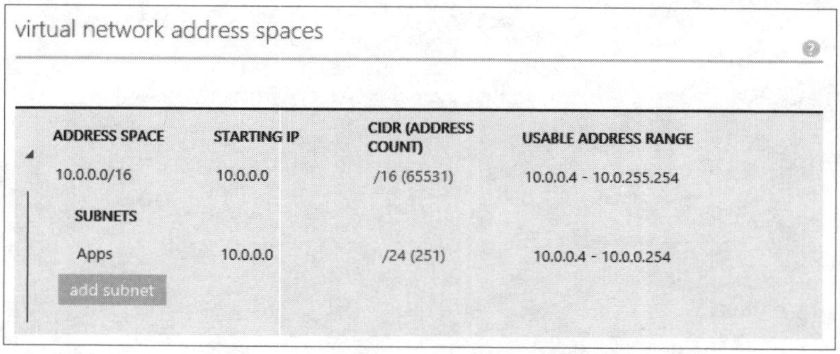

ADDRESS SPACE	STARTING IP	CIDR (ADDRESS COUNT)	USABLE ADDRESS RANGE
10.0.0.0/16	10.0.0.0	/16 (65531)	10.0.0.4 - 10.0.255.254
SUBNETS			
Apps	10.0.0.0	/24 (251)	10.0.0.4 - 10.0.0.254

FIGURE 3-19 Virtual Network configuration in management portal

To deploy a cloud service into the Apps subnet in the virtual network, you need to add a <NetworkConfiguration> element to the cloud service configuration file with settings identifying the Apps subnet in the virtual network. Listing 3-11 shows the necessary configuration to deploy into the network shown in Figure 3-19.

LISTING 3-11 Cloud service configuration with two sites and a virtual application configured in one web role

```xml
<?xml version="1.0" encoding="utf-8"?>
<ServiceConfiguration serviceName="Contoso.CloudService" xmlns="http://schemas.
microsoft.com/ServiceHosting/2008/10/ServiceConfiguration" osFamily="4" osVersion="*"
schemaVersion="2014-06.2.4">
  <Role name="ContosoWebRole">
    <Instances count="3" />
    <ConfigurationSettings>
      ...
    </ConfigurationSettings>
  </Role>

  <NetworkConfiguration>
    <VirtualNetworkSite name="contosoVNET" />
      <AddressAssignments>
        <InstanceAddress roleName="ContosoWebRole">
          <Subnets>
            <Subnet name="Apps"/>
          </Subnets>
        </InstanceAddress>
      </AddressAssignments>
  </NetworkConfiguration>
</ServiceConfiguration>
```

When the cloud service with this configuration is deployed, Azure will identify the network configuration and provision the virtual machine instances in the Apps subnet. Figure 3-20 shows the ContosoVNET where the role instances are allocated.

FIGURE 3-20 Virtual Network dashboard showing web role instances allocated in the Apps subnet

EXAM TIP

When a cloud service is deployed to a Virtual Network, the IP address assigned to the role instances from the subnet of the Virtual Network does not influence the public virtual IP (VIP) address of the cloud service. The public VIP for the cloud service is still assigned an IP address by Azure that is publicly reachable.

Perform a virtual IP swap

Cloud Services have a staging and production environment that you can deploy into. Each cloud service environment is assigned a public virtual IP (VIP). Additionally, each environment will get a URL that can be used to access the deployment in that environment and the URL, as you would expect, resolves to the VIP for that environment.

The staging environment is used for development, testing, and pre-staging before promoting a cloud service to production. When the URL is assigned to the staging environment, a GUID is used to guarantee a unique name. The URL for a cloud service deployment in the staging environment would look something like this: *http://dce415d89890440282edc6b7d79cf090.cloudapp.net*.

The production environment is used for production purposes. Therefore, it's assigned a friendlier URL using the name of the cloud service. For a cloud service named Contoso, the URL would look like *contoso.cloudapp.net*.

A virtual IP (VIP) swap equates to swapping the environment (staging or production) that the VIP and URL are assigned to. Table 3-1 shows the two environments for a cloud service, where Deployment-A is in production and Deployment-B is in staging.

TABLE 3-1 Staging and production environments for two deployments

Environment	VIP	DNS NAME (SITE URL)	Deployment Label
Staging	104.45.225.97	http://dce415d89890440282edc6b7d79cf090.cloudapp.net	Deployment-B
Production	104.45.224.150	http://contoso.cloudapp.net	Deployment-A

After performing a VIP swap, the two environments appear as shown in Table 3-2. Notice that the only change is the deployment that the environment points to.

TABLE 3-2 Staging and production environments for two deployments after swapping

Environment	VIP	DNS NAME (SITE URL)	Deployment Label
Staging	104.45.225.97	http://dce415d89890440282edc6b7d79cf090.cloudapp.net	Deployment-A
Production	104.45.224.150	http://contoso.cloudapp.net	Deployment-B

You can perform a VIP swap in the management portal in the Dashboard page for a cloud service. At the bottom of the page is a Swap button.

Updating a cloud service deployment

A cloud service deployment can be updated in a manner very similar to how the initial deployment to Azure was accomplished, which is, to publish updated versions of the cloud service package (.cspkg) and/or the cloud service configuration (.cscfg).

When you update a deployment, Azure applies the update sequentially across the update domains of your cloud service so as to minimize less availability of instances during the update. This assumes you have a role instance count of two or more for each role in the cloud service.

To update a cloud service using the management portal, go to the Dashboard page of the cloud service, click either the Production or Staging tab, and then select the environment to be updated. At the bottom of the page is an Update button. Clicking the Update button to perform the update as shown in Figure 3-21.

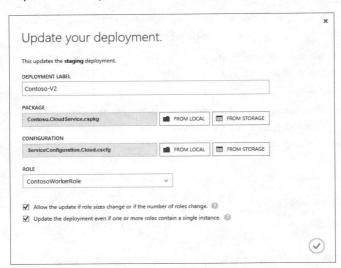

FIGURE 3-21 Dialog in management portal to update a cloud service deployment

While this dialog is very similar to the dialog you used to initially deploy the cloud service, this one has a couple of subtle differences. The first is the Role field, which is a drop-down box allowing you to select the role that is being updated, or all roles in the cloud service. This can be useful if there is just one role being updated as in this case where the ContosoWorkerRole was selected.

The other notable difference is the check box labeled Allow The Update If Role Sizes Change Or If The Number Of Roles Change. By checking this, you're acknowledging that if your update involves any of these conditions, any data in local storage resources will be lost because the service will have to be redeployed.

Updating the cloud service configuration

There may be situations where an update only needs to be applied to the configuration of the cloud service and not the files and binaries of the roles. Some scenarios where this may be desired are:

- You want to change the instance count for a role.
- You need to update <ConfigurationSettings> for a role such as a connection string to an Azure Storage account or a SQL Database instance.

- You need to update the thumbprint for a certificate a role uses.

You can update just the cloud service configuration for an existing deployment in the management portal by opening the Configure page for the cloud service you want to update. At the bottom of the page is an Upload button. Click the Upload button for a prompt for the updated configuration file.

Scaling a cloud service

The scalability story for Cloud Services is unique by virtue of it being comprised of web roles and worker roles. Each role in a cloud service can be independently scaled, thus making scalability for the cloud service highly effective. Scaling a role in a cloud service entails increasing or decreasing the instance count for the role.

EXAM TIP

Unlike other compute stacks in the Azure platform, the ability to scale up or down the virtual machine size for a role instance, such as increasing it to an A7 or decreasing it to a Small, is not possible for Cloud Services. To change the virtual machine size for a role means changing the cloud service definition file and re-deploying the service.

Scaling the instance count for a role in a cloud service can be done manually or automatically using the Autoscale feature.

Manually scaling roles in a cloud service

Using the management portal, go to the Scale page for the cloud service you intend to scale, and click the environment (production or staging) where you want to apply the scaling change. The Summary section shows the roles in the cloud service. This Summary section shows the size of the instance and how many instances are running, as shown in Figure 3-22.

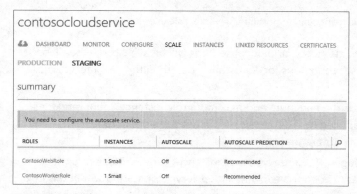

FIGURE 3-22 Scale page in management portal showing Summary section for roles

Further down the page are sections for each role in the cloud service where you can specify the Instance Count for each role independently using the slider control as shown in Figure 3-23.

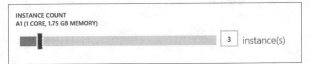

FIGURE 3-23 Slider control in the management portal used to scale a role's instance count

Autoscale roles in a cloud service using metrics

The elasticity promise of cloud computing is recognized through the Autoscale feature in Azure. With Cloud Services, the Autoscale feature enables you to independently scale roles in a cloud service using metrics such as CPU and QUEUE depth.

To configure Autoscale for a cloud service, go to the Scale page for the cloud service and scroll to the role section for the role you want to configure Autoscale for. You can choose to Scale By Metric, as shown in Figure 3-24.

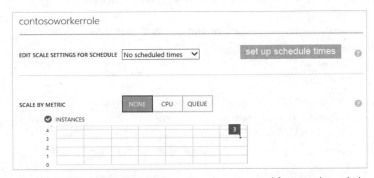

FIGURE 3-24 Scale By Metric in the management portal for a worker role in a cloud service

If you elect to scale by the CPU metric, additional settings will be available in the Management Portal, enabling you to set conditions for Autoscaling based on the CPU metric. These settings are as follows:

- **Instance Range** This is the minimum and maximum role instance count range. As Autoscale actions are applied to the role, Azure will not scale the number of running instances below or above this range.
- **Target CPU** The average CPU range across all instances for the role. Azure will scale instances up or down as needed to keep your cloud service operating within this CPU range.
- **Scale Up By** The number of instances you want Azure to scale up by when scaling up the number of running instances.

- **Scale Up Wait Time**   The number of minutes Azure will wait after scaling your role instance up before applying additional upward Autoscale actions.
- **Scale Down By**   The number of instances you want Azure to scale down by when scaling down the number of running instances.
- **Scale Down Wait Time**   The number of minutes Azure will wait after scaling your role instance down before applying additional downward Autoscale actions.

Figure 3-25 shows the CPU metric Autoscale settings in the Scale page of the management portal.

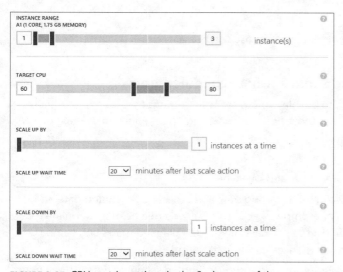

FIGURE 3-25 CPU metric settings in the Scale page of the management portal

If you elect to scale by Queue metric, additional options will be available in the Management Portal, enabling you to set conditions for Autoscaling based on the queue depth. These options are the same as the earlier options for the CPU metric with the exception that the Target CPU setting is replaced by queue-specific settings for Autoscale. The queue settings are as follows:

- **Account Or Namespace**   The name of the Azure Storage account or Service Bus namespace containing the queue you want to scale by.
- **Queue Name**   The name of the queue.
- **Target Per Machine**   The number of queue messages that a single role instance can handle. For example, if your queue averages 6,000 messages per hour and a single role instance is capable of processing 1,000 messages per hour, you would set this value to 1,000. In this example, Autoscale would scale your role instances up to 6 instances or the maximum number allowed in the Instance Range (whichever is lower).

Figure 3-26 shows the queue depth metric Autoscale settings in the Scale page of the management portal. Note that only the queue-specific settings are shown.

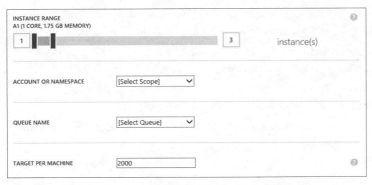

FIGURE 3-26 Queue depth metric settings in the Scale page of the management portal

Autoscale roles in a cloud service using scheduled times

The Autoscale feature in Azure also enables you to set scale settings based on one or more schedules that you define. You have three options for setting up schedule times that you can then configure Autoscale rules for. These options are:

- A recurring schedule for day and night.
- A recurring schedule for weekdays and weekends.
- Specific dates, where you can set a starting date and time, and an ending date and time for a specific event. For example, if your role is a web role hosting an online retail site, you may want to define a specific date range for a planned marketing campaign, where you can increase role instances during that period.

You can choose any combination of the options for setting up schedule times. When you do, you can configure Autoscale to set your role instance count using the schedule times you defined. Figure 3-27 shows the page in the management portal where you can set up your scheduled time for Autoscale.

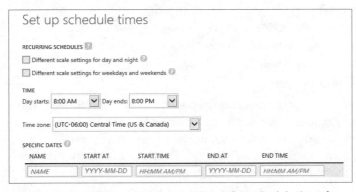

FIGURE 3-27 Page in management portal to define schedule times for use in Autoscale

Creating a Service Bus namespace

Azure Cloud Services that consist of multiple web roles often use some form of messaging to trigger events in a role or to exchange data between the roles. The messaging pattern can be implemented a variety of ways using a variety of services. One messaging service is the Microsoft Azure Service Bus, which offers rich features and messaging patterns such as queues, topics, event hubs, and notification hubs.

Create a Service Bus namespace using the management portal

To create a Service Bus namespace using the management portal, click the Service Bus tab in the left navigation of the management portal. This will open the Service Bus page and list any existing Service Bus namespaces. Use the Create button to create a new namespace, where you can select a name for the namespace, the region, and the type of namespace, as shown in Figure 3-28.

FIGURE 3-28 Adding a new Service Bus namespace using the management portal

Create a Service Bus namespace using Azure PowerShell

You can create a Service Bus namespace using the Azure PowerShell cmdlet New-AzureSBNamespace. This cmdlet does not specify the type for the namespace. Instead, when it creates the namespace, it creates it as a Mixed type. The Mixed type supports all the messaging patterns that Messaging and Notification Hubs support, but in a single namespace. The command as shown here creates a new Service Bus namespace named Contoso-mixed.

```
New-AzureSBNamespace -Name Contoso-Mixed -Location "West US"
```

When specifying the location for a new Service Bus namespace, you should first check to see which locations are available for the current subscription. You can do this by using the Get-AzureSBLocation command as shown here.

```
PS E:\Get-AzureSBLocation | Select Code

Code
--------
Central US
East US
East US 2
North Central US
South Central US
West US
North Europe
West Europe
East Asia
Southeast Asia
Brazil South
Japan East
Japan West
```

Thought experiment
Configure an In-Role Cache

In this thought experiment, apply what you've learned about this objective. You can find answers to these questions in the "Answers" section at the end of this chapter.

You are the IT Administrator for Contoso. You are responsible for managing Contoso's cloud services and virtual machines, which are deployed in a Virtual Network in Azure.

You need to configure one of the cloud services to handle demand fluctuations in a cost effective manner. The cloud service consists of a web role and a worker role. The web role is a public facing web site for Contoso's customers where they can purchase products, get support, and check on shipping and order status. The worker role is not publicly facing and is used for back end processing of orders that it receives from messages sent to an Azure Storage queue. The web role instance count of two is sufficiently handling the demand. However, the worker role routinely falls behind during the day and on weekends when product orders tend to increase. There is only one instance of the worker role. During testing, you determined that the worker role is capable of processing about 300 messages from the queue per hour. During the peak periods, you have observed that the web role adds messages to the queue at a rate of about 6,000 messages per hour.

1. How will you configure the cloud service to handle the workload?

2. Are there any concerns regarding the architecture or deployment that you need to take into consideration as you implement your solution?

Objective summary

- The ServiceConfiguration.Cloud.cscfg file contains configuration settings necessary for the cloud service to run in Azure. The ServiceConfiguration.Local.cscfg file contains configuration settings necessary to run the cloud service in the Azure Compute and Storage Emulators.

- Each role in a cloud service must have at least two role instances for the cloud service to get the 99.95 percent SLA.

- A cloud service in Azure has two environments; staging and production. The staging URL is *http(s)://<guid>.cloudapp.net*. The production URL is *http(s)://<service-name>.cloudapp.net*. To promote a cloud service from the staging environment to the production environment, you should perform a virtual IP (VIP) swap.

- Autoscale can be configured for a cloud service role using either a CPU metric or a queue depth metric. The Instance Range setting defines the minimum and maximum number of role instances that Azure will Autoscale up or down to.

- You can configure Autoscale based on scheduled times for specific day and night settings, weekday and weekend settings, and specific date range settings.

Objective review

Answer the following questions to test your knowledge of the information in this objective. You can find the answers to these questions and explanations of why each answer choice is correct or incorrect in the "Answers" section at the end of this chapter.

1. You need to deploy a new cloud service to Azure using the management portal. Which two files do you need to deploy the cloud service?

    A. Cloud service package (.cspkg)

    B. Cloud service definition (.csdef)

    C. Web.config

    D. Cloud service configuration file (.cscfg)

2. You need to create a Service Bus namespace to support queues and topics. Which type of namespace do you need to create? (Choose all that apply).

    A. Notification Hub

    B. Messaging

    C. Relay

    D. Mixed

3. You need to create a Service Bus namespace to support Notification Hubs. You need to be able to schedule push notifications and also configure Autoscale. Which tier should you choose?

   A. Free

   B. Basic

   C. Standard

   D. Multi-tenancy

Objective 3.3: Monitor Cloud Services

Monitoring is an important part of an application's lifecycle. The Azure platform and features for Cloud Services deliver the information you need to insure your Cloud Services are performing as expected. Monitoring for Cloud Services is very similar to monitoring virtual machines and websites. You can monitor performance counters and configure alerts just the same.

This objective goes beyond the monitoring of Cloud Services and addresses monitoring concepts of other messaging features in the platform that Cloud Services often depend on.

This objective covers how to:
- Monitor a cloud service
- Configure endpoint monitoring
- Monitor a Service Bus queue
- Monitor a Service Bus topic
- Monitor a Service Bus relay
- Monitor a Notification Hub
- Collect diagnostics data

Monitoring a cloud service

The management portal provides a rich user interface for monitoring important performance counter metrics for a cloud service. There are two levels of monitoring for a cloud service that controls how much data can be collected and analyzed. The available levels are minimal (which is the default) or verbose. You can select the level in the Configure page of the cloud service as shown in Figure 3-29. On this page you can also specify the number of retention days for the logs and the connection strings to an Azure storage count for each role in the cloud service.

EXAM TIP

Use a storage account to store monitoring logs that is separate from any storage accounts your cloud service may be using for normal application functions. Azure Storage accounts have scalability targets of 20,000 IOPS/second. So, depending on the level of logging and activity in your cloud service, using the same storage account for logging could exhaust this capacity and potentially have a negative impact on the normal business functions the cloud service performs for users. It may even be necessary to specify different storage accounts for each role to use for logging. Monitor the storage accounts your cloud service uses to insure you are operating within the scalability targets.

FIGURE 3-29 Monitoring section of cloud service Configure page in the management portal

You can view the performance counter metrics in the management portal on the Monitor page for the cloud service. By default, an aggregate of the CPU percentage for each role in the cloud service is displayed in the graph, as shown in Figure 3-30.

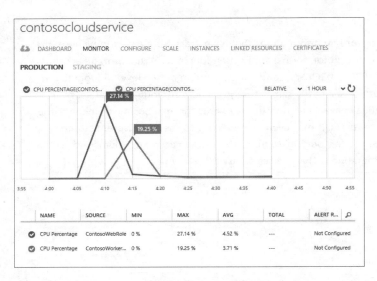

FIGURE 3-30 Monitor page in the management portal for a cloud service with a web role and worker role

At the bottom of the page are options to add or remove other metrics that you may want to monitor. For any of the metrics, you can choose to monitor an aggregate value, which is the value across all role instances for a role, or you can get more granular and look at specific role instance metrics. The metrics available for monitoring will vary depending on your monitoring level (minimal or verbose). With minimal monitoring configured, the available metrics are as follows:

- CPU Percentage
- Disk Read Bytes/Second
- Disk Write Bytes/Second
- Network In
- Network Out

With verbose monitoring configured, additional metrics are available as follows:

- ASP.NET Application Errors Total/Second
- ASP.NET Application Requests/Second
- ASP.NET Requests Queued
- ASP.NET Requests Redetected
- Memory Available
- Web Service Bytes Total/Second
- Web Service IASAPI Extension Requests/Second

Just as with other compute options in the Azure platform, Cloud Services offer the feature to define alerts that can be triggered based on some condition or metric value. To define an alert, in the Monitor page highlight the metric you want to define an alert for and then click the Add Rule button at the bottom of the page. This will give you a dialog to set the conditions for the alert and the action to take. Figure 3-31 shows the dialog configuring an alert if the aggregate CPU sustains an average value of 75 percent or more.

FIGURE 3-31 Dialog in Azure port to configure an alert based on the CPU percentage metric

---

MORE INFO   **MONITORING SOLUTIONS FOR CLOUD SERVICES**

New Relic is a popular third-party monitoring solution that is available directly through the Azure Store with special pricing for Azure users. This tool primarily targets developers because it provides deeper insight into the application's code. It uses an agent that is compiled with the cloud service code and as a result is able to provide more monitoring and diagnostic data than you can get in the Monitor page of the management portal. More information about New Relic can be found at *http://azure.microsoft.com/en-us/documentation/articles/store-new-relic-cloud-services-dotnet-application-performance-management/*.

Configuring endpoint monitoring

Endpoint monitoring is a feature that monitors your cloud service from external geo-distributed locations. If endpoint monitoring is configured, Azure will invoke HTTP requests to specified endpoints of your cloud service from up to three locations around the world. If the response returns an HTTP 200 (OK) and the response is received within 30 seconds, the endpoint is considered healthy. If the endpoint response is an HTTP 400 or higher, or the response takes more than 30 seconds, the endpoint is considered unhealthy.

Endpoint monitoring gives you the capability to monitor your cloud service from locations closest to your customers or from locations that are strategic to the business.

You can configure endpoint monitoring in the Monitor page for a cloud service, as shown in Figure 3-32, where you must define the following properties:

- The name you want to use to for the endpoint being monitored. This can be any name you choose.
- The URL of the endpoint you want Azure to issue HTTP requests against.
- The geo-distributed locations you want Azure to issue the HTTP requests from.

FIGURE 3-32 Endpoint monitoring in the Configure page of the management portal

It is a best practice for the cloud service to have a health check page that checks for the availability of other resources it depends on, such as database, web services, storage accounts, etc. Then, when configuring endpoint monitoring, specify the URL for the health check page. This is more effective in monitoring the health of a service than just invoking the default URL of the cloud service.

Monitoring a Service Bus queue

Monitoring of a Service Bus queue using the management portal is possible by opening the Dashboard page of the queue you want to monitor. To get to the Dashboard page, click the Service Bus namespace that contains the queue and then click the Queues tab at the top of the page to list the queues in the namespace. Next, click the name of the queue to open the dashboard. Figure 3-33 shows the Dashboard page for a Contoso-orders queue.

FIGURE 3-33 Dashboard page in management portal used to monitor a Service Bus queue

You can add metrics to the graph by clicking the More control directly above the graph. The metrics available for monitoring Service Bus queues are as follows:

- Incoming Messages
- Internal Server Errors
- Length
- Server Busy Errors
- Outgoing Messages
- Failed Requests
- Size
- Successful Requests
- Other Errors
- Total Requests

Monitoring a Service Bus topic

Monitoring of a Service Bus topic using the management portal is possible by opening the Monitor page for the topic you want to monitor. To get to the Monitor page, click the Service Bus namespace that contains the topic, and then click the Topics tab at the top of the page to list the topics in the namespace. Next, click the name of the topic, and then click the Monitor tab at the top of the page to open the dashboard. Figure 3-34 shows the Dashboard page for a Contoso-news queue.

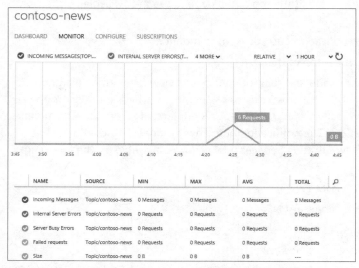

FIGURE 3-34 Monitor page in management portal used to monitor a Service Bus topic

You can add metrics to the graph by clicking the Add Metrics button at the bottom of the Monitor page. The metrics available for monitoring Service Bus topics are the same as for queues.

Monitoring a Service Bus relay

Monitoring a Service Bus relay using the management portal is only possible after a relay has been created using the Service Bus API's. The Service Bus relay is not something you can create and manage in Azure. Instead, it is created by an on-premises web service such as a Windows Communication Foundation (WCF) service that has delegated listening for incoming requests to the Azure Service Bus. This is particularly useful in hybrid scenarios where an existing on-premises web service needs to be accessed from cloud applications. By using the Service Bus relay, the on-premises web service can be securely accessed by clients without having to configure firewall rules or make network configuration changes in the on-premises environment.

The transient nature of Service Bus relays makes monitoring them less prescriptive. Assuming the existence of one or more relays, you can monitor them using the management portal by clicking on the Service Bus namespace that the on-premises application is configured to register the relay in. At the top of the page, click on the relays tab. For each relay present, you can monitor the name of the application that created the relay, the type of relay (HTTP or TCP), and the number of listeners connected to the relay.

Monitoring a Notification Hub

Monitoring a Notification Hub using the management portal is possible by opening the Monitor page for the notification hub you want to monitor using the following steps:

1. Click on the Service Bus namespace that contains the notification hub you want to monitor.

2. Click the Notifications Hub tab at the top of the page to see the available notification hubs.

3. Click the name of the notification hub you want to monitor.

4. Click the Monitor tab at the top of the page.

On the Monitor page you can add and remove metrics and view the metrics in a graph. The metrics for notification hubs include two classes of operations, which are *API calls* and *Notification outcomes*. The API call metrics includes, but is not limited to, create, read, update and delete operations for devices. The notification outcomes includes metrics relating to pushes made to the Platform Notification Services (PNS) and are available for the following platforms:

- Windows Notification Service (WNS)
- Apple Push Notification Service (APNS)
- Google Cloud Messaging (GCM)
- Microsoft Push Notification Service (MPNS)

The number of metrics available is extensive and varies by platform. A full list of metrics that can be monitored is available at *http://msdn.microsoft.com/en-us/library/azure/dn458822.aspx*.

Collecting diagnostics data

You can configure Azure cloud service roles during development to collect telemetry data that can help troubleshoot problems or monitor for performance trends. The configuration of which data to collect is stored in an XML file called Diagnostics.wadcfg and exists for each role in the cloud service, allowing you to have different logging settings for each role. The diagnostics configuration is packaged into the cloud service package (.cspkg) during packaging and deployed into an Azure Storage blob container named Wad-control-container. Application diagnostics code will look in this container to retrieve the diagnostics configuration for the role.

The diagnostics data configured to be collected is stored in an Azure storage account. The type of data that can be collected is shown here:

- IIS HTTP logs
- IIS failed requests logs
- Azure diagnostic infrastructure logs
- Windows event logs
- Performance counters
- Crash dumps
- Custom error logs
- ETW events

Listing 3-12 shows configuration in a Diagnostics.wadcfg file to collect all available telemetry data.

LISTING 3-12 Diagnostics configuration file

```xml
<?xml version="1.0" encoding="utf-8"?>
<DiagnosticMonitorConfiguration configurationChangePollInterval="PT1M"
overallQuotaInMB="4096" xmlns="http://schemas.microsoft.com/ServiceHosting/2010/10/
DiagnosticsConfiguration">
  <DiagnosticInfrastructureLogs />
  <Directories>
    <IISLogs container="wad-iis-logfiles" directoryQuotaInMB="1024" />
    <CrashDumps container="wad-crash-dumps" />
  </Directories>

  <Logs bufferQuotaInMB="1024" scheduledTransferPeriod="PT1M"
scheduledTransferLogLevelFilter="Verbose" />
  <WindowsEventLog bufferQuotaInMB="1024" scheduledTransferPeriod="PT1M"
scheduledTransferLogLevelFilter="Verbose">
    <DataSource name="Application!*" />
  </WindowsEventLog>
  <PerformanceCounters bufferQuotaInMB="512" scheduledTransferPeriod="PT0M">
    <PerformanceCounterConfiguration counterSpecifier="\Memory\Available MBytes"
sampleRate="PT3M" />
    <PerformanceCounterConfiguration counterSpecifier="\Web Service(_Total)\ISAPI
Extension Requests/sec" sampleRate="PT3M" />
```

```
        <PerformanceCounterConfiguration counterSpecifier="\Web Service(_Total)\Bytes Total/
Sec" sampleRate="PT3M" />
        <PerformanceCounterConfiguration counterSpecifier="\ASP.NET Applications(__Total__)\
Requests/Sec" sampleRate="PT3M" />
        <PerformanceCounterConfiguration counterSpecifier="\ASP.NET Applications(__Total__)\
Errors Total/Sec" sampleRate="PT3M" />
        <PerformanceCounterConfiguration counterSpecifier="\ASP.NET\Requests Queued"
sampleRate="PT3M" />
        <PerformanceCounterConfiguration counterSpecifier="\ASP.NET\Requests Rejected"
sampleRate="PT3M" />
      </PerformanceCounters>
</DiagnosticMonitorConfiguration>
```

It is a good practice to use a separate storage account for logging diagnostics data than what your cloud service uses for other purposes. For example, your cloud service may use Azure Storage queues to communicate between roles or blobs to store document files the application uses. Using a separate storage account for logging helps insure your application's performance is not affected due to storage account scalability targets being exceeded.

Thought experiment
Monitoring Cloud Services and Service Bus namespaces

In this thought experiment, apply what you've learned about this objective. You can find answers to these questions in the "Answers" section at the end of this chapter.

You are the IT Administrator for Contoso. You are responsible for monitoring Contoso's Cloud Services and Service Bus namespaces used by the Cloud Services. Users have been complaining that order summary reports generated by one of the worker roles are taking much longer than normal. The worker role retrieves messages from a Service Bus queue, generates a report for the user, stores it in blob storage, and then sends an email notification to the user when the report is ready for them to access. You have observed that shortly after users reported the performance issue, errors are logged that suggests the worker role is running out of memory.

You need to implement a monitoring strategy and diagnostics strategy to help diagnose this issue.

1. What kind of monitoring and logging can you implement to help identify this problem before users do?

2. What kind of data could you collect that would help determine the root cause?

Objective summary

- Cloud service monitoring can be set to minimal (the default value) or to verbose.
- Use endpoint monitoring to monitor your cloud service from up to three geo-distributed locations.
- Service Bus queues do not have a Monitor page in the management portal. The monitoring experience for queues is limited to the Dashboard page and the metrics it makes available.
- Cloud service diagnostics are configured in the Diagnostics.wadcfg file for each role in the cloud service and are stored in the wad-control-container in Azure blob storage for the role to reference at runtime.
- Performance counter data collected for a cloud service is stored in an Azure Storage Table named WADPerformanceCountersTable.
- Event log data collected for a cloud service is stored in an Azure Storage Table named WADWindowsEventLogsTable.

Objective review

Answer the following questions to test your knowledge of the information in this objective. You can find the answers to these questions and explanations of why each answer choice is correct or incorrect in the "Answers" section at the end of this chapter.

1. You need to monitor the queue depth of a Service Bus queue. Which metric can you add to the graph on the Dashboard page for the queue to monitor queue depth?

   A. Incoming Messages

   B. Length

   C. Total Requests

   D. Size

2. You need to collect IIS HTTP logs for a web role. Which file will you use to configure diagnostics data?

   A. Cloud service configuration file

   B. Cloud service definition file

   C. Web.config

   D. Diagnostics.wadcfg

3. You need to monitor the CPU percentage metric for a web role and the available memory metric for a worker role in a cloud service. You need the log files for each web role stored in separate storage accounts. Which two monitoring settings should you configure?

   A. Level

   B. Retention

   C. Diagnostic connection strings

   D. Endpoints

Answers

This section contains the solutions to the thought experiments and answers to the objective review questions in this chapter.

Objective 3.1: Thought experiment

1. The settings you will be adding will be part of a Named Cache and the cloud service using the cache will reference it by name. Therefore, you will need to know the name that the development team is planning to use so you can name the cache correctly. You should also ask the development group whether or not high availability is required.

2. Based on the information provided and the additional information collected, you would configure the cache settings as follows:

   A. **Name**   Set to the name given to you by the development team.

   B. **High availability**   Enabled if needed; otherwise disabled.

   C. **Notifications**   Disabled.

   D. **Eviction policy**   Least recently used (LRU).

   E. **Expiration type**   Sliding Window.

   F. **Time to live**   20.

3. Testing should be done to determine the resources needed to support the changes. Information such as the number of items that will be stored in the cache, the size of the items, and bandwidth used are all things that should be taken into consideration. Using the capacity planning guide spreadsheet will help insure your cache can handle the additional load.

Objective 3.1: Review

4. **Correct answers:** B, D

   A. **Incorrect:** The Managed Cache is a caching service that is managed by Microsoft.

   B. **Correct:** A co-located cache is a valid topology for an In-Role Cache. In this topology, the cache uses the resources of the virtual machines hosting a web or worker role.

   C. **Incorrect:** The Redis Cache is the latest caching service that is managed by Microsoft.

   D. **Correct:** A dedicated cache is a valid topology for an In-Role Cache. In this topology, the cache is hosted on dedicated worker role instances and uses all the virtual machine resources.

5. **Correct answer:** C

   A. **Incorrect:** The osFamily is the property in the <ServiceConfiguration> element that identifies which Windows operating system to use, such as Windows Server 2008 SP2, Windows Server 2008 R2, Windows Server 2012, or Windows Server 2012 R2.

   B. **Incorrect:** The <ConfigurationSettings> element is where role-specific settings are defined, such as the connection string for a storage account the role may depend on.

   C. **Correct:** The osVersion is the property in the <ServiceConfiguration> element that identifies a specific version of operating system to use. You can use the Azure PowerShell cmdlet Get-AzureOSVersion to see the available operating system versions.

   D. **Incorrect:** The <Instances> element is a role-specific setting that indicates how many instances of that role must be created when the service is deployed.

6. **Correct answer:** B

   A. **Incorrect:** The New-AzureServiceRemoteDesktopExtensionConfig cmdlet creates a new RDP extension configuration object, but does not enable it.

   B. **Correct:** The Set-AzureServiceRemoteDesktopExtension cmdlet enables RDP access for the cloud service and optionally, a specific role in the cloud service.

   C. **Incorrect:** The Get-AzureRemoteDesktopFile cmdlet retrieves the .RDP file for a virtual machine to connect to.

   D. **Incorrect:** The Enable-AzureServiceProjectRemoteDesktop cmdlet enables RDP access for a cloud service *project* by adding the settings to the cloud service definition (.csdef) file. The project must be published using the Publish-AzureServiceProject cmdlet for the change to be applied to a running service in Azure.

7. **Correct answer:** A

   A. **Correct:** The Add-AzureCertificate cmdlet should be used to upload the certificate to Azure.

   B. **Incorrect:** The New-AzureCertificateSetting cmdlet creates a setting object used to insert an existing certificate into a new Azure Virtual Machine.

   C. **Incorrect:** The Set-AzureDeployment command is used to set the status, upgrade mode, and configuration settings for an Azure cloud service deployment.

   D. **Incorrect:** The Get-AzureCertificate cmdlet is used to retrieve an existing certificate object from an Azure cloud service.

8. **Correct answers:** A, B, and D

   A. **Correct:** Use the New-AzureReservedIP cmdlet first to reserve an IP address in the region you plan to deploy to cloud service to.

   B. **Correct:** Adding the <NetworkConfiguration> section to the cloud service configuration file and identifying the reserved IP address by name is required to configure the cloud service for the reserved IP address.

   C. **Incorrect:** It is not required to delete any existing cloud service deployments. You can re-deploy the cloud service to use the reserved IP address.

   D. **Correct:** Re-deploying the cloud service with the updated cloud service configuration to the same region the IP address was reserved in is the final step in completing the task.

9. **Correct answer:** B

   A. **Incorrect:** The <ServiceDefinition> element is the root element in the cloud service definition file. However, it is not the XML element that defines network traffic rules.

   B. **Correct:** The <NetworkTrafficRules> element is used to define communication patterns between roles.

   C. **Incorrect:** The <InternalEndpoint> element is used to define an internal endpoint within a <WebRole> or <WorkerRole> element.

   D. **Incorrect:** The <InputEndpoint> element is used to define an external input endpoint within a <WebRole> or <WorkerRole> element.

10. **Correct answer:** A

    A. **Correct:** The <LocalStorage> element is used to define the name, sizeInMB, and cleanOnRecycle properties for the local storage resource.

    B. **Incorrect:** The <LocalResources> element contains a collection of <LocalStorage> elements.

    C. **Incorrect:** The <WebRole> element defines other properties and settings for the web role and the <LocalStorage> and <LocalResources> are defined within the <WebRole> element, but this is not where the properties for local storage are defined.

    D. **Incorrect:** The <Destinations> element contains <RoleEndpoints> which are used to define network traffic rules.

11. **Correct answer:** D

    A. **Incorrect:** The Large instance size does not meet the memory requirement.

    B. **Incorrect:** The ExtraLarge instance size does not meet the memory requirement.

    C. **Incorrect:** The Standard_D13 instance size does meet all the requirements but is not the most cost effective.

    D. **Correct:** The A7 meets all the requirements and is the most cost effective.

Objective 3.2: Thought experiment

1. You should configure Autoscale for the worker role so that it can scale to meet the demand. Since the workload of the worker role is determined by messages in the queue, you should configure Autoscale using the queue depth metric. The worker role is capable of processing about 300 messages per hour so you should set the Target Per Machine setting to 300. The Instance Range should be set to a minimum of 1 and a maximum of 20 based on the data you have. This should handle the peak load of 6,000 messages per hour being added to the queue by the web role.

2. Because the cloud service is deployed into a Virtual Network, you need to insure that that the subnet the cloud service is deployed in has the address space capacity for the additional role instances that will potentially be added as a result of your Autoscale configuration. You should also verify that your Azure subscription has the core capacity to handle the number of instances your worker role will be scaled to. If it is not sufficient, then you will need to contact Microsoft Support to have your core capacity increased. Finally, your business owner will probably ask for a cost analysis or estimate of how much your solution will end up costing. You can estimate the amount of the increase based on the information you have about when peak times occur and by using the Azure pricing calculator at *http://azure.microsoft.com/en-us/pricing/calculator/*.

Objective 3.2: Review

1. **Correct answers:** A, D

   A. **Correct:** The cloud service package file (.cspkg) contains the roles that make up the cloud service.

   B. **Incorrect:** The cloud service definition file (.csdef) is used during the development of the cloud service to define the roles, virtual machine sizes, endpoints and other settings for the role.

   C. **Incorrect:** The Web.config file is a configuration file used by a web role or worker role. It is included as part of the cloud service package for each role in the cloud service.

   D. **Correct:** The cloud service configuration file (.cscfg) contains the configuration for the cloud service.

2. **Correct answers:** B, D

   A. **Incorrect:** The Notification Hub Service Bus namespace supports Notification Hubs.

   B. **Correct:** The Messaging Service Bus support queues, topics, and relays.

   C. **Incorrect:** Relay is not a Service Bus type. However, it is a messaging pattern that is supported by the Messaging and Mixed Service Bus type.

   D. **Correct:** The Mixed Service Bus supports queues, topics, relays, and Notification Hubs.

3. **Correct answer:** C
   A. **Incorrect:** The Free tier does not support Autoscale or the ability to schedule push notifications.
   B. **Incorrect:** The Basic tier supports Autoscale, but it does not support the ability to schedule push notifications.
   C. **Correct:** The Standard tier supports all Notification Hub features. It is the highest tier.
   D. **Incorrect:** Multi-tenancy is a feature available in the Standard tier.

4. **Correct answers:** A, D
   A. **Correct:** The cloud service configuration (.cscfg) contains the configuration needed for the cloud service package (.cspkg).
   B. **Incorrect:** A Web.config file is a configuration file for a web role or worker role and will be included in the cloud service package (.cspkg).
   C. **Incorrect:** The cloud service definition contains configuration used to create the cloud service package (.cspkg)
   D. **Correct:** The cloud service package (.cspkg) contains the files and binaries for the cloud service roles.

Objective 3.3: Thought experiment

1. Set the monitoring level to verbose so you can monitor the aggregate available memory metric for the worker role. Define an alert based on this metric to email you when the available memory falls below a reasonable threshold for an extended period of time. You may want to collaborate with the application developers to understand what a reasonable threshold value should be if you don't already have the data. You may also want to add the Length metric to your monitor to see if the queue depth is increasing as the problem reoccurs.

2. Because you have strong evidence this is a memory-related issue, you should generate a few dump files every 3-5 minutes after you see the problem starting to occur. It is extremely useful to have 2-3 dump files in over a period of 10-15 minutes when debugging memory issues.

Objective 3.3: Review

1. **Correct answer:** B
   A. **Incorrect:** The incoming messages metric indicates the rate at which message are being added to the queue.
   B. **Correct:** The length metric indicates how many messages are in the queue.
   C. **Incorrect:** The total requests metric indicates the number of requests to retrieve messages from the queue.
   D. **Incorrect:** The size metric indicates the total size of all the messages in the queue.

2. **Correct answer:** D

   A. **Incorrect:** The cloud service configuration file does not contain configuration data. It is used to configure things such as the role instance count for roles, osFamily, and osVersion.

   B. **Incorrect:** The cloud service definition file defines the service model for the cloud service.

   C. **Incorrect:** The Web.config file may have some diagnostics settings specific to the application, but it won't have the configuration needed to collect IIS logs for all the role instances for the role.

   D. **Correct:** The Diagnostics.wadcfg contains the necessary configuration settings to capture IIS logs for all role instances.

3. **Correct answers:** A, C

   A. **Correct:** The Level should be set to verbose. Otherwise, you won't be able to add the available memory metric.

   B. **Incorrect:** The Retention setting specifies the number of days logs should be retained.

   C. **Correct:** The Diagnostic connection strings setting should be set so that each role is logging to a separate storage account.

   D. **Incorrect:** The Endpoints setting is used to configure endpoint monitoring from geo-distributed locations.

CHAPTER 4

Implement storage

Implementing storage is one of the most important aspects of building or deploying a new solution using Microsoft Azure. There are several services and features available for use, and each has their own place. Microsoft Azure Storage is the underlying storage for most of the services in Azure. It provides service for storage and retrieval of files and also has services that are available for storing large volumes of data through tables, and a fast reliable messaging service for application developers with queues.

Microsoft Azure SQL Database is another option for storage of relational data. Azure SQL Database allows for easily deploying databases that use the familiar T-SQL language used by SQL Server in an environment with near-zero management overhead.

Microsoft Azure Recovery Services encompasses both Azure Site Recovery and Azure Backup. Azure Site Recovery allows you to protect on-premises servers and clouds by failing over to another physical data center or to virtual machines in Azure. Azure Backup allows you to easily configure data to be protected in the cloud by backing up files and folders to a backup vault stored in Azure.

Objectives in this chapter:

- Objective 4.1: Implement blobs and Azure files
- Objective 4.2: Manage access
- Objective 4.3: Configure diagnostics, monitoring, and analytics
- Objective 4.4: Implement SQL databases
- Objective 4.5: Implement recovery services

Objective 4.1: Implement blobs and Azure files

Azure Storage accounts expose two endpoints to allow file access. The first endpoint is for blob storage. This allows application developers and tools that use the Azure Storage API to store files directly in storage. The second endpoint, Azure files, allows for file access through the Server Message Block (SMB) protocol. This allows you to access files in an Azure Storage account as you would a traditional file share through a mapped drive.

Managing blob storage

Azure blob storage is a service for storing unstructured data such as text files, videos, or as we saw in Chapter 2, virtual hard disk files for virtual machines. A storage account exposes multiple endpoints, one for each of the services it exposes:

- *https://[account name].blob.core.windows.net* (blob)
- *https://[account name].table.core.windows.net* (table)
- *https://[account name].queue.core.windows.net* (queue)
- *https://[account name].file.core.windows.net* (file)

> **NOTE SSL JUST WORKS**
>
> **Each Azure storage endpoint can be accessed via HTTP or HTTPS (SSL) by default. No additional configuration is needed to access blobs through the HTTPS endpoint.**

Figure 4-1 shows some of the concepts of a storage account. Each blob storage account can have one or more containers. Containers are similar in concept to a folder on your computer, in that they are used to group blobs within a storage account. There can be a container at the base of the storage account, appropriately named root, and there can be containers one level down from the root container.

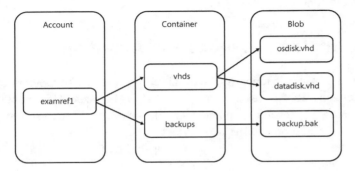

FIGURE 4-1 Azure Storage account entities and hierarchy relationships

The blob service in Azure Storage is based on a flat storage scheme. This means that creating a container one level below the root is the only true level of container. However, you can specify a delimiter as part of the blob name to create your own virtual hierarchy. For example, you could create a blob named /January/Reports.txt and /February/Reports. txt, and filter based on /January or /February in most tools that support Azure Storage. Most third-party storage tools allow you to create folders within a container, but they are actually being clever with the name of the blob itself.

You can create a container through the Microsoft Azure management portal, third-party storage tools, or through the Azure PowerShell cmdlets. To create a container in the Azure management portal, open the storage account by clicking Browse, Storage Accounts, and then the name of your storage account. Within the storage account blade, click the Containers tile, and then click Add, as shown in Figure 4-2. Figure 4-2 also shows the access types that can be set for the container.

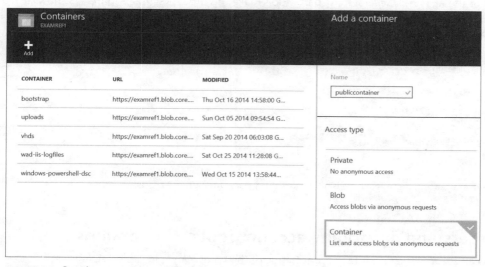

FIGURE 4-2 Creating a container using the Azure management portal

To create a container using the Azure PowerShell cmdlets, use the New-AzureStorageContainer cmdlet, as shown in the following example. To specify the Private access type, specify the value Off to the Permission parameter. The other access types Blob and Container are the same with PowerShell.

```
New-AzureStorageContainer -Name "newcontainer" `
                -Permission Off
```

To create a container at the root of the storage account, specify the special name $root for the container name. This allows you to store blobs in the root of the storage account and reference them via URLs such as *https://[account name].blob.core.windows.net/fileinroot.txt*.

Blobs come in two types:

- **Page blobs**   A collection of 512-byte pages optimized for random read and write operations. The maximum size for a page blob is 1 TB. Virtual machine hard disks are created as page blobs.

- **Block blobs**   Designed for efficient uploading. Block blobs are comprised of blocks that can be written to and committed as a set. The maximum size for a block blob is 200 GB. They are used for files such as videos, images, and text.

Setting metadata with storage

Within Azure Storage, blobs and containers support setting additional metadata properties for both system and user purposes. For instance, a system purpose would be the last modified date of an object, where a user-defined metadata property may be storing the name or IP address of the server that stored the blob for later lookup.

You can set and retrieve the metadata on both containers and blobs through the Azure SDK or the REST API. Several third-party tools make this process simple. Figure 4-3 shows using the third-party tool CloudXplorer to add a custom metadata property named Author with a value of Michael Washam.

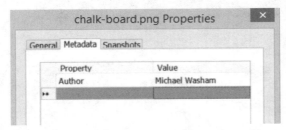

FIGURE 4-3 Setting metadata on a blob using a third-party tool, CloudXplorer

Understanding storage account replication options

You can set an Azure Storage account to one of the types shown in Table 4-1.

TABLE 4-1 Storage account types and their descriptions

Account Type	Description
Standard_LRS (Locally redundant storage)	Makes three synchronous copies of your data within a single datacenter.
Standard_ZRS (Zone redundant storage)	Stores three copies of data across multiple datacenters within or across regions. For block blobs only.
Standard_GRS (Geographically redundant storage)	Same as LRS (three copies local), plus three additional asynchronous copies to a second datacenter hundreds of miles away.
Standard_RAGRS (Read-access geographically redundant storage)	Same capabilities as GRS, plus you have read access to the data in the secondary datacenter.

You can set the type for a storage account through the management portal by clicking the Pricing Tier tile. The tile is available during creation of a storage account by clicking New, Everything, and then Create, and then selecting the tier, as shown in Figure 4-4. You can change the tier later by opening the storage account in the management portal and clicking the Pricing Tier tile.

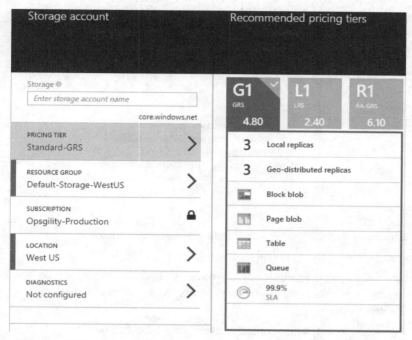

FIGURE 4-4 Setting the pricing tier of a storage account in the management portal

To set the value using the Azure PowerShell cmdlets, use the Type parameter of New-AzureStorageAccount (at creation) or the Set-AzureStorageAccount cmdlets (after creation), as shown in the following example.

```
$accountName = "[storage account name]"
$location    = "West US"
$type        = "Standard_LRS"
New-AzureStorageAccount -StorageAccountName $accountName `
                        -Location $location `
                        -Type $type

$type        = "Standard_RAGRS"
Set-AzureStorageAccount -StorageAccountName $accountName `
                        -Type $type
```

> **NOTE** **STANDARD_ZRS AND BLOCK BLOBS**
>
> You cannot change the Standard ZRS (zone replicated) to any other storage account type and vice versa. Zone replicated storage accounts only support block blobs.

Using the async blob copy service

The async blob copy service is a server side based service that can copy files you specify from a source location to a destination in an Azure Storage account. The source blob can be located in another Azure Storage account, or it can even be outside of Azure as long as the storage service can access the blob directly for it to copy.

To initiate a blob copy, use the Start-AzureStorageBlobCopy cmdlet. This cmdlet accepts either the source URI (if it is external), or as the example below shows, the blob name, container, and storage context to access the source blob in an Azure Storage account. The destination requires the container name, blob name, and a storage context for the destination storage account.

```
$blobCopyState = Start-AzureStorageBlobCopy  -SrcBlob $vhdName `
                                             -SrcContainer $srcContainer `
                                             -Context $srcContext `
                                             -DestContainer $destContainer `
                                             -DestBlob $vhdName `
                                             -DestContext $destContext
```

Let's review the parameters in the preceding example:

- The SrcBlob parameter expects the file name of source file to start copying.

- The SrcContainer parameter is the container the source file resides in.

- The Context parameter accepts a context object created by the New-AzureStorageContext cmdlet. The context has the storage account name and key for the source storage account and is used for authentication.

- The DestContainer is the destination container to copy the blob to. The call will fail if this container does not exist on the destination storage account.

- The DestBlob parameter is the filename of the blob on the destination storage account. The destination blob name does not have to be the same as the source.

- The DestContext parameter also accepts a context object created with the details of the destination storage account including the authentication key.

> **NOTE** **MULTIPLE SUBSCRIPTIONS REQUIRES A CALL TO SELECT-AZURESUBSCRIPTION**
>
> To copy between storage accounts in separate subscriptions, you need to call Select-AzureSubscription between the calls to Get-AzureStorageKey to switch to the alternate subscription.

Here is a complete example of how to use the Start-AzureStorageBlob copy cmdlet to copy a blob between two storage accounts.

```
$vhdName = "[file name]"
$srcContainer = "[source container]"
$destContainer = "[destination container]"
$srcStorageAccount = "[source storage]"
$destStorageAccount = "[dest storage]"
```

```
$srcStorageKey = (Get-AzureStorageKey -StorageAccountName $srcStorageAccount).Primary

$destStorageKey = (Get-AzureStorageKey -StorageAccountName $destStorageAccount).Primary

$srcContext = New-AzureStorageContext -StorageAccountName $srcStorageAccount `
                            -StorageAccountKey $srcStorageKey

$destContext = New-AzureStorageContext -StorageAccountName $destStorageAccount `
                            -StorageAccountKey $destStorageKey

New-AzureStorageContainer -Name $destContainer `
                    -Context $destContext

$copiedBlob = Start-AzureStorageBlobCopy -SrcBlob $vhdName `
                            -SrcContainer $srcContainer `
                            -Context $srcContext `
                            -DestContainer $destContainer `
                            -DestBlob $vhdName `
                            -DestContext $destContext
```

There are several cmdlets, in this example, to discuss further. The Get-AzureStorageKey cmdlet accepts the name of a storage account, and the return value contains the storage account's primary and secondary authentication keys. These values are passed to the New-AzureStorageContext cmdlet, along with the storage account name, and the context object is created. The New-AzureStorageContainer cmdlet is used to create the storage container on the destination storage account. The cmdlet is passed the destination storage account's context object ($destContext) for authentication.

The final call in the example is the call to Start-AzureStorageBlobCopy. To initiate the copy this cmdlet uses the source (Context) and destination context objects (DestContext) for authentication. The return value is a reference to the new blob object on the destination storage account.

The return value of Get-AzureStorageBlobCopyState contains the CopyId, Status, Source, BytesCopied, CompletionTime, StatusDescription, and TotalBytes properties, as shown in Figure 4-5. Use these properties to write logic to monitor the status of the copy operation.

```
$copiedBlob | Get-AzureStorageBlobCopyState
```

```
PS C:\> $copiedBlob | Get-AzureStorageBlobCopyState

CopyId            : b0f359a2-c052-45e6-8471-a882666ca8e9
CompletionTime    :
Status            : Pending
Source            : https://examref1.blob.core.windows.net/uploads/mydatadisk.vhd?sv=2014-02-14&sr=b&sig=kQI5k
                    p982%2FzkjpMMTKnZiIom84qotJdiLK8Tn6xmOmY%3D&se=2014-12-09T16:20:10Z&sp=r
BytesCopied       : 786432000
TotalBytes        : 136367309312
StatusDescription :
```

FIGURE 4-5 Using Get-AzureStorageBlobCopyState to view the status of a blob copy

Configuring, and using, Azure files

The Microsoft Azure file service offers the ability to create file shares (up to 5 TB) that use the SMB version 2.1 protocol directly in an Azure Storage account. The shares can be accessed by both Azure Virtual Machines and Azure Cloud Services using regular file share methods, such as a mapped drive or file I/O APIs and commands. Figure 4-6 shows the hierarchy of files stored in Azure files.

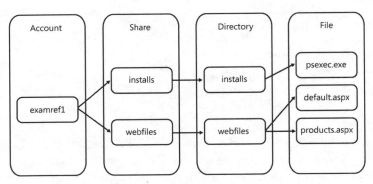

FIGURE 4-6 Azure files entities and relationship hierarchy

There are several common use cases for using Azure files. A few examples include the following:

- Migration of existing applications that require a file share for storage.
- Shared storage of files such as web content, log files, application configuration files, or even installation media.

To create a new file share using the management portal, open the blade for a storage account, click the File Shares tile, and then click Add, as shown in Figure 4-7.

FIGURE 4-7 Adding a new share with Azure files

To create a share using the Azure PowerShell cmdlets, use the following code.

```
$storageAccount = "[storage account name]"
$shareName = "contosoweb"
$storageKey = (Get-AzureStorageKey -StorageAccountName $storageAccount).Primary
```

```
$ctx = New-AzureStorageContext -StorageAccountName $storageAccount `
                              -StorageAccountKey $storageKey
New-AzureStorageShare -Name $shareName -Context $ctx
```

To access a share created in Azure files, you should store the storage account name and key using the Cmdkey.exe utility. This allows you to associate the credentials with the URI to the Azure files share. The syntax for using Cmdkey.exe is shown in the following example.

```
cmdkey.exe /add:[storage account name].file.core.windows.net /user:[storage account
name] /pass:[storage account key]
```

After the credentials are stored, use the net use command to map a drive to the file share, as shown in the following example.

```
net use z: \\examref1.file.core.windows.net\contosoweb
```

> **NOTE AZURE FILES IN PREVIEW**
>
> As of this writing, Azure files is in preview. You can expect many of the features for Azure files described in this book to change.

Using the Import and Export service

The Azure Import and Export service for storage allows you to ship data into or out of an Azure Storage account by physically shipping disks to an Azure datacenter. This service is ideal when it is either not possible or prohibitively expensive to upload or download the data directly.

The first step to import data using the service is to identify the data to import and the physical disk requirements. Each physical disk used must be a 3.5-inch SATA II or III that is no larger than 4 TB. Create a volume for data that is formatted with NTFS for importing data.

The second step is to prepare your drives using the Microsoft Azure Import/Export tool (WAImportExport.exe). This tool is a standalone install downloadable from *http://www.microsoft.com/en-us/download/details.aspx?id=42659*.

To prepare the drive for import, first ensure the source computer has BitLocker enabled so that the data can be encrypted as it is added to the disk. The first session, when preparing the drive, requires several parameters, such as the destination storage account key, the BitLocker key, and the log directory. The following example shows the syntax of using the WAImportExport.exe utility with the PrepImport parameter to prepare the disk for an import job for the first session.

```
WAImportExport PrepImport /sk:<StorageAccountKey> /t: <TargetDriveLetter>
[/format] [/silentmode] [/encrypt] [/bk:<BitLockerKey>] [/logdir:<LogDirectory>]
/j:<JournalFile> /id:<SessionId> /srcdir:<SourceDirectory> /dstdir:<DestinationBlob
VirtualDirectory> [/Disposition:<Disposition>] [/BlobType:<BlockBlob|PageBlob>]
[/PropertyFile:<PropertyFile>] [/MetadataFile:<MetadataFile
```

Subsequent sessions require similar syntax but can omit many of the parameters, as shown in the following syntax example.

```
WAImportExport PrepImport /j:<JournalFile> /id:<SessionId> /srcdir:<SourceDirectory>
/dstdir:<DestinationBlobVirtualDirectory> [/Disposition:<Disposition>]
[/BlobType:<BlockBlob|PageBlob>] [/PropertyFile:<PropertyFile>]
[/MetadataFile:<MetadataFile>]
```

The Azure Import/Export tool creates a journal file that contains the information necessary to restore the files on the drive to the Azure Storage account, such as mapping a folder/file to a container/blob. Each drive used in the import job will have a unique journal file on it created from the WAImportExport.exe tool.

EXAM TIP

To add a single file to the drive and journal file, use the Srcfile parameter instead of the Srcdir parameter.

Create an import job through the management portal after the drive preparation is complete. To create an import job, do the following:

1. Log in to the management portal (*https://manage.windowsazure.com*), open the Azure Storage account you want to import data to by clicking the Storage link on the left navigation, and then click your storage account name.

2. On the Import/Export tab, click Create Import Job at the bottom of the page to open the Create An Import Job Wizard. Figure 4-8 shows the Before You Ship page, which is the wizard's first page.

3. To complete the wizard and create the job, browse to the journal file created during drive preparation and enter the correct contact and shipping information for your drives.

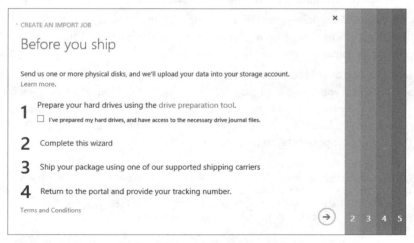

FIGURE 4-8 Creating an import job for the Import/Export Service

To export data, create an export job on the storage account using the management portal. To create an export job, do the following:

1. Open the Azure Storage account you want to export data from using the management portal.

2. On the Import/Export tab, click Create Export Job to open the Create An Export Job Wizard.

3. To complete the wizard and create the job, enter your contact information and shipping information for the data. The wizard prompts you to select the data to be exported. You have the option to export all the data from the storage account, or using two selectors (Starts With and Equal To), specify the path to the data, as shown in Figure 4-9. The path could be a simple container name combined with a partial folder/file name, or the relative path to a specific file in your storage account.

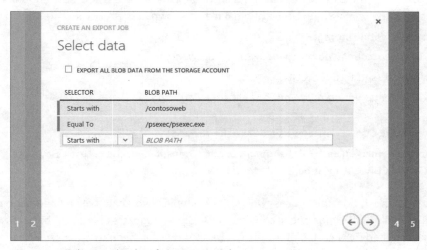

FIGURE 4-9 Selecting the data for an export job

Implementing Content Delivery Network

Use the Azure Content Delivery Network (CDN) to deliver static content such as images, text, or media closer to your users. To store content in a CDN endpoint, create a new CDN endpoint using the management portal (*https://manage.windowsazure.com*) by clicking New, CDN, Quick Create, Set and then set the origin domain to an Azure Storage account, website, or Cloud Service, as shown in Figure 4-10.

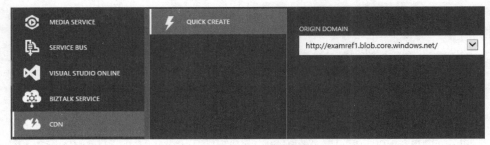

FIGURE 4-10 Creating a CDN endpoint in the management portal

Blobs that are stored in a container with public access enabled will be replicated to the CDN edge endpoints. To access the content within the CDN instead of your storage account, change the URL for the blob to reference the absolute path of the created CDN endpoint combined with the relative path of the original file, as shown in the following:

Original URL within storage

http://storageaccount.blob.core.windows.net/imgs/logo.png

New URL accessed through CDN

http://[CDN endpoint name].vo.msecnd.net/imgs/logo.png

> **NOTE AZURE CONTENT DELIVERY NETWORK AND SSL**
>
> SSL can be enabled on each CDN endpoint to allow transport-level secure access to the object in the CDN. SSL must be enabled per CDN endpoint.

Figure 4-11 shows how this process works. For example, if you had a file named Logo.png that was originally in the imgs public container in Azure Storage, that file could be accessed through the created CDN endpoint. Figure 4-11 also shows the benefits of a user accessing the file from the United Kingdom to the storage account in the West US versus accessing the same file through a CDN endpoint, which will resolve much closer to the user.

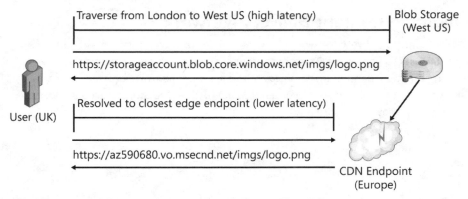

FIGURE 4-11 Accessing content from a CDN instead of a storage account

The additional benefit of using a CDN goes beyond deploying your content closer to users. A typical public-facing web page contains several images and may contain additional media such as .pdf files. Each request that is served from the Azure CDN means it is not served from your website which can remove a significant amount of load.

Managing how long content stays in the CDN is different depending on if your origin domain is from an Azure Storage account, or an Azure cloud service, or an Azure website.

Manage the content expiration through storage by setting the time-to-live (TTL) period of the blob itself. If you don't set a TTL directly, the default value is seven days. This means the content will stay in the CDN for seven days and will then be refreshed (or removed if the content is deleted from storage) at the end of the TTL period.

Using storage explorer tools, you can set the Cache-Control property on the blob files directly or you can also set the property using Windows PowerShell when uploading to storage. The example below shows how you can use the Set-AzureStorageBlobContent cmdlet to upload a set of files (blobs) to a storage account. For the content to be accessible through CDN, the container is set to Container (public). The metadata to control the TTL, and also the content type, is set on each blob as it is uploaded. The max-age attribute is measured in seconds. In the following example, the TTL is set to 86400 seconds, or 1 day.

```
$storageAccount = "[storage account name]"
$storageKey = (Get-AzureStorageKey -StorageAccountName $storageAccount).Primary
$context = New-AzureStorageContext -StorageAccountName $storageAccount `
                                   -StorageAccountKey $storageKey

$filesPath = "C:\CDNContent"
$container = "cdncontent"
New-AzureStorageContainer -Name $container `
                          -Context $context `
                          -Permission Blob


Get-ChildItem $filesPath | foreach {
    $contentType = "img/png"
    $cacheControl = "public, max-age=86400"
    $blobProperties = @{ContentType=$contentType; CacheControl=$cacheControl}

    Set-AzureStorageBlobContent -File $_.FullName `
                                -Container $container `
                                -Context $context `
                                -Properties $blobProperties
}
```

EXAM TIP

You can control the expiration of blob data in the CDN by setting the Cache-Control meta-data property of blobs.

Managing content expiration that is hosted directly in a cloud service or an Azure website requires programmatically setting the cache using the Response.Cache class, or using the <staticContent> element in the Web.config.

To remove content from the CDN altogether, there are two approaches depending on how the content has been added. If the content is stored in storage, you can set the container to private, or delete the content from the container, or delete the container itself. If the content is in a cloud service or an Azure website, you can modify the application to no longer serve the content. You can also delete the CDN endpoint, but that obviously will get rid of other content exposed in the CDN endpoint. Keep in mind that even if the content is deleted from storage, or no longer accessible from your web application, it will remain in the CDN endpoint until its TTL has expired. As of this writing, there is no direct way of purging content from the CDN.

Another technique of controlling information cached in the CDN is using query strings. For instance, if your application hosted in Azure Cloud Services or Azure Websites has a page that generates content dynamically, such as: *http://[CDN Endpoint].vo.msecnd.net/chart.aspx*, click Enable Query Strings on the CDN endpoint configuration page to allow the CDN to cache multiple versions depending on the query string passed in.

In the following example, if the two URLs generated different objects based on the query string passed in, enable query strings to have CDN treat them as separate objects. Without enabling the option, only one object would be cached and incorrect data would be used.

http://[CDN Endpoint].vo.msecnd.net/chart.aspx?chart=2014

http://[CDN Endpoint].vo.msecnd.net/chart.aspx?chart=2013

Configuring custom domains

Both an Azure Storage account and an Azure CDN endpoint allows you to specify a custom domain for accessing blob content instead of using the Azure URLs (*blob.core.windows.net* and *vs.msecnd.net*). To configure either service, you must create a new CNAME record with the DNS provider that is hosting your DNS records.

For example, to enable a custom domain for the *blobs.contoso.com* sub domain to an Azure Storage account, create a CNAME record that points from *blobs.contoso.com* to the Azure Storage account *[storage account].blob.core.windows.net*. Table 4-2 shows an example mapping in DNS.

TABLE 4-2 Mapping a domain to an Azure Storage account in DNS

CNAME RECORD	TARGET
blobs.contoso.com	contosoblobs.blob.core.windows.net

Mapping a domain that is already in use within Azure may result in minor downtime as the domain is updated. If you have an application with an SLA, by using the domain you can avoid the downtime by using a second option to validate the domain. Essentially, you use an intermediary domain to validate to Azure that you own the domain by performing the same process as before, but instead you add an intermediary step of using the asverify subdomain. The asverify subdomain is a special subdomain recognized by Azure. By prepending asverify to your own subdomain, you permit Azure to recognize your custom domain without modifying the DNS record for the domain. After you modify the DNS record for the domain, it will be mapped to the blob endpoint with no downtime.

After the asverify records are verified in the management portal, you then add the correct DNS records. You can then delete the asverify records if you want because they are no longer used. Table 4-3 shows the example DNS records created when using the asverify method.

TABLE 4-3 Mapping a domain to an Azure Storage account in DNS with the asverify intermediary domain

CNAME RECORD	TARGET
asverify.blobs.contoso.com	asverify.contosoblobs.blob.core.windows.net
blobs.contoso.com	contosoblobs.blob.core.windows.net

To enable a custom domain for an Azure CDN endpoint, the process is almost identical. Create a CNAME record that points from *cdn.contoso.com* to the Azure CDN endpoint *[CDN endpoint].vo.msecnd.net*. Table 4-4 shows mapping a custom CNAME DNS record to the CDN endpoint.

TABLE 4-4 Mapping a domain to an Azure CDN endpoint in DNS

CNAME RECORD	TARGET
cdncontent.contoso.com	az691789.vo.msecnd.net

The cdnverify intermediate domain can be used just like the asverify for storage. Use this intermediate validation if you're already using the domain with an application because updating the DNS directly can result in downtime. Table 4-5 shows the CNAME DNS records needed for verifying your domain using the cdnverify subdomain.

TABLE 4-5 Mapping a domain to an Azure CDN endpoint in DNS with the cdn intermediary domain

CNAME RECORD	TARGET
cdnverify.cdncontent.contoso.com	cdnverify.az691789.vo.msecnd.net
cdncontent.contoso.com	az691789.vo.msecnd.net

> **NOTE SSL IS NOT SUPPORTED WITH CUSTOM DOMAINS**
>
> As of this writing, using SSL with custom domains and third-party certificates is not supported for the Azure Storage Service or Azure CDN.

Objective summary

- Each Azure Storage account exposes several endpoints for storing data. These are: blobs, tables, queues, and files. Each endpoint can be accessed via HTTP and HTTPS.

- Blobs are stored in containers in a storage account. Within each container, you can optionally create a virtual hierarchy by appending folder names to the name of a blob /January/Reports.txt, for example.

- Both blob and containers support metadata. This a set of name/value pairs. Some metadata is created and managed by Azure, and some properties can be set or created by a user.

- Use the async blob copy service to copy blobs between storage accounts even if they are in different subscriptions. You can also use the Start-AzureStorageBlobCopy and Get-AzureStorageBlobCopyState cmdlets to copy blobs between storage accounts.

- Use the Azure Import/Export service to import large amounts of data that is too time or cost-prohibitive to upload over the Internet.

- Use the Content Delivery Network (CDN) to distribute content close to customers. The CDN can be used with content in an Azure Storage account, an Azure website, or an Azure cloud service.

Objective review

Answer the following questions to test your knowledge of the information in this objective. You can find the answers to these questions and explanations of why each answer choice is correct or incorrect in the "Answers" section at the end of this chapter.

1. How can you monitor the status of an asynchronous blob copy?

   A. Use the management portal to monitor its progress.

   B. Use the Get-AzureStorageBlobContent cmdlet.

   C. Use the Get-AzureStorageBlob cmdlet.

   D. Use the Get-AzureStorageBlobCopyState cmdlet.

2. To enable a custom domain on an Azure Storage account where the domain is already in use by an application hosted in Azure, which DNS records must be created?

   A. An A record in your custom domain that points to the IP address of your Azure Storage account.

   B. A CNAME record that points to the FQDN of your Azure Storage account.

   C. A CNAME record that points to the FQDN of your Azure Storage account with as-verify prepended to both the custom domain and the FQDN of the Azure Storage account.

   D. Custom domains are not supported with Azure Storage.

3. How do you control how long a blob is stored in the Azure CDN using blob storage?

   A. Set the time-to-live (TTL) on the Azure CDN endpoint in the management portal.

   B. Set the Cache-Control metadata property for each blob.

   C. Delete the content from the Azure Storage account to immediately remove it from the CDN.

   D. Use the Set-AzureStorageBlobContent cmdlet to remove the blob from the CDN.

4. How must an Azure Storage account be configured to automatically replicate virtual machine disks to a remote Azure region and have it accessible in the replicated region?

   A. Standard_LRS - (Locally redundant storage)

   B. Standard_ZRS - (Zone redundant storage)

   C. Standard_GRS - (Geographically redundant storage)

   D. Standard_RAGRS - (Read-access geographically redundant storage)

Objective 4.2: Manage access

There are several techniques for controlling access to objects within an Azure Storage account. Using the authentication key and storage account name is one technique. Granting access using a shared access signature or via a policy to allow granular access with expiration is another technique. In addition to granting access, understanding how to update (roll) storage keys for security purposes and revoking access is of vital importance.

Managing storage account keys

By default, every request to an Azure Storage account requires authentication. The only exception was briefly mentioned in Objective 4.1, which discussed that, by setting the security policy, you can optionally enable anonymous access at the container level for blob storage. The available options for this security policy are described in Table 4-6.

TABLE 4-6 Container permissions and resulting access

Access Type	Resulting access
Private/Off	No anonymous access (default)
Blob	Access blobs via anonymous requests
Container	List and access blobs via anonymous requests

There are several options available for authenticating users, which provide various levels of access. The first type of authentication is by using the Azure Storage account name and authentication key. With the storage account name and key, you have full access to everything within the storage account. You can create, read, update, and delete containers, blobs, tables, queues, and file shares. You have full administrative access to everything other than the storage account itself (you cannot delete the storage account or change settings on the storage account, such as its type).

To access the storage account name and key, open the storage account from within the management portal and click the Keys tile. Figure 4-12 shows the primary and secondary access keys for the Examref1 storage account. With this information, you can use storage management tools or command-line tools like Windows PowerShell and AzCopy.exe to manage content in the storage account.

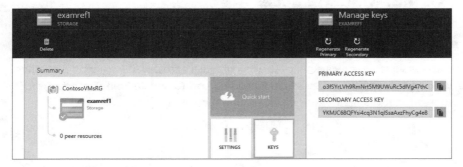

FIGURE 4-12 Access keys for an Azure Storage account

Each storage account has a primary and a secondary key. The reason there are two keys is to allow you to modify applications to use the secondary key instead of the first, and then regenerate the first key using the management portal or the New-AzureStorageKey PowerShell cmdlet. This technique is known as *key rolling*, and it allows you to reset the primary key with no downtime for applications that access storage using the authentication key directly.

> **NOTE** **SPECIAL CARE MAY BE NEEDED WHEN REGENERATING KEYS**
>
> When regenerating the key for a storage account that is hosting Azure Virtual Machines, ensure that you shut the virtual machines down before regenerating the key. If you don't shut them down, you will have to redeploy the virtual machines. If you're using Azure Media Services, you will have to re-sync the key of any storage account being used by Azure Media Services after the key regeneration.

Creating, and using, shared access signatures

A Shared Access Signature (SAS) is a URI that grants access to specific containers, blob, queues, and tables. Use a SAS to grant access to a client that should not have access to the entire contents of the storage account but that still requires secure authentication. By distributing a SAS URI to these clients, you can grant them access to a resource for a specified period of time, with a specified set of permissions.

The following example shows how to create a SAS URI using the Azure PowerShell cmdlets. The example creates a storage context using the storage account name and key that is used for authentication, and to specify the storage account to use. The context is passed the New-AzureStorageBlobSASToken cmdlet, which is also passed the container, blob, and permissions (read, write, and delete), along with the start and end time that the SAS URI is valid for.

```
$account = "[storage account name]"
$key = (Get-AzureStorageKey -StorageAccountName $account).Primary
$context = New-AzureStorageContext -StorageAccountName $account `
                            -StorageAccountKey $key

$startTime = Get-Date
$endTime = $startTime.AddHours(4)
New-AzureStorageBlobSASToken -Container "secure" `
                        -Blob "reports1.xlsx" `
                        -Permission "rwd" `
                        -StartTime $startTime `
                        -ExpiryTime $endTime `
                        -Context $context
```

Figure 4-13 shows the output of the script. After the script executes, notice the SAS token output to the screen.

```
PS C:\>
$account = "examref1"
$key = (Get-AzureStorageKey -StorageAccountName $account).Primary
$context = New-AzureStorageContext -StorageAccountName $account
                                   -StorageAccountKey $key

$startTime = Get-Date
$endTime = $startTime.AddHours(4)

New-AzureStorageBlobSASToken -Container "secure"
                             -Blob "reports1.xlsx"
                             -Permission "rwd"
                             -StartTime $startTime
                             -ExpiryTime $endTime
                             -Context $context
?sv=2014-02-14&sr=b&sig=8qLv51D3ahgw9Zoyf9vhVfSvOuVdak%2Fdh1gIHmb6plI%3D&st=2014-11-29T12%3A17%3A50Z&se=2014-1
1-29T16%3A17%3A50Z&sp=rwd

PS C:\>
```

FIGURE 4-13 Creating a Shared Access Token

This is a query string that can be appended to the full URI of the blob or container the SAS URI was created with, and passed to a client (programmatically or manually). Use the SAS URI by combining the full URI to the secure blob or container and appending the generated SAS token. The following example shows the combination in more detail.

The full URI to the blob in storage.

```
http://examref1.blob.core.windows.net/secure/reports1.xlsx
```

The combined URI with the generated SAS token.

```
http://examref1.blob.core.windows.net/secure/reports1.xlsx?sv=2014-02-14&sr=b&sig=8qL
v51D3ahgw9Zoyf9vhVfSvOuVdak%2Fdh1gIHmb6plI%3D&st=2014-11-29T12%3A17%3A50Z&se=2014-11-
29T16%3A17%3A50Z&sp=rwd
```

Using a stored access policy

Creating a shared access signature is fine for many operations, but in some cases you may want to create a SAS token based off of a predefined policy instead of creating the token using ad-hoc permissions and expiration periods. A stored access policy allows you to define the permissions, start, and end date for access to the container. Figure 4-14 shows using the third-party tool Azure Management Studio by Cerebrata to create two stored access policies.

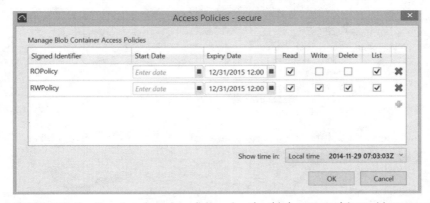

FIGURE 4-14 Creating stored access policies using the third-party tool Azure Management Studio

To use the created policies, reference them by name during creation of a SAS token using third-party tools as shown previously, or with the Policy parameter of the New-AzureStorageBlobSASToken, New-AzureStorageContainerSASToken, New-AzureSTorageTableSASToken, or New-AzureStorageQueueSASToken Azure Windows PowerShell cmdlets.

Thought experiment

Securing access to files in Azure Storage

In this thought experiment to apply what you have learned about this objective. You can find answers to these questions in the "Answers" section at the end of this chapter.

You are the web administrator for Contoso. You want to allow a number of files stored in Azure Storage to be anonymously downloaded from the Internet. You want to share a second set of files within the same storage account on an as-needed basis and only for a specific period of time.

1. What is the best approach to allow anonymous access to the first set of files?

2. Using Windows PowerShell, how could you solve the access issue for the second set of files?

Objective summary

- By default, all requests to an Azure Storage account require authentication in the form of using the storage account name and the shared access key.

- You can enable anonymous access to blobs by setting the security policy of the container to blob or container.

- Create a Shared Access Signature (SAS) to allow access to a resource within storage with specific permissions (read, write, and delete) and a start time and expiration time.

- A stored access policy can be created separately to define the parameters of access, and then be referenced when creating a SAS Token.

Objective review

Answer the following questions to test your knowledge of the information in this objective. You can find the answers to these questions and explanations of why each answer choice is correct or incorrect in the "Answers" section at the end of this chapter.

1. To allow anonymous access to a blob in Azure Storage but not the ability to enumerate other blobs in the same container, which permission should be set?

    A. Container

    B. Blob

    C. Private/Off

    D. Anonymous access is not allowed because all requests to storage require authentication.

2. To regenerate a key on an Azure Storage account what steps, if any, should be taken with virtual machines using the storage account? (Choose all that apply.)

    A. Nothing, regenerating an Azure Storage account key does not require additional steps for virtual machines.

    B. Re-sync the key for the Azure Virtual Machine in the management portal.

    C. Redeploy the virtual machine after the key has been regenerated if the virtual machine was not shut down before regeneration.

    D. Shut the virtual machine down before regenerating the key.

3. Which cmdlet can be used to temporarily share a blob in Azure Storage?

    A. Set-AzureStorageBlobContent

    B. Get-AzureStorageBlob

    C. New-AzureStorageBlobSASToken

    D. New-AzureStorageKey

Objective 4.3: Configure diagnostics, monitoring, and analytics

For any application that is deployed in the cloud, and that also has a dependency on storage, understanding how to enable Azure Storage Diagnostics is critical to ongoing operations. Azure Storage Diagnostics provides the ability to capture metrics and log data. You can use this information to analyze storage service usage, diagnose issues with requests made against the storage account, and to improve the performance of applications that use a service. Diagnostics also allows for a configurable retention period to automatically manage the storage of the data generated. Like other services in Azure, the Azure Storage Service also provides built-in monitoring and alerting capabilities to provide alerts on configurable thresholds.

> **This objective covers how to:**
> - Configure Azure Storage Diagnostics
> - Analyze diagnostic data
> - Enabling monitoring and alerts

Configuring Azure Storage Diagnostics

The first step to enable diagnostics on an Azure Storage account is to open the storage account properties and click on any of the metrics already on the storage account, such as the TotalRequests Today tile. In the new blade that opens, click the Diagnostics button at the top of the blade. This will open another blade where you can enable diagnostics, select the metrics you wish to capture, as well as the logging and retention settings. Figure 4-15 shows the management portal configuration for enabling storage diagnostics on the storage account.

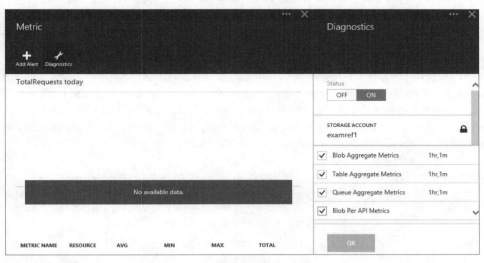

FIGURE 4-15 Enabling diagnostics for an Azure Storage account

You can also enable and configure storage diagnostics by using the Set-AzureStorageServiceLoggingProperty and Set-AzureStorageServiceMetricsProperty Azure PowerShell cmdlets.

In the following example, the Set-AzureStorageMetricsProperty cmdlet enables hourly storage metrics on the blob service with a retention period of 30 days and at the ServiceAndApi level. The next call is to the Set-AzureStorageServiceLoggingProperty cmdlet, which is also configuring the blob service and a 30-day retention period but is only logging delete operations.

```
$account = "[storage account name]"
$key = (Get-AzureStorageKey -StorageAccountName $account).Primary
$context = New-AzureStorageContext -StorageAccountName $account `
                                   -StorageAccountKey $key
Set-AzureStorageServiceMetricsProperty -ServiceType Blob `
                                       -MetricsType Hour `
                                       -RetentionDays 30 `
                                       -MetricsLevel ServiceAndApi `
                                       -Context $context
Set-AzureStorageServiceLoggingProperty -ServiceType Blob `
                                       -RetentionDays 30 `
                                       -LoggingOperations Delete `
                                       -Context $context
```

Metrics data is recorded at the service level and at the service and API level. At the service level, a basic set of metrics such as ingress and egress, availability, latency, and success percentages, which are aggregated for the Blob, Table, and Queue services, is collected. At the service and API level, a full set of metrics that includes the same metrics for each storage API operation, in addition to the service-level metrics, is collected. Statistics are written to a table entity every minute or hourly depending on the value passed to the MetricsType parameter (the management portal only supports using hour).

Logging data is persisted to Azure blob storage. As part of configuration, you can specify which types of operations should be captured. The operations supported are: All, None, Read, Write, and Delete.

Analyzing diagnostic data

After you have enabled and configured diagnostics for capture, the next step is to understand how to retrieve the data and understand what it means. Metrics data is captured in several tables in the storage account being monitored. Table 4-7 lists the names of the tables created, and where the data for hourly and minute metrics is created per service.

TABLE 4-7 Container permissions and resulting access

Metrics type	Table names
Hourly	$MetricsHourPrimaryTransactionsBlob
Hourly	$MetricsHourPrimaryTransactionsTable
Hourly	$MetricsHourPrimaryTransactionsQueue
Minute	$MetricsMinutePrimaryTransactionsBlob
Minute	$MetricsMinutePrimaryTransactionsTable
Minute	$MetricsMinutePrimaryTransactionsQueue
Capacity	$MetricsCapacityBlob (blob service only)

To view the data, you can programmatically access table storage, or use a tool that can return data from Azure tables, such as Visual Studio or some of the third-party storage tools. Figure 4-16 shows using Visual Studio to view raw metric data in table storage.

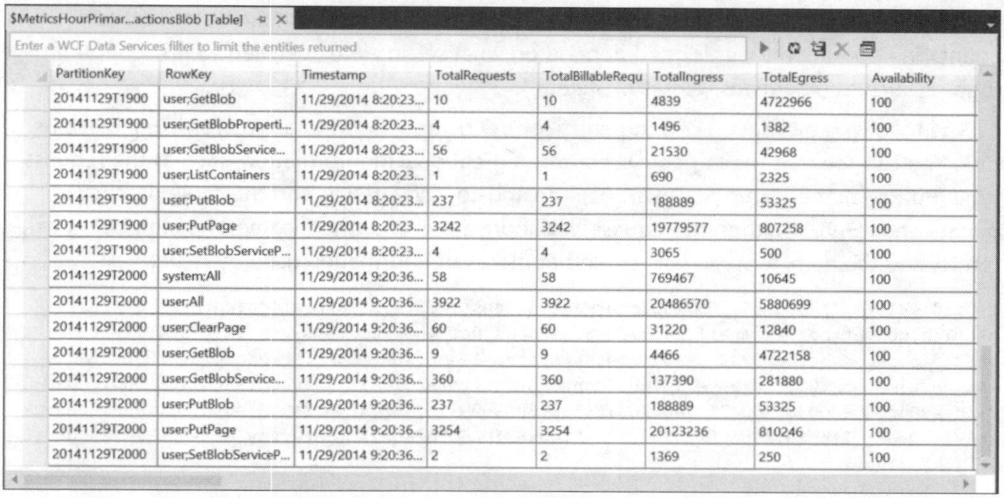

$MetricsHourPrimar...actionsBlob [Table]

Enter a WCF Data Services filter to limit the entities returned

PartitionKey	RowKey	Timestamp	TotalRequests	TotalBillableRequ	TotalIngress	TotalEgress	Availability
20141129T1900	user;GetBlob	11/29/2014 8:20:23...	10	10	4839	4722966	100
20141129T1900	user;GetBlobProperti...	11/29/2014 8:20:23...	4	4	1496	1382	100
20141129T1900	user;GetBlobService...	11/29/2014 8:20:23...	56	56	21530	42968	100
20141129T1900	user;ListContainers	11/29/2014 8:20:23...	1	1	690	2325	100
20141129T1900	user;PutBlob	11/29/2014 8:20:23...	237	237	188889	53325	100
20141129T1900	user;PutPage	11/29/2014 8:20:23...	3242	3242	19779577	807258	100
20141129T1900	user;SetBlobServiceP...	11/29/2014 8:20:23...	4	4	3065	500	100
20141129T2000	system;All	11/29/2014 9:20:36...	58	58	769467	10645	100
20141129T2000	user;All	11/29/2014 9:20:36...	3922	3922	20486570	5880699	100
20141129T2000	user;ClearPage	11/29/2014 9:20:36...	60	60	31220	12840	100
20141129T2000	user;GetBlob	11/29/2014 9:20:36...	9	9	4466	4722158	100
20141129T2000	user;GetBlobService...	11/29/2014 9:20:36...	360	360	137390	281880	100
20141129T2000	user;PutBlob	11/29/2014 9:20:36...	237	237	188889	53325	100
20141129T2000	user;PutPage	11/29/2014 9:20:36...	3254	3254	20123236	810246	100
20141129T2000	user;SetBlobServiceP...	11/29/2014 9:20:36...	2	2	1369	250	100

FIGURE 4-16 Viewing Azure Storage Diagnostics metric data using Visual Studio

> ***MORE INFO*** **METRICS SCHEMA**
>
> **You can read the full schema for captured metrics at *http://msdn.microsoft.com/en-us/library/azure/hh343264.aspx*.**

Logging data is stored in blob storage within the storage account in a container named $logs. Figure 4-17 shows the contents of the $logs container using Visual Studio to enumerate the files within the $logs container (you could use Windows PowerShell or a third-party storage tool as well). Each blob stored in the container starts with the service name (Blob, Table, and Queue).

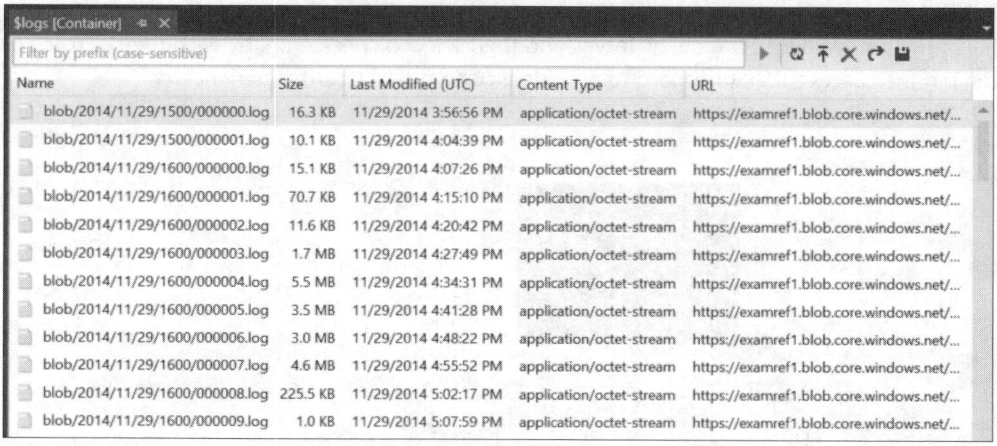

$logs [Container]

Filter by prefix (case-sensitive)

Name	Size	Last Modified (UTC)	Content Type	URL
blob/2014/11/29/1500/000000.log	16.3 KB	11/29/2014 3:56:56 PM	application/octet-stream	https://examref1.blob.core.windows.net/...
blob/2014/11/29/1500/000001.log	10.1 KB	11/29/2014 4:04:39 PM	application/octet-stream	https://examref1.blob.core.windows.net/...
blob/2014/11/29/1600/000000.log	15.1 KB	11/29/2014 4:07:26 PM	application/octet-stream	https://examref1.blob.core.windows.net/...
blob/2014/11/29/1600/000001.log	70.7 KB	11/29/2014 4:15:10 PM	application/octet-stream	https://examref1.blob.core.windows.net/...
blob/2014/11/29/1600/000002.log	11.6 KB	11/29/2014 4:20:42 PM	application/octet-stream	https://examref1.blob.core.windows.net/...
blob/2014/11/29/1600/000003.log	1.7 MB	11/29/2014 4:27:49 PM	application/octet-stream	https://examref1.blob.core.windows.net/...
blob/2014/11/29/1600/000004.log	5.5 MB	11/29/2014 4:34:31 PM	application/octet-stream	https://examref1.blob.core.windows.net/...
blob/2014/11/29/1600/000005.log	3.5 MB	11/29/2014 4:41:28 PM	application/octet-stream	https://examref1.blob.core.windows.net/...
blob/2014/11/29/1600/000006.log	3.0 MB	11/29/2014 4:48:22 PM	application/octet-stream	https://examref1.blob.core.windows.net/...
blob/2014/11/29/1600/000007.log	4.6 MB	11/29/2014 4:55:52 PM	application/octet-stream	https://examref1.blob.core.windows.net/...
blob/2014/11/29/1600/000008.log	225.5 KB	11/29/2014 5:02:17 PM	application/octet-stream	https://examref1.blob.core.windows.net/...
blob/2014/11/29/1600/000009.log	1.0 KB	11/29/2014 5:07:59 PM	application/octet-stream	https://examref1.blob.core.windows.net/...

FIGURE 4-17 Enumerating log data with Visual Studio

Each file within the container has a list of the operations performed on the storage account. The operation types logged depend on what setting was specified when configuring logging such as (All, Reads, Writes or Deletes).

The following example is of a log entry for I/O being written to an Azure virtual machine disk. You can see that the log entry captures a great deal of information, such as the request type (PutPage), the status (Success/201), the end-to-end latency, and the server latency in milliseconds (9,9), whether the request was anonymous or authenticated, the blob being written to, and the date, as well as several other pieces of information used by Azure.

```
1.0;2014-11-29T23:06:05.5053130Z;PutPage;Success;201;9;9;authenticated;examref1;exa
mref1;blob;"http://examref1.blob.core.windows.net/vhds/contoso-vms-VM2-2014-11-12.
vhd?comp=page&amp;se=9999-01-01&amp;sk=system-1&amp;sp=rw&amp;sr=b&amp;sv=2014-02-
14&amp;timeout=10";"/examref1/vhds/contoso-vms-VM2-2014-11-12.vhd";aae8f4cf-0001-00a8-
25dc-a994c2000000;0;100.71.140.160:63488;2009-09-19;562;4096;249;0;4096;"ItKHEuiZJbSVLk
2KRV1dlQ==";"ItKHEuiZJbSVLk2KRV1dlQ==";"0x8D1DA4030740017";Saturday, 29-Nov-14 23:06:06
GMT;;"XDrive_1.1";;
```

MORE INFO **STORAGE ANALYTICS LOG FORMAT**

For more details about the storage analytics log format, see *http://msdn.microsoft.com/ en-US/library/azure/hh343259.aspx.*

Enabling monitoring and alerts

Enabling monitoring on Azure Storage is a similar experience to other services such as Virtual Machines. The first step is to enable diagnostics to capture data that can be monitored. The second step is to configure charts in the management portal and enable alerts for the criteria you are interested in. Figure 4-18 shows some of the default metrics for the storage account. To enable other metrics, open the storage account properties in the management portal. Right-click one of the default monitoring metrics, such as TotalRequests Today, click Edit Chart, select the service (Blob, Queue, or Table), and then select a check mark by each metric. You can pin the chart to the Startboard to provide a custom dashboard experience.

FIGURE 4-18 Monitoring metrics for an Azure Storage account

Add an alert by clicking the Alerts tile, and then clicking Add Alert. Figure 4-19 shows the Alert Rules page in the management portal, where you can select the Resource (blob, queue, or table), and specify the alert name and description, along with the actual metric to alert on. In this example, the value in the Metric drop-down is set to capacity and (not shown) is the threshold and condition. The Condition is set to Greater Than, and the Threshold is set to 5497558138880 (5 TB in bytes). Each alert can be configured to email the administrator or co-administrator of the subscription, or a specific email address.

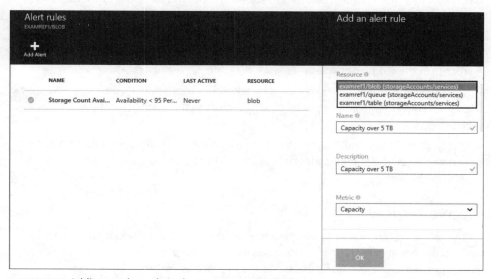

FIGURE 4-19 Adding an alert rule in the management portal

Thought experiment

Monitoring storage account capacity

In this thought experiment, apply what you've learned about this objective. You can find answers to these questions in the "Answers" section at the end of this chapter.

You are the IT administrator for Contoso. You need to have an alert emailed to a monitored inbox anytime one of several storage accounts you are responsible for reaches 5 TB.

1. What steps need to be taken to enable monitoring?
2. What settings should be applied when creating an alert?

Objective summary

- To monitor a storage account, enable Azure Diagnostics through the management portal, or through Windows PowerShell.
- The Set-AzureStorageServiceMetricsProperty cmdlet allows you to specify the metrics logging configuration per service. You can also set the logging level and retention period.
- The Set-AzureStorageServiceLoggingProperty cmdlet allows you to specify the logging configuration per service. You can also set which operations should be logged and a retention period.
- Captured metrics are stored in the table storage of the Azure Storage account being monitored, with table names that begin with $Metric. Captured logs are stored in blob storage in the $logs container.
- You can configure a custom dashboard by adding metrics within the management portal on the Azure Storage account or by pinning a chart to the management portal Start-board.
- Add alerts by specifying the metric to monitor and then configuring a threshold. An alert can email the administrators or co-administrators of the subscription or a custom email address.

Objective review

Answer the following questions to test your knowledge of the information in this objective. You can find the answers to these questions and explanations of why each answer choice is correct or incorrect in the "Answers" section at the end of this chapter.

1. Where is captured metric data stored?

    A. A blob container named $metrics.

    B. A blob container named $logs.

    C. In a series of tables that begin with $Metric.

    D. In a SQL database outside of the storage account.

2. Where is captured log data stored?

    A. A blob container named $metrics.

    B. A blob container named $logs.

    C. In a series of tables that begin with $Metric.

    D. In a SQL database outside of the storage account.

3. Which cmdlet can you use to change the retention period of captured log data for the table service?

    A. Set-AzureStorageServiceLoggingProperty

    B. Set-AzureStorageServiceMetricsProperty

    C. Set-AzureStorageAccount

    D. The retention period can only be set through the management portal.

Objective 4.4: Implement SQL databases

Microsoft Azure SQL Database is a relational database-as-a-service designed for predictable performance, scalability, and business continuity, with minimal management requirements.

> **This objective covers how to:**
> - Choose a service tier
> - Implement point-in-time recovery
> - Implement geo-replication
> - Scalability strategies
> - Importing and exporting data

Choosing a service tier

SQL Database has several service tiers that can be configured for predictable performance depending on the performance and size needs of your database. You can select the service tier at database creation time, or you can change the tier after database creation. Each service tier has one or more performance levels that can also be dialed up or down depending on the range of levels available within the service tier.

Performance levels are measured by the number of Database Throughput Units (DTUs) they support. DTUs provide a way to describe the relative capacity of a performance level based on a blended measure of CPU, memory, reads, and writes. Each SQL Database server can have a maximum of 1,600 DTUs. The number of DTUs available to your database is defined at the service tier and performance level you have selected for that specific database. Another key element of choosing a service tier is the maximum size of a database. As of this writing, the supported range starts from a maximum size of 2 GB, all the way to 500 GB.

When measuring performance, Microsoft uses the Azure SQL Database Benchmark (ASDB). The ASDB measures the throughput of a performance level using a mix of operations common in online transaction processing (OLTP) workloads. The ASDB also allows for measuring the predictability of the service tier and performance level combination. The response time varies depending on the service. For more information about the ASDB, see *http://msdn.microsoft.com/en-us/library/azure/dn741336.aspx#benchmark*.

Table 4-8 provides a comparison of the capabilities and benchmark numbers for Azure SQL Database per service tier along with the predictability measurement. See *http://msdn.microsoft.com/en-us/library/azure/dn741336.aspx* for the latest comparison of capabilities between service tiers.

TABLE 4-8 Performance characteristics for Azure SQL Database by service tier

Service Tier / Perfomance level	DTU	DB SIZE (MAX)	Worker threads (MAX)	sessions (MAX)	BenchmarK rate	predictability
Basic	5	2 GB	30	300	16,600 transactions per hour	Good
Standard S0	10	250 GB	60	600	521 transactions per minute	Better
Standard S1	20	250 GB	90	900	934 transactions per minute	Better
Standard S2	50	250 GB	120	1,200	2,570 transactions per minute	Better
Premium P1	100	500 GB	200	2,400	105 transactions per second	Best
Premium P2	200	500 GB	400	4,800	228 transactions per second	Best
Premium P3	800	500 GB	1,600	19,200	735 transactions per second	Best

In addition to performance, predictability, and database size, business continuity capabilities are enabled based on the service tier. Consider these capabilities when you're deciding on a service tier for your database. Table 4-9 shows the business continuity features that are specific to a service tier. See *http://msdn.microsoft.com/en-us/library/azure/hh852669.aspx* for the latest on business continuity features.

TABLE 4-9 Business continuity features for Azure SQL Database by service tier and recovery objective

Feature Name	Basic	Standard	Premium
Point-in-time restore	Any restore point within the past 7 days	Any restore point within the past 14 days	Any restore point within the past 35 days
Geo-restore	RTO < 24 hours RPO < 24 hours	RTO < 24 hours RPO < 24 hours	RTO < 24 hours RPO < 24 hours
Standard geo-replication	Not included	RTO < 2 hours RPO < 30 minutes	RTO < 2 hours RPO < 30 minutes
Active geo-replication	Not included	Not included	RTO < 1 hour RPO < 5 minutes

Recovery time objective (RTO) and recovery point objective (RPO) as used in Table 4-9 are defined as follows:

- **Recovery time objective** Maximum downtime before the application is fully functional after a failure.

- **Recovery point objective** Maximum amount of most recent data changes (time interval) the application could lose before it is fully functional after a failure.

Changing service tier or performance levels is an online operation. This allows you to monitor performance metrics, such as CPU Percentage, DTU Percentage, and Data IO Percentage, as well as the storage capacity of your database. If these metrics consistently show that you are close to the top of the capacity, you can decide to move to the next service or performance tier. If you are consistently near the bottom of these metrics, you could choose to go to a smaller service tier or performance level, assuming your database size and business continuity requirements supported it. You can configure all these metrics through the management portal.

Implementing point-in-time recovery

Point-in-time restore is a core feature that is part of Basic, Standard, and Premium service tiers. Basic databases can be recovered back to seven days, Standard databases back to 14 days, and databases in the Premium tier can be recovered up to 35 days. The feature works by selecting a point to restore from, and then restoring to a new database. Point-in-time restore does not allow you to overwrite an existing database or provide the ability to selectively merge changes.

Figure 4-20 shows the management portal during the recovery of an active database after clicking the Restore menu item. To implement a point-in-time restore of an active database, log in to the management portal, open the database, click the Restore menu item, and then select the restore point you want to restore the database to.

FIGURE 4-20 Performing a point-in-time restore using the management portal

To restore a deleted database using the management portal, create a new SQL database by clicking New, SQL Database, and then change the Select Source option to Backup, and then refer to the deleted database to restore from, as shown in Figure 4-21. You can then select the service tier and performance level within the Pricing Tier option.

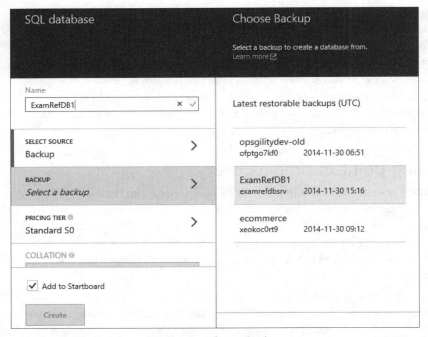

FIGURE 4-21 Creating a new SQL database from a backup

You can also use the Azure PowerShell cmdlets to recover a deleted database or revert to a point-in-time backup for an active database. Use the Get-AzureSqlRecoverableDatabase cmdlet and the SQL Database server name to identify the databases that have been deleted and are recoverable. The following example enumerates all the recoverable databases from a specified SQL Database server.

```
Get-AzureSqlRecoverableDatabase –ServerName $sqlServer
```

After identifying the available databases that are available for recovery, you next either use the Start-AzureSqlDatabaseRecovery cmdlet, or the Start-AzureSqlDatabaseRestore cmdlets. The difference between the two cmdlets is the Start-AzureSqlDatabaseRecovery cmdlet only allows for recovering a deleted database (the last backed up), and the Start-AzureSqlDatabaseRestore cmdlet allows restoring a deleted database (specify the deletion date using the SourceDatabaseDeletionDate parameter), or allows performing a point-in-time restore on an active database with the PointInTime parameter.

The following example shows how you can use the Start-AzureSqlDatabaseRestore cmdlet to recover a database to a specific point-in-time.

```
$recoveryPoint = "Sunday, November 30, 2014 4:55:00 PM"
$sqlServer     = "examrefdbsrv"
$sourceSqlDB   = "ExamRefDB1"
$targetSqlDB   = "ExamRefDBRestored"
```

```
$op = Start-AzureSqlDatabaseRestore -SourceServerName $sqlServer `
                                    -SourceDatabaseName $sourceSqlDB `
                                    -PointInTime $recoveryPoint `
                                    -TargetServerName $sqlServer `
                                    -TargetDatabaseName $targetSqlDB
```

> **NOTE** **RESTORE TO A NEW DATABASE**
>
> A database must be restored to a new database for a point-in-time restore.

The operation can be monitored by passing the RequestID property of the returned operation object to the Get-AzureSqlDatabaseOperation cmdlet, as shown in the following example.

```
$ctx = New-AzureSqlDatabaseServerContext -ServerName $sqlServer `
                                         -UseSubscription
Get-AzureSqlDatabaseOperation -ConnectionContext $ctx `
                              -OperationGuid $op.RequestID
```

Figure 4-22 shows the output of a restore operation using the Get-AzureSqlDatabaseOperation cmdlet.

```
PS C:\> $ctx = New-AzureSqlDatabaseServerContext -ServerName examrefdbsrv -UseSubscription

PS C:\> Get-AzureSqlDatabaseOperation -ConnectionContext $ctx -OperationGuid $op.RequestID


DatabaseName    : ExamRefDBRestored
Name            : DATABASE RESTORE
State           : COMPLETED
PercentComplete : 100
StartTime       : 11/30/2014 5:11:06 PM
LastModifyTime  : 11/30/2014 5:12:39 PM
```

FIGURE 4-22 Viewing the status of a restore operation

Implementing geo-replication

SQL Database geo-replication is a business continuity feature that allows you to replicate changes from a primary to one, or potentially multiple, secondary databases. (The multiple database option is available with the Premium service tier only).

There are two types of geo-replication with SQL Database, standard geo-replication, which is available in the Standard service tier, and active geo-replication, which is available with the Premium service tier.

Standard geo-replication

With standard geo-replication, you can configure a single replication partner. Standard replication asynchronously replicates committed transactions to the secondary database in a pre-determined region. With standard geo-replication, the secondary database is offline except for the replication traffic.

To create a secondary replica with standard geo-replication enabled, open a database that is configured for the Standard service tier in the management portal, and then click the Geo Replication tile. The next step is to click the secondary location octagon, as shown in Figure 4-23. The gray octagons mark where regions are unavailable for the secondary database. A green octagon indicates the region that is available for use, and a blue octagon indicates the region is selected. Select the secondary location, and then select either an existing or new SQL Database server by clicking the Server Name option. With standard geo-replication, you can select one pre-determined region for your secondary database. For information about updated region-to-region mapping, see *http://msdn.microsoft.com/en-us/library/azure/dn758204.aspx*.

FIGURE 4-23 Creating a secondary replica for standard geo-replication

You can also enable the secondary database using Windows PowerShell. The following example shows how to create a secondary database.

```
$sqlPrimaryServer   = "[primary server name]"
$sqlSecondaryServer = "[secondary server name]"
$sqlDB              = "[database name]"
Start-AzureSqlDatabaseCopy -ServerName $sqlPrimaryServer `
                           -DatabaseName $sqlDB `
                           -PartnerServer $sqlSecondaryServer `
                           -ContinuousCopy `
                           -OfflineSecondary
```

> **NOTE** **SQL DATABASE SERVER MUST EXIST WHEN ADDING A REPLICA USING WINDOWS POWERSHELL**
>
> When creating a secondary database using Windows PowerShell, the remote SQL Database server must already be created. You can create a SQL Database server using the New-AzureSqlDatabaseServer cmdlet.

In the event of an outage in the Azure region where your primary database running SQL Database is hosted, you can failover to the secondary database by clicking the Stop Now button in the management portal on the secondary database. This action stops replication immediately with the primary database and brings the secondary database online as a read/write database.

> **IMPORTANT POTENTIAL DATA LOSS WHEN STOPPING REPLICATION**
>
> Stopping replication on the primary database does not wait for in-flight transactions to complete. There may be data loss.

You will need to adjust applications to use the secondary database either by programmatically handling failover with multiple connection strings, or by updating the connection string to the secondary database. Figure 4-24 shows the management portal with the secondary database replication options open.

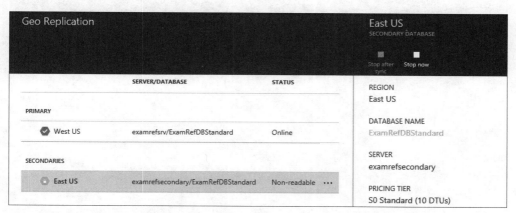

FIGURE 4-24 Options for stopping replication on a secondary with standard geo-replication

You can use the Stop-AzureSqlDatabaseCopy cmdlet to break the continuous copy relationship with the primary database. With standard geo-replication, you must specify the ForcedTermination parameter because planned termination is only supported with active geo-replication as the example below shows.

```
Stop-AzureSqlDatabaseCopy -ServerName $sqlPrimaryServer `
                -PartnerServer $sqlSecondaryServer `
                -DatabaseName $sqlDB `
                -ForcedTermination
```

Active geo-replication

Active geo-replication is only available with a database set to a Premium service tier. With active geo-replication, you can create up to four secondary databases. Unlike standard geo-replication, the secondary databases can be actively used for read-only workloads. Active geo-replication also allows you to place the secondary database replicas in any region you have access to. This means, if you want a secondary database replica in the same region as the primary database for low-latency read-only access, you can do that.

To create a secondary replica with active geo-replication enabled, open a database that is configured for the Premium service tier in the management portal, and click the Geo Replication tile. Next, click an available region octagon. Figure 4-25 shows using the management portal to add multiple secondary replicas for the SQL database. In the diagram, the blue octagon is the location of the primary database. The green empty octagons indicate the locations that are available for adding secondary databases. A green filled icon with a check mark indicates an active secondary database, and a green filled icon without a check mark indicates a secondary database that has initiated replication. The blue lines indicate where replication is active (solid), or where it is starting (dashed).

FIGURE 4-25 Adding secondary replicas with active geo-replication

Use the Start-AzureSqlDatabaseCopy cmdlet to add a secondary database replica just like you do with standard geo-replication. To make the database online with read-only access, omit the OfflineSecondary parameter, as the following example shows.

```
$sqlPrimaryServer   = "[primary server name]"
$sqlSecondaryServer = "[secondary server name]"
$sqlDB              = "[database name]"
Start-AzureSqlDatabaseCopy -ServerName $sqlPrimaryServer `
                -DatabaseName $sqlDB `
                -PartnerServer $sqlSecondaryServer `
                -ContinuousCopy
```

To make a secondary database stand-alone and writable for reasons such as failover, or migration of the database to a separate region, you must first stop the continuous replication from the primary database.

Figure 4-26 shows the options available to you for stopping replications, which are as follows:

- **Stop After Sync**   This option refers to a *planned termination*. This option is useful in the event of a planned failover (or migration) where data loss is unacceptable. If you select this option, all transactions committed on the primary database are committed on the secondary database, and then continuous copy is stopped.

- **Stop Now**   This option is for an *unplanned termination* (or a *forced* termination). This option is designed for when either the primary database or secondary database are not accessible. With this option, the service does not wait for transactions to complete, and terminates the relationship immediately.

> **IMPORTANT   DATA LOSS IN AN UNPLANNED TERMINATION**
>
> Be aware that the unplanned termination option for stopping replication can result in irrecoverable data loss.

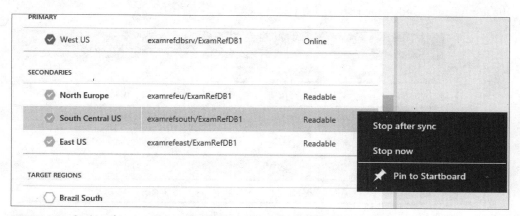

FIGURE 4-26 Options for stopping replication to a secondary database with active geo-replication

Just like standard geo-replication, you can use the Stop-AzureSqlDatabaseCopy cmdlet to break the continuous copy relationship with the primary database in active geo-replication. However, active geo-replication does support planned termination so you do not have to specify the ForcedTermination parameter unless needed.

```
Stop-AzureSqlDatabaseCopy -ServerName $sqlPrimaryServer `
                -PartnerServer $sqlSecondaryServer `
                -DatabaseName $sqlDB
```

Scalability strategies

Several options are available for applications that need to scale beyond what the highest SQL Database service tier can offer for a single database.

Scaling out with active geo-replication is an option to consider if an application can be designed to use secondary databases for read-only queries. This allows you to load-balance queries across up to four SQL database instances.

Another option is designing a database using a custom partitioning scheme. Data partitioning involves storing portions of a database across several database stores. Partitioning usually involves the following distinct types:

- Horizontal partitioning
- Vertical partitioning
- Hybrid partitioning

Horizontal partitioning (also referred to as *sharding*) involves designing an application and multiple databases (or, *shards*) to contain a portion of the database on multiple instances. Sharding is a common technique for architecting an application where the scalability requirements of a given data set are beyond what a single database can offer. Figure 4-27 shows a simplified example where a table is partitioned across three SQL database instances where the last name is used as the partition key.

First Name	Last Name	Profile
Kim	Abercombie	30 KB (binary)
Shaun	Beasley	30 KB (binary)
Victor	Freitas	30 KB (binary)
David	Jaffe	30 KB (binary)
Peter	Saddow	30 KB (binary)
Michael	Washam	30 KB (binary)

FIGURE 4-27 An example of horizontal partitioning (sharding)

Vertical partitioning involves splitting some portions of the data into multiple distinct data stores. This technique has the advantage of distributing application load across multiple services that are each optimized for storage of the specific data. Figure 4-28 shows a common approach of vertical partitioning where the record data is stored in the SQL database instance, but binary data, such as images, is stored in a separate storage account and only a reference is stored in the SQL database.

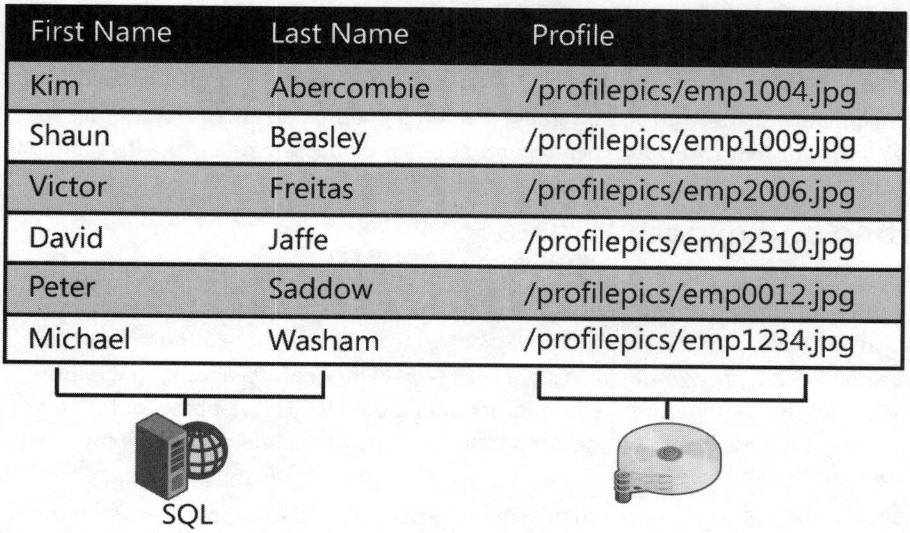

FIGURE 4-28 An example of vertical partitioning

The final approach is hybrid partitioning. This approach involves using a combination of horizontal partitioning (multiple shards) and separate data sources to take advantage of the scalability capabilities for each type of data. Figure 4-29 shows a combination of the diagrams shown in Figures 4-27 and 4-28. The table data is split across multiple SQL database shards, and the binary blob data is stored in Azure blob storage.

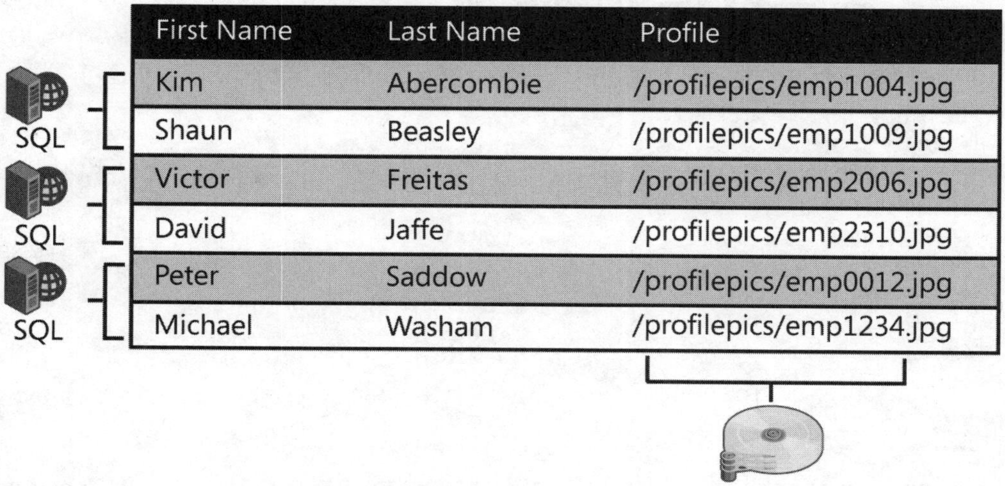

FIGURE 4-29 An example of hybrid partitioning

The scaling strategy you choose depends greatly on the application and the data you are storing. As of this writing, a recent addition to SQL Database that is in preview is Azure SQL Database Elastic Scale. Elastic Scale is a set of .NET libraries that can be used to ease the burden of managing multiple shards with SQL Database. For more information about Elastic Scale, see *http://azure.microsoft.com/en-us/documentation/articles/sql-database-elastic-scale-get-started/.*

Importing and exporting data

SQL Database supports the ability to import and export data using the BACPAC format. A BACPAC file is an entity that encapsulates all of the objects (tables, stored procedures, views, and so on) along with the data in the database into a file. For more information about BACPAC, see on MSDN: *http://msdn.microsoft.com/en-us/library/ee210546.aspx.* The Import and Export Service is the preferred method for migrating data to SQL Database, or for archival purposes. For business continuity, geo-replication and point-in-time restore are the most appropriate options.

To export a database, log in to the management portal, click SQL Databases, open the database to export, and then click Export. Figure 4-30 shows the configuration options for exporting the database. You must create or select an Azure Storage account because it will be used as the medium to export the data.

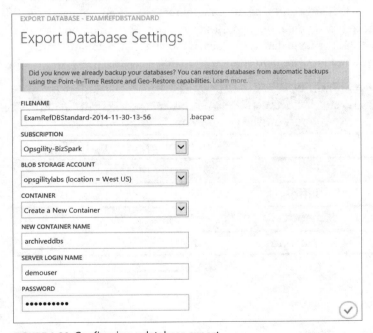

FIGURE 4-30 Configuring a database export

To import a database from a BACPAC file from on-premises, first export it from SQL Server, and then upload it to an Azure Storage account (preferably in the same region as the database server you will import to). Next, in the management portal, click New > Data Services > SQL Database, and then click Import. Figure 4-31 shows the dialog box within the management portal to specify the BACPAC URL in Azure Storage, and the remaining configuration options.

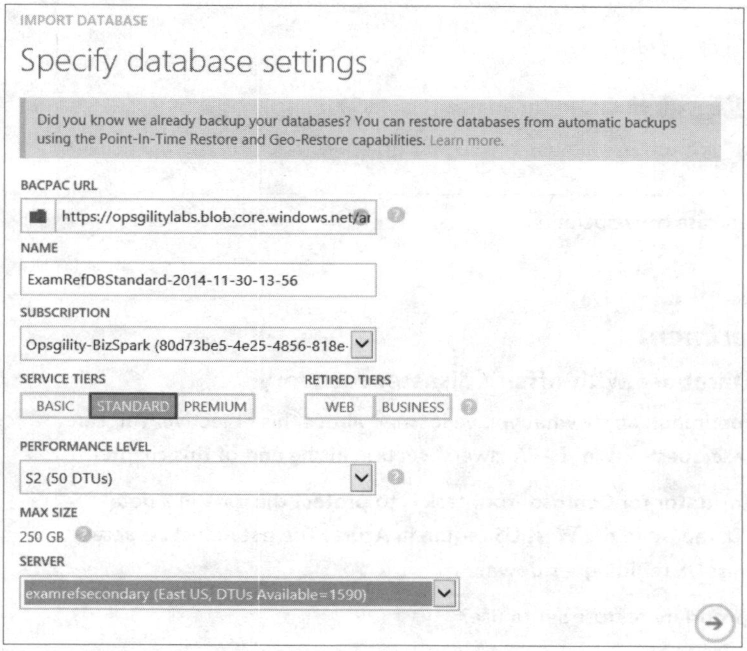

FIGURE 4-31 Configuring a database for import

> **MORE INFO** **EXPORTING DATA FROM SQL SERVER**
>
> Exporting data from SQL Server is beyond the scope of this book. However, MSDN documentation is available to help you with the process. See *http://msdn.microsoft.com/en-us/library/hh213241.aspx*.

An export performs a bulk copy of the data in each table in the database. This does not guarantee the transactional consistency of the exported data. If the data is active at the time of export (not transactional consistent), you can use the Copy SQL Database feature to make a copy of the database first and then export the copy. For an example, see Figure 4-32.

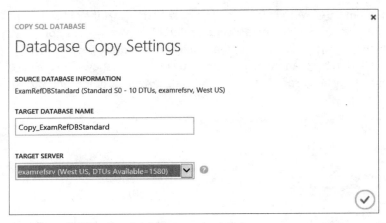

FIGURE 4-32 Setting up a database copy operation

Thought experiment

Deploy a SQL Database with offsite disaster recovery

In this thought experiment, apply what you've learned about this objective. You can find answers to these questions in the "Answers" section at the end of this chapter.

You're the IT administrator for Contoso. Your task is to protect the data in a database running SQL Database in the West US region in Azure. The data must be accessible in case the West US region goes down.

1. What is the appropriate feature set to use?

2. What is the minimum service tier in SQL Database needed for this requirement?

Objective summary

- SQL Database has three service tiers (Basic, Standard, and Premium) and each service tier has one or more performance levels. Each service and performance tier has a defined set of resources measured by Database Throughput Units (DTU).

- Point-in-time recovery is available for all service tiers. Basic databases can be recovered back to 7 days, Standard back to 14 days, and Premium up to 35 days.

- Standard geo-replication allows you to add a single SQL Database replica to a predetermined Azure region that is considered offline except for replication traffic. To bring the replica online, the continuous copy connection must first be broken. Standard geo-replication is only available for Standard and Premium service tiers.

- Active geo-replication allows you to add up to four SQL Database replicas in any region your subscription has access to. The replicas may be used for read-only workloads for increased scale or reporting. Active geo-replication is only available for premium service tiers.

- Use the database Import/Export tool to import a BACPAC file previously exported from SQL Server or another SQL Database. The export feature can be used to export a database to an Azure Storage account for archival or migration back to on-premises.

Objective review

Answer the following questions to test your knowledge of the information in this objective. You can find the answers to these questions and explanations of why each answer choice is correct or incorrect in the "Answers" section at the end of this chapter.

1. You have a single database that is 300 GB. What is the minimum service tier needed for the database?

   A. Basic

   B. Premium

   C. Standard

   D. None, the maximum database size is 150 GB.

2. How many SQL Database replicas are supported with geo-replication using a Standard service tier?

   A. 4

   B. 2

   C. 1

   D. None, geo-replication is not supported with the Standard service tier.

3. Which partitioning schemes involves using multiple data stores?

   A. Hybrid

   B. Horizontal

   C. Vertical

   D. None, partitioning only applies to data in the same data store.

Objective 4.5: Implement recovery services

Azure Recovery Services encompasses Azure Site Recovery and Azure Backup. Site Recovery provides the ability to protect System Center Virtual Machine Manager (VMM) clouds by replicating the virtual machines within to a separate cloud in a remote physical datacenter or to Azure Virtual Machines. Azure Backup is a backup solution that can integrate with Windows Server Backup, Data Protection Manager, or it can be used as a stand-alone tool to back up data to an Azure Storage account. For the exam, this objective focuses on implementing Azure Backup.

> **This objective covers how to:**
> - Protect servers with Azure Backup

Protecting servers with Azure Backup

To use Azure Backup, the first step is to create an Azure Backup Vault. To create an Azure Backup Vault, log in to the management portal, click New, click Backup Vault, click Quick Create, and then specify a name for the vault and the region, and then click Create Vault. Figure 4-33 shows an excerpt of the management portal while Azure Backup Vault creation is in progress.

FIGURE 4-33 Creating an Azure Backup Vault using the management portal

After the backup vault is created, download the vault credentials by clicking the Vault Credentials link in the Quick Glance section of the vault's dashboard. The vault credentials are valid for two days. After the expiration, you must download the credentials again through the management portal. You will need to copy the credentials to the server to protect them because they will be required during the agent installation to register the server.

> **EXAM TIP**
>
> **Downloading vault credentials is a relatively new feature. Previously, you were required to generate a self-signed certificate using a tool like Makecert.exe and upload it to the vault, as well as deploy it on the servers that are protected. The certificate is used to identify the vault and authenticate clients.**

The next step is to download the correct Azure Backup Agent. Within the Quick Glance section of the vault's dashboard, the following agent downloads are available:

- Azure Backup Agent for Windows Server and System Center Data Protection Manager (supported on Windows Server 2008 R2 with SP1, Windows Server 2012, Windows Server 2012 R2)
- Azure Backup Agent for Windows Server Essentials (supported on Windows Server 2012 Essentials, Windows Server 2012 R2, Windows Server 2012 R2 Essentials).

Install the downloaded agent on the server that will be protected. Figure 4-34 shows the first screen of the installer, which requires you to specify an installation path and a secondary path that will be used for cache. The cache setting defaults to a path on the drive C. You can change this setting to point to another disk to avoid IO contention on the operating system disk. If you're running the agent on a virtual machine in Azure, you can also reference the temporary disk D. The cache disk size should be at least 10-15 percent of the space required for data storage of your backups. The remainder of the setup allows you to specify proxy settings and Microsoft Update opt-in.

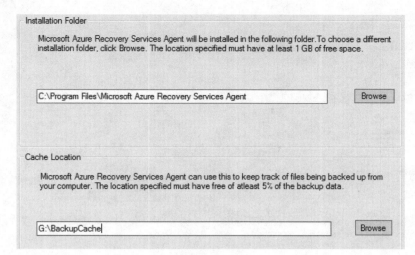

FIGURE 4-34 Installing the Azure Backup Agent

On the last dialog box of the install, click the Register Server button to launch the Register Server Wizard. Figure 4-35 shows the initial dialog box of the Register Server Wizard. Browse to the vault credentials created from the management portal. The credentials are used to identify the vault and to authenticate your server.

EXAM TIP

Configuring the agent with vault credentials is a relatively new process. Previous versions of the wizard prompted you to browse for a self-signed certificate, which performed the same function (vault identification and authentication).

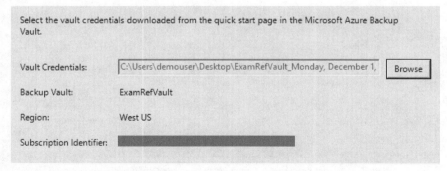

FIGURE 4-35 Specifying vault credentials for the Azure Backup Agent

Azure Backup encrypts all backup data at rest. Figure 4-36 shows the screen to generate the passphrase used to encrypt and decrypt the backup. Ensure the passphrase is secure because if it is lost, your backup data cannot be recovered.

Backups are encrypted to protect the confidentiality of your data.

Generate or type a passphrase to encrypt and decrypt backups from this server.

Enter Passphrase (minimum of 16 characters)

| ************************************** | (36) | | Generate Passphrase |

Confirm Passphrase

| ************************************** | (36) |

Enter a location to save the passphrase

| G:\passphrase | ▼ | | Browse |

⚠ If your passphrase is lost or forgotten, the data cannot be recovered. Microsoft Online Services does not save or manage this passphrase. It is strongly recommended you save your passphrase to an external location like a USB drive or network drive.

FIGURE 4-36 Setting the passphrase for backup encryption

To schedule a backup, click the Azure Backup or Azure Backup shell (PowerShell) icons. If you are using Windows Server Backup or Data Protection Manager (DPM), Azure Backup is integrated into their management consoles and is available when either application is launched.

Figure 4-37 shows the Azure Backup Wizard where you can specify items to backup. It is important to understand that Azure Backup only works with files and folders. For bare metal or VSS-related backups, you must use another tool such as DPM. You can configure Azure Backup to protect the backup from the other tool.

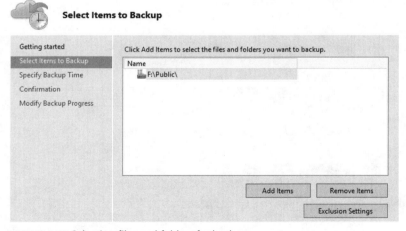

FIGURE 4-37 Selecting files and folders for backup

As part of the backup configuration, select the folders and files that should be protected. The maximum amount of data that can be backed up is 1.5 TB per volume. You can also specify a list of file types, folders, or files to exclude from backup. Figure 4-38 shows the options that are available for scheduling backups and for setting a retention policy. A synchronization (backup) with Azure Backup can occur daily or weekly, up to three times per day.

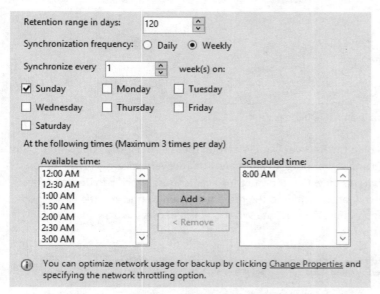

FIGURE 4-38 Scheduling a backup using the Azure Backup Schedule Backup Wizard

Click the Change Properties link at the bottom of the Actions pane of the Azure Backup application to configure bandwidth usage throttling. This allows you to configure periods of time that can use less bandwidth so Azure Backup does not impact other operations. Figure 4-39 shows the Throttling tab to make these changes. Specify work hours and non-work hours, and then specify the maximum bandwidth to use for each setting.

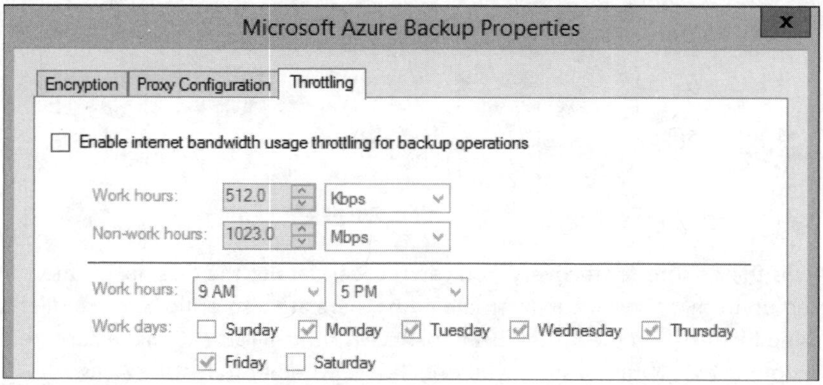

FIGURE 4-39 Configuring bandwidth usage throttling

After the backup schedule is created, you can force a backup by clicking the Backup Now link in the Azure Backup user interface. Figure 4-40 shows the protected items in the backup vault after a successful backup.

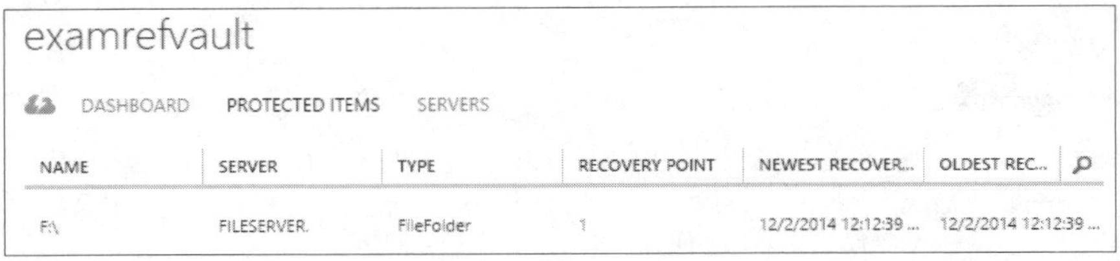

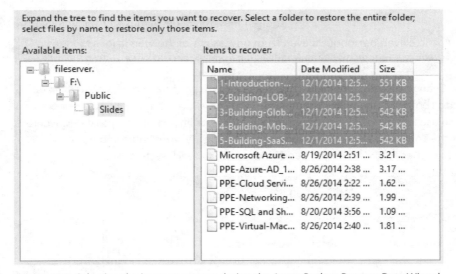

FIGURE 4-40 Protected items in an Azure Backup Vault

Recover data by launching the Recover Data Wizard in the Azure Backup application. Data can be recovered to the same server or as an alternate. The recovery wizard allows you to select volumes that are backed up within the vault. You can choose specific folders and files to restore or use the search feature built into the recovery wizard to find specific files. Figure 4-41 shows the fourth step in the Recover Data Wizard, which allows you to select specific files from the vault to recover.

FIGURE 4-41 Selecting the items to recover during the Azure Backup Recover Data Wizard

Figure 4-42 shows the options for recovery. You can recover data to the original location where it was backed up from, or specify an alternate path. There are also options for conflict resolution if the same files exist on the target location. Access control lists (ACLs) are captured as part of the backup process. During restore, you can choose whether to restore ACLs.

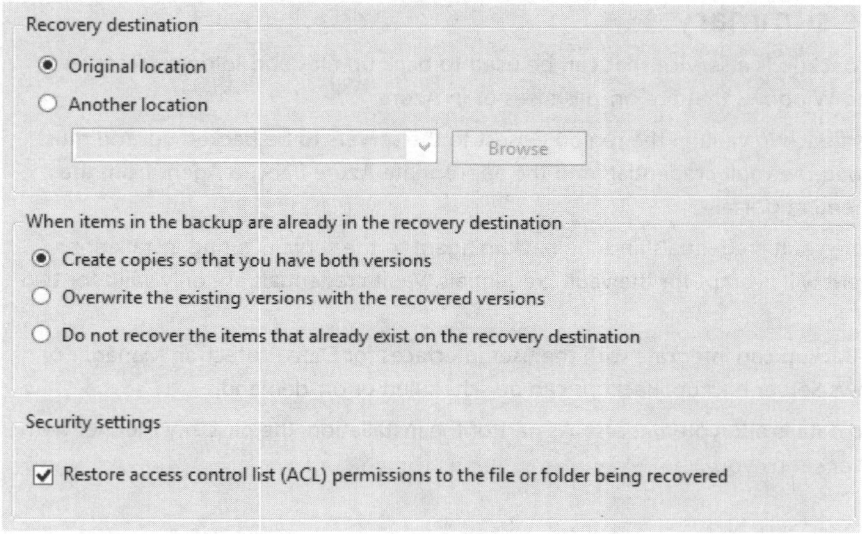

Recovery destination

◉ Original location

○ Another location

[⌄] [Browse]

When items in the backup are already in the recovery destination

◉ Create copies so that you have both versions

○ Overwrite the existing versions with the recovered versions

○ Do not recover the items that already exist on the recovery destination

Security settings

☑ Restore access control list (ACL) permissions to the file or folder being recovered

FIGURE 4-42 Options available for recovery

MICROSOFT VIRTUAL ACADEMY **SQL DATABASE AND AZURE STORAGE COURSES**

Microsoft Virtual Academy offers free online courses delivered by industry experts, including courses relevant to this exam. We recommend SQL Database for Business-Critical Cloud Applications and Azure Storage - Design and Implementation Jump Start. You can access the courses at *http://www.microsoftvirtualacademy.com/training-courses/azure-sql-database-for-business-critical-cloud-applications* and *http://www.microsoftvirtualacademy.com/training-courses/windows-azure-storage-design-and-implementation-jump-start*.

Thought experiment

Protect a file server with Azure Backup

In this thought experiment, apply what you've learned about this objective. You can find answers to these questions in the "Answers" section at the end of this chapter.

You are the IT administrator for Contoso, and you are tasked with protecting the data in an on-premises computer running Windows Server. The volume of the data is 2 TB. The network is busy between the hours of 9:00 to 17:00 so you want to minimize traffic but also protect files during this time.

1. What if anything must be done about the size of the data on the volume to protect it with Azure Backup?

2. What can be done to ensure that the network is not hindered by backups during the work day and still protect files?

Objective summary

- Azure Backup is a service that can be used to back up files and folders on servers running Windows that are on-premises or in Azure.
- Create a backup vault in the region closest to the servers to be backed up. You must download the vault credentials and the appropriate Azure Backup Agent from the management portal.
- Copy the vault credentials and the backup agent to the server. During installation, the agent will prompt for the vault credentials. Vault credentials are only valid for two days.
- Azure Backup can integrate with the user interfaces for Data Protection Manager or Windows Server backup. Backups can be scheduled or on-demand.
- Backup data is encrypted at rest. As part of the installation, the pass key is either generated or set by you.

Objective review

Answer the following questions to test your knowledge of the information in this objective. You can find the answers to these questions and explanations of why each answer choice is correct or incorrect in the "Answers" section at the end of this chapter.

1. What is the maximum volume size that Azure Backup can protect?
   - **A.** 800 MB
   - **B.** 1 TB
   - **C.** 1.5 TB
   - **D.** 64 TB

2. How much storage should be allocated for the cache location?
   - **A.** 10-15 percent of the size of the data to be backed up
   - **B.** 50 GB
   - **C.** 50 percent of the size of the data to be backed up
   - **D.** 1 GB

3. Which agent should be installed if you are running Windows Server 2012 Essentials?
   - **A.** Azure Backup Agent for Windows Server and System Center Data Protection Manager.
   - **B.** Azure Backup Agent for Windows Server Essentials
   - **C.** Azure Backup Agent for Data Protection Manager
   - **D.** None, Windows Server 2012 Essentials is not supported

Answers

This section contains the solutions to the thought experiments and answers to the objective review questions in this chapter.

Objective 4.2: Thought experiment

1. The first set of files should be put into a container with Blob or Container permissions set.
2. The second set of files should be shared out using a Shared Access Signature with an expiration set.

Objective 4.2: Review

1. **Correct answer:** B

    A. **Incorrect:** Container permission allows an anonymous user to enumerate and read all of the blobs in the container.

    B. **Correct:** Blob permission allows an anonymous user to read all of the blobs in the container but not enumerate them.

    C. **Incorrect:** Private/Off requires users to authenticate to the storage account and does not work for anonymous users.

    D. **Incorrect:** Anonymous access can be enabled through the Blob or Container permissions.

2. **Correct answers:** C, D

    A. **Incorrect:** Regenerating the key for a storage account hosting virtual machines can require changes such as shutting down the virtual machine first, or redeploying the virtual machine.

    B. **Incorrect:** There is no way to re-sync the key for virtual machines.

    C. **Correct:** If the virtual machines were not shut down prior to regenerating the key, redeployment is required.

    D. **Correct:** Shutting down the virtual machines before regenerating the key is the best approach.

3. **Correct answer:** D

    A. **Incorrect:** The Set-AzureStorageBlobContent cmdlet is used to upload a blob to Azure Storage.

    B. **Incorrect:** The Get-AzureStorageBlob cmdlet is used to enumerate blobs in a container.

    C. **Incorrect:** The New-AzureStorageBlobSASToken cmdlet is used to generate a SAS token used with Shared Access Signatures.

    D. **Correct:** The New-AzureStorageKey cmdlet is used to regenerate keys on an Azure Storage account.

Objective 4.3: Thought experiment

1. Enable diagnostics on the Azure Storage accounts and track metrics for blob storage.

2. Create an alert on the capacity metric and set the threshold to over 5497558138880 bytes.

Objective 4.3: Review

1. **Correct answer:** C

   A. **Incorrect:** Metric data is stored in a series of tables that begin with $Metric.

   B. **Incorrect:** Metric data is stored in a series of tables that begin with $Metric.

   C. **Correct:** Metric data is stored in a series of tables that begin with $Metric.

   D. **Incorrect:** Metric data is stored in a series of tables that begin with $Metric.

2. **Correct answer:** B

   A. **Incorrect:** Storage log data is stored in a blob container named $logs in the storage account being monitored.

   B. **Correct:** Storage log data is stored in a blob container named $logs in the storage account being monitored.

   C. **Incorrect:** Storage log data is stored in a blob container named $logs in the storage account being monitored.

   D. **Incorrect:** Storage log data is stored in a blob container named $logs in the storage account being monitored.

3. **Correct answer:** A

   A. **Correct:** The Set-AzureStorageServiceLoggingProperty cmdlet can modify the retention policy for log settings for the Blob, Table, or Queue service of the storage account.

   B. **Incorrect:** The Set-AzureStorageServiceMetricsProperty cmdlet can modify the retention policy for the metric settings for the Blob, Table, or Queue service of the storage account.

   C. **Incorrect:** The Set-AzureStorageAccount cmdlet is used to modify the label and type of a storage account.

   D. **Incorrect:** The retention policy can be set with PowerShell and the management portal.

CHAPTER 5

Implement an Azure Active Directory

Microsoft Azure Active Directory is the identity and access management solution for the Microsoft Azure platform. Organizations can use Azure Active Directory to configure access to applications used by the organization, manage users and groups, configure Multi-Factor Authentication (MFA) for users, identify irregular sign-in activity using advanced machine learning algorithms, extend existing on-premises Windows Server Active Directory implementations to Azure Active Directory, and empower users to manage their identity settings.

Objectives in this chapter:
- Objective 5.1: Integrate an Azure AD with existing directories
- Objective 5.2: Configure the Application Access Panel
- Objective 5.3: Integrate an app with Azure AD

Objective 5.1: Integrate an Azure AD with existing directories

Integrating Azure Active Directory with existing directories is one of the most common tasks for an IT professional because most organizations have an existing on-premises directory and/or online directory that the business depends on. Azure Active Directory is by no means intended to be a replacement for existing directories. It is a directory service that is specifically designed for the cloud, and, in particular, the Microsoft Azure platform. As such, it delivers services and features that can augment existing directory solutions to handle cloud-based identity and access needs for an organization.

Azure Active Directory is offered in either a Free, Basic, or Premium edition. The Basic and Premium editions offer advanced enterprise features, an unlimited number of directory objects, and SLAs. The content in this chapter discusses features and services of Azure Active Directory without regard for which edition the feature is offered in. Details about which features are available with each edition are available at *http://msdn.microsoft.com/en-us/library/azure/dn532272.aspx*.

Implementing directory synchronization

Many organizations have a significant investment in their on-premises infrastructure that includes a Windows Server Active Directory used to manage users, groups, and other resources in the organization. This on-premises directory provides the identity and access capabilities needed by IT professionals to support their business operations on-premises.

As these organizations move workloads to Azure and leverage cloud applications to support their business, it is common for organizations to seek ways to leverage their on-premises investment in Windows Server Active Directory. Organizations do this to provide similar identity and access capabilities for their cloud environment in Azure.

Directory synchronization addresses the needs of IT professionals seeking to extend their on-premises Windows Server Active Directory to Azure Active Directory. It reduces the administration costs that would otherwise be associated with managing users and groups in different environments. It also promotes a more positive user sign-in experiences for users accessing applications in their on-premises environment and cloud applications running in Azure.

Azure Active Directory supports directory synchronization of users and groups under four scenarios. The scenario best suited for your environment will depend on your on-premises infrastructure and authentication requirements for your users. These scenarios and a description of each are shown in Table 5-1.

TABLE 5-1 Directory synchronization scenarios supported by Azure Active Directory

scenario	description
Directory synchronization	Synchronizes on-premises users and groups to Azure Active Directory. Synchronization occurs on scheduled intervals to synchronize changes made in the on-premises directory.
Directory synchronization with password sync	An extension to the directory synchronization scenario that synchronizes a hash of a user's on-premises password to Azure Active Directory. This enables users to authenticate to Azure Active Directory using the same credentials they use to authenticate to their on-premises directory.

> **MORE INFO** **CHOOSING THE RIGHT DIRECTORY SYNCHRONIZATION SCENARIO**
>
> Each directory synchronization scenario offers unique benefits. Additionally, the time and complexity involved in implementing a scenario can vary. A decision matrix is available for you to learn what you can accomplish with each scenario, and also the requirements for each scenario at *http://msdn.microsoft.com/en-us/library/azure/jj573649.aspx*.

Currently there are two tools used to implement directory synchronization, which are as follows:

- Azure Active Directory Synchronization tool (DirSync)
- Azure Active Directory Synchronization Services (AAD Sync)

Which tool you use also depends on the scenario you are implementing and the synchronization features that your scenario requires. AAD Sync should be the tool you look to first because this is the tool Microsoft is making investments in going forward. DirSync was the first directory integration tool released and is still required for some scenarios.

> **MORE INFO CHOOSING THE RIGHT DIRECTORY SYNCHRONIZATION TOOL**
>
> Microsoft is clear in their messaging that AAD Sync will eventually be the single synchronization tool for synchronizing your on-premises directory to Azure Active Directory. At the time of this writing, there are features in DirSync and Microsoft Forefront Identity Manager (FIM) 2010 R2 that have not yet been implemented in AAD Sync. A breakdown of which features are supported by which tool can be found at *http://msdn.microsoft.com/en-us/library/azure/dn757582.aspx*.

Enable directory integration

Regardless of the directory synchronization scenario you are implementing, the first task will be to enable directory synchronization for your Azure Active Directory. This can be accomplished in the Azure management portal by going to the Directory Integration page of your directory and setting the Directory Sync field to Activated, as shown in Figure 5-1.

FIGURE 5-1 Activating directory synchronization for an Azure Active Directory

After directory sync is activated for your directory, you can proceed with the implementation of one of the directory synchronization scenarios. As shown previously in 5-1, there are four directory synchronization scenarios supported by Azure Active Directory. The following scenarios are the most common, and therefore the focus for the next two sections:

- Directory synchronization with password sync
- Directory synchronization with single sign-on

Configure directory synchronization with password sync

Configuring directory synchronization with password sync is the simplest of the supported directory synchronization scenarios. It does not provide a true single sign-on experience for users, but it does enable users to sign-in using the same username and password that they use in their on-premises environment. For many organizations, this is sufficient to meet their authentication requirements for cloud applications if Active Directory Federation Services (AD FS) is not already configured on-premises.

> **NOTE** **DIRECTORY SYNCHRONIZATION WITH PASSWORD SYNC REQUIRES DIRSYNC**
>
> At the time of this writing, the new AAD Sync tool does not support directory synchro-nization with password sync. Therefore, DirSync is required for this scenario. The Azure management portal references it in the Directory Integration page after activating directory synchronization.

To get started with this scenario, the Azure management portal will open step three on the Directory Integration page where you activated directory synchronization. Click the download link for the directory sync tool and save it to either the on-premises domain controller, or a domain joined server that will be dedicated to running directory synchroniza-tion. The download is a single executable called DirSync.exe. After copying this to the target server in your on-premises environment, run DirSync.exe to start the installation.

> **NOTE** **DIRSYNC REQUIRES .NET FRAMEWORK 3.5 SP1**
>
> If the target server you download DirSync.exe to is running Windows Server 2012 or later, you may get an error when trying to run DirSync if it detects that .NET Framework 3.5 SP1 is not installed. On Windows Server 2012 and newer, this version of the .NET Framework is not installed by default. Therefore, it may be necessary for you to enable this feature before proceeding with the DirSync installation.

The DirSync installation is a wizard-driven experience that starts by prompting you for two sets of credentials that DirSync needs to configure directory synchronization. The credentials needed are as follows:

- The credentials for a *global administrator* in the Azure Active Directory
- The credentials for a *domain administrator* in the Windows Server Active Directory

The rest of the options are check boxes to enable or disable a feature of directory synchro-nization, such as Hybrid Deployment or Password Synchronization. The goal of this section of the objective is to configure password synchronization; therefore, this option must be checked in the wizard, as shown in Figure 5-2.

FIGURE 5-2 Enabling the Password Synchronization feature during DirSync installation

After exiting the DirSync Installation Wizard, DirSync will continue running in the background as a Windows Service and periodically synchronize objects from the on-premises Windows Server Active Directory to the Azure Active Directory. The name of the service is Windows Azure Directory Sync Service.

EXAM TIP

Directory synchronization can be invoked on-demand by using the Start-OnlineCoExistence-Sync Windows PowerShell cmdlet that is installed as part of the DirSync installation. Optionally, you can pass the FullSync switch to the command if you want to invoke a full directory synchronization. Otherwise, it will only synchronize the changes since the last synchronization occurred. The script to import the module containing the cmdlet is installed at C:\Program Files\Windows Azure Active Directory Sync\DirSync\ImportModules.ps1. You must execute this script first for the cmdlets to be available.

You can get a list of all of the configuration cmdlets installed by executing the command Get-Command -All -Module "Microsoft.Online.Coexistence.PS.Config" | Select Name.

Invoking directory synchronization on demand is useful in scenarios where you need a change in the director to be synchronized immediately, such as removing a user from the on-premises directory.

Verifying that directory synchronization is working is a matter of simply checking the Users and/or Groups page of the directory in the management portal. Users that are synchronized from the on-premises Windows Server Active Directory will appear as sourced from the Local Active Directory, as shown in Figure 5-3. You can also check the event log on the server running DirSync to see logs recorded by DirSync. This will be covered in further detail in the Monitor Azure Active Directory section of this text.

FIGURE 5-3 Users page of a directory with directory synchronization configured

The default configuration for this scenario synchronizes user passwords *from* the Windows Server Active Directory *to* the Azure Active Directory. In the event that a user needs to reset his or her password, an administrator of the on-premises directory would have to reset the password for the user. Resetting user passwords is one of the most common IT tasks costing organizations time and money, and Azure Active Directory offers a feature to combat this through its self-service password reset (SSPR) feature. The SSPR feature enables you to define password reset policies for users in a way that gives the organization great control over how password resets are performed, while empowering users to complete the task on their own. This feature is available for Azure Active Directory Basic and Premium, and is enabled and configurable in the management portal, as shown in Figure 5-4.

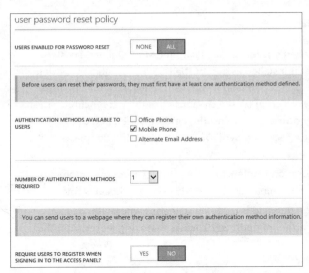

FIGURE 5-4 Configuring password reset policies for users in the management portal

DirSync with password sync includes a feature called *password write-back* that can be enabled for an Azure Active Directory with SSPR enabled. With this feature, password resets performed in Azure Active Directory can be persisted back to the on-premises Windows Server Active Directory. The DirSync installation includes the following Windows PowerShell cmdlets to enable or disable this feature as shown here:

- Enable-OnlinePasswordWriteback
- Disable-OnlinePasswordWriteback

Before running these cmdlets, you must first run the Windows PowerShell script at %ProgramFiles%\Azure Active Directory Sync\DirSyncConfigShell.psc1 with elevated admin rights. Additional information, potential requirements, and troubleshooting steps for the password write-back feature are available at *http://msdn.microsoft.com/en-us/library/azure/dn688249.aspx*.

Configure directory synchronization with single sign-on

Configuring directory synchronization with single sign-on results in a better user experience for users than the password-sync scenario discussed in the previous section because it provides true single sign-on for the users. In this scenario, if a user is already authenticated in their on-premises environment, the user will not be prompted to re-authenticate when accessing cloud applications protected by Azure Active Directory. This is the most significant difference for users, as compared to the password sync scenario described earlier. In that scenario, the user would be prompted to sign-in when accessing cloud applications even if the user was already authenticated in their on-premises environment.

The single sign-on experience this configuration delivers is made possible by the fact that users *always* authenticate to their on-premises Windows Server Active Directory, whether they are accessing resources on-premises or in the cloud. In other words, there is no synchronization of hashed passwords to Azure Active Directory. Instead, users are prompted to authenticate at a security token service (STS) on-premises. Active Directory Federation Service (AD FS) is such a service and must be installed in the on-premises environment to implement this scenario.

> **MORE INFO**   **AZURE ACTIVE DIRECTORY CONNECT (AAD CONNECT)**
>
> Microsoft has developed a tool called Azure Active Directory Connect that addresses the complexities of implementing directory synchronization. At the time of this writing, AAD Connect is in a Beta version and can be downloaded via the Microsoft Connect program at *https://connect.microsoft.com/site1164/program8612*.
>
> AAD Connect is a wizard that takes care of configuring DirSync, installing the necessary perquisites, and configuring your environment for either directory synchronization with password sync or directory synchronization with single sign-on. The single sign-on scenarios are popular choices for many customers configuring directory synchronization because it provides the best user experience when signing in. However, installing and configuring AD FS to support the single sign-on scenarios is not a trivial task. The Azure Active Directory team developed this tool to simplify the implementation of directory synchronization. AAD Connect will even verify the configuration for you so that you have confidence that the implementation was done correctly.
>
> To learn more about the initial Beta version features and how to use AAD Connect, read the post on the Active Directory Team Blog at *http://blogs.technet.com/b/ad/archive/2014/08/04/connecting-ad-and-azure-ad-only-4-clicks-with-azure-ad-connect.aspx*. The documentation for AAD Connect provides more details about the capabilities of the tool at *http://msdn.microsoft.com/en-us/library/azure/dn832695.aspx*.

Implementing this scenario requires the high-level tasks below. Each of these tasks are broken down further into several steps that must be completed.

- Have a custom domain configured for the Azure Active Directory that you are going to integrate with.
- Have an SSL certificate that can be used when communicating with the AD FS server in the on-premises domain.
- AD FS deployed.
- A trust setup between AD FS and Azure Active Directory.
- Directory synchronization (not password sync) installed and configured.

Assuming AD FS will be used for the on-premises STS, step-by-step instructions and guidance is available at *http://msdn.microsoft.com/en-us/library/azure/jj205462.aspx*.

If you have the required SSL certificates and servers available for the required federation servers and proxy servers, the AAD Connect tool will configure everything for you. This will be the recommended path for implementing this scenario for users who don't already have AD FS or another third-party STS implemented in their environment.

Integrating Azure Active Directory with Office 365

Although Microsoft Azure and Microsoft Office 365 are marketed and sold as separate subscriptions, there is one service that ties the two together, and that service is Azure Active Directory. If you are an Office 365 subscriber, you already have an Azure Active Directory, whether you have an Azure Subscription or not. That is because the directory you get with Office 365 is actually a tenant in Azure Active Directory. However, that does not mean you have the full set of services an Azure Subscription offers. To be able to provision services and resources in Microsoft Azure requires that you have an Azure subscription.

If you have an Office 365 subscription and an Azure subscription, the Azure Active Directory from your Office 365 can be integrated with your existing Azure subscription.

If you have an Azure subscription but don't have an Office 365 subscription, Office 365 can be added to your Azure subscription through the Application Gallery.

No matter which of these scenarios applies, integrating an Azure Active Directory from an Office 365 subscription with an Azure subscription offers your organization some important benefits, including the following:

- Authorized users in the Azure Active Directory can provision resources in the Azure subscription.
- Application access to software as a services (SaaS) applications that the organization depends on can be managed in the management portal for users in the directory.
- Applications an organization develops in-house can be protected such that only authenticated users in the directory can access them.

Sign up for Azure as an organization using Office 365 organization accounts

If you already have an Office 365 subscription but not an Azure subscription, the easiest way to add an Azure subscription for your organization is to go to *http://azure.com* and click the link to start a free trial subscription. When the sign in page appears, you should click the Sign In With Your Organizational Account link, as shown in Figure 5-5.

FIGURE 5-5 Sign up for Microsoft Azure using an existing organizational account

After clicking the link to sign in, using your organizational account, complete the process as follows:

1. Provide your contact information. Some of the fields will be pre-populated from your directory in Office 365 for you.

2. Provide mobile verification as a second authentication step.

3. Provide payment information.

4. Agree to the terms for an Azure subscription.

After completing these steps, the Azure subscription will be created, your directory from Office 365 will be accessible in the management portal, and you will be added as a service administrator on the Azure subscription. Optionally, you can add co-administrators to the Azure subscription so others in your organization can provision services in the Azure subscription. No further action is needed to integrate your Office 365 directory with your Azure subscription.

Integrate an Office 365 directory with an existing Azure subscription

If you already have an Office 365 subscription and an Azure subscription obtained from a Microsoft Account, you can integrate the Office 365 directory with the Azure subscription by adding an *existing directory* to your Azure subscription. To accomplish this, sign in to the management portal using your Microsoft account credentials associated with the Azure subscription. Next, click New, App Service, Active Directory, Directory, and Custom Create.

This opens a dialog box to add a directory. Change the drop-down box for the directory field to Use Existing Directory, as shown in Figure 5-6.

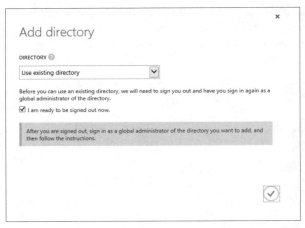

FIGURE 5-6 Add an existing directory to an Azure subscription

This approach requires you to sign out of the management portal and sign back in using the organizational account of a global administrator in the Office 365 directory. The reason you must sign back in as a global administrator of the directory is that Azure will add your Microsoft account to the directory as a global administrator and associate the directory with your Azure subscription, which requires the permissions of a global administrator to complete.

> **MORE INFO**   **AZURE ACTIVE DIRECTORY USER ACCOUNTS**
>
> Azure Active Directory (and Office 365) offers several different administrator roles that can be assigned to users in the directory. This is useful in organizations where designating certain functions to other users is desired.
>
> The following administrator roles can be assigned to users in the directory:
>
> - **Billing administrator**   This role can purchase Azure services, manage subscriptions and support tickets, and monitor service health.
> - **Global administrator**   This role has access to all administrative features in the directory and can assign other administrator roles.
> - **Password administrator**   This role can reset passwords for users and other password administrators. This role may not reset passwords for a global administrator. This role can also manage service requests and monitor service health.
> - **Service administrator**   This role can manage service requests and monitor service health.
> - **User administrator**   This role can reset password for users, manage user accounts, user groups, and service requests.
>
> Complete details about these administrator roles, and any applicable constraints, can be found at *http://msdn.microsoft.com/library/azure/dn468213.aspx*.

After completing this step, your Office 365 directory will be the default directory associated with your Azure subscription. You will be able sign in to the management portal using your organizational account and provision services in the Azure subscription. No further action is needed to integrate your Office 365 directory with your Azure subscription.

EXAM TIP

An administrator role in Azure Active Directory, such as a global administrator, does not automatically have permission to provision services and resources in an Azure subscription. Only service administrators and co-administrators can provision services and resources in an Azure subscription. A global administrator has administrative permissions to the directory and all functions in the Office 365 Admin portal.

To add a user as a co-administrator for an Azure subscription, go to the settings section in the management portal, click the Administrators tab, and then click Add at the bottom of the page.

Adding Office 365 to an existing Azure subscription

If you have only an Azure subscription, you can add Office 365 for your organization by signing up for Office 365 using the organizational account credentials for a global administrator user in your Azure Active Directory. Unless you have created a different Azure Active Directory in your Azure subscription, the Default Directory that came with your Azure subscription will be used to purchase the Office 365 subscription.

Adding Office 365, using your existing Azure Active Directory, can be accomplished by going to *https://portal.office.com*. Sign in using the credentials for a global administrator in your directory. After signing in you will be in the Office 365 Admin portal. Because you don't have an Office 365 subscription associated with the Azure Active Directory you signed in with, you will be prompted to purchase services, as shown in Figure 5-7.

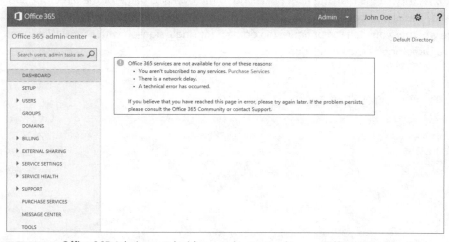

FIGURE 5-7 Office 365 Admin portal with an option to purchase an Office 365 subscription

Proceeding through the options to purchase an Office 365 subscription will result in an Office 365 subscription that is backed by the Azure Active Directory in your Azure subscription. Just as in the previous scenarios, the Office 365 subscription will be integrated with the Azure Active Directory. Users and groups can be created using the management portal or the Office 365 Admin portal.

Configuring a custom domain

Each Azure subscription is assigned a default directory and DNS name on the shared domain *.onmicrosoft.com. For example, if you signed up for an Azure subscription using the name Contoso, the default directory and DNS name for your Azure subscription is *contoso.onmicrosoft.com*. Although this assigned domain is a fully functional domain, it isn't necessarily user friendly. Users would have to sign in using a sign in name, such as john.doe@contoso.onmicrosoft.com, which has the disadvantages of having to type in a rather long domain and also not being intuitive for a user in the Contoso directory.

By adding a custom domain to your directory, you can significantly improve the user sign-on experience for users in the directory. If you own the *contoso.com* domain, and associate it to your Azure directory, users would be able to sign in using a sign in name, such as john.doe@contoso.com.

Configuring a custom domain involves the following steps:

1. Obtain ownership of a domain if you don't already have one.
2. Add the domain to your Azure directory.
3. Update DNS records at the domain registrar.
4. Verify the domain in the management portal.
5. Change the primary domain for the directory.

Assuming the ownership of a domain has been established, the next step is to add the domain to the directory. In the management portal, go to the Domains page for the directory, and then click Add. This action opens a dialog box where you can specify the name of the domain and indicate whether you plan to configure the domain for single sign-on with a local Windows Server Active Directory, as shown in Figure 5-8.

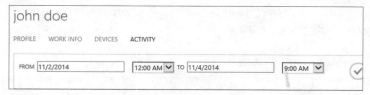

FIGURE 5-11 Specifying criteria for a user sign-in activity report in the management portal

You can also run a sign-in activity report for a group of users. To view sign-in activity for a group, click the group you want to retrieve the report for in the Groups page, and follow the same steps.

Whether your report is for a single user or a group, the information on the report will be comprised of the following:

- The date and time the sign in occurred.
- The application the user accessed. This could be an Office 365 application or an application registered in the directory for the organization, such as a SaaS application or a custom developed application.
- The user's IP address.
- The user's location, such as city and state.
- The type of client the user was running, such as Windows 8.

You can view the report in the management portal, or you can download it as a .csv file.

Azure reports

Azure Active Directory reports are an extremely useful monitoring tool that you can use to gain visibility into potential security risks for your organization, user activities such as sign in, password resets, and application usage.

The reports are available in the reports page of the directory in the management portal. They are organized into three groups of reports, which are *anomalous activity, activity logs*, and *integrated applications*. You can view the reports directly in the management portal or download them as .csv files.

> **MORE INFO** **AZURE ACTIVE DIRECTORY REPORTS AVAILABILITY**
>
> Some of the reports are only available in the Azure Active Directory Premium offering, such as advanced anomaly reports that use machine learning technology, and reports that provide advanced application usage.
>
> Information about which reports are available in the Free, Basic, and Premium offerings is available at *http://msdn.microsoft.com/en-us/library/azure/dn283934.aspx*.

Anomalous activity reports are used to report sign in activity that Azure Active Directory found to be inconsistent with normal activity. Data in the report does not necessarily mean there is a security risk. Ultimately, that is for you decide. These reports are designed to bring this information to your attention so you can make informed decisions about how to respond. Table 5-2 lists the anomalous activity reports available.

TABLE 5-2 Anomalous reports for Azure Active Directory

Report name	description
Sign ins from unknown sources	May indicate an attempt to sign in without being traced.
Sign ins after multiple failures	May indicate a successful brute force attack.
Sign ins from multiple geographies	May indicate that multiple users are signing in with the same account.
Sign ins from IP addresses with suspicious activity	May indicate a successful sign in after a sustained intrusion attempt.
Sign ins from possibly infected devices	May indicate an attempt to sign in from possibly infected devices.
Irregular sign in activity	May indicate events anomalous to users' sign in patterns.
Users with anomalous sign in activity	Indicates users whose accounts may have been compromised.

Activity log reports are used to report sign in activity, location of a user during sign in, the IP address of the user, and password reset activities. Table 5-3 lists the activity log reports available.

TABLE 5-3 Activity log reports for Azure Active Directory

Report name	description
Audit	Audited events in your directory.
Password reset activity	Provides a detailed view of password resets that occur in your organization.
Password reset registration activity	Provides a detailed view of password reset registrations that occur in your organization.
Groups activity	Provides an activity log to all group-related activity in your directory.

The integrated applications reports are where you can identify application usage trends and account provisioning events related to users being granted or denied access to SaaS applications. Table 5-4 lists the integrated applications reports.

TABLE 5-4 Integrated applications reports for Azure Active Directory

Report name	description
Application usage	Provides a usage summary for all SaaS applications integrated with your directory. This report is based on the number of times users have clicked the application in the Access Panel.
Account provisioning activity	Provides information pertaining to the provisioning of user or group access to a SaaS application.
Account provisioning errors	Use this to monitor errors that occur during the synchronization of accounts from SaaS applications to Azure AD.

Notifications

The notifications feature for Azure Active Directory Premium users enables administrators to be notified via email when anomalous sign in activity is detected. The email in the alert includes a link to a report identifying the situation and requires that the user viewing the report be both a co-administrator on the Azure subscription, and a global administrator for the directory. Additional notifications pertaining to password reset activity are also configurable in the Configure page of the directory in the management portal, as shown in Figure 5-12.

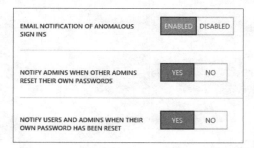

FIGURE 5-12 Configuring notifications in the management portal

Cloud App Discovery

Cloud App Discovery is a service you can use to discover cloud applications being used from within your organization. Unlike the application usage reports that report on application usage for applications you have provisioned in your Azure Active Directory, this service discovers applications that are being used that have not been provisioned in your directory. At the time of this writing, this service is in preview.

Cloud App Discovery is available at *https://appdiscovery.azure.com*. To get started using the service, you need to sign in using the organization credentials of a global administrator in the directory. The service works by collecting data from user's computers about which cloud applications they are accessing and using. This is accomplished through an agent that you must download and install on the users' machines you want to collect data for. The agent software runs on the user's computer as a service called the Microsoft Cloud App Discovery Endpoint Agent and captures application usage on the machine. The agent periodically transfers the application usage data for the machine to the Cloud App Discovery service. You can download the agent from the Cloud App Discovery portal.

The Cloud App Discovery portal provides information about applications that have been discovered, the users that are accessing those applications, and application usage metrics such as the number of requests made to an application, the volume of data, and number of users. Using the management portal you can manage the applications discovered, proceed to add the application to your Azure Active Directory, and provision user and group access to it. Alternatively, you may decide the application is not suitable for the organization and take action to restrict access to it. Figure 5-13 shows a portion of the management portal where apps and users have been discovered.

FIGURE 5-13 Cloud App Discovery portal

Monitoring directory synchronization

DirSync records events in the Windows Application Event Log. The source of the logs is Directory Synchronization. DirSync runs on an automatic schedule of every three hours, and the password sync extension runs on a schedule of every 30 minutes. Therefore, many of the logs will be a result of these scheduled synchronizations.

Part of the DirSync installation includes the Synchronization Service Manager from Microsoft Forefront Identity Manger (FIM) 2010 R2. It is located at C:\Program Files\Windows Azure Active Directory Sync\SYNCBUS\Synchronization Service\UIShell\msiiclient.exe.

NOTE SYNCHRONIZATION SERVICE MANAGER CLIENT INSTALLATION

The installation of this tool during the DirSync installation does not set up the required security groups to run it, as you would normally get in a full FIM installation. As a result, when you run the tool, you're likely to get an error indicating your account is not a member of a required security group. The security group missing is the MIISAdmins group. Therefore, you must create this group and add your user account to the group to use the tool. For more information about this issue and detailed steps to correct it, see *http://support.microsoft.com/kb/2791422*.

The advantage that Synchronization Service Manager provides is clickable links on directory synchronization events to see details of the object synchronized. As an example, when a user is updated, you will be able to see all the attributes for the user that were updated, such as the display name, surname, upn, and more, This level of detail does not exist in the event logs. Using this tool to monitor synchronization only works for adding, updating, or deleting directory objects. It does not display information for password sync events. Figure 5-14 shows the Synchronization Statistics window in the Synchronization Service Manager client for a single directory object that was added, and a directory object that was updated. Notice in the Staging section, the Adds and Updates are linkable and clicking either will display the details for that directory object.

Synchronization Statistics	
Staging	
Unchanged	0
Adds	1
Updates	1
Renames	0
Deletes	0
Discovery	
Filtered Objects	0
Inbound Synchronization	
Projections	1
Joins	0
Filtered Disconnectors	0
Disconnectors	0
Connectors with Flow Updates	2
Connectors without Flow Updates	0
Filtered Connectors	0
Deleted Connectors	0
Metaverse Object Deletes	0
Outbound Synchronization	**Windows Azure Active Directory Connector**
Export Attribute Flow	2
Provisioning Adds	1

FIGURE 5-14 Synchronization Statistics window in the Synchronization Service Manager client

In some cases it may be necessary to turn on additional logging that is not captured in the event log or discoverable through the Synchronization Service Manager. For example, if there are synchronization errors occurring, it may be necessary to see the result of each action occurring in the context of the synchronization. You can use the following Windows PowerShell cmdlets to enable or disable logs for directory synchronization and password synchronization.

- Enable-DirSyncLog
- Disable-DirSyncLog
- Enable-PasswordSyncLog
- Disable-PasswordSyncLog

When enabling logging, you can also indicate the desired *TraceLevel* for the logs, which can be Error, Info, Verbose, or Warning.

Thought experiment
Configure directory integration

In this thought experiment, apply what you've learned about this objective. You can find answers to these questions in the "Answers" section at the end of this chapter.

You are the IT administrator for Contoso. Contoso has an existing on-premises environment with Windows Server Active Directory and Active Directory Federation Services (AD FS) already configured. Contoso wants to extend their on-premises directory to Azure Active Directory. Users need to be able to sign in to on-premises applications and cloud applications running in Azure using the same username and password. Contoso also wants users to be able to change their password and reset their password without requiring the assistance of an administrator.

1. Which directory integration solution would you recommend and why?
2. What tools would you use to implement the solution?
3. Would Contoso need to change their Azure Active Directory tier?

Objective summary

- The default DNS name for an Azure Active Directory is assigned on the shared domain *.onmicrosoft.com.
- Verifying a custom domain can be done by adding either a TXT or an MX record to your domain name registrar. TXT records are the preferred method assuming that the domain registrar supports it. It is possible to have multiple domain names for a directory but only one domain can be the primary domain.
- Azure Active Directory Sync (AAD Sync) supports directory synchronization for multi-forest environments.
- Configuring directory synchronization with single sign-on requires an on-premises security token service (STS) be installed. In a Windows environment, this will generally be Active Directory Federation Services (AD FS), but other third-party products, such as Shibboleth, are also supported. The AAD Connect tool can be used to implement this scenario.

- A trust relationship between Azure Active Directory and the on-premises STS in the directory synchronization with single sign-on is required because Azure AD will externalize the authentication of users accessing the cloud application to the local STS. If a user is already authenticated in their on-premises environment, an authentication token will be issued by the STS without prompting the users again for credentials.

- The password write-back feature of directory synchronization with password sync requires the premium version for Azure AD.

- Azure Active Directory is offered in three tiers: Free, Basic, and Premium. The 99.9 percent SLA is only available in the Basic and Premium offerings.

Objective review

Answer the following questions to test your knowledge of the information in this objective. You can find the answers to these questions and explanations of why each answer choice is correct or incorrect in the "Answers" section at the end of this chapter.

1. You need to give a user in your Azure Active Directory full administrative access. Which administrator role should you assign the user?

   A. Global administrator

   B. User administrator

   C. Password administrator

   D. Billing administrator

2. You have a user in your Azure Active Directory that needs permissions to create a virtual machine in the Azure subscription. What should you do to support this requirement?

   A. Assign the global administrator role to the user.

   B. Assign the user administrator role to the user.

   C. Add the user as a co-administrator on the Azure subscription.

   D. Add the user as a service administrator on the Azure subscription.

3. You need to verify a custom domain for an Azure Active Directory. Which type of DNS record can you add to your domain registrar to accomplish this? (Choose two.)

   A. CNAME (Alias)

   B. TXT (Text)

   C. MX (Mail Exchanger)

   D. A (Host)

4. You have configured directory synchronization with password sync between your on-premises Windows Server Active Directory and your Azure Active Directory. Which Windows PowerShell cmdlet should you use to allow password resets in Azure Active Directory to be persisted back to your on-premises directory?

A. Enable-MSOnlinePasswordSync

B. Enable-PasswordSyncLog

C. Enable-DirSyncLog

D. Enable-OnlinePasswordWriteBack

5.   You have removed a user from your on-premises directory that is configured for directory synchronization with your Azure Active Directory. You need for this change to be synchronized immediately. Which Windows PowerShell cmdlet will you use?

A. Start-OnlineCoexistenceSync

B. Set-DirSyncConfiguration

C. Enable-DirSyncLog

D. Set-FullPasswordSync

6.   You need to implement directory synchronization with single sign-on for a multi-forest environment. Which tool should you use?

A. . DirSync

B. AAD Sync

C. AAD Connect

D. Synchronization Service Manager

Objective 5.2: Configure the Application Access Panel

The Azure Active Directory application access capabilities support integrating a directory with well-known software as a service (SaaS) applications that many organizations rely on for their day-to-day business needs. By integrating with these applications using Azure Active Directory, IT professionals are able to centrally manage access to the applications for users and groups in the organization. As applications are added to the directory, users are able to see and start the applications they have been assigned access to using the Access Panel.

> **MORE INFO**   **AZURE ACTIVE DIRECTORY SAAS APPLICATIONS**
>
> The number of applications that can be integrated with Azure AD increases frequently. At the time of this writing, over 2,400 applications are available for organizations to use. Microsoft provides a gallery of all the applications available at *http://azure.microsoft.com/ en-us/marketplace/active-directory/*. Using the gallery, you can search for applications by name, or browse through the applications by category.

Adding SaaS applications to Azure Active Directory

The Applications page of an Azure Active Directory is where you can see and manage applications that have been added to your directory. At the bottom of this page is an Add button that will open an intuitive interface you can use to add a new SaaS application. Choose the option to Add An Application From The Gallery, and you will be able to select from the many applications available, as shown in Figure 5-15.

FIGURE 5-15 Application Gallery in the management portal

Configuring access to SaaS applications

Configuring user access to a SaaS application will vary depending on the sign in capabilities of the application. Azure Active Directory supports *single sign-on* and automatic *user provisioning* for third-party SaaS applications. Applications from the gallery will support one or both.

After an application has been added to the directory, the management portal provides a quick start guide on the steps needed to integrate it with your directory, as shown in Figure 5-16.

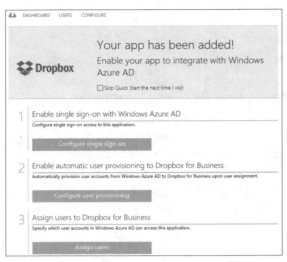

FIGURE 5-16 Quick start guide to adding Dropbox for Business to Azure AD

> **MORE INFO** **CONFIGURING USER ACCESS TO SAAS APPLICATIONS**
>
> Given the number of applications available in the application gallery, it's not feasible to provide step-by-step instructions for every application. The management portal does a nice job guiding you through the broader configuration tasks required for each application, such as configuring single sign-on, user provisioning, and assigning user access. There are also step-by-step tutorials for some common SaaS applications at *http://msdn. microsoft.com/en-us/library/azure/dn308590.aspx#BMK_Tutorials*.

Single sign-on

Azure Active Directory supports two modes for single sign-on, which are *federation-based* and *password-based*. Both modes provide a single sign-on experience for the user but differ on the credentials used to sign in to the SaaS application.

Federation-based single sign-on requires that users authenticate to Azure Active Directory using their organizational account credentials to access the application. In other words, a federated trust exists between Azure Active Directory and the SaaS application. In this mode, the SaaS application redirects users to sign in using an application (protocol) endpoint from your Azure Active Directory. The application endpoint used will depend on the protocol supported by the SaaS application. Azure Active Directory supports the WS-Federation, SAML-P, and OAuth protocols and therefore provides the expected sign-in and sign-out endpoints for each. This mode also requires that a certificate be uploaded to the third-party SaaS application that it will use to validate authentication tokens issued by Azure Active Directory. The management portal provides the application endpoint URL and certificate during the configuration process, both of which will be needed when configuring the SaaS application for single sign-on.

> **NOTE EXISTING SINGLE SIGN-ON**
>
> Many applications that support the federation-based single sign-on mode will also have an option for existing single-sign-on. The difference with this option is that Active Directory Federation Services (AD FS) and other third-party on-premises STSs are used to configure single sign-on with the SaaS application. This option is ideal for organizations that already have a SSO solution implemented in their on-premises environment.

Password-based single sign-on uses the username and password from the third-party SaaS application to sign in the user. In this mode, the user authenticates to the SaaS application using his or her credentials for the application, not Azure Active Directory. The credentials for the user are encrypted and securely stored in Azure AD, such that an authenticated user is able to get a single sign-on experience through a browser extension that retrieves the credentials from Azure AD and presents them to the application for the user.

Automatic user provisioning

Some applications enable you to configure automatic user provisioning whereby user accounts for the application are automatically added or removed as users are added or removed from the Azure Active Directory. The setup experience for this feature varies by application, but it generally involves signing in to the third-party application using administrative credentials and granting permission to Azure AD to provision user accounts in the application.

> **MORE INFO MANAGING AZURE ACTIVE DIRECTORY USING WINDOWS POWERSHELL**
>
> The objectives discussed in this chapter are easily accomplished using the management portal and most are one-time configurations not worthy of being automated. Still, it is possible to achieve many of these administrative tasks using the Azure Active Directory Module for Windows PowerShell.
>
> Before you can install the Azure Active Directory Module for Windows PowerShell, you must first install the Microsoft Online Sign-in Assistant for IT Professionals. Details about downloading, installing, and using the Azure Active Directory Module are available at *http://msdn.microsoft.com/en-us/library/azure/jj151815.aspx*.

Assigning user access to applications

After configuring the application for single sign-on or user provisioning, you can proceed to the final step, which is to assign user access to the application. Managing access to the application is done in the Users page for the application, as shown in Figure 5-17, where access can be assigned for a user, removed for a user, and the user's account settings can be edited, such as in the case of password-based single sign-on.

FIGURE 5-17 Managing access to the Box application using the management portal

> **MORE INFO   ASSIGNING ACCESS FOR A GROUP TO A SAAS APPLICATION**
>
> One of the benefits of the Azure Active Directory Basic and Premium editions is the ability to assign or remove access to applications using groups. This can save you considerable time when you're managing application access for a large group of users. Information about how to assign application access for a group is available at *http://msdn.microsoft. com/en-US/library/azure/dn621141.aspx*.

Accessing applications from the Access Panel

SaaS applications added to Azure Active Directory are available to users in the directory through the Access Panel. The Access Panel is a portal, separate from the management portal, where users can see and launch the applications they have been assigned access to. Users can sign in to the Access Panel at *https://myapps.microsoft.com* using their organizational account credentials. They can launch applications that they have access to from the Applications page in the management portal, as shown in Figure 5-18.

FIGURE 5-18 Access Panel showing SaaS applications available for a user

Customizing the Access Panel and sign-in page

The Access Panel and the sign-in page users use to authenticate are generalized such that they can be used by all Azure Active Directory tenants. In the Premium edition of Azure Active Directory, you can apply customized branding to the sign-in page and Access Panel for your users to display your organization's logo, custom messaging, and colors. These customization features are available in the Configure page of the directory under the Directory Properties section. In Customize Branding, you can apply the desired customizations, as shown in Figure 5-19.

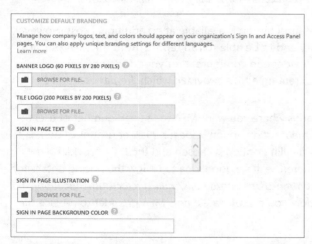

FIGURE 5-19 Customizing branding for the sign-in page and Access Panel

The customization options that are applicable to the Access Panel are limited to the banner logo. The banner logo and the other settings apply to the sign-in page.

Configuring Multi-Factor Authentication

Multi-Factor Authentication (MFA) is an effective way to add additional security to applications and resources. Multi-Factor Authentication in Azure AD works by first challenging the user for a valid username and password during sign in. If successfully authenticated, the second leg of authentication begins by challenging the user to verify he or she using a *mobile app, phone call*, or *text message*. This layered approach to authentication increases security by challenging you during sign in for something known, such as a password, and something you have, such as a mobile device. Having one without the other is not sufficient to gain access to a system protected by MFA.

> **MORE INFO**   **AZURE MULTI-FACTOR AUTHENTICATION SERVICE SOLUTIONS**
>
> Microsoft Azure Multi-Factor Authentication is a service that you can use to add additional security to resources in the cloud and in on-premises environments. This objective discusses adding MFA to Azure AD to secure access to Azure, Microsoft Online Services such as Office 365, and SaaS applications integrated with the directory. Details about the kinds of solutions that can be implemented for an on-premises environment using the Azure Multi-Factor Authentication service are available at *http://msdn.microsoft.com/en-us/library/azure/dn249466.aspx*.

MFA for administrators of an Azure subscription is available at no additional cost. However, to extend MFA to users of the directory and to be able to run reports from the MFA portal requires that you create a new MFA provider and configure it for your directory. You can choose from two billing options when creating a MFA provider, which are *per user* and *per authentication*.

The *per user* option is ideal in scenarios where you want MFA for a fixed number of users that authenticate regularly. The *per authentication* option is ideal for larger groups of users that authenticate less frequently. After a billing option is chosen and the MFA provider has been created, it cannot be changed. Therefore, it's a good idea to review the pricing details for each option at *http://azure.microsoft.com/en-us/pricing/details/multi-factor-authentication/*. If you do need to change the billing option, you must create a new MFA provider to replace the existing one.

Create a Multi-Factor Authentication provider

To create a new MFA provider using the management portal, select the Multi-Factor Auth Provider option under Application Services when creating a new resource, as shown in Figure 5-20.

FIGURE 5-20 Creating a Multi-Factor Authentication provider

Configuring a Multi-Factor Authentication provider

The Azure Multi-Factor Authentication service is configurable through a separate portal that you can reach from the management portal. To access the Azure MFA portal, highlight the directory in the management portal and click the Multi-Factor Auth Providers tab at the top of the page. Select the MFA provider, and then click Manage .

The Azure MFA portal is where you can run MFA usage reports and configure settings for how the Azure MFA service will be used for your organization, as shown in Figure 5-21.

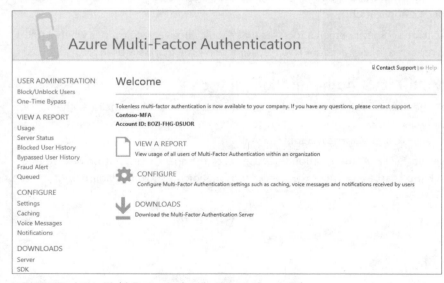

FIGURE 5-21 Azure Multi-Factor Authentication service portal

In the Configure section, the following options are available:

- **Settings**   Configure the number of attempts to allow during a MFA call, the phone number to be used for caller ID, the ability to empower users to submit fraud alerts, and whether to block a user's account after submitting a fraud report.

- **Caching**   Set up a cache such that, after a user has successfully authenticated, subsequent authentication attempts within the time period specified for the cache will automatically succeed. A cache can be defined as one of three types as follows and multiple caches can be configured for a MFA provider:

  - **User**   A user who has previously authenticated will be automatically authenticated on subsequent authentication attempts within the cache seconds specified.

  - **User, authentication type, application name**   A user who has previously authenticated will be automatically authenticated on subsequent authentication attempts within the cache seconds specified if the user is using the same type of authentication and accessing the same application.

  - **User, authentication type, application name, IP address**   A user who has previously authenticated will be automatically authenticated on subsequent authentication attempts within the cache seconds specified if the user is using the same type of authentication, accessing the same application, and is from the same IP address. This type of cache is only applicable for on-premises MFA servers and line of business applications developed using the MFA SDK.

- **Voice Messages**   Replace the standard messages used during MFA calls with your own custom messages. The voice message can be used to replace message types such as greeting, retry, fraud greeting, and more. The voice message can also be applicable to a specific application.

- **Notifications**   Specify email addresses that should receive notifications when a fraud alert is reported, a user account is locked, or a one-time bypass is used.

Enabling Multi-Factor Authentication for users

Multi-Factor Authentication can be enabled for users using a separate Multi-Factor Authentication portal. You can access this portal from the management portal by going to the Users page for your directory, and clicking Manage Multi-Factor Auth.

To enable Multi-Factor Authentication for a user, click the check mark button next to the user. Next, click the Enable link under the Quick Steps section, as shown in Figure 5-22.

FIGURE 5-22 Enabling Multi-Factor Authentication for a user

After enabling Multi-Factor Authentication for a user, the user's MFA status is updated to *Enabled*. It is a subtle but important distinction to note that MFA for the user is not being enforced yet. At this stage, the service has only been enabled for the user. To be enforced requires that user configuration for additional security verification be completed, which is the topic of the next section.

User configuration for additional security verification

A user that has been enabled for MFA will be prompted at the next sign in that an administrator has required the user to set up the account for additional security verification to be used during Multi-Factor Authentication. During this process, the user is able to select the contact method to be used during Multi-Factor Authentication, which can be one of the following:

- Mobile phone
- Office phone
- Mobile application

Depending on the method selected, the user will then be able to provide the additional information needed. For example, when choosing the mobile phone method, the user is then prompted to provide the phone number and whether to be contacted via text message or phone call from the Multi-Factor Authentication service, as shown in Figure 5-23.

FIGURE 5-23 Setting up additional security verification using the mobile phone contact method

After the user has verified the settings in step two, the Multi-Factor Authentication status for the account is updated to Enforced, and the user will start getting prompted for MFA during sign in.

> **MORE INFO   APPLICATION PASSWORDS WITH AZURE MULTI-FACTOR AUTHENTICATION**
>
> For non-browser applications such as Microsoft Outlook and Lync, MFA is not supported. As a result, users who have MFA configured can't access such applications using just their organizational account credentials. Application passwords are created during additional security verification for users indicating they use non-browser applications. By updating an application to use the generated application password instead, a user is able to bypass Multi-Factor Authentication when signing in to use the application. More information about application passwords, applications that support using them, and how they are created is available at *http://msdn.microsoft.com/en-us/library/azure/dn270518.aspx#howapppassword*.

Federating with Facebook and Google ID

When adding users to Azure Active Directory, you typically add users to your organization. As an example, if the organization is Contoso, as a user is added you assign a username, such as jayhamlin@contoso.com.

It's also possible to add a user to the directory using their identity with a social identity provider such as Facebook, Google, and others. These are referred to as *federated identity providers* and are the authority for that user's identity. To add an external user to your directory, set the type of user to User With An Existing Microsoft Account, and then enter the email address associated with the user's Microsoft account.

> **MORE INFO   MICROSOFT ACCOUNTS**
>
> Microsoft accounts are used by many popular Microsoft applications, online services, and devices such as Skype, OneDrive, Xbox Live, Windows Phone, Surface, and more. Therefore, users already using these apps, services, and devices already have a Microsoft account. That account can be used to add them as external users to an Azure Active Directory. Users that don't already have a Microsoft account can get one at *http://microsoft.com/account* using any email address they already have, such as a Facebook, Google ID, or other email addresses. Users can then be added to an Azure Active Directory but use their existing email address when signing in.

EXAM TIP

When an external user of a directory signs in to access an application protected by Azure Active Directory, the user authenticates to the federated identity provider, not Azure Active Directory.

Adding a user to a directory using a Microsoft account is useful in situations where you want to grant access to applications for users who are not part of the organization but may be contracted to work on short-term project assignments. This has the benefit of these users being able to use existing credentials to access applications rather than being given new credentials to keep up with. When the user no longer needs access to the applications, you can remove the user's account from Azure Active Directory. The user's Microsoft account continues to work as it always has for other online applications and services.

Thought experiment

Configure a SaaS application for single sign-on

In this thought experiment, apply what you've learned about this objective. You can find answers to these questions in the "Answers" section at the end of this chapter.

You are the IT administrator for Contoso and responsible for installing and managing SaaS applications for the organization. Contoso has purchased a SaaS application subscription from an ISV and wants users in Contoso to be able to access and use the application using their Contoso credentials.

You have already confirmed that the SaaS application is in the Azure application gallery. You also have confirmed that the SaaS application supports federated single sign-on.

1. How will you add the SaaS application to the Contoso Azure Active Directory?

2. How should you configure single sign-on for the application?

Objective summary

- Azure Active Directory is the identity provider for users added to a directory as a new user in the organization. In this scenario, the organization owns and manages the user's identity. For users added to a directory using a Microsoft account, the user and the federated identity provider where the account was created own and manage the user's identity.

- A user added to a directory using a Microsoft account will not be able to use the Access Panel to see and launch applications assigned to him or her. Instead, the user must access the application URL and sign in using credentials associated with the account.

- A multi-factor authentication provider is available as either a per user or per authentication billing plan.

- SaaS applications added to a directory support single sign-on or automatic user provisioning configurations. For single sign-on, options may include password-based, federation-based, and existing single sign-on.

- The sign-in page and Access Panel can be custom branded for Azure Active Directory Premium users. You can apply localized branding settings for all or selected settings to support users in different locales.

Objective review

Answer the following questions to test your knowledge of the information in this objective. You can find the answers to these questions and explanations of why each answer choice is correct or incorrect in the "Answers" section at the end of this chapter.

1. How can Azure Active Directory users see, and launch, the applications they have been granted access to? (Choose all that apply.)

   A. management portal

   B. Active Directory Portal

   C. Access Panel

   D. "My Apps" from the Apple App Store

2. Which of the following are valid contact methods for Multi-Factor Authentication users? (Choose all that apply.)

   A. Mobile phone

   B. Office phone

   C. Email

   D. Mobile application

3. Which two single sign-on modes does Azure Active Directory support for SaaS applications?

   A. Automatic user provisioning

   B. Password-based

   C. Active Directory Federation Service (AD FS)

   D. Federation-based

4. What is the URL where users can access the Access Panel?

   A. *https://myapps.microsoft.com*

   B. *https://portal.azure.com*

   C. *http://azure.microsoft.com/en-us/marketplace/active-directory*

   D. *http://account.windowsazure.com/organization*

Objective 5.3: Integrate an app with Azure AD

Organizations that develop their own line-of-business (LOB) applications can protect access to those applications using Azure Active Directory. The type of LOB application that can be integrated with Azure Active Directory can vary. It can be a web application that users access using their browser, or a desktop client application that is installed on the user's computer. It may be a web service lacking a user interface that other LOB applications depend on to provide a complete solution. It could also be an application that has capabilities to create, edit, or even delete objects in the directory.

The process for integrating an application developed in-house requires careful coordination between the IT professional managing the Azure Active Directory, and the application developer responsible for developing the application. The content in this objective draws attention to the skills and knowledge the IT professional needs to integrate these kinds of applications with Azure Active Directory and configure application permissions.

> **This objective covers how to:**
> - Add a web application or web service
> - Add a native application
> - Configure graph API permissions for an application

Add a web application or web service

The process of integrating either a web application or web service with Azure Active Directory using the management portal begins the same way. In the Applications page of your directory, click Add at the bottom of the page and choose the option to Add An Application My Organization Is Developing. This action launches a wizard where you can provide a name for the application and also indicate the type of application, as shown in Figure 5-24. The name can be anything you want it to be. Notice that for the application type, web application and web service (also known as web API) are considered one and the same.

FIGURE 5-24 Adding a web application or web service to Azure Active Directory

After choosing the application type for Web Application And/Or Web API, the second and final page in the wizard prompts you for the application's sign-on URL and the application ID URI, as shown in Figure 5-25. The sign-on URL is the URL that clients will use to access the application. The application ID URI is a URI that uniquely identifies the application in your Azure Active Directory. The URI can be anything you want as long as it is unique to your directory and a valid URI.

FIGURE 5-25 Specifying the sign-on URL and application ID URI

MORE INFO **SIGN-ON URL AND APPLICATION ID URI**

A subtle distinction between the sign-on URL and the application ID URI is the use of a URL for one and a URI for another. Many times these two terms, URL and URI, are used interchangeably. However, they are very different in their definition.

The uniform resource locator (URL) identifies a resource on the web and can be used to access that resource using, for example, your browser.

The uniform resource identifier (URI) identifies a resource. Usually the resource is a resource on the web, but it doesn't have to be.

A good blog discussing the relationship between URLs, URIs, and uniform resource names (URNs) is available at *http://www.cloudidentity.com/blog/2013/03/02/url-urn-uri-oh-my/*.

By completing the wizard to add the application you have created only the infrastructure that Azure Active Directory needs to support authenticating users of your application. Beyond the four settings you provided previously for this application, Azure Active Directory has also configured additional settings in your directory that application developers will need to build the application. This is where the careful coordination between the IT professional and application developer begins.

The application developer needs the following settings to develop and configure the application that will be protected by Azure Active Directory.

- **Application ID URI** The URI that you provided in the Add Application Wizard for the application. The application developer will use this in the code and/or configuration to associate the application with this entry in the directory.

- **Reply URL** By default, this is the sign-on URL you provided in the Add Application Wizard for the application. When Azure Active Directory issues a security token for a user of the application, it redirects the client back to the application URL so that the token can be presented to the application and validated.

- **Application endpoints** Endpoints that application developers can reference in the application code and/or configuration that are used to sign in and sign out users of the application.

The first two settings can be retrieved in the Single Sign-On section of the Configure page for the application, as shown in Figure 5-26. To get to the Configure page, click the application in the Applications page, and then click the Configure tab.

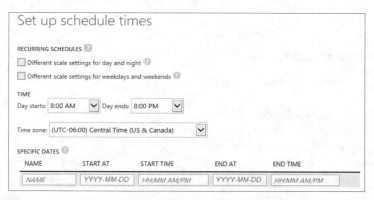

FIGURE 5-26 Single Sign-On section of the Configure page for an application in Azure Active Directory

The application endpoints can be accessed from the management portal by clicking View Endpoints.The application endpoints are the same for all applications in your Azure Active Directory. However, they are unique to each tenant (or organization) in Azure Active Directory. Azure Active Directory supports the following protocols and makes available application endpoints for each, as shown in Table 5-5.

TABLE 5-5 Protocols and application endpoints supported by Azure Active Directory

Protocol	application endpoints
WS-Federation	https://login.windows.net/<tenant>/wsfed
SAML-P	https://login.windows.net/<tenant>/saml2
OAuth	https://login.windows.net/<tenant>/oauth2/token https://login.windows.net/<tenant>/oauth2/authorize

The <tenant> in the URL for the application endpoints above is a GUID/ID assigned to your tenant (or organization) in Azure Active Directory and therefore referred to as *tenant specific endpoints*. Application developers use these application endpoints in code and/or configuration to externalize the authentication of users to Azure Active Directory. Which endpoint is used depends largely on the type of application being developed and the authentication requirements for the application. Figure 5-27 shows all of the application endpoints available for a tenant in Azure Active Directory.

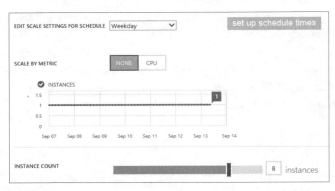

FIGURE 5-27 Application endpoints for an Azure Active Directory

In addition to the application protocol endpoints shown previously in Table 5-2, Azure Active Directory publishes additional tenant-specific endpoints that application developers may require when developing applications protected by Azure Active Directory. These are the federation metadata document and graph API endpoints.

The federation metadata document is an XML document that describes the security token service (STS) that is responsible for issuing SAML tokens to authenticated users. The URL for the STS is unique for each tenant in Azure Active Directory and is of the form *https://sts.windows.net/<tenant>*. This document also contains the certificate that Azure Active Directory will use to sign the tokens it issues and is one of the primary means by which applications validate tokens that are presented by clients accessing the application. If an application receives a token signed by an issuer other than the one it has externalized authentication to, then it can deny access to the application. The remainder of the federation metadata document describes the application endpoints for the WS-Federation and SAML-P protocols.

You can view the contents of the federation metadata document by opening the endpoint URL in a browser. However, it is more common that application development tools such as Visual Studio consume the metadata document because developers build applications using WS-Federation or SAML-P. The tools in Visual Studio, and other developer tools, take care of the extremely intricate configuration details required for the application to externalize authentication to Azure Active Directory by extracting the necessary information from the federation metadata document.

The graph API endpoint is used by applications to retrieve additional properties of directory objects such as users and security groups. It is also used by applications to create, edit, or even delete directory objects if the application has been configured with permissions to do so. This endpoint will be discussed further in the Configure Graph API permissions for an application section.

Enable access to a web application or web service from other applications

Many applications are architected in a way that allows certain features of the application to evolve and be versioned independently while collectively providing a complete solution for the business. For example, a web application that users interact with in a browser may have a dependency on a set of web services (or web APIs) that are used to send and receive data to a database, or perform business logic for the web application.

For a web service to be accessible from other applications registered in the directory, its application manifest must be updated to allow it. The application manifest is used to configure properties for an application that the management portal does not provide a user interface for. Enabling access to a web service from another application is one example where the application manifest has to be edited and can be done as follows:

1. Go to the Applications page in the management portal.
2. Click the name of the application whose manifest you want to edit.

3. At the bottom of the page, click Manage Manifest, and then select the Download Manifest option.

4. Save the manifest file to your local computer.

5. Edit the file using a text editor such as Notepad.

6. In the management portal, click Manage Manifest, and select the Upload Manifest option.

7. Click the check mark to upload the edited manifest file.

The application manifest is a JSON-formatted file. Listing 5-1 illustrates the default manifest for a web service added to Azure Active Directory.

LISTING 5-1 Application manifest for a web application/web service added to Azure Active Directory

```
{
  "allowActAsForAllClients": null,
  "appId": "7f12aa02-123f-4599-ad5d-f9851e36ce84",
  "appMetadata": {
    "version": 0,
    "data": []
  },
  "appRoles": [],
  "availableToOtherTenants": false,
  "displayName": "Contoso Support Web Service",
  "errorUrl": null,
  "groupMembershipClaims": null,
  "homepage": "https://contoso.com/support-api",
  "identifierUris": [https://contoso-support-api
    https://contoso-support-api
  ],
  "keyCredentials": [],
  "knownClientApplications": [],
  "logoutUrl": null,
  "oauth2AllowImplicitFlow": false,
  "oauth2AllowUrlPathMatching": false,
  "oauth2Permissions": [],
  "oauth2RequirePostResponse": false,
  "passwordCredentials": [],
  "publicClient": null,
  "replyUrls": [
    https://contoso.com/support-api
  ],
  "requiredResourceAccess": [
    {
      "resourceAppId": "00000002-0000-0000-c000-000000000000",
      "resourceAccess": [
        {
          "id": "311a71cc-e848-46a1-bdf8-97ff7156d8e6",
          "type": "Scope"
        }
      ]
    }
  ],
```

```
  "samlMetadataUrl": null,
  "defaultPolicy": [],
  "extensionProperties": [],
  "objectType": "Application",
  "objectId": "1688c779-e30b-4dea-9433-ea71bb44dced",
  "deletionTimestamp": null,
  "createdOnBehalfOf": null,
  "createdObjects": [],
  "manager": null,
  "directReports": [],
  "members": [],
  "memberOf": [],
  "owners": [],
  "ownedObjects": []
}
```

To allow this application to be accessible from other applications registered in Azure Active Directory requires that the *oauth2Permissions* node be updated with the property settings to allow access to it. Listing 5-2 illustrates the change to the oauth2Permissions node to allow full-delegated user access to the application.

LISTING 5-2 An abbreviated application manifest with oauth2Permissions added

```
… abbreviated …
  "oauth2AllowImplicitFlow": false,
  "oauth2AllowUrlPathMatching": false,
  "oauth2Permissions": [
    {
      "adminConsentDescription": "Allow the app full access to the Contoso Support Web
API on behalf of the signed-in user",
      "adminConsentDisplayName": "Have full access to the Contoso Support Web API",
      "id": "C39B0282-F0F4-431D-941B-777DC456C962",
      "isEnabled": true,
      "origin": "Application",
      "type": "User",
      "userConsentDescription": "Allow the application full access to the Contoso
Support Web API on your behalf",
      "userConsentDisplayName": "Full access to Contoso Support Web API",
      "value": "user_impersonation"
    }],
  "oauth2RequirePostResponse": false,
…  abbreviated …
```

With this edit in place, another application in Azure Active Directory will be able to see and configure access to this application if needed, which you see in the subsequent section where adding a native application to Azure Active Directory is discussed.

Adding a native application

Integrating a native application with Azure Active Directory using the management portal begins with a similar process to what you learned in the previous section for web applications and web services.

1. Go to the Applications page of your directory.
2. Click Add at the bottom of the page.
3. Choose the option to Add An Application My Organization Is Developing.
4. In the first page of the Add Application Wizard, provide a name for the application and select the option to indicate the application is a Native Client Application.
5. In the second page of the Add Application Wizard, provide a Redirect URI. This is a URI that uniquely identifies the application in your Azure Active Directory. It can be anything you want as long as it is unique to your directory and a valid URI.

As before, by completing the wizard to add a native application you have created the infrastructure that Azure Active Directory needs to authenticate users of your application. For native applications, an application developer needs the following settings to develop and configure the native application that will be protected by Azure Active Directory:

- **Redirect URI**   The URI you provided in the second page of the Add Application Wizard.
- **Client ID**   An identifier that Azure Active Directory generates and is used to identify the native application. Application developers use the Client ID in the application when accessing the graph API or other web APIs registered in Azure Active Directory.

You can get both of these values from the Properties section of the Configure page for the application, as shown in Figure 5-28.

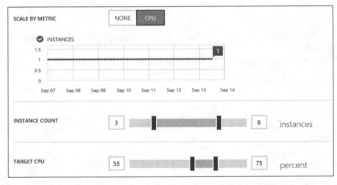

FIGURE 5-28 Properties of a native client application added to Azure Active Directory

Configure access to other applications

Native applications added to Azure Active Directory use the OAuth application endpoints to acquire an access token for a specified resource such as a web service application registered in the same directory. However, adding the native client application to Azure Active Directory does not mean the application has permissions to access the web service. Additional configuration must be added in Azure Active Directory to allow the native application to access the web service. This configuration is easily added using the management portal.

1. Go to the Applications page of your directory.

2. Click the name of the native application.

3. Click the Configure tab at the top of the page.

4. In the Permissions To Other Applications section, select the application you want to enable access to from the native application in addition to the appropriate permissions.

Figure 5-29 is an example of a native application being configured with permissions to a web service also registered in Azure Active Directory.

FIGURE 5-29 Configuring permissions to other applications for a native application

MORE INFO **OAUTH 2.0 IN AZURE ACTIVE DIRECTORY**

When a native application accesses a web application or web service registered in Azure Active Directory, it does so using the Authorization Code Grant type. This is part of the OAuth 2.0 Authorization Framework specification available at *http://tools.ietf.org/html/rfc6749*.

The Authorization Code Grant flow makes use of the two OAuth application endpoints provided by Azure Active Directory by first obtaining an authorization code from the OAuth 2.0 authorization endpoint, and then later exchanging it for a token it obtains from the OAuth 2.0 token endpoint.

Additional information about how OAuth 2.0 is used in Azure Active Directory and best practices for application developers is available at *http://msdn.microsoft.com/en-us/library/azure/dn645545.aspx*.

Configuring graph API permissions for an application

The graph API is used by applications that need access to read directory objects in Azure Active Directory or to create, update, and delete objects. For example, an application may need to query the directory to determine a user's manager in the organization or add the user to a particular security group. Azure Active Directory supports these kinds of application requirements, but your application must be configured with the necessary permissions to allow it as this goes beyond the default settings that provide single sign-on support for users.

The graph API is available for both web applications/web services and native applications, and can be configured via application permissions or delegated permissions.

Application permissions may be assigned to access the directory without a user context and are only available for web applications/web services. Delegated permissions are used to access the directory as the user signed in to the application and are available for both web applications/web services and native applications.

Permissions to access the graph API can be added to the configuration for an application using the management portal by selecting either the Read Directory Data or Read And Write Directory Data permission for the Windows Azure Active Directory application. Figure 5-30 illustrates setting the Read And Write Directory Data permission for a web application added to the directory.

FIGURE 5-30 Setting Graph API permissions for an application in Azure Active Directory

Thought experiment

Configure a line-of-business application in Azure Active Directory

In this experiment, apply what you've learned about this objective. You can find answers to these questions in the "Answers" section at the end of this chapter.

You are the IT administrator for Contoso and are responsible for managing the line-of-business applications developed by the development team at Contoso. A new web application has been developed for users to manage their benefit enrollment using their browsers. Per the application developers, the new benefits portal needs to be able to retrieve all properties for a sign-in user to pre-populate information for users on certain pages. The new benefits portal also includes a web service that the web application must be able to access.

1. What steps will you take to add the application to Azure Active Directory?

2. How will you configure the applications to meet the two requirements given to you by the development team?

Objective summary

- For SaaS applications configured using federation-based single sign-on, users are automatically signed in using their organizational account information in Azure Active Directory.

- For SaaS applications configured using password-based single sign-on, users are automatically signed in using their account information from the application. In this scenario, the user account information is securely stored in Azure Active Directory.

- Azure Active Directory provides application endpoints for WS-Federation, SAML-P, and OAuth 2.0 protocols. Azure Active Directory supports security token formats SAML and JWT.

- The oauth2Permissions array node in a web service application's manifest can be edited to allow the web service to be accessed from other applications registered in the directory, such as web applications or a native applications.

- The graph API is used by applications to create, read, update, or delete directory objects in Azure Active Directory. An application must be configured for either the Read Directory Data or Read And Write Directory Data permissions to use the graph API.

Objective review

Answer the following questions to test your knowledge of the information in this objective. You can find the answers to these questions and explanations of why each answer choice is correct or incorrect in the "Answers" section at the end of this chapter.

1. Which protocols does Azure Active Directory provide application endpoints for? (Choose all that apply.)

   A. WS-Federation

   B. Federation metadata document

   C. SAML-P

   D. OAuth 2.0

2. Which application setting in Azure Active Directory is used to uniquely identify a web application that has been added to the directory?

   A. Sign-on URL

   B. Reply URL

   C. Application ID URI

   D. Name

3. What is the URL for the security token service (STS) endpoint that issues a SAML token for an authenticated user?

   A. *https://sts.windows.net/<tenant>*

   B. *https://login.windows.net/<tenant>/saml2*

   C. *https://login.windows.net/<tenant>/wsfed*

   D. *https://graph.windows.net/<tenant>*

4. A developer building a web application for your organization needs the certificate that your Azure Active Directory uses to sign SAML tokens. Which application endpoint should you provide the developer?

   A. WS-Federation sign-on endpoint

   B. SAML-P sign-on endpoint

   C. Graph API endpoint

   D. Federation metadata document endpoint

Answers

This section contains the solutions to the thought experiments and answers to the objective review questions in this chapter.

Objective 5.1: Thought experiment

1. You should recommend the Directory Sync with single sign-on solution for Contoso. Because they already have Active Directory Federation Services (AD FS) installed and configured in their on-premises environment, much of the heavy work to implement this solution is already done. This solution also delivers a true single sign-on solution because users will not be challenged for credentials when accessing cloud applications if they are already authenticated in their on-premises environment. Finally, Contoso may find comfort in knowing that this solution does not sync hashes of user passwords to Azure AD because users will always authenticate using the AD FS endpoints running on-premises.

2. The AAD Connect tool should be used to implement the solution. It provides an intuitive wizard that will download and install the prerequisites such as .NET Framework 3.5, Microsoft Online Services Sign-in Assistant, and the Azure Active Directory PowerShell module. This tool will also enable directory integration in your Azure Active Directory, install and configure the AAD Sync tool, and then verify that single sign-on is configured and working correctly between the on-premises directory and Azure Active Directory.

3. For users to change their password or reset their password and have the new password persisted back to their on-premises directory, Azure Active Directory Premium edition is required.

Objective 5.1: Review

1. **Correct answer:** A

    A. **Correct:** A global administrator has full administrative access to the directory.

    B. **Incorrect:** A user administrator can manage users, groups, and reset password for other users in the directory.

    C. **Incorrect:** A password administrator can reset passwords for other users and other password administrators.

    D. **Incorrect:** A billing administrator can purchase services, manage service requests, and monitor service health.

2. **Correct answer:** C

    A. **Incorrect:** Assigning the global administrator role to the user would give the user full access to the directory, but would not allow the user to provision services in the Azure subscription.

B. **Incorrect:** Assigning the user administrator role to the user would enable the user to manage users and groups in the directory, but would not allow the user to provision services in the Azure subscription.

C. **Correct:** Adding the user as a co-administrator on the Azure subscription would allow the user to create a virtual machine in the Azure subscription and provision other resources as needed.

D. **Incorrect:** Adding the user as a service administrator on the Azure subscription would allow the user to create a virtual machine and other resources in the Azure subscription. However, this would also give the user access to billing and other features beyond what is required.

3. **Correct answers:** B and C

A. **Incorrect:** A CNAME record is used to map a domain name to another domain name.

B. **Correct:** Azure supports custom domain verification for an Azure Active Directory using a TXT record entry in your domain name registrar.

C. **Correct:** Azure supports custom domain verification for an Azure Active Directory using a MX record entry in your domain name registrar.

D. **Incorrect:** An A (host) record is used to specify an IP address a domain name should resolve to.

4. **Correct answer:** D

A. **Incorrect:** Enable-MSOnlinePasswordSync is the cmdlet used to enable the password synchronization feature for DirSync. It has the same effect as checking the option to enable password synchronization during installation of the DirSync tool.

B. **Incorrect:** Enable-PasswordSyncLog is the cmdlet used to enable logging for the password synchronization extension of DirSync.

C. **Incorrect:** Enable-DirSyncLog is the cmdlet used to enable logging for DirSync.

D. **Correct:** Enable-OnlinePasswordWriteBack is the cmdlet used to enable the password write-back feature.

5. **Correct answer:** A

A. **Correct:** Start-OnlineCoexistenceSync is the cmdlet used to perform an on-demand synchronization.

B. **Incorrect:** Set-DirSyncConfiguration is used to apply configuration settings for directory synchronization.

C. **Incorrect:** Enable-DirSyncLog is the cmdlet used to enable logging for DirSync.

D. **Incorrect:** Set-FullPasswordSync is used to force a full sync the next time the synchronization service is started.

6. **Correct answer:** B

   A. **Incorrect:** DirSync is used for single-forest directory synchronization.

   B. **Correct:** AAD Sync is the tool that supports configuring directory synchronization in a multi-forest environment.

   C. **Incorrect:** The AAD Connect tool currently does not support multi-forest environments. This feature is on the roadmap for the tool though.

   D. **Incorrect:** The Synchronization Service Manager is a FIM client that can be used to monitor synchronization events.

Objective 5.2: Thought experiment

1. You should add the SaaS application to the Contoso Azure Active Directory using the management portal. In the applications page for the Contoso directory, you can add an application from the application gallery simply by selecting it in the application gallery. The management portal then guides you through the steps necessary to configure the application.

2. You should configure single sign-on using the Windows Azure AD Single Sign-On option in the wizard used to configure SSO. This establishes federation between Contoso's Azure Active Directory and the SaaS application. Another alternative would be to use the Existing Single Sign-On option. However, this would only be advisable if Contoso already had Active Directory Federation Services installed and configured in their on-premises environment.

Objective 5.2: Review

1. **Correct answers:** C and D

   A. **Incorrect:** The management portal is where co-administrators of an Azure subscription can provision resources.

   B. **Incorrect:** The Active Directory Portal is where global administrators can manage users and is often used by administrators of Office 365 subscriptions.

   C. **Correct:** The Access Panel is where users can see and launch applications they have been assigned access to.

   D. **Correct:** The My Apps application from the Apple App Store can be used for users of iOS 7 devices.

2. **Correct answers:** A,B, and D

   A. **Correct:** Mobile phone is a valid contact method and can be configured to receive a text message or a phone call.

   B. **Correct:** Office phone is a valid contact method.

C. **Incorrect:** Email is not a valid contact method when configuring Multi-Factor Authentication. It is used in the first leg of authentication though when authenticating using a username and password.

D. **Correct:** Mobile application is a valid contact method. When choosing this option, you are prompted to download the application to a device and activate it using a passcode provided. The supported device types are Windows Phone, Android, and iOS devices.

3. **Correct answers:** B and D

A. **Incorrect:** Automatic user provisioning is used to provision user accounts in the SaaS application because users are provisioned in Azure Active Directory.

B. **Correct:** Password-based single sign-on uses the user's credentials with the SaaS application to authenticate.

C. **Incorrect:** Active Directory Federation Services can be a token provider in a single sign-on configuration, but it is not one of the single sign-on modes.

D. **Correct:** Federation-based single sign-on uses the user's credentials in Active Directory to authenticate when accessing the SaaS application.

4. **Correct answer:** A

A. **Correct:** The URL *https://myapps.microsoft.com* is the URL for the Access Panel.

B. **Incorrect:** The URL *https://poral.azure.com* is the URL for the management portal.

C. **Incorrect:** The URL *http://azure.microsoft.com/en-us/marketplace/active-directory* is the URL for the Azure Active Directory applications gallery.

D. **Incorrect:** The URL *https://account.windowsazure.com/organization* is the URL to sign up for an Azure Subscription as an organization rather than as an individual.

Objective 5.3: Thought experiment

1. Use the management portal to add the application to Azure Active Directory. In the applications page of the management portal, click the Add button to start the Add Application Wizard. Add the web application using the type web application and/or web API. Repeat this for the web service so that you have two applications registered in Azure Active Directory. Provide the development team with the application endpoints for your Azure Active Directory and the application ID URI and reply URL for both applications.

2. The web service will need to be exposed such that the web application can be configured to access it on behalf of the signed-in user, which can be done by adding the oauth2Permissions configuration to the application manifest for the web service.

3. Using the management portal, configure the web application to access the graph API by assigning a delegated permission to read directory data for the existing Windows Azure Active Directory application. Add a second application permission setting for the web service and select the permission level that was added in the web service's application manifest file.

Objective 5.3: Review

1. **Correct answers:** A, C, and D

   A. **Correct:** The WS-Federation endpoint is used often for browser-based web applications and provides user sign in and sign out support.

   B. **Incorrect:** The federation metadata document endpoint contains metadata for the Azure Active Directory tenant, such as the certificate used to sign the security tokens it issues.

   C. **Correct:** SAML-P provides support for the SAML 2.0 web browser single sign-on and sign-out profiles.

   D. **Correct:** Azure Active Directory supports the OAuth 2.0 protocol via the OAuth 2.0 token endpoint and the OAuth 2.0 authorization endpoint.

2. **Correct answer:** C

   A. **Incorrect:** The sign-on URL is the URL where clients can access the application using a browser or other web tool.

   B. **Incorrect:** The reply URL is where Azure Active Directory will redirect the user to after a client has been authenticated and authorized to access the application.

   C. **Correct:** The application ID URI is used to uniquely identify an application added to Azure Active Directory.

   D. **Incorrect:** The name setting is only a friendly name chosen for the application and can be any value. The name is displayed in the applications page of Azure Active Directory for each application.

3. **Correct answer:** A

   A. **Correct:** The URL *https://sts.windows.net/<tenant>* is a tenant-specific endpoint where SAML tokens are issued.

   B. **Incorrect:** The URL *https://login.windows.net/<tenant>/saml2* is the application endpoint used to sign in and sign out users using the SAML-P protocol.

   C. **Incorrect:** The URL *https://login.windows.net/<tenant>/wsfed* is the application endpoint used to sign in and sign out users using the WS-Federation protocol.

   D. **Incorrect:** The URL *https://graph.windows.net/<tenant>* is the graph API application endpoint used by applications to perform CRUD operations on directory objects in Azure Active Directory.

4. **Correct answer:** D

   A. **Incorrect:** The WS-Federation sign-on endpoint is where unauthenticated users of an application configured for WS-Federation are redirected to sign in.

   B. **Incorrect:** The SAML-P sign-on endpoint is where unauthenticated users of an application configured for SAML-P are redirected at to sign in.

   C. **Incorrect:** The Graph API endpoint is used by applications to read and/or write data in the Azure Active Directory.

   D. **Correct:** The federation metadata document endpoint points to the metadata document for the Azure Active Directory, which contains the certificate used to sign SAML tokens.

CHAPTER 6

Implement virtual networks

Azure Virtual Networks provide the infrastructure for deploying workloads that require an advanced network configuration. Virtual networks provide support for hybrid network connectivity from Azure to your on-premises network, or to other virtual networks in Azure. Azure Virtual Networks also provide support for deploying intranet or n-tier workloads using the internal load balancer. Workloads, such as Active Directory, are also enabled in the cloud using features only supported in virtual networks (such as subnets and static IP addresses). This chapter will focus on virtual networks, how to create them, configure them, as well as focusing on key hybrid technologies.

Objectives in this chapter:

- Objective 6.1: Configure a virtual network
- Objective 6.2: Modify a network configuration
- Objective 6.3: Design and implement a multi-site, or hybrid, network

Objective 6.1: Configure a virtual network

Configuring an Azure virtual network involves network design skills such as specifying the address spaces (ranges) to use, and dividing the network into subnets. In addition to designing the network itself, several features can only be enabled through virtual networks. These features include static IP addresses, internal load balancing, and Active Directory domain join. Virtual machines (VMs) and cloud services (web and worker roles) both have different techniques for deployment into a virtual network.

> **This objective covers how to:**
> - Create and configure a virtual network
> - Deploy a virtual machine into a virtual network
> - Deploy a cloud service into a virtual network
> - Configure internal load balancing

Creating and configuring a virtual network

Azure virtual networks can be created through the Azure management portal or by importing the network configuration defined in XML using the Azure PowerShell cmdlets, or the service management API.

To create a new virtual network using the Azure management portal, complete the following:

1. Specify the name of the virtual network and the region to create it in, as shown in Figure 6-1.

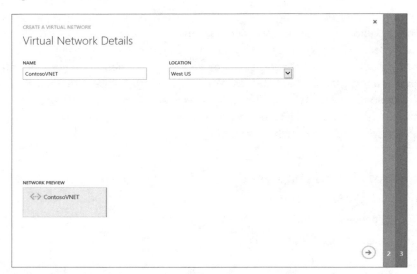

FIGURE 6-1 Specifying the virtual network name and location in the Create A Virtual Network Wizard

> **NOTE AFFINITY GROUPS NO LONGER REQUIRED**
>
> Previously, in an affinity group, creating a virtual network was required, but this requirement is going away and moving towards the region model for more flexibility.

2. On the DNS Servers And VPN Connectivity page, specify a DNS server by adding its name and IP address to the configuration. A DNS server in an Azure Virtual Network can refer to an IP address of a DNS server on-premises, in an Azure virtual machine, or even an external DNS service. All virtual machines and cloud services (web and worker roles) will be automatically assigned the DNS configuration specified in the virtual network.

3. On the DNS Servers And VPN Connectivity page, you may specify whether the virtual network will use hybrid connectivity using point-to-site or site-to-site connectivity, or use the Microsoft Azure ExpressRoute service. This step is optional because not all virtual networks will use these options. Figure 6-2 shows the virtual network configuration at this stage.

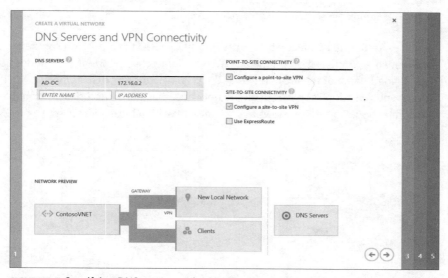

FIGURE 6-2 Specifying DNS servers, point-to-site connectivity, or site-to-site connectivity for a virtual network in the Create A Virtual Network Wizard

4. Figure 6-3 shows that the next step is to define the address space of the point-to-site configuration of the network. This stage of the creation process only appears if point-to-site connectivity was previously selected in step 2. The IP addresses in this range will be assigned to clients connecting to your networking through individual VPN connections.

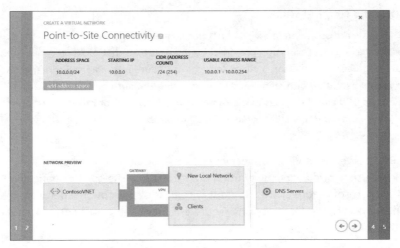

FIGURE 6-3 Setting the address space for point-to-site clients

5. Because site-to-site connectivity was previously selected in step 2, you can define the local network configuration on the Site-To-Site Connectivity page. This includes the user defined name of the local network, the public IP address of a supported VPN device, and the address spaces of all the networks that will be accessible through this connection. Figure 6-4 shows a local network with a local address space of 172.16.0.0/12.

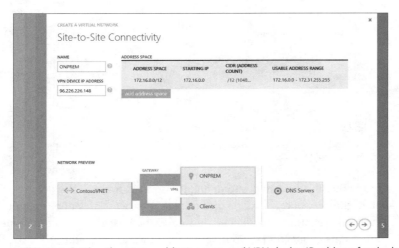

FIGURE 6-4 Setting the name, address space, and VPN device IP address for the local network

6. On the Virtual Network Address Spaces page, shown in Figure 6-5, define the address spaces and subnets of the virtual network. These are the private IPs that all resources (virtual machines and cloud service web and worker roles) will be assigned when deployed into this virtual network.

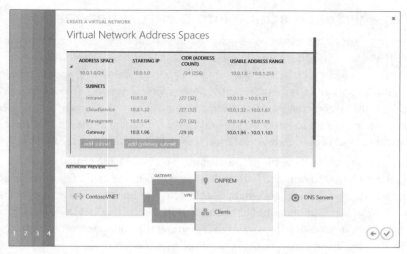

FIGURE 6-5 Final configuration of the ContosoVNET virtual network

EXAM TIP

Recently, a change has been implemented to allow virtual networks to use any IP address range you want inside of your virtual networks. Previously, the IP address ranges (or address spaces) defined inside of an Azure virtual network could only use IP ranges defined in RFC 1918. This RFC includes IP addresses in the following ranges:

- 10.0.0.0 – 10.255.255.255 (10.0.0.0/8)

- 172.16.0.0 – 172.31.255.255 (172.16.0.0/12)

- 192.168.0.0 – 192.168.255.255 (192.168.0.0/16)

EXAM TIP

You can also specify DNS at the cloud service level using the New-AzureDNS and New-AzureVM cmdlets. This approach allows finer control for assigning DNS servers than specifying DNS at the virtual network level. The settings only apply to virtual machines within the cloud service and can only be set when the first virtual machine is created in the cloud service. Here is a partial example so that you can see the usage:

```
$dns1 = New-AzureDns -Name "AD-DC1" -IPAddress "172.168.0.2"
$dns2 = New-AzureDns -Name "AD-DC2" -IPAddress "172.168.0.3"
New-AzureVM -DnsSettings $dns1,$dns2 (other parameters)
```

Deploying a virtual machine into a virtual network

The Azure management portal allows you to create a virtual machine in an existing virtual network, specify the subnet, and optionally specify a static IP address. The virtual network cannot be changed on a virtual machine after creation (without deleting it and re-creating it from disks), so it is important to remember to specify the virtual network to use during virtual machine creation. Also, when creating multiple virtual machines in the same cloud service (domain name), it is important to know that the first virtual machine in the cloud service sets the virtual network for all subsequent virtual machines in that same cloud service.

When creating a virtual machine using the management portal, the virtual networks available to you are filtered to only show the virtual networks in the same subscription and location as the virtual machine you are creating. To create a virtual machine and specify a virtual network, click New, Optional Config, Network, and then you select the virtual network, subnet, and optionally a static IP address. Figure 6-6 shows the configuration of a new virtual machine in the ContosoVNET virtual network, with the management subnet specified, and the static IP address 10.0.1.68 assigned.

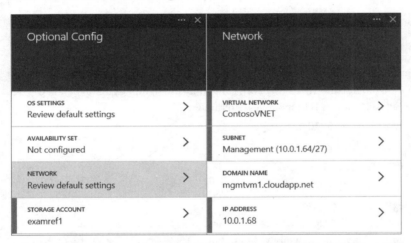

FIGURE 6-6 Using the management portal to specify virtual network configuration

To specify the virtual network when provisioning from Windows PowerShell, use the VNetName and SubnetNames parameters of the New-AzureQuickVM cmdlet. The virtual network is set for all virtual machines in the same cloud service when the first virtual machine is created in the cloud service. The following example shows creating a virtual machine in the ContosoVNET and Management subnet using the New-AzureQuickVM cmdlet. This cmdlet does not support specifying a static IP address.

```
$vnetName = "ContosoVNET"
$subnet   = "Management"
New-AzureQuickVM -Windows `
                 -ServiceName $serviceName `
                 -Name $vmName `
                 -ImageName $imageName `
```

```
                    -AdminUsername $adminUser `
                    -Password $password `
                    -Location $location `
                    -InstanceSize $size `
                    -SubnetNames $subnet `
                    -VNetName $vnetName
```

The following example shows how to configure the network configuration using the New-AzureVM creation method. The example uses the Set-AzureStaticVNetIP and Set-AzureSubnet cmdlets to specify the network configuration. It also specifies the virtual network name using the VNetName parameter of the New-AzureVM cmdlet.

```
$vnetName = "ContosoVNET"
$subnet   = "Management"
$staticIP = "10.0.1.68"
New-AzureVMConfig -Name $vmName `
                  -InstanceSize $size `
                  -ImageName $imageName |
Add-AzureProvisioningConfig -Windows `
                            -AdminUsername $adminUser `
                            -Password $password |
Set-AzureStaticVNetIP -IPAddress $staticIP |
Set-AzureSubnet -SubnetNames $subnet |
New-AzureVM -ServiceName $serviceName `
            -Location $location `
            -VNETName $vnetName
```

EXAM TIP

The static IP address must reside in the IP range of the subnet you assign to the virtual machine, and it can't be assigned to another virtual machine. For example, the subnet specified in Figure 6-6 (10.0.1.64/27) supports a range of IP addresses: 10.0.1.64 - 10.0.1.95. The first four IP addresses in a subnet are always reserved in Azure. This means the first IP available for assignment is 10.0.1.68. Static IP addresses can be specified on an existing virtual machine by updating the virtual machine configuration with the Set-AzureStaticVNetIP cmdlet.

Active Directory domain join

Active Directory domain join isn't specifically called out in this objective, but virtual network connectivity is a key dependency for the feature to work. When creating a virtual machine using a Windows-based image, you can specify that the virtual machine automatically join a Windows Server Active Directory domain at creation.

To successfully enable Active Directory domain join, the virtual machine must be deployed into an existing virtual network that has an Active Directory-enabled DNS server specified as part of the virtual network configuration (this can also be specified at the cloud service level using the New-AzureDNS cmdlet). The domain controller can be on-premises and connected via site-to-site, or ExpressRoute, or it can be a domain controller running in a virtual machine in a virtual network in Azure that is reachable from the virtual machine that you are creating.

To domain join a virtual machine, specify the domain name, and provide a domain account (user name and password) with permission to join the computer account to the domain. Using Windows PowerShell you can optionally specify an organizational unit (OU) for the new computer object to be created in. To specify the domain parameters, it's important to use the WindowsDomain parameter of the Add-AzureProvisioningConfig cmdlet instead of using the Windows parameter, as shown in previous examples. The following is a complete example of using Windows PowerShell to domain join a virtual machine.

```
$adminUser        = "[admin user name]"
$adminPassword    = "[admin password]"
$domainUser       = "[domain admin user name]"
$domainPassword   = "[domain user password]"
$ou               = 'OU=AzureVMs,DC=fabrikam,DC=com'
$domain           = "contoso"
$fqdnDomain       = "contoso.com"
$imageFamily      = "Windows Server 2012 R2 Datacenter"
$imageName        = Get-AzureVMImage |
                        where { $_.ImageFamily -eq $imageFamily } |
                        sort PublishedDate -Descending |
                select -ExpandProperty ImageName -First 1

New-AzureVMConfig -Name $vmName `
                -InstanceSize $size `
                -ImageName $imageName |
Add-AzureProvisioningConfig -WindowsDomain `
                    -AdminUsername $adminUser `
                    -Password $adminPassword `
                    -Domain $domain `
                    -JoinDomain $fqdnDomain `
                    -DomainUserName $domainUser `
                    -DomainPassword $domainPassword `
                    -MachineObjectOU $ou |
Set-AzureSubnet -SubnetNames $subnet |
New-AzureVM -ServiceName $serviceName `
                -Location $location `
                -VNETName $vnetName
```

Deploying a cloud service into a virtual network

You can deploy Azure Cloud Services to a virtual network by defining the network configuration in the ServiceConfiguration.cscfg file prior to deployment.

This example shows an example network configuration of a cloud service with two worker roles: WebRole and WorkerRole. The virtual network name is specified using the VirtualNetworkSite element. Each role can be assigned a specific subnet by specifying it in the AddressAssignments element. It is possible to specify multiple subnets for each role. If the IP addresses in the first subnet are depleted, new instances of your web or worker role will automatically use IP addresses from the next subnet if one is specified.

```
<NetworkConfiguration>
  <VirtualNetworkSite name="ContosoVNET" />
```

```
<AddressAssignments>
  <InstanceAddress roleName="WebRole" >
    <Subnets>
      <Subnet name="CloudService"></Subnet>
    </Subnets>
  </InstanceAddress>
  <InstanceAddress roleName="WorkerRole" >
    <Subnets>
      <Subnet name="CloudService"></Subnet>
    </Subnets>
  </InstanceAddress>
</AddressAssignments>
</NetworkConfiguration>
```

After the network configuration is defined, simply deploy the cloud service to the same region as the virtual network using the management portal or the New-AzureService and New-AzureDeployment cmdlets.

Configuring internal load balancing

Azure Virtual Networks support deploying load-balanced virtual machines using a private IP address from your virtual network as the virtual IP (VIP). This functionality supports deploying intranet workloads and even load balancing middle-tier applications. The internal load balancer can only be specified when the virtual machine is created by using Windows PowerShell.

To configure the internal load balancer, do the following:

1. Identify an IP address from a subnet on a virtual network in your subscription. The following example creates several variables that define the configuration from the previously created virtual network.

   ```
   $vip       = "10.0.1.30"
   $lbName    = "web"
   $subnet    = "Intranet"
   $vnetName = "ContosoVNET"
   The nextasd
   ```

2. Create a load balancer configuration object using the New-AzureInternalLoadBalancerConfig cmdlet and specify the configuration.

   ```
   $ilb = New-AzureInternalLoadBalancerConfig -InternalLoadBalancerName $lbName `
                                   -StaticVNetIPAddress $vip `
                                   -SubnetName $subnet
   ```

3. Specify the name of the load balancer to each load-balanced endpoint in the set. The following example creates two virtual machine configuration objects. Each configuration has a load-balanced endpoint added using the Add-AzureEndpoint cmdlet. The internal load balancer name is specified with the InternalLoadBalancer name parameter.

   ```
   $vm1 = New-AzureVMConfig -ImageName $ImageName -Name "lb1" `
                       -InstanceSize Small |
   ```

```
            Add-AzureProvisioningConfig -Windows `
                                        -AdminUsername $adminUser `
                                        -Password $password |
        Set-AzureSubnet -SubnetNames $subnet |
        Add-AzureEndpoint -Name "web" -Protocol tcp -LocalPort 80 `
                          -PublicPort 80 -LBSetName "weblbset" `
                          -InternalLoadBalancerName $lbName `
                          -DefaultProbe
$vm2 = New-AzureVMConfig -ImageName $ImageName -Name "lb2" `
                         -InstanceSize Small |
        Add-AzureProvisioningConfig -Windows `
                                    -AdminUsername $adminUser `
                                    -Password $password |
        Set-AzureSubnet -SubnetNames $subnet |
        Add-AzureEndpoint -Name "web" -Protocol tcp -LocalPort 80 `
                          -PublicPort 80 -LBSetName "weblbset" `
                          -InternalLoadBalancerName $lbName `
                          -DefaultProbe
```

4. Create the virtual machines using the New-AzureVM cmdlet. The internal load balancer configuration created earlier must be passed to the InternalLoadBalancerConfig cmdlet as shown in the following example.

```
New-AzureVM -ServiceName $serviceName `
            -Location $location `
            -VNetName $vnetName `
            -VMs $vm1, $vm2 `
            -InternalLoadBalancerConfig $ilb
```

Thought experiment

Deploying an intranet workload using virtual machines

In this thought experiment, apply what you've learned about this objective. You can find answers to these questions in the "Answers" section at the end of this chapter.

You are the network administrator of Contoso. You are deploying an Active Directory domain controller in an Azure virtual machine. You want to ensure that the IP address does not change and that virtual machines added to the virtual network will be able to resolve the domain name.

1. How should you configure the IP address of the domain controller?

2. How should you configure the virtual network to allow new virtual machines to resolve the domain name?

Objective summary

- The virtual network can only be assigned when the first virtual machine is created into a domain name/cloud service. Additional virtual machines deployed into the same domain name/cloud service will inherit this virtual network. Using Windows PowerShell, the VNetName parameter of the New-AzureQuickVM or New-AzureVM cmdlets can be used when you create the first virtual machine.

- A virtual machine's subnet can be specified at creation time or changed later using the Windows PowerShell cmdlet Set-AzureSubnet.

- When a static IP address is required for a solution, don't set it in the operating system. You must set the static IPs using the management portal or using the Set-AzureSetVNetIP cmdlet.

- If an Active Directory DNS server is specified in your virtual network configuration and the Active Directory domain controller is reachable from the virtual network, you can domain join a virtual machine at creation time using the Azure Preview Portal or the Azure PowerShell cmdlets.

- A cloud service can be deployed into a virtual network by specifying the network configuration in the ServiceConfiguration.cscfg file. The cloud service must be deployed into the same region as the virtual network.

- The internal load balancer is configured by specifying an IP address from a virtual network and referenced with each load-balanced endpoint. The internal load balancer configuration is referenced in the New-AzureVM cmdlet.

Objective review

Answer the following questions to test your knowledge of the information in this objective. You can find the answers to these questions and explanations of why each answer choice is correct or incorrect in the "Answers" section at the end of this chapter.

1. Which of the address spaces is valid for an Azure virtual network? (Choose all that apply.)
   A. 192.168.0.0/16
   B. 10.0.0.0/8
   C. 172.0.0.0/8
   D. 172.16.0.0/12

2. You have defined the subnet 10.0.1.0/24. Which IP address would be valid for the VIP of an internal load balancer configuration?
   A. 10.0.1.0
   B. 10.0.0.1
   C. 10.0.1.100
   D. 10.0.1.3

3. Which Windows PowerShell cmdlet is used to specify the static IP address of an Azure virtual machine?

   A. New-AzureVM

   B. Add-AzureProvisioningConfig

   C. Set-AzureStaticVNetIP

   D. Set-AzureSubnet

Objective 6.2: Modify a network configuration

Azure virtual networks can be configured using the management portal, Windows Power-Shell, or, of course, the Azure REST API. This objective covers how to modify the network configuration and also covers some of the settings you can change on virtual machines, such as the static IP address and even the subnet.

> **This objective covers how to:**
> - Import and export network configuration
> - Changing the configuration of an existing network configuration

Importing and exporting network configuration settings

The network configuration of an Azure subscription can be exported as an XML file. You can modify the XML file using a text or XML editor, or programmatically, and then import it into the subscription. There are several reasons you would want to modify the network configuration. For instance, if you need to add a new virtual network or modify the configuration in an automated fashion, it's possible to retrieve the configuration, modify the XML file, and then import it all programmatically. Configuring multi-site, or virtual network to virtual network configurations, requires modifying the configuration file directly.

The network configuration file can be imported or exported directly from the management portal or from Windows PowerShell. To export the network configuration file using the management portal, click Networks on the left navigation, and then click Export. To export the network configuration file using Windows PowerShell, call the Get-AzureVNETConfig cmdlet and pass the path and filename to the ExportToFile parameter as the following example shows.

```
Get-AzureVNetConfig -ExportToFile "C:\ExamRef\NetConfig.xml"
```

> **MORE INFO** **AZURE VIRTUAL NETWORK CONFIGURATION SCHEMA**
>
> You can modify the network configuration. Use the schema documented on MSDN at
> *http://msdn.microsoft.com/en-us/library/azure/jj157100.aspx.*

After the network configuration is specified in the XML file, use the management portal to import the file by clicking New, Network Services, Virtual Network, and then click Import, and browse to the XML file. To import the network configuration file using Windows PowerShell, use the Set-AzureVNETConfig cmdlet, as shown in the following example.

```
Set-AzureVNetConfig -ConfigurationPath "C:\ExamRef\NetConfig.xml"
```

Review the configuration of the virtual network created in Objective 6-1. The following excerpt from the virtual network's parent element <NetworkConfiguration> focuses on the most relevant portion of the configuration.

```
<VirtualNetworkConfiguration>
<Dns>
  <DnsServers>
    <DnsServer name="AD-DC" IPAddress="172.16.0.2" />
  </DnsServers>
</Dns>
<LocalNetworkSites>
  <LocalNetworkSite name="ONPREM">
    <AddressSpace>
      <AddressPrefix>172.16.0.0/12</AddressPrefix>
    </AddressSpace>
    <VPNGatewayAddress>96.226.226.148</VPNGatewayAddress>
  </LocalNetworkSite>
</LocalNetworkSites>
<VirtualNetworkSites>
  <VirtualNetworkSite name="ContosoVNET" Location="West US">
    <AddressSpace>
      <AddressPrefix>10.0.1.0/24</AddressPrefix>
    </AddressSpace>
    <Subnets>
      <Subnet name="Intranet">
        <AddressPrefix>10.0.1.0/27</AddressPrefix>
      </Subnet>
      <Subnet name="CloudService">
        <AddressPrefix>10.0.1.32/27</AddressPrefix>
      </Subnet>
      <Subnet name="Management">
        <AddressPrefix>10.0.1.64/27</AddressPrefix>
      </Subnet>
      <Subnet name="GatewaySubnet">
        <AddressPrefix>10.0.1.96/29</AddressPrefix>
      </Subnet>
    </Subnets>
    <DnsServersRef>
      <DnsServerRef name="AD-DC" />
    </DnsServersRef>
    <Gateway>
      <VPNClientAddressPool>
        <AddressPrefix>10.0.0.0/24</AddressPrefix>
      </VPNClientAddressPool>
      <ConnectionsToLocalNetwork>
        <LocalNetworkSiteRef name="ONPREM">
          <Connection type="IPsec" />
```

```
        </LocalNetworkSiteRef>
      </ConnectionsToLocalNetwork>
    </Gateway>
  </VirtualNetworkSite>
</VirtualNetworkSites>
</VirtualNetworkConfiguration>
```

The VirtualNetworkConfiguration element is the parent element to the <Dns> element, which contains the DNS servers for the virtual network. It also includes the <LocalNetworkSites>, which contains the list of local networks to connect to. The VirtualNetworkConfiguration element is also the parent of the <VirtualNetworkSites> element, which holds all of the virtual networks in your subscription.

Each <VirtualNetworkSite> element specifies the name of the virtual network and the region (you can specify an AffinityGroup, but Azure is moving towards using regions for virtual networks instead). Within the <VirtualNetworkSite> element is a list of the address spaces, subnets, and references to DNS servers and local networks. As you can see, the DNS servers and local networks are associated with a virtual network but are not part of the virtual network itself. This is more apparent in the management portal because both DNS and local networks have separate UIs for management. To manage existing local networks or DNS server references in the management portal, click Networks on the left navigation, and then click Local Networks or DNS Servers, as shown in Figure 6-7.

FIGURE 6-7 Using the management portal to view virtual networks, local networks, and DNS server settings

Changing an existing network configuration

You should be aware of a few rules about changing resources that are part of the network configuration of an Azure subscription. One rule to remember is that each Azure subscription has quotas for different types of services. You can add new virtual networks, DNS servers, and local networks as long as you stay within your subscription quotas. To view your subscription quotas, use the Get-AzureSubscription cmdlet with the ExtendedDetails parameter.

Another rule is you can remove DNS servers, local networks, or virtual networks from your subscription as long as they don't have any resources in use. For DNS and local networks, there can be no existing virtual networks referencing them. A virtual network cannot be deleted while there are virtual machines, cloud service instances, or a gateway provisioned.

Another set of rules to understand is what you can and can't change on a provisioned virtual network. For instance, you can enable point-to-site connectivity, site-to-site connectivity, or ExpressRoute on an existing virtual network. Point-to-site and site-to-site are not compatible on the same virtual network with ExpressRoute. You can add, remove, or modify the subnet configuration as long as no virtual machines, cloud service instances, or gateways are provisioned in the subnet. Finally, you can add or remove DNS references to a virtual network that already exists. However, be aware that any existing virtual machines or cloud service instances will not see the DNS configuration changes until they have been restarted.

The last rule relates to the virtual network configuration of a virtual machine. You cannot change the virtual network of an existing virtual machine without deleting and re-creating it from the disk. However, you can change the virtual machine's subnet, assign a static IP address, and also add a load-balanced endpoint as long as the internal load balancer configuration was specified when the first virtual machine in the cloud service was created.

To change any of these settings on a virtual machine use the Azure PowerShell cmdlets. For example, to change the virtual machine's subnet, first retrieve the current virtual machine configuration with a call to the Get-AzureVM cmdlet. Next, pass the returned configuration through the Windows PowerShell pipeline operator to the Set-AzureSubnet cmdlet, which modifies the configuration with the updated subnet name. The modified configuration is then passed to the Update-AzureVM cmdlet, as shown in the following example.

```
Get-AzureVM -ServiceName $serviceName -Name $vmName |
    Set-AzureSubnet -SubnetNames $newSubnet |
    Update-AzureVM
```

> **NOTE   A REBOOT IS REQUIRED TO CHANGE A SUBNET**
>
> Changing the subnet or static IP address of a virtual machine will cause the virtual machine to reboot.

Thought experiment
Automating a virtual network deployment

In this thought experiment, apply what you've learned about this objective. You can find answers to these questions in the "Answers" section at the end of this chapter.

You are the network administrator with Contoso. You are tasked with moving a virtual machine in the ContosoVNET virtual network to another subnet. You also need to move a virtual machine that is not on the virtual network (but in the same region) to the virtual network.

1. What steps need to be taken to change the subnet of the virtual machine in the virtual network?

2. What steps need to be taken to move the existing virtual machine not in the virtual network to be deployed in the virtual network?

Objective summary

- You can modify the network configuration of an Azure subscription using the management portal or Windows PowerShell.
- Use the Get-AzureVNETConfig cmdlet to view or save the existing network configuration.
- Use the Set-AzureVNETConfig cmdlet to update the network configuration. This cmdlet accepts a parameter (ConfigurationPath) to an XML file for the entire network configuration of the subscription.
- The schema for Azure network configuration is documented on MSDN at *http://msdn. microsoft.com/en-us/library/azure/jj157100.aspx*.
- You can change the static IP address of a virtual machine using the Set-AzureStaticVNetIP cmdlet. This requires a reboot of the virtual machine.
- You can change the subnet of a virtual machine using the Set-AzureSubnet cmdlet. This requires a reboot of the virtual machine.
- You can add or remove a DNS server from a virtual network. Existing virtual machines or cloud service instances will need to be restarted to see the update.
- You cannot remove a subnet if virtual machines or cloud service web and worker role instances are actively deployed that reference them.
- You cannot remove a local network or DNS server entry if a virtual network references them.

Objective review

Answer the following questions to test your knowledge of the information in this objective. You can find the answers to these questions and explanations of why each answer choice is correct or incorrect in the "Answers" section at the end of this chapter.

1. You need to add a new virtual network to the XML file programmatically. Which element do you add?

    A. <VirtualNetworkSites>

    B. <VirtualNetworkSite>

    C. <NetworkConfiguration>

    D. <VirtualNetwork>

2. You have programmatically added the virtual network to the network configuration XML file. Which Windows PowerShell cmdlet do you use to update the configuration?

    A. Set-AzureVNetConfig

    B. Set-AzureVNetGateway

    C. Update-AzureVM

    D. Set-AzureSubnet

3. You add a new DNS server to your virtual network configuration, but the existing virtual machines cannot resolve names using the DNS server. What must you do to solve the problem?

   A. You cannot add a DNS server to an existing virtual network.

   B. Specify the IP address of the DNS server on the network adapter in the virtual machine.

   C. Reboot the virtual machines.

   D. Create the DNS reference using the New-AzureDNS cmdlet.

Objective 6.3: Design and implement a multi-site or hybrid network

There are several options for enabling hybrid network connectivity to Azure Virtual Network. The point-to-site option is useful for connecting individual computers to Azure using a VPN client with support for SSTP. Enabling site-to-site connectivity provides the ability to connect entire networks using secure IPSEC VPN. Using Azure ExpressRoute allows you to connect through either an Internet Exchange Provider or a Network Service Provider using a private dedicated circuit. Each of these options has their own merits and usually fairly distinct use cases.

This objective covers how to:
- Identify the appropriate connectivity solution
- Implement a point-to-site VPN
- Implement a site-to-site VPN
- Implement a virtual network-to-virtual network VPN

Identifying the appropriate connectivity solution

Azure Virtual Networks offer three distinct technologies for enabling hybrid connectivity. You should understand when to use each of the following options:

- **Point-to-site connectivity** This option allows individual client machines to connect to your Azure virtual network using a traditional VPN client with the Secure Socket Tunneling protocol (SSTP) (up to 128 clients per virtual network). It doesn't require an IPSEC VPN device as site-to-site connectivity does, because each connection is established between the virtual network and an individual client computer. This option is great for remote secure administration, development, and test. However, it isn't designed for connecting application tiers because the VPN client connection requires a user to log in to the computer and manually connect. A point-to-site connection re-quires a dynamically routed gateway to be created on the Azure Virtual Network. The gateways bandwidth is 80 Mbps.

- **Site-to-site connectivity**   This option is the most common solution for enabling hybrid connectivity. It requires an IPSEC-based VPN solution such as a device, or even a software solution like Microsoft Routing and Remote Access Service (RRAS). The site-to-site option allows you to define one or more on-premises networks by specify-ing the address ranges in Classless Inter-Domain Routing (CIDR) format. The connec-tion is established using a shared authentication key between the VPN device and the gateway created in Azure. The gateway can be configured for static or dynamic routing and, just like point-to-site connectivity, the gateway's bandwidth is 80 Mbps.

- **Azure ExpressRoute**   This option makes it easy to establish dedicated and private circuits between your datacenter and Microsoft Azure using a third-party provider such as an Internet Exchange Provider (IXP) or a Network Service Provider (NSP). Your existing infrastructure can be located on-premises in your datacenter, or co-located in one of several participating provider locations. ExpressRoute allows you to extend your infrastructure to Microsoft Azure by providing private, reliable, high-speed connectiv-ity between your infrastructure and the cloud.

With ExpressRoute, your circuit is isolated using industry standard VLANs to allow pri-vate, secure access to resources deployed in Microsoft Azure Virtual Networks and also to provide connectivity to Microsoft Azure public services. ExpressRoute comes in two models: The exchange provider model and the network service provider model. Figure 6-8 shows at a high level the differences in architecture. In the exchange provider model, you establish a crossover connection from a cage in the co-location datacenters, and establish a connection by using a router with BGP support. In the network service provider scenario, ExpressRoute integrates the connection into a new or existing MPLS-based wide area network.

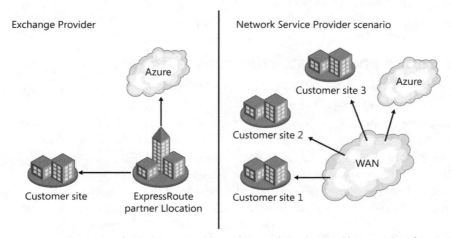

FIGURE 6-8 Comparing the Exchange Provider and Network Service Provider scenarios of Azure ExpressRoute

Table 6-1 shows some of the key differences between the two ExpressRoute provider models.

TABLE 6-1 Comparing ExpressRoute provider scenarios

Features	Network service providers	Exchange providers
Bandwidth options	10 Mbps, 50 Mbps, 100 Mbps, 500 Mbps, 1 Gbps	200 Mbps, 500 Mbps, 1Gbps, 10Gbps
Routing	Managed by the provider	Managed by the customer
High availability	Provider offers redundant connectivity	Customer must establish a pair of cross connects through the Exchange provider
MPLS support	Yes	No
Multi-site	Yes	No

EXAM TIP

Compatibility between a point-to-site or site-to-site enabled virtual network and an ExpressRoute circuit may make an appearance on the exam. At the time of this writing, these technologies are incompatible and cannot be used on the same virtual network with an ExpressRoute-enabled virtual network.

Implementing a point-to-site VPN

Point-to-site connectivity solutions are relatively easy to implement. We have already taken the first steps in Objective 6.1 by enabling point-to-site on the virtual network and creating a subnet named GatewaySubnet (the management portal does this for you). If you define the network using the XML configuration only, you will need to add the GatewaySubnet with a subnet size of at least a /29.

The other portion of the point-to-site configuration was also configured in the management portal and that is defining the IP range for the VPN client connections. This is the <VPNClientAddressPool> element, shown in Objective 6.2.

The final step is to create the gateway itself. You can do this using the management portal or using the New-AzureVNetGateway cmdlet. The management portal does not ask what type of gateway to use if point-to-site is already configured on the virtual network. Instead, it creates a dynamic routing gateway when you click Create Gateway.

Creating the gateway through Windows PowerShell requires you to specify the GatewayType parameter and specify DynamicRouting, as well as the name of the virtual network, as shown in the following example.

```
New-AzureVNetGateway –VNetName "ContosoVNET" –GatewayType DynamicRouting
```

After creating the gateway, you must create a set of certificates to authenticate VPN clients to the point-to-site gateway, as follows:

1. Create a self-signed root certificate. The following example shows how to make this certificate using makecert.exe.

```
makecert -sky exchange -r -n "CN=P2SRootCert" -pe -a sha1 -len 2048 -ss My
.\P2SRootCert.cer
```

2. Create a client certificate based on the root certificate using a similar command as shown in the following example.

```
makecert.exe -n "CN=P2SClient" -pe -sky exchange -m 96 -ss My -in "P2SRootCert"
-is my -a sha1
```

3. Upload the self-signed root certificate to the Azure gateway. At the time of this writing, there is no Windows PowerShell cmdlet to accomplish this task and it must be done using the management portal. To upload to the management portal, click Networks in the left navigation, click the virtual network name, and then click Certificates to see the Upload A Root Certificate link, as shown in Figure 6-9.

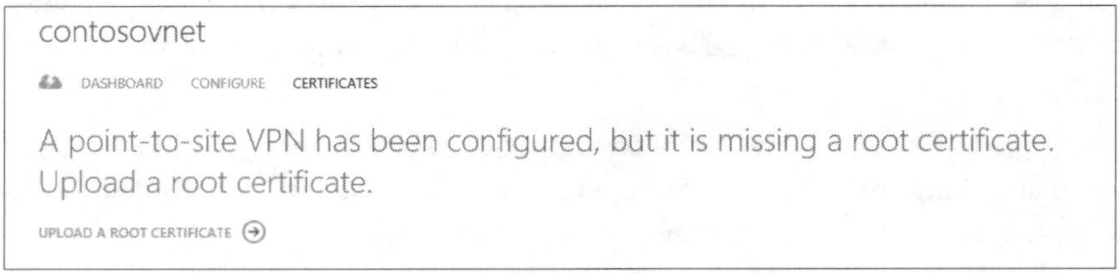

contosovnet

DASHBOARD   CONFIGURE   **CERTIFICATES**

A point-to-site VPN has been configured, but it is missing a root certificate. Upload a root certificate.

UPLOAD A ROOT CERTIFICATE ⊕

FIGURE 6-9 The location in the management portal to upload the root certificate for point-to-site connectivity

4. The other certificate that was created is located in your personal certificate store. Export the client certificate created in step 2, and then install it on the client machine that will connect to the gateway.

To export the certificate, run certmgr.msc, navigate to Personal, Certificates, and right-click the certificate issued to P2SClient. Click All Tasks and then click Export. Ensure you select Export The Private Key and specify a password. Finally, specify the path and filename for the exported certificate. Install the certificate on the client computer that will connect to the Azure gateway by double-clicking the generated .pfx file.

5. Install the VPN client package. In the management portal, open the virtual network with point-to-site enabled by clicking the Networks link in the left navigation, click the name of the virtual network, and then click the download link for the appropriate package (64-bit or 32-bit) for your client operating system. The download links available are shown in Figure 6-10.

FIGURE 6-10 Location in the management portal to download the client VPN package

The download consists of a generated executable with the name in the format {guid}.exe. Because the executable is generated on the fly, it isn't signed. As a result, you will first need to unblock the executable for it to be able to run. Right-click the .exe file name, click Properties, and then click Unblock (or use the Unblock-File Windows PowerShell cmdlet).

After you run the script, a new VPN connection will be available on your client computer. Figure 6-11 shows a VPN connection to the ContosoVNET virtual network. After you click Connect, the connection is established. The client computer can access resources on the virtual network using the internal IP address of the resource using the secure VPN connection instead of accessing it through the cloud service VIP.

FIGURE 6-11 The VPN connection created by installing the point-to-site client package

Figure 6-12 shows the virtual network dashboard for the ContosoVNET virtual network after the VPN client has connected.

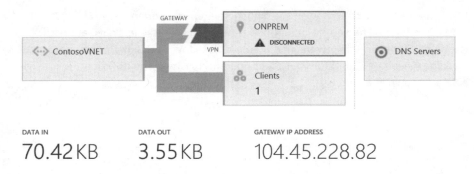

DATA IN
70.42 KB

DATA OUT
3.55 KB

GATEWAY IP ADDRESS
104.45.228.82

FIGURE 6-12 Virtual network status in the management portal

Implementing a site-to-site VPN

Site-to-site virtual private networks are a flexible option when it comes to providing connectivity in Microsoft Azure. Site-to-site supports the ability to connect one or more networks between on-premises and Azure. For instance, you can connect multiple on-premises network offices to one or more virtual networks, and you can provide connectivity to other virtual networks in Azure (even in different regions).

To connect a local network to Azure, you must have a supported device or software-based VPN solution. Microsoft is continually adding new solutions that have been tested and validated. For a current list of supported VPN solutions, see this MSDN article, *http://msdn.microsoft.com/library/azure/jj156075.aspx.*

As we saw in Objective 6.1 (Figure 6-4), you can define the local network during virtual network creation by specifying a name, a public IP address of a supported VPN device, and the address spaces that define the local network.

The next step to designing a site-to-site virtual private network is to decide on the address space you will use in your Azure Virtual Networks. Following is the configuration shown in Figure 6-5, which we will continue using as an example:

- Name: ONPREMISE
- VPN DEVICE IP: 96.226.226.148
- ADDRESS SPACE: 172.16.0.0/12

> *NOTE* **PLANNING ADDRESS SPACES**
>
> As part of this planning exercise, it is important to understand that the address spaces in your Azure virtual networks cannot overlap with addresses in your local networks or any other virtual networks in Azure that may be connected in the future.

The next step is to create a gateway. The gateway for a site-to-site VPN can be set to static routing or dynamic routing. Supportability of the gateway type depends on the device or software solution chosen. For more information about the supported solutions and to identify whether your device supports static or dynamic routing, see *http://msdn.microsoft.com/en-us/library/azure/jj156075.aspx*.

From a capabilities perspective, you should know that dynamic routing gateways are required to implement multi-site, point-to-site, and virtual network to virtual network connections. Static gateways are currently restricted as one local network to one virtual network within Azure.

Let's use an example of connecting to a server running the Routing and Remote Access Service (RRAS) for site-to-site connectivity. Figure 6-13 shows a diagram of the virtual network that was created in Objective 6.1, and then extended with point-to-site connectivity in Objective 6.2. To establish the connection between the ContosoVNET and the ONPREMISE network, we must configure the Routing and Remote Access Service in Windows Server 2012 or later.

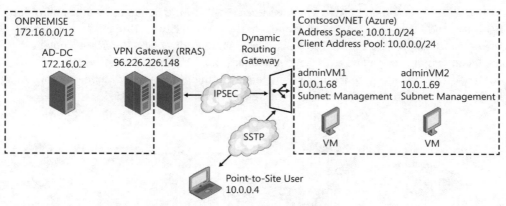

FIGURE 6-13 Network architecture of a site-to-site and point-to-site connected virtual network

To configure the RRAS service, log in to the management portal, open the dashboard for the ContosoVNET virtual network, and then click Download VPN Device Script in the Quick Glance section of the management portal. Figure 6-14 shows the resulting Download A VPN Device Configuration Script dialog box. Select the vendor (as of this writing, Cisco, Juniper, and Microsoft Corporation are available), select the platform, and then select the operating system.

FIGURE 6-14 Downloading a VPN device configuration script

In the case of selecting RRAS, a Windows PowerShell script is generated that contains the necessary code to configure RRAS to connect to the Azure gateway. The script verifies that the required features are installed and ultimately calls the Add-VPNS2SInterface cmdlet with the IP address of your gateway, the remove subnet (10.0.1.0/24 in this case), and the shared authentication key. After the script has completed execution, the Azure dashboard shows that both site-to-site and point-to-site are connected, as shown in Figure 6-15.

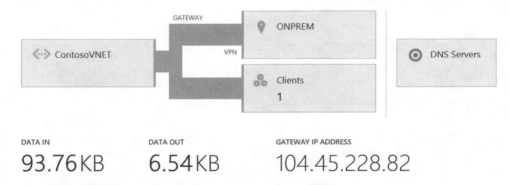

FIGURE 6-15 A virtual network with site-to-site and point-to-site connected

Implementing a virtual network-to-virtual network VPN

To implement virtual network-to-virtual network connectivity, you must define a second virtual network with address spaces that do not overlap any other virtual networks that will be connected. You can create this second virtual network in the same or a different subscription and in any Azure region you have access to.

To implement a virtual network-to-virtual network VPN, do the following:

1. Create a secondary virtual network. Use the management portal by clicking New, Network Services, Virtual Network, and Custom Create. For example, Figure 6-16 shows a secondary virtual network named ContosoVNETEast that is deployed in the East US region. The address space is 10.0.2.0/24 so it does not overlap with the range of 10.0.1.0/24, which was used to define the virtual network ContosoVNET in the West US region.

ADDRESS SPACE	STARTING IP	CIDR (ADDRESS COUNT)	USABLE ADDRESS RANGE
10.0.2.0/24	10.0.2.0	/24 (251)	10.0.2.4 - 10.0.2.254
SUBNETS			
Intranet	10.0.2.0	/27 (27)	10.0.2.4 - 10.0.2.30
CloudService	10.0.2.32	/27 (27)	10.0.2.36 - 10.0.2.62
Management	10.0.2.64	/27 (27)	10.0.2.68 - 10.0.2.94
add subnet			

FIGURE 6-16 Network design for ContosoVNETEast

2. Define two local networks. The first, ContosoVNETLocal will be considered a local network to the ContosoVNETEast virtual network, and the ContosoVNETEast virtual network will be considered a local network to ContosoVNETLocal. To add a local network in the management portal, click New, Network, Virtual Network, and then click Add Local Network, as shown in Figure 6-17.

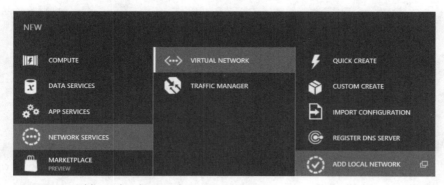

FIGURE 6-17 Adding a local network

3. Define the IP addresses and address spaces for the new local network ContosoVNETLocal. Figures 6-18 and 6-19 show how to define a new local network for the first virtual network by specifying the VPN Device IP and the Address Spaces. In Figures 6-18 and 6-19, the VPN device IP address and address space matches the values for the ContosoVNET virtual network.

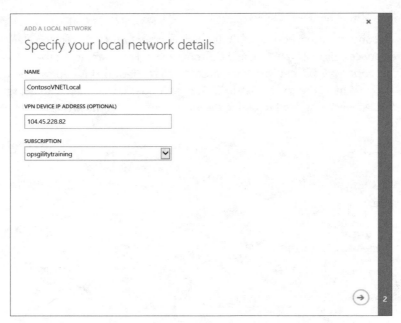

FIGURE 6-18 Specifying the VPN device IP address and local network name

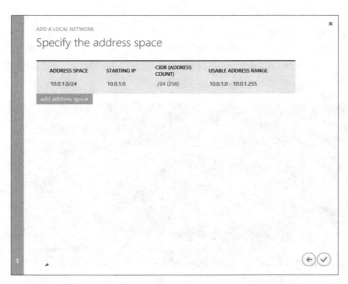

FIGURE 6-19 Defining the address space for the ContosoVNETLocal local network

4. Create the local network for the second virtual network, which in this example is
   ContosoVNETEast. This is the same process used to create the ContosoVNETLocal local
   network, as shown in Figures 6-18 and 6-19, except when prompted for the gateway
   IP address, 0.0.0.0 is specified because the gateway hasn't been created yet. For this

example, the name of the local network is ContosoVNETEastLocal. Figure 6-20 shows the additional local networks that are created alongside the original ONPREM local network that point to the Microsoft Routing and Remote Access Service server.

VIRTUAL NETWORKS	LOCAL NETWORKS	DNS SERVERS	
NAME	ADDRESS SPACE		VPN GATEWAY ADDRESS
ONPREM	172.16.0.0/12		96.226.226.148
ContosoVNETLocal	10.0.1.0/24		104.45.228.82
ContosoVNETEastLocal	10.0.2.0/24		0.0.0.0

FIGURE 6-20 The local network configuration for the ContosoVNET and ContosoVNETEast virtual networks

5. To configure both virtual networks to connect, modify the XML network configuration file directly. As of this writing, neither the management portal or the Azure Preview Portal directly supports configuring multi-site virtual networks, so the first step is to export the network configuration file for your subscription. To export using the management portal, click Networks on the left navigation, and then click Export. The network configuration for the local addresses created in the earlier steps will look similar to the following XML representation.

```xml
<LocalNetworkSite name="ContosoVNETEastLocal">
  <AddressSpace>
    <AddressPrefix>10.0.2.0/24</AddressPrefix>
  </AddressSpace>
  <VPNGatewayAddress>0.0.0.0</VPNGatewayAddress>
</LocalNetworkSite>
<LocalNetworkSite name="ContosoVNETLocal">
  <AddressSpace>
    <AddressPrefix>10.0.1.0/24</AddressPrefix>
  </AddressSpace>
  <VPNGatewayAddress>104.45.228.82</VPNGatewayAddress>
</LocalNetworkSite>
<LocalNetworkSite name="ONPREM">
  <AddressSpace>
    <AddressPrefix>172.16.0.0/12</AddressPrefix>
  </AddressSpace>
  <VPNGatewayAddress>96.226.226.148</VPNGatewayAddress>
</LocalNetworkSite>
```

EXAM TIP

A virtual network can have up to 10 local networks associated with it. A local network can be a network that is on-premises or another Azure Virtual Network.

6. Associate the ContosoVNET virtual network with the ContosoVNETEastLocal local network. In the network configuration XML file, make a new <LocalNetworkSiteRef> in the ContosoVNET virtual network that references the ContosoVNETEastLocal local

network. This is the process to add a reference to a secondary local network for multi-site virtual networks. It does not matter whether the local network is another virtual network in Azure, or an on-premises network. It is still considered "local" to the virtual network being configured. The following example shows in bold the changes needed for the configuration change.

```xml
<VirtualNetworkSite name="ContosoVNET" Location="West US">
  <AddressSpace>
    <AddressPrefix>10.0.1.0/24</AddressPrefix>
  </AddressSpace>
  <Subnets>
    <Subnet name="Intranet">
      <AddressPrefix>10.0.1.0/27</AddressPrefix>
    </Subnet>
    <Subnet name="Data">
      <AddressPrefix>10.0.1.32/27</AddressPrefix>
    </Subnet>
    <Subnet name="Management">
      <AddressPrefix>10.0.1.64/27</AddressPrefix>
    </Subnet>
    <Subnet name="GatewaySubnet">
      <AddressPrefix>10.0.1.96/29</AddressPrefix>
    </Subnet>
  </Subnets>
  <DnsServersRef>
    <DnsServerRef name="AD-DC" />
  </DnsServersRef>
  <Gateway>
    <VPNClientAddressPool>
      <AddressPrefix>10.0.0.0/24</AddressPrefix>
    </VPNClientAddressPool>
    <ConnectionsToLocalNetwork>
      <LocalNetworkSiteRef name="ONPREM">
        <Connection type="IPsec" />
      </LocalNetworkSiteRef>
      <LocalNetworkSiteRef name="ContosoVNETEastLocal">
        <Connection type="IPsec" />
      </LocalNetworkSiteRef>
    </ConnectionsToLocalNetwork>
  </Gateway>
</VirtualNetworkSite>
```

7. Configure the association of the ContosoVNETEast virtual network to the ContosoVNETLocal local network. To associate using the management portal, open the virtual network properties, and then click Configure at the top of the page. Next, select the ContosoVNETLocal local network from the LocalNetwork drop-down list box. The changes needed in the following XML configuration file are the addition of the GatewaySubnet and the <Gateway> element. The gateway element references the previously created ContosoVNETLocal local network. The required changes are in bold below.

```xml
<VirtualNetworkSite name="ContosoVNETEast" Location="East US">
  <AddressSpace>
    <AddressPrefix>10.0.2.0/24</AddressPrefix>
```

```
          </AddressSpace>
          <Subnets>
            <Subnet name="Intranet">
              <AddressPrefix>10.0.2.0/27</AddressPrefix>
            </Subnet>
            <Subnet name="CloudService">
              <AddressPrefix>10.0.2.32/27</AddressPrefix>
            </Subnet>
            <Subnet name="Management">
              <AddressPrefix>10.0.2.64/27</AddressPrefix>
            </Subnet>
            <Subnet name="GatewaySubnet">
              <AddressPrefix>10.0.2.96/29</AddressPrefix>
            </Subnet>
          </Subnets>
          <Gateway>
            <ConnectionsToLocalNetwork>
            <LocalNetworkSiteRef name="ContosoVNETLocal">
              <Connection type="IPsec" />
            </LocalNetworkSiteRef>
            </ConnectionsToLocalNetwork>
          </Gateway>
        </VirtualNetworkSite>
```

> **NOTE** **THE IP ADDRESS FOR THE SECOND GATEWAY IS CREATED LATER**
>
> The IP address of the ContosoVNETEast gateway is not defined yet because it has not been created yet.

8. Import the updated configuration using the management portal or with the Set-AzureVNETConfig Windows PowerShell cmdlet. To import using the management portal, click New, Network Services, Virtual Networks, click Import, and then browse to the modified NetworkConfig.xml. To import the configuration using Windows PowerShell use the Set-AzureVNetConfig cmdlet as shown in the following example.

```
Set-AzureVNetConfig -ConfigurationPath C:\ExamRef\NetworkConfig.xml
```

9. After the network configuration has been set, create the gateway in the ContosoVNETEast virtual network. To create the gateway in the management portal, click Networks on the left navigation, click the name of the virtual network, click Dashboard, and then finally click Create Gateway and select a Dynamic Routing gateway. Because this is a virtual network-to-virtual network configuration, the gateway must be of type DynamicRouting because StaticRouting does not support virtual network-to-virtual network connectivity. The following example shows using the New-AzureVNetGateway cmdlet to create the gateway.

```
New-AzureVNetGateway -VNetName "ContosoVNETEast" -GatewayType DynamicRouting
```

10. After the gateway is created, find the gateway IP address for ContosoVNETEast by opening the dashboard of the ContosoVNETEast virtual network. Then, update the configuration for the ContosoVNETEastLocal local network to use the new IP address.

To make the update using the management portal, click Local Networks, highlight the local network, and then click Edit. You can then specify the updated VPN Gateway Address. Figure 6-21 shows the updated configuration.

VIRTUAL NETWORKS	LOCAL NETWORKS	DNS SERVERS	
NAME		**ADDRESS SPACE**	**VPN GATEWAY ADDRESS**
ONPREM		172.16.0.0/12	96.226.226.148
ContosoVNETLocal		10.0.1.0/24	104.45.228.82
ContosoVNETEastLocal		10.0.2.0/24	104.45.151.30

FIGURE 6-21 Local network configuration with the updated gateway IP address for the ContosoVNETEast virtual network specified

11. The final step is to set the shared authentication keys between the two virtual networks. The following example uses the Set-AzureVNetGatewayKey cmdlet on each virtual network, referencing the local network for each, and specifying the same shared key. After the keys are set, the Azure gateways negotiate connectivity with each other to establish the IKE session.

```
Set-AzureVNetGatewayKey -VNetName ContosoVNET `
                -LocalNetworkSiteName ContosoVNETEastLocal `
                -SharedKey A1b2C3D4

Set-AzureVNetGatewayKey -VNetName ContosoVNETEast `
                -LocalNetworkSiteName ContosoVNETLocal `
                -SharedKey A1b2C3D4
```

Figure 6-22 shows the dashboard for the ContosoVNET virtual network after the virtual network ContosoVNETEast (local network name ContoVNETEastLocal) is connected.

CONNECTION	STATUS	DATA...	DATA...	ALLOCATED IP ADDRESSES COU...	
ONPREM	✓ Connected	70886	40096	0	
ContosoVNETEastLocal	✓ Connected	240	552	0	
VPNClientConnection	✓ Connected	108442	7648	1	

FIGURE 6-22 The network status for the ContosoVNET virtual network with multiple sites connected

> **NOTE MULTIPLE SUBSCRIPTIONS ARE SUPPORTED**
>
> In this example, the secondary network ContosoVNETEast could also have been in a secondary Azure subscription.

Figure 6-23 shows the final architecture of the network configuration. The ContosoVNET virtual network is configured to connect to the ONPREMISE network and the ContosoVNETEast network in a multi-site configuration. The ContosoVNETEast virtual network connects to the ConsotoVNET virtual network using virtual network-to-virtual network.

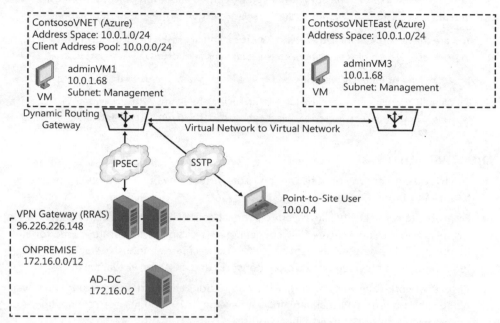

FIGURE 6-23 Network architecture of the ContosoVNET and ContosoVNETEast virtual networks configured for multi-site and virtual network-to-virtual network

EXAM TIP

Routing and architecture could be included in the exam. The solution in Figure 6-22 shows how to connect an on-premises network to a virtual network in Azure, and then connect the virtual network located in the West US region to a virtual network in the East US region. It is important to understand that virtual networks do not support transitive routing. This means you cannot reach the ONPREMISE network from ContosoVNETEast through ContosoVNET. You would need to create a connection from ONPREMISE to ContosoVNETEast for direct connectivity.

MICROSOFT VIRTUAL ACADEMY   **MICROSOFT AZURE IAAS DEEP DIVE JUMP START**

Microsoft Virtual Academy offers free online courses delivered by industry experts, including a course relevant to this exam. We recommend the Microsoft Azure IaaS Deep Drive Jump Start. You can access the course at *http://www.microsoftvirtualacademy.com/training-courses/windows-azure-iaas-deep-dive-jump-start*.

Thought experiment

Connecting multiple branch offices to a virtual network

In this thought experiment, apply what you've learned about this objective. You can find answers to these questions in the "Answers" section at the end of this chapter.

You are the network administrator with Contoso. You are tasked with connecting two of Contoso's branch office locations to a virtual network hosted in Microsoft Azure.

1. What type of gateway will you need to create on the Azure Virtual Network?

2. What IP address ranges are available for use within an Azure virtual network? What should you consider when choosing the ranges for the Azure virtual network?

Objective summary

- The hybrid connectivity options with an Azure virtual network are point-to-site, site-to-site, and ExpressRoute.

- Point-to-site connectivity allows you to connect an individual computer to an Azure virtual network using a secure VPN connection. A self-signed certificate is used for authentication. Site-to-site connectivity allows you to create an industry standard IPSEC VPN connection between one or more networks and an Azure virtual network.

- Virtual network-to-virtual network IPSEC connections can span Azure regions and even Azure subscriptions. A virtual network can have up to 10 local network connections (to on-premises sites or other virtual networks).

- Azure ExpressRoute allows direct connectivity to Azure through Exchange providers or network service providers that are ExpressRoute partners.

- The ExpressRoute Exchange provider scenario allows you to connect your hardware co-located at an Exchange provider directly to Azure with port speeds from 200 Mbps to 10 Gbps. The customer is responsible for providing two routers configured in a highly available configuration and must set up BGP routing to route traffic to Azure. The ExpressRoute network service provider scenario allows you to connect an MPLS-based wide area network to Azure. Network service providers handle the management of the routing.

- To configure a site-to-site network, each virtual network must have a static or dynamic routing gateway created. A dynamic routing gateway is required for multi-site, point-to-site, and virtual network-to-virtual network connectivity.

- When designing the address spaces for a site-to-site virtual network, the address spaces should not overlap with the local network regardless of whether it is on-premises or another virtual network in Azure.

Objective review

Answer the following questions to test your knowledge of the information in this objective. You can find the answers to these questions and explanations of why each answer choice is correct or incorrect in the "Answers" section at the end of this chapter.

1. Which cmdlet can you use to set the shared authentication key on an Azure virtual network?

   A. Set-AzureVNetGatewayKey

   B. Set-AzureVNetGateway

   C. Set-AzureVNetConfig

   D. New-AzureVNetGateway

2. Which gateway type should you create to enable point-to-site connectivity?

   A. Static Routing

   B. Dynamic Routing

   C. No gateway is needed

   D. IPSEC

3. You have implemented two virtual networks: One in the West US and the other in the East US Azure region. Using site-to-site virtual networks, you must provide connectivity between the virtual networks and to both networks from your on-premises location. Where should the site-to-site connections be created?

   A. One connection between the virtual networks and one connection to the on-premises location to either virtual network.

   B. One connection between the virtual networks and one connection to each of the virtual networks from the on-premises location.

   C. This scenario is not supported using site-to-site connectivity.

   D. Only one connection from on-premises to either of the virtual networks.

Answers

This section contains the solutions to the thought experiments and answers to the objective review questions in this chapter.

Objective 6.1: Thought experiment

1. The domain controller should be deployed into a virtual network and a static IP address should be specified.

2. The IP address of the DNS server for Active Directory should be specified for the virtual network DNS server. Deploy more than one domain controller within an availability set for redundancy.

Objective 6.1: Review

1. **Correct answers:** A, B, and D

   A. **Correct:** This address space is valid for RFC 1918 and Azure Virtual Networks.

   B. **Correct:** This address space is valid for RFC 1918 and Azure Virtual Networks.

   C. **Incorrect:** This address space is not valid for RFC 1918 and thus is not valid for an Azure virtual network.

   D. **Correct:** This address space is valid for RFC 1918 and Azure Virtual Networks.

2. **Correct answer:** C

   A. **Incorrect:** The IP address 10.0.1.0 is on the same subnet as 10.0.1.0/24. However, Azure reserves the first four IP addresses of a subnet and this would be a reserved IP, so it is not valid.

   B. **Incorrect:** The IP address 10.0.0.1 is not part of the 10.0.1.0/24 subnet.

   C. **Correct:** The IP address 10.0.1.100 is part of the 10.0.1.0/24 subnet and is not reserved by Azure. This would be a usable address for the internal load balancer.

   D. **Incorrect:** The IP address 10.0.1.3 is on the same subnet as 10.0.1.0/24. However, Azure reserves the first four IP addresses of a subnet and this would be a reserved IP, so it is not valid.

3. **Correct answer:** C

   A. **Incorrect:** The New-AzureVM cmdlet is used to create a virtual machine.

   B. **Incorrect:** The Add-AzureProvisioningConfig cmdlet is used to specify the provisioning configuration for a virtual machine created from an image.

   C. **Correct:** The Set-AzureStaticVNetIP cmdlet is used to set the static IP of a virtual machine.

   D. **Incorrect:** The Set-AzureSubnet cmdlet is used to set the subnet of a virtual machine.

Objective 6.2: Thought experiment

1. Use the Azure PowerShell cmdlets, call Get-AzureVM to retrieve the virtual machine configuration object, specify the new subnet with the Set-AzureSubnet cmdlet, and call Update-AzureVM to complete.

2. The virtual machine must be deleted with the option of retaining the disks. After the virtual machine is deleted, re-create it from the previously retained disks.

Objective 6.2: Review

1. **Correct answer:** B

   A. **Incorrect:** The <VirtualNetworkSites> is the parent element that contains the virtual networks for the network configuration.

   B. **Correct:** The <VirtualNetworkSite> element is the element that defines a virtual network in the network configuration.

   C. **Incorrect:** The <NetworkConfiguration> element is the root element for the subscription's network configuration.

   D. **Incorrect:** The <VirtualNetwork> element is not part of the network configuration schema.

2. **Correct answer:** A

   A. **Correct:** The Set-AzureVNetConfig cmdlet is used to set the network configuration. It accepts the path to the full network configuration as an XML file.

   B. **Incorrect:** The Set-AzureVNetGateway cmdlet is used to set the state of an Azure gateway.

   C. **Incorrect:** The Update-AzureVM cmdlet is used to update the configuration of an Azure virtual machine.

   D. **Incorrect:** The Set-AzureSubnet cmdlet is used to assign the subnet to a virtual machine.

3. **Correct answer:** C

   A. **Incorrect:** You can add DNS servers to the configuration of an existing virtual network.

   B. **Incorrect:** You should not specify the DNS server on the network adapter within the guest operating system. The settings within the guest operating system can change if the virtual machine is moved to a different physical server in the datacenter due to a resize or hardware failure.

   C. **Correct:** Azure Virtual Machines and web and worker role instances will need to be rebooted to see the addition of a new DNS server.

   D. **Incorrect:** The New-AzureDNS cmdlet creates a DNS entity that can be referenced when creating the first virtual machine in a cloud service.

Objective 6.3: Thought experiment

1. Creating a dynamic routing gateway is required to enable multi-site connectivity to a virtual network.

2. Address ranges from RFC 1918 are the only supported ranges for Azure Virtual Networks. Address ranges should not overlap other networks in on-premises networks or with other virtual networks you may connect the virtual network to.

   ```
   10.0.0.0 - 10.255.255.255 (10.0.0.0/8)
   172.16.0.0 - 172.31.255.255 (172.16.0.0/12)
   192.168.0.0 - 192.168.255.255 (192.168.0.0/16)
   ```

Objective 6.3: Review

1. **Correct answer:** A

   A. **Correct:** The Set-AzureVNetGatewayKey cmdlet can be used to set the shared authentication key for a virtual network gateway.

   B. **Incorrect:** The Set-AzureVNetGateway cmdlet is used to set the state of an Azure gateway.

   C. **Incorrect:** The Set-AzureVNetConfig cmdlet is used to set the network configuration for an Azure subscription.

   D. **Incorrect:** The New-AzureVNetGateway cmdlet is used to create an instance of a gateway.

2. **Correct answer:** B

   A. **Incorrect:** Static routing gateways do not support point-to-site connectivity.

   B. **Correct:** Dynamic routing gateways are required to implement point-to-site connectivity.

   C. **Incorrect:** A dynamic gateway is required to implement point-to-site connectivity.

   D. **Incorrect:** IPSEC is a protocol used for some types of virtual private networks.

3. **Correct answer:** B

   A. **Incorrect:** This option is not valid because the on-premises location requires connectivity to both virtual networks. This solution only connects the on-premises site to one virtual network.

   B. **Correct:** This option is correct because the on-premises location requires connectivity to both virtual networks. This solution provides a connection from on-premises to both virtual networks.

   C. **Incorrect:** This scenario is supported with site-to-site connectivity.

   D. **Incorrect:** A connection must be made between the on-premises location and both virtual networks as well as a connection between the virtual networks.

Index

A

AAD. *See* Azure Active Directory (AAD)
AAD Sync tool 269
access control
   for Azure Storage account 229–234
   backing up and restoring ACLs 260–261
Access Panel, for SaaS applications 292–293
Active Directory Federation Service 273–274
active geo-replication 247–249
activity log reports 282
administrator roles, for Azure Active Directory 276, 277
affinity groups 320
alerts
   for Azure Storage accounts 238–239
   for cloud services 198–199
   for endpoint failures 36
   for events 38
   for performance counter metrics 37–38
Always On setting 11
analytics
   for Azure Storage accounts 236–238
   configuring 39–40
anomalous activity reports 281
application diagnostic logs
   enabling 28–30
   location of 30
   retrieving 30–32
   streaming 32–34
Applicationhost.config file 169–170
application settings
   configuring 11–13
   environment variables for 12
APPSETTING_ environment variables 12
A record, for DNS 14–15, 17
ASDB (Azure SQL Database Benchmark) 241
async copy service, for blob storage 218–219

authentication
   for Azure Active Directory 294–300
   for Azure Storage accounts 230–231
Autoscale
   configuring with metrics 46
   configuring with schedules 44–45
awverify CNAME record 15
Azure Active Directory (AAD) 267
   activity log reports 282
   administrator roles for 276, 277
   anomalous activity reports 281
   Cloud App Discovery 283–284
   custom domain for 278–280
   directory synchronization 268–274, 284–286
   domain join 325–326
   editions of 267
   federated identity providers for 298–299
   integrated application reports 282
   integrating with Office 365 274–278
   LOB applications, integrating 301–312
   monitoring 280–286
   Multi-Factor Authentication for 294–298
   notifications for 283
   SaaS applications, integrating 288–293
   user and group activity sign-in reports 280
Azure Active Directory Connect 273
Azure Backup 255–262
   Backup Agent for 256
   Backup Vault for 256
   Backup Wizard for 258
   Recovery Data Wizard 260–261
   Register Server Wizard 257
Azure cloud services
   configuration, updating 188
   custom domain, configuring 160–161
   deploying 182–186
   deployment, updating 187–189

L

load balancing
   for virtual networks 327–328
load balancing method, Azure Traffic Manager 18–19
LOB (line-of-business) applications
   enabling access from other applications 305–307
   graph API permissions for, configuring 309–310
   native applications, integrating with Azure Active
      Directory 307–309
   web applications or services, integrating with Azure
      Active Directory 301–307
Locally-redundant storage (LRS) option 216
local storage, for cloud services
   configuring 170–172
location of Azure website
   availability of 3
   specifying 4
logging. *See* diagnostics data
LRS (Locally-redundant storage) option 216

M

Managed Cache 160
Management Portal. *See* Azure Management Portal
messaging services. *See* Microsoft Azure Service Bus;
   See Azure Service Bus
MFA (Multi-Factor Authentication) 294–298
   additional security verification with 297–298
   enabling 296–297
   provider for, configuring 295–296
   provider for, creating 294–295
MFA portal 295, 296
Microsoft accounts 298–299
Microsoft Azure Active Directory (AAD). *See* Azure Active
   Directory (AAD)
Microsoft Azure Cloud Services 151. *See* Azure Cloud
   Services
   cloud services created with. *See* Azure cloud services
Microsoft Azure IaaS Deep Drive Jump Start 349
Microsoft Azure Recovery Services 255
Microsoft Azure Service Bus. *See* Service Bus
Microsoft Azure SQL Database. *See* Azure SQL Database
Microsoft Azure subscription
   adding Office 365 to 277–278
   adding to Office 365 subscription 275
   core capacity 153
   integrating Office 365 directory with 275–277

Microsoft Azure Virtual Networks. *See* Azure virtual
   networks
Microsoft Azure Websites 1. *See also* Azure websites
   websites created with. *See* Azure websites
Microsoft Office 365. *See* Office 365
Microsoft Virtual Academy 40, 349
monitoring. *See also* diagnostics data; *See also* alerts;
   diagnostics data
   alerts 198–199
      for endpoint failures 36
      for events 38
      for performance counter metrics 37–38
   analytics
      for Azure Storage accounts 236–238
      configuring 39–40
   Azure Active Directory 280–286
   Azure Storage 238–239
   cloud services 196–199
   deployments (website endpoints) 36–37
   endpoints 199–200
   Service Bus queue 200–201
   Service Bus relay 202
   Service Bus topic 201
   services 38–39
   website resources 34–35
Multi-Factor Authentication. *See* MFA
MX record, verifying custom domains using 279
My Apps application 293
MySQL
   connection string for 11–12
MYSQLCONNSTR_ environment variables 12

N

name of Azure website
   availability of 3
   specifying 4
.NET Framework Version setting 11
network traffic rules
   for cloud services, configuring 166–168
New-AzureDeployment cmdlet 327
New-AzureDNS cmdlet 323
New-AzureQuickVM cmdlet 324
New-AzureReservedIP cmdlet 164
New-AzureSBNamespace cmdlet 193
New-AzureService cmdlet 327
New-AzureStorageAccount cmdlet 217
New-AzureStorageBlobSASToken cmdlet 231–232
New-AzureStorageContainer cmdlet 215

About the authors

 MICHAEL WASHAM is a Microsoft MVP specializing in Microsoft Azure and is the founder and CEO of Opsgility (www.opsgility.com), a leader in instructor-led and on-demand training for Microsoft Azure and enterprise computing. Prior to starting Opsgility, Michael was a fifteen year Microsoft veteran, and while at Microsoft, Michael's roles included being a Senior Program Manager on the Microsoft Azure Runtime team and a Senior Technical Evangelist for Microsoft Azure Infrastructure Services. Michael was the original developer of the Microsoft Azure PowerShell cmdlets and is a globally recognized speaker for conferences such as TechEd and BUILD. When not focused on cloud computing Michael spends time with his wife and kids in the north Texas area.

 RICK RAINEY is a Microsoft Azure Insider and Advisor, Certified Trainer (MCT), blogger (*http://rickrainey.com*) and an Azure community enthusiast. At Microsoft, he worked closely with Microsoft Premier Enterprise customers, Independent Software Vendors, and Microsoft Engineering to design and develop applications for the Microsoft Azure platform. Today, he is the owner and CEO of CloudAlloc (*http://www.cloudalloc.com*), a provider of services and tools designed to achieve maximum business value from applications and infrastructure workloads running in the cloud.

Professional services and tools
designed to maximize your
investment in the cloud.

Cloud Solution Architectures

Development & Implementation

Solution Support

Training

www.cloudalloc.com   info@cloudalloc.com

Capacity
Planning

Scalability

Hybrid
Connectivity

Enterprise Software
Training from the
EXPERTS

1-866-833-3878

www.opsgility.com

Free ebooks

From technical overviews to drilldowns on special topics, get *free* ebooks from Microsoft Press at:

www.microsoftvirtualacademy.com/ebooks

Download your free ebooks in PDF, EPUB, and/or Mobi for Kindle formats.

Look for other great resources at Microsoft Virtual Academy, where you can learn new skills and help advance your career with free Microsoft training delivered by experts.

Microsoft Press

Now that you've read the book...

Tell us what you think!

Was it useful?
Did it teach you what you wanted to learn?
Was there room for improvement?

Let us know at http://aka.ms/tellpress

Your feedback goes directly to the staff at Microsoft Press,
and we read every one of your responses. Thanks in advance!